*The California School of Professional Psychology
Handbook of Multicultural Education, Research,
Intervention, and Training*

CSPP

*The California School
of Professional Psychology*

Handbook of Multicultural Education, Research, Intervention, and Training

Edited by
Elizabeth Davis-Russell

Foreword by Connell F. Persico

JOSSEY-BASS
A Wiley Company
www.josseybass.com

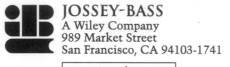

JOSSEY-BASS
A Wiley Company
989 Market Street
San Francisco, CA 94103-1741

www.josseybass.com

Jossey-Bass books and products are available through most bookstores. To contact Jossey-Bass directly, call (888) 378-2537, fax to (800) 605-2665, or visit our website at www.josseybass.com.

Substantial discounts on bulk quantities of Jossey-Bass books are available to corporations, professional associations, and other organizations. For details and discount information, contact the special sales department at Jossey-Bass.

We at Jossey-Bass strive to use the most environmentally sensitive paper stocks available to us. Our publications are printed on acid-free recycled stock whenever possible, and our paper always meets or exceeds minimum GPO and EPA requirements.

Credits are on p. 345

Library of Congress Cataloging-in-Publication Data

The California School of Professional Psychology handbook of multicultural education, research, intervention, and training / [edited by] Elizabeth Davis-Russell.
    p. cm.
    Includes bibliographical references and index.
    ISBN 0-7879-5763-1
    1. Cross-cultural counseling. 2. Cultural psychiatry. 3. Psychologists—Training of—Social aspects. I. Title: Handbook of multicultural education, research, intervention, and training. II. Davis-Russell, Elizabeth. III. California School of Professional Psychology.

BF637.C6 C27   2002
150′.7—dc21   2002016069

HB Printing 10 9 8 7 6 5 4 3 2 1   FIRST EDITION

CONTENTS

FOREWORD

Increasing access to higher education has always required alterations to the content, processes, and structures of institutions. For the pioneers, making the necessary changes requires will and fortitude. For those who see the need to do something, it is helpful to have models and evidence of prior successes.

In March 1991 a small group of faculty, students, and administrators from the California School of Professional Psychology (CSPP) met in Napa, California to formulate an agenda for transforming an established professional psychology curriculum into one that would flow from multicultural perspectives, thereby increasing the number of faculty and students of color within the school, and creating an institution-wide structure to assess and comment on the school's commitment to multiculturalism. The MERIT Institute was born, and, through the work of its members on the four CSPP campuses, defined the competencies a professional psychologist must master to be an ethical and effective practitioner, opened up training and service delivery to additional underserved people, substantially improved the number and quality of psychologists of color in the United States, and prepared Euro-Americans for practicing in a diverse society.

This handbook presents some of the learning that has occurred over the past decade as a result of the MERIT Initiative within CSPP. The four components of MERIT are Multicultural Education, Research, Intervention, and Training. Thus, Part One of this handbook speaks to context, standards, skills, and resources useful in the classroom education of professional psychologists. Part Two addresses some of the critical knowledge required for conducting appropriate multicultural research. Part Three speaks to critical variables for effective intervention with clients of color. Part Four addresses important issues in the training of culturally competent psychologists.

It is our hope that you find this handbook to be of service as you work with diverse populations and, possibly, modify the content of the educational programs in which you participate. Creating a society that serves the needs of its people in a just and equitable way remains an unalterable goal. Being a part of the MERIT initiative that altered the direction and soul of an institution has been an honor as well as humbling. I wish you the same joy and camaraderie we have shared along the way.

San Francisco, California   Connell F. Persico, Ph.D.
February 2002   Senior Vice President
                                     Alliant International University

PREFACE

In 1982 Bernal and Padilla surveyed clinical psychology programs to determine the status of the training of clinical psychologists for work with ethnic minorities. Recently, Bernal and Castro (1994) replicated and extended this study, sending their survey to all APA-accredited doctoral programs in clinical psychology. One hundred four of the programs returned completed questionnaires. From their responses, Bernal and Castro conclude that progress in multicultural training over the past decade has been mixed. There are some positive trends. When these results are compared to the 1982 survey results, the 1994 survey found that programs providing minority-related courses had increased by 20 percent, and programs requiring such courses increased by 17 percent. Furthermore, 10 percent more programs in 1994 reported that faculty are engaged in multicultural research (Ponterotto, Casas, Suzuki, & Alexander, 1995).

Lest we begin to rest on our laurels, the signs of progress are not overwhelming. Bernal and Castro (1994) highlight that a substantial percentage of programs do not even have the basics to conduct minority training.

In school psychology, Rogers, Ponterotto, Conoley, and Wiese (1992) examined the results of curriculum surveys completed by training directors at 121 doctoral and nondoctoral school psychology programs. These showed that 60 percent of the programs offer at least one course in multicultural issues, and 63 percent of the programs offered two to five courses.

Suarez-Balcazar, Durlak, and Smith (as cited in Bernal & Castro, 1994) surveyed 56 community psychology graduate programs. Their findings revealed that 48 percent of programs required at least one multicultural course; 87 percent indicated that relevant fieldwork experiences were available to interested students; and in 70 percent of programs, multicultural research was being conducted.

D'Andrea and Daniels as cited in D'Andrea, Daniels, and Heck (1991) developed a conceptual stage model of training thought to reflect different types and levels of multicultural counseling training. The authors found that a majority of counseling programs is operating at the cross-cultural Awakening stage, which is the second stage. Very few programs are found to be operating at the third and fourth stages, the Cultural Integrity and Infusion stages, respectively.

The above data indicate that the programs that are educating and training future faculty, supervisors, and therapists have not sufficiently incorporated multiculturally relevant curricula and practices to produce culturally competent professionals in these areas. This raises a number of questions about how training is conducted. How do we educate and train people from underrepresented groups within the United States? How do we prepare others to work with them? Dana (1998) points out: "Historically, quality mental health care in the United States has largely depended on a common language and the shared beliefs that contribute to a process of mutual understandings between providers and clients. These shared beliefs derive from a Eurocentric construction of reality" (p. 15).

The good news is that we have made progress since I was a doctoral student in a clinical psychology program in the 1980s, and my program offered one course that dealt with multicultural issues. The bad news is that there are programs that still do not address these significant issues or tend to marginalize them. It is inconceivable that in the twenty-first century, given the diversity that is inherently part of this nation and of higher education, programs in psychology and related disciplines still have not integrated cultural competence into their models of education and training. Many of us have worked tirelessly to bring these issues to the forefront. Having begun my teaching career in the City University of New York where I introduced a course (the first of its kind at the college, not without controversy) on Black Psychology: Black Perspectives, I continued at each subsequent institution to develop courses and programs in multicultural psychology. My journey took me to the California School of Professional Psychology (CSPP), where I saw an institutional commitment to diversity. The institution was one of the pioneers in this area. This handbook is a testimony to some of the work done at CSPP.

In 1989, as part of the ongoing work in diversity, the faculty, administrators of the four campuses of the California School of Professional Psychology, and the System Office conceived the Multicultural, Education, Research, Intervention, and Training (MERIT) Institute during a retreat in the Napa Valley. The original purpose was to provide a systemwide organizational structure that could be used to galvanize the efforts of the faculty toward promoting multicultural education, research, training, and services across the CSPP. Given its institutional commitment to diversity, CSPP now had a vehicle to assume a leadership role in the field in particular, and in higher education. The MERIT Institute developed and implemented multicultural competency standards, and ensured that in the training of professional psychologists, there was a campus, institutional, educational, and training ethos that reflected respect for the importance of diversity. It also committed itself to presenting the institution's multicultural activities to the broader communities. This handbook represents the efforts of some of CSPP's faculty, alumni, and administrators.

While much has been written within the last two decades, there have been few approaches addressing the complexity of the issues in multiculturalism and the variability that exists amongst the populations usually designated as underrepresented. Parham points out in Ponterotto, Casas, Suzuki, and Alexander (1995) that we seem to be "caught in a state of inertia or a quandary about how to proceed with the diversity movement" (p. ix). This handbook is designed as one way to move us out of that inertia or quandary. It is intended to be broad, encompassing how we teach, conduct research, and intervene to produce change in the lives of individuals, families, groups, and organizations. It is inspired by our classroom experiences, research experiences, and clinical experiences. It is not the final word, but is designed to bring to the arena our wisdom after many years of work. Multiple voices are heard in this handbook. Some are more seasoned than others who bring fresh perspectives. What unites us all is our commitment to elevating what we see as critical issues in our work, relationships, and treatment of culturally different persons. Any similarity to actual people is purely coincidental. We hope that this handbook will stimulate you, the reader, so that more voices are joined in this commitment. We invite you to join us.

References

Bernal, M. E., & Padilla, A. M. (1982). Status of minority curricula and training in clinical psychology. *American Pschologist, 37,* 780–787.

Bernal, M. E., & Castro, F. G. (1994). Are clinical psychologists prepared for service and research with ethnic minorities? Report of a decade of progress. *American Psychologist, 49,* 797–805.

Dana, R. H. (1998). *Understanding cultural identity in intervention and assessment.* Thousand Oaks, CA: Sage.

D'Andrea, M., Daniels, J., & Heck, R. (1991). Evaluating the impact of multicultural counseling training. *Journal of Counseling Development, 70,* 145–150.

Ponterotto, J. G., Casas, J. M., Suzuki, L. A., & Alexander, C. M. (1995). *Handbook of multicultural counseling.* Thousand Oaks, CA: Sage.

Rogers, M. R., Ponterotto, J. G., Conoley, J. C., & Wiese, M. J. (1992). Multicultural training in school psychology: A national survey. *School Psychology Review, 21,* 603–616.

ACKNOWLEDGMENTS

In writing such a book, there are many whose works are not reflected in the pages, but who have made significant contributions to the book. One runs the risk of omitting some because the list is extensive. I would like to call attention to and acknowledge the work of Dr. Judith Albino, president of Alliant International University, who through her foresight, negotiated with Jossey-Bass for the publication of this book. I would also like to acknowledge the founding faculty and administrators of the Multicultural, Education, Research, Intervention, and Training (MERIT) Institute. Through those days spent at Napa Valley, they worked not only to establish a vehicle through which California School of Professional Psychology's (CSPP) commitment to diversity could become manifested, they also continued to monitor the institution to ensure that the commitment was "in our blood." Part of that group became the MERIT Council and others were added to the Council. Council members, past and present also are acknowledged for their dedication to "keeping the institution honest."

The book would not be a reality without the contributors. I would like to acknowledge their willingness, in very busy times, to submit their work to bring this project to fruition. And finally, my acknowledgment goes to Donna Williams for her diligence in typing the manuscript and pursuing the authors for their materials. Many thanks to Donna.

Dedication

As a graduate student and later as a professor, I engaged with others in lengthy discussions about Abraham Maslow's definition of "peak experiences" during the Self Actualization stage. Those discussions didn't produce definite conclusions, but I think that in one's lifetime, there are profound experiences that have the effects of altering the course of one's life. Sometimes they are experiences in which one feels at "one" with the universe, and at other times they make one feel discordant with the universe. I became inspired to be a teacher and helper thanks to my paternal grandmother, Caldonia Davis, as I traveled with her to places where roads had not yet been built. My grandmother worked to educate hundreds who would otherwise not have been educated. I don't know if she experienced Maslow's "peak experiences," but as I watched the rescue workers during the aftermath of the horrifying events of September 11, 2001, in New York City, working tirelessly to save the lives of others, certain images were indelibly etched on my memory. One was of two African American women, bloodied, clutching each other, helping each other. In the frailty of the moment, yet with their commitment to helping each other, in my grandmother's commitment and dedication to educate those without opportunity, and in the heroism of the rescue workers, we find the essence of what makes us human. This is the lesson that my grandmother was trying to teach me; to give of one's self *selflessly*. So, to her memory, to those two African American women, and to the rescue workers of the World Trade Center, who taught us such valuable lessons, I dedicate this book.

Elizabeth Davis-Russell

*The California School of Professional Psychology
Handbook of Multicultural Education, Research,
Intervention, and Training*

PART ONE

EDUCATION

CHAPTER ONE

Psychology and the Reach of Multiculturalism in American Culture

Leena Banerjee

This year my older son played on a baseball team in West Coast suburbia in the Junior League that was composed of mostly, but not exclusively, Minority teens from different cultures. Their coaches and managers were Minorities as well. They played with other teams through the season that were also mixed and often Minority dominated. In one game in another town, they played against an all-White team with White coaches, managers, and umpires. My son's team felt that the umpires calls were repeatedly biased in favor of the other team. During half time, his coach said to them that they would have to give two hundred percent in this game because the umpires were from where the other team was from, implying that they could not depend on a fair shake. My son's team won the game but came away with a feeling that, in order to win, they had to overcome unfair obstacles. Without knowing the story from the perspective of the other team, I was, nonetheless, struck by how differences of color or race in the interface had produced perceptions and experiences of division and even injustice in the course of ordinary community life. Indeed, integrating diversity in just, foresighted ways remains one of the most important social issues of our times.

In the progressive democratization of the United States, multiculturalism has been a prominent force in the public mind since the Civil Rights Era. In the public sphere, there has been a focus on diversity in the most ephemeral of senses—the diversity of appearance (popularized as race)—not the complexities of culture. As the appearance of our workplaces and some of our educational and other institutions have begun to change and diversify, public conversations on race have become muted, as indeed discrimination and oppression have become more subtle, but no less pernicious, and no less of a challenge. Strickland (2000) places appropriate emphasis on the issue when she characterizes difference as something that can still be a life and death issue in this society.

In the public mind, the United States of America's national cultural identity continues to be considered in terms of a White center (with an extension cord to Western Europe, some would argue, in Kanellos, 1997) and a cluster of hyphenated Minority identities on the periphery (Banerjee, 2000). This center-periphery configuration (Mukherjee, 1997), communicates the value-laden difference between who is central, part of the fabric and definition of national identity and culture, and who is not. Social Darwinism responsible for this hierarchy among cultures has now become very subtle in the United States. In Germany, German Turks can never be seen as German (Zack, 1998). In America, shedding the substance of ethnic culture, not necessarily the identification, can allow a person to be seen as an American. Is this kind of cultural "removal" (Saldivar, 1990) a desirable way to integrate diversity?

Examples of this center-periphery reality can be readily found in daily life by anyone who wishes to be observant. Recently, I went on a field trip to visit an art museum in Pasadena, California, with my second grader's class. The beautifully refurbished Norton Simon Museum boasts a small but recognized collection of European art and a rather extensive South Asian collection. The European art displayed prominently and beautifully at the entrance and all through the upstairs delighted the children who took turns spontaneously striking the poses of Degas's ballerina sculptures. The Asian art also displayed beautifully in the cavernous downstairs brought a similar response from the children who got together in twos and threes to strike the poses of the ancient sculptures of gods and goddesses with multiple limbs. In the text of the museum brochures, its art collection was described in sections divided into fourteenth–seventeenth, seventeenth–eighteenth, and nineteenth–twentieth centuries, covering European art but failing to state that it was European, a safe cultural assumption. At the end, after this chronological presentation, a section was added on South Asian art, standing by itself, unintegrated—even in the dimension of historical time—an exotic element, outside the center. When arguing for integrative multiculturalism, it is unnecessary to take the position that multiculturalism, itself, constitutes an absolute good for society. From a pragmatic and relative standpoint however, in the context of a free and heterogeneous society, it can be argued to be psychologically, socially, and politically good because it can allow healthy self-owning, a basis for egalitarianism and unification (Banerjee, 2000), which can lead to the maturation of democracy. Without a comprehensive, integrative, plural paradigm, a plural people can't see themselves equitably reflected in the national identity and culture and can't count on qualifying as equally legitimate members. Representation of diversity in terms of appearance alone without accompanying cultural contexts, can't adequately provide this mirror.

Multiculturalism is the idea of a plural paradigm that allows retention and transformation of cultural identity through individual or collective choice rather than implicit or explicit coercion, thereby extending to each individual and group an essential dignity. It fosters a climate of humanism and provides depth and resilience to a culture through access to its collective memories, better perspective on oneself and others, collective wisdom and collective narrative stories that may in turn be shared, exchanged, or blended freely in the exigencies of survival. Loss of cultural identity is a loss of cultural capital and a loss of opportunity to interact with multiple sources of meaning and expanded cultural resources.

The gap in American culture between a multicultural ideology and a cultural credo of pluralism continues to be wide. Without such a cultural credo, heterogeneous groups can't identify with each other in the way different members of a family can identify with each other and the family as a whole and retain their individualities. Without mutual familiarity, reciprocal identifications and owning, and a climate of connection and belonging together, across-the-board participation in the democratic process suffers. Political accountability of peoples' representatives to uphold the public interests also suffers. The political process becomes more vulnerable to parochialism, ethnopolitics, and special-interest politics unchecked by countervailing forces representing larger interests, commitments to social equality, and justice. Gaps in the socioemotional integration of a nation prevent the development of authentic common ground and full democratic participation, instead they feed mistrust, fracture, injustice, and discontent.

THE MULTICULTURAL PARADIGM AND PSYCHOLOGY

Within psychology, multiculturalism has been contributing to a richer understanding of human life (Fowers & Richardson, 1996), and is now recognized as a prominent thread in psychological theory, research, practice, and training with continued active efforts being made to make it a defining feature of the profession (Sue, Bingham, Porche-Burke, & Vasquez, 1999).

Articulate analyses of the status and challenges facing multicultural research within the scientific paradigm are available (Sue, 1999). Substantial development of alternative paradigms that utilize other routes to knowledge (such as qualitative enquiry, spirituality, intuition, essence of reality contained in metaphors, stories, and parables) awaits us in an undetermined future. Articulation of the epistemologies and methodologies of such paradigms will reflect multicultural infusion and expansion of the culture of the field in a fundamental way. These paradigms will also represent and better fit the cultural orientation toward truth seeking among many peoples including, but not solely, many ethnic Minority peoples and serve as complements to the almost singularly utilized and dominating positivist scientific paradigm.

The larger and deeper challenge is that psychology is necessarily nested in the larger processes and realities of the society in which surface multiculturalism, enduring homogenization, voluntary segregation, division, and now classism as the new face of segregation, are prominent. This poses dilemmas for us to be and to train researchers and practitioners who uphold and advance multiculturalism in professional work, when in the process of surviving and becoming successful in this society, we continue to be subject to powerful, but subtle, contrary, and assimilative forces. Minority students are especially at risk for facing such dilemmas. Psychological literature is full of references to intergenerational conflicts between successive generations of Minority families and explained by concepts such as degrees of acculturation (Wakil, Siddique, & Wakil, 1981; Panat & Banerjee, 1994; Gardetta, 1998). It is as if it's not only understandable, but justifiable, for these conflicts to be the special burden of Minority families. So long as the center is not struggling at a deeper cultural level (beyond appearance and its nuances) with owning its diversity and integrating it at the center of society, these familial and psychic conflicts will continue to be the special burden of minority families. In psychology, the emerging dynamic constructivist approach to understanding the influence of dual cultures in individuals demonstrates that recent culturally based contextual primes influence the thinking of individuals by affecting the choice of cultural orientation that is used (Hong, Morris, Chiu, & Benet-Martinez, 2000). A cultural context without rich and representative plurality of primes will then tend to significantly decrease access to domain-specific cultural knowledge. Indeed, this is the reality in the mainstream of American culture.

Any academic discipline and a society exert mutual, reciprocal influences on one another. Psychology has provided understandings of culturally based differences in self-construal for quite some time (Kitayama & Marcus, 1994). Psychology can contribute by developing a multicultural paradigm that not only provides a platform of visibility for marginalized and oppressed groups, but moves to a next evolutionary step of attending to more complex, subtle, and wide-reaching cultural oppressions, as well as the crying need for a more satisfactory framework for cohesiveness, and social integration.

An activist psychology can critique existing constructs unexamined for the cultural assumptions from which they originate, and define new constructs to re-imagine identity and culture that integrate universal with indigenous elements. A stellar example of this kind of work is the theoretical formulation on attachment theory by Rothbaum, Weisz, Pott, Miyake, and Morelli (2000). They point out that attachment theory has considered cultural influences only at its periphery. Interestingly, this practice also mirrors the overall situation with national cultural identity and multiculturalism. The authors—by contrasting Western and Japanese cultures as they relate to the three main tenets of attachment theory, namely sensitivity, competence, and secure base—show the differences in conceptualization and meaning of each by culture. For example, in the case of the sensitivity hypothesis, Western parents valuing independence and autonomy show sensitivity in response to a child's needs. This practice provides the child space and opportunity to act as an autonomous person as well as reinforcement of bonding needs by a responsive parent. Japanese parents valuing interdependence and emotional closeness show sensitivity by anticipating the child's needs. This practice teaches contextual sensitivity that is needed for harmonious adaptation to close relationship contexts as well as reinforces bonding needs. The authors carefully argue that a lack of understanding of indigenous cultures in such ways has lead to research that has focused on superficial cultural differences in sensitivity, such as caregiver proximity when children are exploring or the timing of independence training. Despite the insights, testability, and relevance of attachment theory for some sections of American culture, such research practices advertently or inadvertently perpetuate oppression of other parts of the culture by shaping the awareness, knowledge base, mentalities, and behaviors of people in terms of the dominant culture and in ignorance of other cultures. The question is how can cultural heterogeneity be preserved, promoted, and better understood if the ingrained and relentless forces of homogenization in the culture are not also concomitantly addressed? How can the passage of a robust multiculturalism into the fabric of the profession and the larger culture be facilitated?

PAST PARADIGMS: A BRIEF HISTORY

Anglo-Conformity, the Melting Pot, and Early Pluralism are the paradigms in chronological order that predated Multiculturalism in defining national cultural identity in the United States. In other words, these approaches influenced the way in which we have viewed who an American is, what American culture consists of, what the available options for constructing individual and communal self-views in a national cultural context are, and how these constructions, in turn, affect the possibilities for relatedness with those in- and outside defined subgroups.

Anglo-Conformity, which originated in seventeenth-century America, was popularized in the nineteenth century and came into full force in the early part of the twentieth century. It was based on the Social Darwinistic belief that peoples of Northern and Western Europe were the most evolved, therefore, peoples from Southern and Eastern Europe who were lower on the evolutionary order were expected to assimilate and adopt the mores of the superior groups. The inferiority of peoples of color was simply assumed and the possibilities for their assimilation were greatly restricted. The central aim of this approach appeared to be the forging of a unity among diverse people; a unity, which was perceived to be continually threatened by the influx of immigrants with diverse cultures, languages, national origins, and religions. The possible psychological losses and negative effects from complete denial of one's collective identity was not considered by proponents of this approach. In addition, hierarchical superiority attributed to Anglo-Conformity and Whiteness; promoted through cultural ideals of Whiteness; unequal treatment of nonWhites in society; exclusion of nonWhites from positions of public authority and visibility and the imposition of White cultural rules and norms on all; and created a legacy of a "damaged culture" (McIntosh, 1998, p. 148) and divided society, with "invisible knapsacks of privilege" and "unearned entitlements" for Whites (pp. 147, 151).

Anglo-Conformity, a racist and culturally imperialist approach, promoted the underlying notion of hierarchy with respect to culture, a notion that is still with us. As an approach, it became even more forceful when rival approaches came on the scene. Fairchild's (1926) *The Melting Pot Mistake* and Grant's (1916) *Passing of a Great Race*, are two examples of the persuasive zeal with which this approach was argued in the public forum.

One of the rival approaches to Anglo-Conformity was the Melting Pot approach, first introduced in a play by the same name written by a Jewish immigrant named Israel Zangwill (1929). The play conveyed the idea that a common American identity was being created by God beyond the feuds of Europe. The Melting Pot advocated the gradual assimilation of old ethnicities to become a new ethnicity, namely, American. However, the idea of the Melting Pot was impeded by the hierarchical and negative attitudes toward cultural differences that assimilationism had already set in place. The assimilation process favored the cultures of Northern and Western Europeans over others, so these ethnicities could give up the old culture, so to speak, and contribute to defining the new. Others such as post-1882 European immigrants from Southern and Eastern Europe, who were perceived as threats to the society and culture, and seen as being "dull of brain" with the potential to "lower the standards of living" (Turner, 1920, p. 278), could give up the old and adopt the new. Our attitudes towards Hispanic immigration today, leaving out the issue of legal versus illegal immigration as a distracter in this context, are an eerie echo of those same negative attitudes toward difference.

In summary, it could be argued that the Melting Pot succeeded in some measure in melting the differences between early European immigrants producing the English-speaking, European American representation of mainstream America familiar to us today. White American identity invented through the processes of assimilation and fusion in the United States, was eloquently described in

Dixon's 1902 novel, *The Leopard's Spots*. The protagonist in the novel gave a winning speech and claimed the gubernatorial nomination by declaring that his constituents were descended not only from the Anglo and the Saxon, but also the Roman, the Spartan, and the Celt, and that their fusion created the White race (Michaels, 1995). Such a construction of ethnic identity, popularized in the United States as racial identity, that was imposed from the top and did not rise up organically from below, is an example of Weberian ideationalization and is politically conspiratorial in nature (Weber, 1967).

Early Pluralism, a forerunner of Multiculturalism, presented that American public and civic life were ethnically neutral and that private life was ethnically determined. Proponents of Cultural Pluralism included such people as John Dewey and Horace Kallen. They were strongly critical of Anglo-Conformity and the Melting Pot approaches. They declared the practice of teaching pride of race to be undemocratic and instead, promoted the teaching of Cultural Pluralism to young children. Kallen (1925) wrote of ethnicities' passage in the United States as moving through four stages. First, there is assimilation prompted by the awareness that differences handicap people in their economic struggle and aspirations. Second, after economic progress is achieved, assimilation stops or slows because prior experiences of discrimination militate against it and give impetus to linguistic, spiritual, and other expressions of ethnicity. Third, there is an ethnic group focus and differences are highlighted. Fourth, difference changes in status from being a disadvantage to being a valued distinction, allowing the cacophony of diversity to be established in the culture. Today, different groups may place themselves in stages one, two, or three of Kallen's stages, but stage four still eludes us.

Researchers reported from the field that cultures were being eroded and languages being lost in the United States, but not a sense of ethnicity or a way of categorizing oneself with connection to certain aspects of historical collective identity (Glazer & Moynihan, 1963, 1975). There has, in fact, been a rise in dissociative ethnic self-categorizations despite sufficient behavioral assimilation, indicating a functional autonomy between culture and identification (Hutnik, 1991). This, in some sense, is like saying that if you had a pot of gold to start with, you are left with the pot and have lost the gold (for ethnic Minority groups), or have lost both the pot and the gold (for the fused European mainstream). Researchers also reported that despite mobility and behavioral assimilation, a common American identity, or a sense of belonging together was not occurring in the society (Glazer & Moynihan, 1975).

Cultural neutrality of the United States' public sphere has been questioned and has been argued to be a blend of Northern and Western European cultures instead (Zack, 1998). Thus, Italians, Irish, Jewish, Polish, and other Europeans— as well as more recently non-Europeans—have joined the mainstream by becoming a different ethnicity, that is, the mainstream blend, at least in their educational or professional endeavors. However, anti-Semitic and anti-Asian sentiment has abounded in reaction to the assimilative success of these groups. In an era of falling crime rates for example, hate crimes towards South Asians have been rising dramatically. Do trends such as these suggest the continuing expectation that the United States' elite is White, Anglo-Saxon and Protestant (WASP)?

In conclusion, Anglo-Conformity, it would seem, won out. With its simpler implications for social policy, it remained a powerful and popular paradigm embedded in the mentality and practices of the mainstream (Hutnik, 1991). The political and economic benefits of this paradigm for White Americans may be obvious, but the cultural, social, and psychic costs of the process are not often considered. McGoldrick (1998) described these issues in the following words:

> I grew up not knowing that I had a cultural background at all. This of course was probably because I could "pass" for a member of the dominant group . . . As my mother put it when I began asking questions, "We're Americans now Monica, our ancestors were just peasants. What difference does it make where we came from?" She recalled her later journey in the following words: "It was not until the mid-1970s that I realized that I was Irish. Through my interests in Murray Bowen's theory, I had begun to explore my roots and inspired a trip by our whole family to Ireland. I was overwhelmed when I landed in Ireland by the feeling that I had come home. Everywhere I seemed to see my relatives, people who related in the way my family did, using humor, teasing, and ridicule to keep others in line or to maintain distance in male-female relationships, failing to talk about the most important things that were happening: giving someone the "silent treatment." Suddenly patterns that I had experienced all my life had a context. It was not that my family was crazy, it was Irish. It was a transformative experience that has never left me. I still think of Ireland as home in some deep way and coming to define myself as Irish-American has been an affirmation at the deepest sense of my belonging. Much that I thought was strange or eccentric, I now see has meaning because of our cultural history" (p. 217).

For European Americans, the story of the systematic removal of such cultural contexts that provide psychological resources, opportunities for meaning, and resiliency occurred as a result of using a process relying on dominance as a way to define national cultural identity and achieve unity, creating uniformity instead with the bonus of a place at the top. For ethnic minority groups, dominance or the workings of present-day Social Darwinistic forces continue and can be seen in the inverse relationship between degree of ethnic retention and generation of residence as well as socioeconomic status. The lack of equal acceptance of minority cultures due to the lack of centrality of Cultural Pluralism in the society, leads to the shedding of authentic culture; ways of dressing, greeting, eating, interacting with others, language, customs, myths, symbols, and numerous other resources and sources of collective wisdom. This pattern cuts across Ogbu's (1989) voluntary and involuntary immigrant groups. School achievement of children from voluntary immigrant groups may be much stronger than that of children from involuntary immigrant groups who have suffered a history of oppression from the dominant group in the United States, but both groups face significant struggles in the process of their adjustment, mobility aims, and socialization of their children in America to retain and integrate into the main currents of everyday life in society, substantive and meaningful aspects of their cultures.

UNITY IN DIVERSITY AS A NEXT EVOLUTIONARY FOCUS FOR MULTICULTURALISM: A FOCUS ON THE DUAL NEEDS FOR DISTINCTIVENESS AND COHESIVENESS

Kallen's (1925) conceptualization of ethnicities' passage in the United States traversed four stages as mentioned earlier. To these four, a fifth stage is proposed that builds on the fourth's assumptions of owning diversity and moving on to a stage of unity in diversity established through meaningful exchange, leading to consensus and core cohesion along with the preservation of differences. In a vastly heterogeneous society such as ours is today, it is possible to have too much difference (Tyler & Smith, 1999). Emphasis on diversity alone can generate too much fear of differences, particularly in a society that has been historically diversity phobic and accustomed to dominance and uniformity as ways to deal with it and create the framework of the culture. At the same time, some present-day manifestations of multiculturalism deserve scrutiny. These include the processes rendering diversity hollow so that substantial aspects of culture are wiped out in the process of making a life and moving up in the society, leaving ethnic self-categorizations functionally autonomous from knowing ethnic culture and from being and behaving ethnic. These also include approaches to diversity that remain ephemeral because diversity of appearance, popularized as race, has been sufficient to satisfy criteria for pluralism.

Three key principles in an evolving integrative multiculturalism are offered as follows:

1. Owning diversity
2. Forging cohesion and unity
3. Holding the dialectical tension between diversity and cohesion

Owning Diversity

The anthropological dictum has long been that cultures like animal species have a high extinction rate and that cultural variation, like biological variation, is a key to survival (Cohen, 1998).

Bringing diversity in would mean a gradual incorporation of surface markers such as language and dress in the public domain, transforming the climate of uniformity to plurality. In an environment of at least some lived and expressed cultural diversity and exchange (on the lines of surface markers), the stage may be better set for dialogue and consensus building in areas such as mythology, literature, holidays, other customs and aspects of culture (primary markers). Social reformers, intellectuals, artists, even the media, religious leaders, and politicians can promote pluralism by bringing the art, music, dance, heroines, heroes, folklore, philosophy, customs of the periphery to the center and center to the periphery till these distinctions gradually disappear, creating interaction, familiarity, and knowledge where dominance, ignorance, exclusivity, and alienation prevail. In current mainstream life, McIntosh (1998) describes the prevailing mentality of arrogance and dominance in the following words: "I can remain oblivious of the language and customs of the persons of color who constitute the world's majority without feeling in my culture any penalty for such oblivion" (p. 149).

This mentality of cultural ignorance without penalty comes from the dominance dynamics of assimilationism, which feeds ethnocentric hubris based on assumptions of cultural superiority making it irrelevant to be familiar with the plural or culturally unfamiliar. It is a major barrier to overcome in the removal of cultural oppression, distance and division and to prepare the ground for sowing the seeds of pluralism more fitting for a democratic, heterogeneous people. Social Psychology research informs us that peoples who feel treated with respect, fairness, and value in their societies create and maintain positive social identities and a willingness to contribute to the collective (Tyler & Smith, 1999). It is all of us who stand to gain from bringing diversity into the center.

Forging Unity

Mahatma Gandhi's paradigm of nonviolence which he argued was not only an individual but also a social virtue, provides an interesting perspective on national unification. Gandhi proposed the idea of an oceanic circle to replace the idea of hierarchy because he argued that hierarchy and integration are essentially incompatible. He described (Gandhi, 1963) hierarchy as a "pyramid with the apex sustained by the bottom," and an oceanic circle as a structure of "ever widening, never ascending circles." In this circle, he went on to say, the center will be "the individual always ready to perish for the village, the latter ready to perish for the circle of villages, till at last, the whole becomes one life composed of individuals never aggressive in their arrogance but ever humble sharing the majesty of the oceanic circle of which they are integral units. Therefore, the outermost circumference will not yield power to crush the inner circle but give strength to all within and derive its own from the center" (p. 53). To use the circle as a metaphor for social processes of forging unity, we have to shift in our thinking from using the culturally familiar linear to a less culturally familiar circular paradigm and attendant values about what makes us good and strong, and, therefore, what processes we employ to attain valued goals.

A framework of absolute and relative morality is also useful to consider here (see Table 1.1). Absolute morality grows out of core, universal needs of all human beings to eat, enjoy health and health care, to have peace and freedom from abuse, to participate in community life that satisfies social and psychological needs and preserves myths and symbols so long without harming others (Cohen, 1998). Relative morality grows out of arbitrary foci and values of different cultures and can be broken down into areas of essential and inessential conformity, distinguishing between areas of necessary conformity for practical and not hegemonic reasons and areas of nonconformity and freedom. Using this framework, relative essentials such as driving on the right side of the road (Cohen), or speaking English as the national language could be identified. Relative inessentials such as learning and speaking multiple languages in the public domain; using multiple ways of greeting people from different cultures such as bowing, shaking hands, folding palms, and so on in the public domain; using multiple formats for gathering for professional work such as on the floor on Tatami mats, Zabutons and low tables, on carpeted floors with "gaddis" or floor cushions, and around the customary conference tables and chairs, could also be

Table 1.1. Contrasting Frameworks

	Hierarchy	Egality
VALUES	Use of diversity-simplifying concepts such as race for social differentiation and description of identity. Focus on differences only and necessarily in a hierarchical, competitive way, yielding winners and losers, more and less favored.	Use of complex concepts such as culture delineating clusters of patterns for social differentiation and description of identity. Focus on differences as well as commonalities. Construct complexity defies easy determination of winners and losers.
PROCESS	Dominance-submission, overt or covert.	Exchange and reciprocity.
OUTCOME	Cultural uniformity, homogeneity, removal of cultural contexts, differences and resources.	Cultural integration based on consensus on democratic absolutes and agreed upon essentials, as well as diversity of inessentials.

identified. This framework can be useful in forging a unity based on absolutes and some consensually agreed upon relative essentials, leaving a wide area of nonconformity and diversity of other relative inessentials, encouraging pluralism to grow in the fabric of the culture and replace homogeneity. As globalization continues, opportunities for a marriage between multiculturalism and internationalism increase as does the possibility of indigenous psychologies from around the globe enriching and informing domestic multiculturalism and vice versa. Crucial to such an evolving, integrative multiculturalism's knowledge base will be enquiry into the conditions and processes that allow a heterogeneous, democratic people to achieve a meaningful cohesiveness and the freedom to create a more plural culture.

Unity in Diversity: Holding the Dual Needs for Distinction and Cohesion

Diversity without the temperance of unity for American peoples contains the dangers of fragmentation, lack of connection and even ethnic violence. Optimal distinctiveness theory, an offshoot of self-categorization theory indicates that people have an intrinsic tendency to balance the needs to be similar to others and to be distinct and unique (Brewer & Pickett, 1999). Holding the two needs together in large and small social contexts means a commitment to dealing with complexity, not simplification; the discomfort of ambiguity, not the comfort of familiar arbitrary dichotomies; and the desire for long-term integrative outcomes. The conceptual means of self-definition for holding the said dualities can be one example among many in a set of mechanisms to consider in this context (Banerjee, 2000).

Conceptual means of self-definition grow out of philosophical approaches and political agendas that generate the particular labels, categories, and processes that are then purposefully used. When a section of society employs the approach of needing no name, for instance, it is generally because its members enjoy the privilege of being among those who name everything (George, 1997). This is the kind of privilege that has allowed successive groups of European Americans, as well as heterosexuals to pass through the public sphere unobstructed and unnoticed for difference. Another nonconstructive practice in this naming and identifying process is the Western attempt to confer identity by contrast, emphasizing differences and exclusivity, which, in turn, results in the same practice being followed by Minority groups to establish counter exclusiveness (Sen, 2000).

In the process of immigration to the United States, I have personally lost the privilege of being among those who name everything. It is a privilege that I have chosen to lose. In my pre-immigration life, I had the experience of a social context where privilege came for no good reason. In my post-immigration life, I have had the experience of a social context where discrimination comes for no good reason. The place in which I now stand in the fullness of the experiences of my life, with access to both kinds of contexts, I own as a unique place from which to give my voice to the cause of democratic social change.

Race, a biologically fictitious term, has been principally used to label difference and identity in America and relies on unchangeable aspects of appearance, namely chromatics and physiognomy (Banerjee, 2000). Race as a term pulling for color, can invite stereotyping and a heightened sense of differences (Banerjee). These perceptions of dissimilarity can, in turn, be a precondition to moral exclusion and acts of further injustice (Opotow, 1990). Culture may be a more suitable term for self-definitional purposes of a free and diverse people mindful of the dual needs for cohesion and distinction. It is a broad, inclusive concept, which can include multiple dimensions including color, region, class, language, customs, belief systems, gender, ability, and sexual orientation (Banerjee). The use of a complex, multilayered concept for self-definitional purposes can also influence a societal mentality toward American national cultural identity in a more complex, realistic, and inclusive direction. It can encourage people to own their own diversity and engage with others at least a little before labeling them, thus moving beyond the surface of appearances. In the process of moving from identifying people in terms of discrete racial categories to clusters of patterns across continuous dimensions, people can draw bases for commonality as well as difference between themselves and others. Culture is also an alterable and adaptable concept, one that can be changed if desired, unlike skin color or physical features. Flexible, alterable concepts are more amenable to a mentality of integration than fixed, unalterable ones.

In the context of the United States Census, the slowly increasing range of choices of racial categories could be replaced with an exhaustive, multilayered list of cultural identifiers (see Exhibit 1.1). One layer could include identifiers such as Salvadorian American, Swedish American, Chinese American, and so on. Another layer could include identifiers such as Muslim American, Jewish American, Protestant (Presbyterian) American, and so on. Yet another layer could include identifiers such as homosexual, heterosexual, bisexual, and so on. Other layers could include gender and ability until all potential layers of diversity are included. People could check off as many categories as apply in each layer, yielding a fuller, more accurate, more fluid, and more permeable representation of identity, and a better basis for owning commonalities as well as distinctiveness. People of mixed heritage have already spearheaded an effort to do this kind of thing with regard to ethnicity. This could, in turn, translate into more fluid, less rigid, less divisive identity politics, dissolving the constructed majority and its hierarchical position of dominance and making more fluid majority-minority groupings that coalesce, dissolve, and reconfigure based on the specific issues in question. Any prospect of dismantling the established hierarchy may be daunting for members of the majority receiving unearned entitlements

Exhibit 1.1   Key Principles and Processes in an Integrative Multicultural Paradigm.

Principle: Owning diversity

Processes
- Reflecting on homogenizing cultural influences on individual, familial, and communal selves
- Bringing in multilingualism
- Bringing in diversity of dress in the public sphere
- Building on diversity of surface markers, for example, language and dress to bring in diversity of primary markers, for example, customs, celebrations, official holidays, mythology, heroines and heroes, art, and so on
- Placing value on experiential multicultural knowledge, skills, and attitudes in place of cultural ignorance that is widespread and commonplace due to assimilationism and homogenization, which have fed fear of difference and that limit freedom of awareness and choice

Principle: Forging unity and cohesion

Processes
- Using the circle as a metaphor for nonlinear, democratic, and multicultural values replacing the pyramid or ladder as metaphor for linear, capitalist values
- Examining and experientially bringing to awareness universally held values and bases for commonality
- Placing value on experiential cultural exchange and reciprocity, such that boundaries are seen as permeable and the border as a place of resource to replace overt or covert cultural hegemony and widespread voluntary segregation
- Developing consensus on a moral framework of some shared absolutes and relative essentials as well as diversity of relative inessentials

Principle: Holding the dialectical tension between diversity and cohesion

Processes
- Developing new concepts and constructs to define and represent culture and identity that have the complexity and adaptability to contain these dualities to replace concepts that confer identity by contrast and maintain exclusivity from one another
- Encouraging flexible, encompassing mentalities toward culture, such that differences and similarities are both actively sought
- Reflecting on the challenges of holding the dialectical tension between tradition

from majority membership. Any prospect of losing racial categories that have provided a mechanism to redress inequalities can also be resisted by minorities. The longer-term goals of forging a better sense of belonging together and a more just system are the kind of motives that can carry this kind of change forward.

Strong residues of Anglo-Conformity remain with us today, framing the backbone of our culture and identity even as Multiculturalism has entered the fray. The obstacles to the passage of Multiculturalism into the culture include insufficient reflection on the dominance and removal approach to defining culture that comes from Anglo-Conformity, lack of attention to means for enjoying reasonable cohesion, and the lack of attention to means for dealing with inevitable cultural conflicts. Other obstacles include Multiculturalism's emphasis on watertight groups evoking tribalism rather than integration, the related focus on surface differences such as color and physiognomy in place of the complexities and richness of culture, and insufficient attention to the center-periphery reality of minority cultures relative to the majority. Expansion of the multicultural paradigm is argued for to include the idea of unity in diversity, to examine how diversity can more effectively be brought into the center, how cohesion can be reasonably aimed for, and the tension between the two constructively and comfortably maintained. These ideas are offered as a scholarly meditation in a narrative voice, guided by a social justice agenda for further reflection and use in the contexts of training, research, advocacy, and public policy discussion.

References

Banerjee, L. (2000). What's in a name and other thoughts on social categorizations in America. *The Community Psychologist, 33*(2), 16–18.

Brewer, B., & Pickett, C. L. (1999). Distinctiveness motives as a source of the social self. In T. R. Tyler., R. M. Kramer, & O. P. John (Eds.), *The psychology of the social self* (pp. 71–87). Mahwah, NJ: Lawrence Erlbaum.

Cohen, M. (1998). *Culture of intolerance: Chauvinism, class and racism in the United States.* New Haven CT, London: Yale University Press.

Fairchild, H. (1926). *The melting pot mistake.* Boston: Little Brown.

Fowers, B., & Richardson, F. (1996, June). Why is multiculturalism good? *American Psychologist,* 609–621.

Gandhi, M. (1963). *Village Swaraj.* Ahmedabad: Navajivan Publishing House.

Gardetta, D. (1998). School daze. *Los Angeles Times Magazine,* pp. 16–36.

George, R. (1997). From expatriate aristocrat to immigrant nobody: South Asian racial strategies in the Southern Californian context. *Diaspora, 6*(1), 31–60.

Glazer, N., & Moynihan, D. P. (1963). *Beyond the melting pot.* Cambridge: MIT Press.

Glazer, N., & Moynihan, D. (Eds.). (1975). *Ethnicity: Theory and experience,* Cambridge: Harvard University Press.

Grant, M. (1916). *The passing of the great race.* New York: Scribner.

Hong, Y., Morris, M., Chiu, C., & Benet-Martinez, V. (2000). Multicultural minds, a dynamic constructivist approach to culture and cognition. *American Psychologist, 55*(7), 709–720.

Hutnik, N. (1991). *Ethnic minority identity, a social psychological perspective.* Oxford: Clarendon Press.

Kallen, H. (1925). *Culture and democracy in the United States.* New York: Arno Press.

Kanellos, N. (1997). An American multicultural response. In I. Reed (Ed.), *MultiAmerica: Essays on cultural war and cultural peace.* New York: Viking Press.

Kitayama, S., & Markus, H. R. (1994). Culture and self: The way we view ourselves. In D. Matsumoto (Ed.), *People: Psychology from a cultural perspective.* Prospect Heights, IL: Waveland Press.

McGoldrick, (Ed.). (1998). *Re-visioning family therapy, race, culture and gender in clinical practice.* New York: Guilford Press.

McIntosh, P. (1998). White privilege: Unpacking the invisible knapsack. In M. McGoldrick (Ed.), *Re-visioning family therapy, race, culture and gender in clinical practice.* New York: The Guilford Press.

Michaels, W. (1995). *Our America, nativism, modernism and pluralism.* Durham: Duke University Press.

Mukherjee, B. (1997). Beyond multiculturalism: Surviving in the nineties. In I. Reed (Ed.), *MultiAmerica: Essays on cultural war and cultural peace.* New York: Viking Press.

Ogbu, J. (1989). *Cultural models and educational strategies of non-dominant peoples.* 1989 Catherine Molony Memorial Lecture, New York, City College Workshop Center.

Opotow, S. (1990). Moral exclusion and injustice: An introduction. *Journal of Social Issues, 46*(1), 1–20.

Panat, S., & Banerjee, L. (1994, October). *Conflicting allegiances: Indian womens' struggle to bridge generations and reach a common identity.* South Asian Womens' Conference: Forging New Identities in America, UCLA, Los Angeles, CA.

Rothbaum, F., Weisz, S., Pott, M., Miyake, K., & Morelli, G. (2000). Attachment and culture, security in the United States and Japan. *American Psychologist, 55*(10), 1093–1104.

Saldivar, R. (1990). *Chicano narrative: Dialectics of difference.* Madison, WI: University of Wisconsin.

Sen, A. (2000). *East and West: The reach of reason.* New York Review of Books, July 20, 2000.

Strickland, B. (2000). Misassumptions, misadventures, and the misuse of psychology. *American Psychologist, 55*(3), 331–338.

Sue, S. (1999). Science, ethnicity and bias, where have we gone wrong? *American Psychologist, 54*(12), 1070–1077.

Sue, D., Bingham, R., Porche-Burke, L., & Vasquez, M. (1999). The diversification of psychology, a multicultural revolution. *American Psychologist, 54*(12), 1061–1069.

Turner, F. (1920). *The frontier in American history.* New York: Holt & Co.

Tyler, T., & Smith, H. (1999). Justice, social identity and group processes. In T. R. Tyler., R. M. Kramer, & O. P. John (Eds.), *The psychology of the social self* (pp. 71–87). Mahwah, NJ: Lawrence Erlbaum.

Wakil, S., Siddique, C., & Wakil, F. (1981). Between two cultures: A study in the socialization of children of immigrants. *Journal of Marriage and the Family, 4,* 929–940.

Weber, M. (1967). *Economy and society.* New York: Bedminter Press.

Zack, N. (1998). *Thinking about race.* Belmont, CA: Wadsworth Publishing Co.

Zangwill, I. (1929). *The melting pot.* New York: Maxmillan.

CHAPTER TWO

A Metastructure for Multicultural Professional Psychology Education and Training

Standards and Philosophy

Diane Adams

The multicultural faculty of one professional school, the California School of Professional Psychology (CSPP) elected to adopt multicultural competency standards as a "next step" move in building upon an increased capacity to be multiculturally responsible and competent. Some of the foundation for this move was laid at the Puerto Rico Conference of the National Council of Schools of Professional Psychology (NCSPP) in 1990 (Stricker et al., 1990). The conference addressed the priority multicultural concerns of professional schools at that time. Conference participants were concerned about how to increase multicultural student and faculty representation, and how to introduce multicultural content into existing curricula for all students. First step efforts, made in the 1980s and early 1990s by CSPP faculty to address these concerns, paid off and led to the possibility for more substantive changes in the ways to teach and practice multicultural psychology. However, the movement toward multiculturalism in professional schools sometimes threatened colleagues because proposed changes, and differing perspectives, challenged fundamental worldviews and beliefs about the role of psychologists, their values, standards, practices, and methods of education.

Some of the proposed changes included a focus on alternative interventions of individual psychotherapy and traditional quantitative research methods and the application of a sociopolitical perspective to practice and theory (Duran, Guillory, & Villanueva, 1990). Schools of professional psychology were called upon to include a focus on the social context of problems, on prevention and health promotion in communities (Adams, 1994), and to include social action, quasi-experimental, and qualitative evaluation and research methods in their curricula, in addition to traditional interventions and methods. As time went on, changes brought about in the health care climate from managed health care (Frank & VandenBos, 1994; Hersch, 1995) and shifts in national funding priorities, made such changes in professional psychology, despite resistance, seem inevitable. Reluctantly, but perceiving it as necessary for survival, the profession as a whole began to grapple seriously with changes in role identity, practice, education, and training.

In this chapter, stages in the development of multicultural psychology within professional psychology are reviewed, and the controversy and dialogue that accompanied changes in curricula and institutions are discussed. This dialogue took place around some of the basic premises of multicultural psychology. Those basic premises are identified here as (1) a culturally pluralistic philosophy; (2) a psychosocial and sociopolitical perspective on development and treatment, which includes the influences of racism and oppression; and (3) a community and systems intervention strategy in addition to individual intervention strategies. The history and theoretical bases of these premises are described and posited as an organizing metastructure for education, training, and practice in professional psychology.

A set of multicultural competency standards crafted by the Multicultural Education, Research, and Training (MERIT) Institute of a professional school (MERIT, 1993) was the starting point for discussion and development of the proposed metastructure. Several of these competencies seemed pivotal to a construct of multicultural psychology. In this chapter, the theoretical bases underlying some of these competencies are identified and posited as essential components of multicultural psychology. Concepts from social psychology, community psychology, public health, education, and social welfare are seen as particularly germane to the practice of multicultural professional psychology. These concepts include the notion of a just society (Albee, 1986; Sue, Arredondo, & McDavis, 1992) and the idea that the goal of interventions is to empower individuals and communities (Rappaport, 1987). The notion that psychologists have no role to play as social change agents is challenged, and professional psychologists are seen as having a legitimate role to play in social and political activism and in social commentary and reform, both within the public sector and within organized psychology.

STAGES IN THE DEVELOPMENT OF MULTICULTURAL PSYCHOLOGY IN PROFESSIONAL SCHOOLS

Multicultural curriculum models: Davis-Russell (1990) and Jackson (1990) reviewed and recommended Copeland's (1982) four training models for psychology curricula. These models are used here both as descriptions of course work organization and descriptions of different stages in the historical development of multicultural curricula within psychology institutions. The four models were as follows:

- The separate-course model
- The area-of-concentration model
- The interdisciplinary model
- The integration model

Early development in the introduction of multicultural content into curricula was marked by the introduction of one multicultural course, called the separate-course model. The area-of-concentration model and the integration model are considered to be more developed stages in multicultural curriculum implementation. Using the area-of-concentration model, a sequence of multicultural courses is implemented as a separate area of concentration. Alternatively or simultaneously using the integration model, multicultural content is integrated in a comprehensive manner into existing courses. The interdisciplinary model poses a different alternative altogether. Using this model, students take course work in other disciplines outside of the clinical psychology curriculum, such as sociology, anthropology, or political science.

Issues in Implementation of Curriculum Models

While the integrated training model appeared to be more advanced and an ideal goal for curriculum change, this ideal was not often realized, particularly when the faculty expected to integrate such content lacked expertise in multicultural psychology, or were resistant to the idea. In these instances the integration of multicultural content was minimal at best, and, at worst, negatively modeled, or even misrepresented the concept of valuing diversity. In retrospect, it seems that the success of the integrated model hinged on the provision of multicultural training and development experiences for all faculty. Particularly, faculty needed multicultural training in the specific content and clinical areas they were teaching in the curriculum and in managing the racial dialogue taking place in the classroom as the institution and the curriculum began to diversify.

Initially, there were fears that the area-of-concentration model would result in "separateness," or the isolation of multicultural faculty and students from their peers and retard the integration of multicultural content throughout the curriculum. This latter fear proved not to be true. The simultaneous existence of the area-of-concentration model and the integration model seemed to facilitate the integration of multicultural content and added to the institution in other ways. At CSPP the area of concentration aided in attracting and retaining faculty with multicultural expertise and interest, which in turn with their interaction and collaboration, helped with the development of multicultural awareness and competence among other faculty. Fears of isolation and separatism resulting from the area-of-concentration model seemed to have been unfounded. Although conflicts arose that were divided along racial lines (or outlook), as the institution actively pursued the goal of multiculturalism, it was normal for separate viewpoints and disparate perceptions to arise when diverse racial, ethnic, and cultural groups would interact. It is debatable what influence if any the area-of-concentration model had on this process. Constant dialogue between all the constituencies of the campus community seemed to be the answer, and needed to be built in, and not take place only in response to crisis.

Multicultural Institutional Development

As multiculturalism advanced in professional schools it became apparent that multicultural curriculum development and multicultural institutional development were linked. With the introduction of a critical mass of diverse students and faculty there was a press for changes in the institution to accommodate them. This often led to changes in curriculum that called for, or were accompanied by changes in institutional policies and procedures. As institutions moved from being monocultural to endorsing an affirmative action position and grappling with true multiculturalism, policy change often preceded attitude change, or even a clear understanding of the issues. Highlen (1994) described similar stages and processes of multicultural development in departments of psychology as these institutions moved from being monocultural to multicultural. A considerable amount of controversial dialogue usually accompanied both institutional change and the introduction of multicultural courses into psychology curricula. Early on, the basic philosophical premise that seemed to underlie arguments against the inclusion of specific multicultural content were beliefs, expressed directly and indirectly, in the value of assimilation and sameness, and in the universal applicability of psychology theory and practice. Arguments in support of change included society's changing sociodemographics, the inadequacy of services for multicultural clients, the alternative value of pluralism, and ethnocentrism as one possible negative outcome of valuing sameness. The philosophical resolution that emerged from this dialogue established one of the basic premises of multicultural psychology, the recognition and valuing of cultural diversity.

Toward a Metastructure for Multicultural Professional Psychology: A Culturally Pluralistic Philosophy

Pedersen (1991b) made the point that if multicultural psychology is to be considered a theory, definitions of multiculturalism need to include "broadly defined social system variables, such as ethnographic, demographic, status and affiliation" (p. 7). One of the distinctions of a multicultural perspective "is that it implies a wide range of multiple groups without grading, comparing, or ranking them as better or worse than one another and without denying the very distinct and complimentary or even contradictory perspectives that each group brings with it" (Pedersen, 1991a, p. 4). Pedersen (1991b) also emphasized the utility of culture as an organizing frame and advised against definitions of multiculturalism restricted to race, nationality, or ethnicity. As culture encompasses such variables as world views, morals, values, and styles of relating, as well as habits, behaviors, and preferences, Pedersen (1991b) suggested that culture then becomes the organizing frame for understanding behavior.

There is controversy over Pedersen's (1991b) suggestion that multiculturalism be broadly defined, and how inclusive the term is or should be. Intellectually there is a commitment to honoring and respecting all diversity. At the same time there is the fear that broad definitions of the term will detract from the pressing and unique concerns of oppressed ethnic and racial groups. This fear is fueled by perceptions, accurate and inaccurate, of still prevalent reluctance among Euro-Caucasians to acknowledge, understand, or grapple personally with the interactional dynamics or psychological effects of racism, oppression, and domination. There is the need to include as part of the definition of multicultural psychology an explicit theoretical perspective which aids in understanding the dynamics of racism, oppression, and other sociopolitical forces on individual development. Such a perspective is equally critical for understanding the psychology of other oppressed groups. Including such a perspective as a necessary and defining component of multicultural psychology may help obviate the need for ongoing discussions about the inclusive and exclusiveness of the term. While knowledge of culture and the valuing of diversity are essential components of a multicultural perspective, they are insufficient for understanding the psychology of people of color or other oppressed groups. Theories that incorporate concepts and processes which explain and describe oppression and racism are necessary, not only in understanding personality development, behavior, and individual adaptation, but also in understanding organizations, institutions, and decision-making processes.

Multicultural Competency Standards Set the Stage

At the same time that multicultural issues were being debated in educational institutions, this debate was also taking place in professional psychology organizations. In this arena, challenges to justify the need for a multicultural psychology were answered by outlining the moral and ethical responsibilities of psychologists. As an outcome of this dialogue, multicultural competency was defined and standards and guidelines for competent practice were proposed. The statements made about multicultural competency contained both the seeds of a comprehensive theoretical framework at the same time that they emphasized the need to develop such a framework. Burn (1992) proposed alternate competency statements to those developed by the American Association for

Counseling and Development [AACD] (1988) and noted: "Although it is not feasible for a large number of counselors to become intimate with a broad spectrum of differing cultures, it is possible to instill in all counselors a foundation from which to appreciate and consider the unique cultural circumstances that influence the behaviors of the client" (Burn, 1992, p. 582). This statement suggested that there was such a foundation or framework. In the American Psychological Association (APA) guidelines for providers of psychological services to diverse populations (American Psychological Association [APA], 1990) the statement was made that service providers needed a sociocultural framework that considered "diversity of values, interactional styles, and cultural expectations in a systematic fashion" (p. 1). "The guidelines didn't articulate such a framework but went on to describe knowledge, skills, and abilities critical to multicultural competency; emphasizing, among other things, the importance of culture, ethnicity, and race on development; and the impact of socioeconomic and political factors on the development of culturally and ethnically diverse groups" (pp. 2–4). Sue, Arredondo, and McDavis (1992) proposed that "what needs to occur is a philosophical change in the premise of counseling that incorporates a movement toward inclusiveness, altruism, community, care and justice" (p. 481). Ibrahim and Arredondo (1986) spoke to the need "to develop a culturally determined world view that includes values, belief systems, life styles, and modes of problem solving and decision making" (p. 349).

Since this chapter was first written Adams (1994) and Sue, Ivey, and Pedersen (1996) went further and articulated a comprehensive theory of Multicultural Counseling and Therapy (MCT). This work and others preceding it contributed to identifying the essential perspectives or components for the theoretical basis of multicultural psychology. It is critical to further articulate this theoretical basis, particularly as it applies to practice, education, and training in professional psychology.

Development and Implementation of Multicultural Competency Standards in a Professional School

The experiences of one group of faculty in developing multicultural courses and content for the curricula at a professional school of psychology serves as a starting point for discussion. The faculty of the MERIT Institute of CSPP elected to move in the direction of adopting multicultural competency standards. These competency standards contained core concepts that further articulate a conceptual basis for multicultural professional psychology. Of the twenty-eight individuals involved in crafting the competencies, twenty-one were faculty involved in teaching multicultural psychology, the other seven comprised the faculty administrators and staff. Of the total twenty-eight, twelve were African American, six Asian, six Euro-Caucasian and four Latino(a). The comprehensiveness of the competencies in encompassing the unique histories, development, and needs of diverse multicultural groups is reflective, and probably a byproduct of the diversity among the group of individuals who participated in crafting them. It was also a byproduct of the consensus model of decision making used in negotiating the final content of the competencies. In the consensus model, different viewpoints are heard, negotiated, and integrated. In the course of the discussions that accompanied the creating of the competency statements, different voices rose at different times to make sure that the language used captured the modes of thinking, world views, and themes significant for understanding different ethnic groups.

A CURRICULUM EXAMPLE: IMPLEMENTATION OF MULTICULTURAL COMPETENCIES

The multicultural competencies are comprehensive, covering many different content areas, and designed specifically for implementation in education and training programs in clinical psychology. They are sequential, with a set of standards identified for each year level of the program and they build upon previous models (Davis-Russell, 1990). Year one of the competencies is targeted at attitudes about multicultural populations. Year two is targeted at knowledge about multicultural populations. Year three is targeted at skills attainment, intervention, research, and scholarly critiques. Years four and five are targeted at advanced clinical skills and professional projects or research skills. The decision to sequence the multicultural competencies in the way that they were sequenced, with year one focused on acquiring an awareness of attitudes and biases, was based on other established models for teaching multicultural content (Locke, 1986; Pedersen, 1988), and also on the experiences of faculty teaching such content in courses to students without having first addressed issues of awareness. In these instances, the lack of awareness of attitudes about racism, or awareness of the ways in which factors such as racism and ethnocentrism affect perceptions and judgments, not only interfered with learning multicultural content, but also contributed to the misapplication of such concepts.

Presently, courses which teach racism awareness and the psychology of intercultural differences have been positioned first in curricula at CSPP. Two different types of such courses are offered on different campuses, one primarily experiential and focused on racism in a workshop format, the other combines simultaneous presentation of didactic and experiential content and includes other forms of oppression in addition to racism. Courses focused on theory, research, and literature are considered knowledge based and positioned in the second year of training. Clinical practica experience, combined with additional courses in professional practice with multicultural populations, are considered skill focused and expected in the third year. The fourth and fifth years concentrate on continued professional internship and practica training combined with advanced courses in multicultural issues. Additionally the dissertation or doctoral project incorporates multicultural perspectives in the conceptualization, design, and implementation, which is considered an advanced skill.

Initial implementation of these curriculum competencies suggest that it might be useful to identify minimal and advanced competencies for each year level. All students would be expected to achieve minimal competency, with advanced competency training available to those who elect it. So for example, in years four and five minimal competency in research might focus on acquiring knowledge of multicultural ethical and professional considerations in the reporting of research findings, sample selection and characteristics, and general issues in research design and instrument selection; while advanced competency in this area would focus on incorporating multicultural perspectives in the conceptualization, design, and implementation of the dissertation and doctoral project or on conducting research with multicultural populations or on issues of concern to those populations.

FUNDAMENTAL CHALLENGES TO TRADITIONAL WAYS OF THINKING ABOUT PSYCHOLOGY

There were particular competency statements that received a great deal of discussion and inspired considerable expressions of affect. These competencies emerged as critical in individuals thinking about multicultural psychology. They felt strongly about them because they thought it crucially important to include them in the competency statements. They are presented here as key perspectives for establishing the theoretical basis of a clinical multicultural psychology.

One of these competencies is to "develop awareness of the dynamics of power and oppression as they relate to domination and racism" (MERIT Institute, 1993, p. 1). Another is "knowledge of the operation of sociopolitical systems within the United States and their treatment of multicultural populations including the impact of individual, cultural, and institutional racism upon the development of personality identity and world views" (p. 3). Moving beyond the sociopolitical system of the United States, another is to "further develop competencies in the treatment of an ethnic/racial group(s) other than one's own and to develop an understanding of how sociopolitical systems and power relationships in a global society impact such cases" (p. 5). An additional competency statement that generated little discussion, but nevertheless poses a challenge for traditional ways of thinking and emerges as critical for formulating a multicultural psychology, is to "attain advanced skills in institutional interventions which can be used on behalf of multicultural populations, for example, advocacy, case management, community intervention, interdisciplinary approaches, and grassroots and community based strategies (self-help groups)" (p. 5).

At the first writing of this chapter (Adams, 1994), these skills and competencies were thought of more as clinical interventions. Since then it has become increasingly clear that the application of the knowledge and skills called for in these competencies are applicable to professional activities and relationships within organized psychology. Psychologists have a role to play in shaping social policy, social commentary, and reform in the public arena. However, it did seem quite clear at the time to the individuals involved in crafting the competencies, that the call for social and political awareness and alternative interventions, posed a fundamental challenge to many colleagues' beliefs concerning the purview of psychology and the role of psychologists in clinical practice.

An Integrative Metastructure

These competencies represented a statement of the core knowledge and skills seen as critical for multicultural competencies. In their focus on international and local political systems, power relationships, and alternative interventions they illustrated a distinction between traditional clinical psychology and multicultural psychology. Inherent in these statements was the recognition of society's impact on psychological development and human behavior and the effects of injustice and oppression on the human condition. Extrapolating from these statements, and adding the concept of cultural pluralism previously reviewed, three basic components of a theory for multicultural clinical psychology emerge. They are (1) a culturally pluralistic philosophy, which has been discussed and reviewed in a previous section; (2) a psychosocial and sociopolitical perspective on development and treatment, which includes the influences of racism and oppression; and (3) a community- and systems-intervention strategy in addition to individual intervention strategies. These three aspects of multicultural clinical psychology are offered as an integrative metastructure. Within the metastructure, knowledge of racism is emphasized as important in understanding individual development and human behavior, and the use of empowering interventions is seen as the goal of practice.

In the latter two areas, the sociopolitical perspective and the community intervention strategies, have been less explored. These areas can be considered frontiers in multicultural clinical psychology, particularly in education and training programs, and more attention will be paid to them here. In discussing these two areas, some concepts are reviewed from the fields of community psychology of primary prevention of psychopathology and of education. Additionally a sociopolitical perspective is seen as important for understanding behavior and understanding individual development. It is argued that without a sociopolitical perspective behavior can be misconstrued and labeled as deviant.

Psychosocial and Sociopolitical Perspectives on Development: A Clinical Example

In some professional schools, in clinical psychology there has been a traditional focus on the individual and on intrapsychic phenomena. In multicultural professional psychology, perspectives on individual development have evolved with a focus on the interrelationships between society and the individual and the interaction between intrapsychic and extrapsychic phenomena. This distinguishes multicultural psychology in professional, clinical programs from multicultural counseling psychology, which is more cognitively based. The following framework is suggested for establishing a psychosocial perspective for development. It is important to be able to distinguish between intrapsychic and extrapsychic sources of stress. Additionally, in establishing a psychosocial perspective for development, it is necessary to place the individual within the context of society and describe the socioeconomic and environmental context in which the individual's behaviors, thoughts, and feelings developed.

For example, problems that a second generation Chinese American woman might present in treatment could best be understood if viewed from a psychosocial and sociopolitical context. Within this context, the history of the Chinese American experience of racism, marked by discriminatory immigration laws, low-income, hard labor, menial jobs, social isolation, and physical assault is important (Hsu, 1971; Takaki, 1989). These manifestations of racism had an intergenerational effect from first generation to second generation because they affected family structure, child rearing patterns, gave birth to Chinatowns, and affected how the second generation children of these families interfaced with the world and also how they felt about themselves (Louie, 1994).

Additionally, using a psychosocial and sociopolitical perspective, it would be important to be aware of Confucianism, and other aspects of traditional Chinese culture, in relationship to gender role expectations as well as the individual woman's level of acculturation (Berry & Kim, 1988; Hsu, 1970). All of these factors will be salient in understanding conflicts expressed by the individual and her experience of her self and her world. These variables will also be important in understanding coping, adaptation, and functional and dysfunctional behavior.

Multicultural clinical psychology tends to be interdisciplinary in the knowledge base it draws upon, using theory and approaches from fields such as history, sociology, political science, and anthropology to understand behavior in social context.

Racism, Individual Development, Coping, and Adaptation

Racism and other theories of oppression are important considerations for understanding the individual development, coping, and adaptation of people of color and other oppressed groups, exerting at least as much of an influence as culture. Racism affects the individuals relationship to the self (for example, self-esteem, self-concept, and sense of racial identity) (Cross, 1978; Parham, 1989). When racism poses a threat to basic survival, for example, the threat and reality of physical assault and unemployment, or restricts the types of opportunities individuals have to realize their aspirations, it challenges the individual to find equilibrium in adaptation. Racism also affects development because it distorts perceptions and shifts the context of interactions, making it difficult to know what it is or is not or what is real and what is not, for both victim and perpetrator (Comer 1980; Delaney, 1980). This aspect of racism makes racism awareness training and education an important component of multicultural competence. Racism is not only manifest individually, but also institutionally as a byproduct of certain institutional practices; and culturally as well in the elevation and denigration of one race's culture and heritage over another's (Jones, 1972). Lack of knowledge of the effects of racism colonization or oppression on individuals can result in victim blaming and difficulty in distinguishing between coping, adaptation, and dysfunction. There are important distinctions to be made for treatment.

MULTICULTURAL PROFESSIONAL PSYCHOLOGY, COMMUNITY AND SOCIAL JUSTICE

It is a well-known fact (Gooden, 1989; Neighbors, 1990) that conditions in multicultural communities play a central role in determining the development and quality of life for multicultural individuals. Racism—institutional, cultural, and individual—accounts for, and perpetuates these conditions. Take for example, the plight of young African American men: the continued escalating death toll—Black-on-Black homicide is the number one killer (Hawkins, 1989); their consistent overrepresentation in special education programs (Kunjufu, 1989); the growing school dropout rate, second only to Latin males (Kozol, 1991; Kunjufu, 1989); and increased substance abuse and overrepresentation in the prison population (Moore, 1993; Singleton, 1989). Within this context, the community and community conditions become a legitimate area of interest and target for interventions in multicultural psychology. The interest in community and the amelioration of social problems within multicultural communities, poses a challenge to clinical psychology's preoccupation with psychopathology and individual treatment (Alpert, 1985), and, as such, represents a basic divergence in orientation. In multicultural professional psychology there is more of an interest in prevention and health promotion as a way to intervene and improve the quality of life and mental health of people of color.

Research and theory in the fields of community psychology, public health, and in the primary prevention of psychopathology—as well as in education—have the potential to significantly contribute to the development of community intervention strategies and increased understanding of the influences of sociopolitical factors on development in multicultural psychology. Lorion (1991) noted that psychology is uniquely positioned to pursue the requisite solutions to the nation's community health problems and also noted that there is a great deal of ambivalence in the field about doing so. This ambivalence stems from a lack of credibility regarding the relationship between such things as poverty, unemployment, racism, and mental health and the still-existing belief that society and concepts of social justice are outside the realm of psychology practice and theory.

Albee (1986) defined a just society as one in which basic human needs are met, unnecessary stress is reduced, individual competence is utilized, and psychopathology and disease are minimized. Barriers to a just society occur when there is arbitrary and excessive use of power to maintain the status quo among other things. Forces, which are barriers to a just society, help to define what may potentially be a generically useful definition of sociopolitical influences. Sociopolitical forces identified by Albee that significantly block efforts to reduce, change, prevent, or treat mental health problems are "exploitation, imperialism, excessive concentration of economic power, nationalism, institutions that perpetuate powerlessness, hopelessness, poverty, discrimination, sexism, racism, and ageism" (p. 894). "These forces are globally significant and systematic in promoting the status quo, rewarding conformity and perpetuating injustice through control and influence exerted on the world's communication systems, especially mass media and educational systems, and by deliberately distributing rewards for conformity and for the support of injustice" (p. 894). In a just society, everyone has the same basic rights, such as political liberties or the right to hold property. In an unjust society, social and economic inequalities are arranged so that they are "to the greatest benefit of the least advantaged" (p. 897). Efforts to create a just society include working to change social and political structures and redistribute power.

There is an interrelationship between injustice, individual development, and general health and well-being. Albee (1986) noted that "epidemiological studies find clear correlations between most forms of 'psychopathology' and factors such as emotionally damaging infant and childhood experiences, poverty, and degrading life experiences" (p. 891). Wallerstein (1992) presented compelling evidence that powerlessness is a risk factor for disease, noting that lifestyle factors only partially explain disease, and also that social class, rather than race, may plausibly explain the differences in health status between certain ethnic or racial groups and Euro-Caucasians. "In sum . . . studies in socioeconomic status, occupational health, and stress suggest that being poor, low in the hierarchy, without control, and living in chronic hardship . . . is . . . a broad risk factor that increases susceptibility to higher morbidity and mortality rates" (p. 199).

Using this framework, powerlessness and empowerment are important concepts for designing community as well as individual intervention strategies. Wallerstein (1992) examined the phenomenon of powerlessness in the social and political science literature and proposed a definition. Alternately it has been referred to as alienation, victim blaming, learned helplessness, internalized oppression, or hidden injuries. Using definitions offered by Wallerstein it can be said to be subjective, that is a perceived phenomenon, based on individual expectancy or belief. In this definition, powerlessness is internalized and intrapsychic. Powerlessness is also an objective (extrapsychic) phenomenon or reality "where people with little or no political and economic power lack the means to gain greater control and resources in their lives" (p. 108).

COMMUNITY INTERVENTIONS: EMPOWERMENT, MODEL, AND STRATEGY

The concept of powerlessness provides a bridge to the strategy, or according to Rappaport (1987), theory of empowerment. He defined empowerment as conveying "both a psychological sense of personal control or influence and a concern with social influence, political power and legal rights. It is a multilevel construct applicable to individual citizens as well as to organizations and neighborhoods; it suggests the study of people in context" (p. 121).

Psychological empowerment (Wallerstein, 1992) merges the intrapsychic construct of self-efficacy and the drive for mastery, and competence, with actual skill development and participation in social action. Empowerment can happen on the level of individual change or by changing the social setting itself. Wallerstein noted that empowerment does not necessarily mean that one group gains what another group loses but that empowerment "can expand power as people mobilize to control their personal and community lives" (p. 203).

However, it is important to note that all prevention interventions are not necessarily empowering. In fact, prevention programs may contribute to victim blaming, deficit comparisons, patronizing, and other such undesirable outcomes. It's important to identify intervention strategies that aren't only consistent with the concept of empowerment but are culturally sensitive and consistent with multicultural groups conceptualizations of community. This conceptualization often emphasizes interdependence, interconnectedness, and extended kinship. One such strategy is collaboration. Collaboration as it's used here refers to partnerships between professionals, academic institutions, and community groups and organizations for the purpose of intervening in or preventing health problems. The role of professionals in empowering collaborations in communities is to be facilitative without taking over, to participate in the defining of needs without dictating what those needs are, to acknowledge that the skills and knowledge of community residents is no less valuable than their own "expertise," and to avoid the fostering of dependence by such mechanisms as withholding information and promoting hierarchical structures (Gruber & Trickett, 1987; Katz, 1984; Serrano-Garcia, 1984).

Another empowering intervention strategy which has received considerable attention in the fields of education and social work but not in clinical psychology, is Freire's (1978) pedagogy of the oppressed. Freire's work as a Brazilian educator was not only highly successful in teaching literacy to slum dwellers in Brazil but also motivated them for political activism and social involvement (Brigham, 1977). Freire's model of education provides empowering strategies useful for health education and community participation.

Freire (1978) recognized that "individuals' health problems were indicators of injustice, oppression, and inequity in society, and that although individuals were not to blame for them, they were basically free to alter the present and structure the future" (p. 23). Education for critical consciousness contributes to empowerment by bringing people together around (1) a critical problem termed community organizing; (2) codifying and problem solving termed critical consciousness; and then (3) developing personal and social action plans. The central premise for professionals in Freire's pedagogy is that education is not neutral. Educational interventions can reinforce powerlessness or empower individuals to question and challenge those forces that keep them powerless (Wallerstein, 1992). Freire's work provides methods for empowering education interventions.

Freire's model of education for critical consciousness, and the other ideas presented here, provide theoretical perspectives and have practical implications for those aspects of multicultural clinical psychology that are concerned with prevention, community, and the effects of racism, oppression, and domination on the general health and well-being of individuals. The passage of time has indicated that these concerns are not only critical for multicultural psychology practice but for the profession as a whole, and that it is time for professional psychology to move toward a more socially responsible and responsive practice. This does not mean that we need to abandon traditional perspectives or interventions. It does require some fundamental changes in our ways of thinking in our education and training programs, which in the end, may improve the profession rather than threaten or dismantle basic principles as some seem to fear.

References

Adams, D. (1994). A new metastructure for multicultural psychology education and training: Standards and philosophy. *Proceedings of the National Council of Schools and Programs of Professional Psychology, Midwinter Conference on Standards of Education in Professional Psychology, Cancun, Mexico, Jan. 25–29*, 203–212.

Albee, G. W. (1986). Toward a just society. *American Psychologist, 41*, 891–898.

Alpert, J. L. (1985). Change within a profession: Change, future, prevention, and school psychology. *American Psychologist, 40*, 1112–1121.

American Association for Counseling and Development. (1988). *Ethical standards.* Alexandria, VA: Author.

American Psychological Association. (1990). *Guidelines for providers of psychological services to ethnic, linguistic, and culturally diverse populations.* Washington, DC: Author.

Berry, J. W., & Kim, U. (1988). Acculturation and mental health. In P. R. Dasen, J. W. Berry, & N. Sartorious (Eds.), *Health and cross-cultural psychology: Toward applications* (pp. 207–236). Newbury Park, CA: Sage.

Brigham, T. (1977). Liberation in social work education: Applications from Paulo Freire. *Journal of Education for Social Work, 13*(3), 5–11.

Burn, D. (1992). Ethical implications in cross-cultural counseling and training. *Journal of Counseling and Development, 70*, 578–583.

Comer, J. P. (1980). White racism: Its root, form, and function. In R. L. Jones (Ed.), *Black psychology* (pp. 361–366). New York: Harper & Row.

Copeland, E. J. (1982). Minority populations and traditional counseling programs: Some alternatives. *Counselor Education and Supervision, 21*, 187–193.

Cross, W. E. (1978). The Cross and Thomas models of psychological Nigrescence: A review. *Journal of Black Psychology, 5*(1), 13–19.

Davis-Russell, E. (1990). Incorporating ethnic minority issues into the curriculum: Myths and realities. In G. Stricker, E. Davis-Russell, E. Bourg, E. Duran, W. R. Hammond, J. McHolland, K. Polite, & B. E. Vaughn (Eds.), *Towards ethnic diversification in psychology education and training* (pp. 171–177). Washington, DC: American Psychological Association.

Delaney, L. T. (1980). The other bodies in the river. In R. L. Jones (Ed.), *Black psychology* (pp. 376–383). New York: Harper & Row.

Duran, E., Guillory, B., & Villanueva, M. (1990). Third and fourth world concerns: Toward a liberation psychology. In G. Stricker, E. Davis-Russell, E. Bourg, E. Duran, W. R. Hammond, J. McHolland, K. Polite, & B. E. Vaughn. (Eds.), *Toward ethnic diversification in psychology education and training.* Washington, DC: American Psychological Association.

Frank, R. G., & VandenBos, G. R. (1994). Health care reform: The 1993–1994 evolution. *American Psychologist, 49*(10), 851–854.

Freire, P. (1978). *Pedagogy of the oppressed.* New York: The Seabury Press.

Gooden, W. E. (1989). Development of black men in early adulthood. In R. L. Jones (Ed.), *Black adult development and aging* (pp. 63–90). Berkeley, CA: Cobb & Henry Publishers.

Gruber, J., & Trickett, E. J. (1987). Can we empower others? The paradox of empowerment in the governing of an alternative public school. *American Journal of Community Psychology, 15*(3), 353–371.

Hawkins, D. (1989). Intentional injury: Are there no solutions? *Law, Medicine and Health Care, 17*(1), 32–44.

Hersch, L. (1995). Adapting to health care reform and managed care: Three strategies for survival and growth. *Professional Psychology: Research and Practice, 26*(1), 16–26.

Highlen, P. (1994). Racial/ethnic diversity in doctoral programs of psychology: Challenge for the twenty-first century. *Applied and Preventative Psychology, 3,* 91–108.

Hsu, F.L.K. (1970). *Americans and Chinese: Purpose and fulfillment in great civilizations.* Garden City, NY: The Natural History Press.

Hsu, F.L.K. (1971). *The challenge of the American dream: The Chinese in the United States.* Belmont, CA: Wadsworth.

Ibrahim, F. A., & Arredondo, P. M. (1986). Ethical standards for cross-cultural counseling: Counselor preparation, practice, assessment, and research. *Journal of Counseling and Development, 64,* 349–352.

Jackson, J. S. (1990). The therapeutic equation and cross-cultural psychology. In G. Stricker, E. Davis-Russell, E. Bourg, E. Duran, W. R. Hammond, J. McHolland, K. Polite, & B. E. Vaughn (Eds.), *Towards ethnic diversification in psychology education and training* (pp. 203–210). Washington, DC: American Psychological Association.

Jones, J. M. (1972). *Prejudice and racism.* New York: Random House.

Katz, R. (1984). Empowerment and synergy: Expanding the community's healing resources. In J. Rappaport, C. Swift, & R. Hess (Eds.), *Studies in empowerment: Steps toward understanding and action.* New York: Haworth Press.

Kozol, J. (1991). *Savage inequalities.* New York: Crown.

Kunjufu, J. (1989). *Critical issues in education of African Americans.* Chicago: African American Images.

Locke, D. C. (1986). Cross-cultural counseling issues. In A. J. Palmo & W. J. Weikel (Eds.), *Foundations of mental health counseling* (pp. 119–137). Springfield, IL: Charles C. Thomas.

Lorion, R. P. (1991). Prevention and public health: Psychology's response to the nation's health care crisis. *American Psychologist, 46,* 516–519.

Louie, C. (1994). *Breaking down the walls of jade: A study of acculturation and second-generation Chinese-American women.* Unpublished doctoral dissertation, California School of Professional Psychology, Alameda, CA.

Multicultural Education, Research and Training Institute. (1993). *Multicultural competencies for CSPP students.* Unpublished manuscript, California School of Professional Psychology (CSPP), Alameda, CA.

Moore, R. (1993, October 13). Federal drug laws snare blacks, whites walk free. *Final call* (pp. 5, 7).

Neighbors, H. W. (1990) The prevention of psychopathology in African Americans: An epidemiological perspective. *Community Mental Health Journal, 26*(2), 167–179.

Parham, T. A. (1989). Across the life cycle. In R. L. Jones (Ed.), *Black adult development and aging* (pp. 151–166). Berkeley, CA: Cobb & Henry.

Pedersen, P. B. (1988). *A handbook for developing multicultural awareness.* Alexandria, VA: American Association for Counseling and Development.

Pedersen, P. B. (1991a). Introduction to part 1: A conceptual framework. In P. B. Pedersen (Ed.), Multiculturalism as a fourth force in counseling [Special issue]. *Journal of Counseling and Development, 70,* 5.

Pedersen, P. B. (1991b). Multiculturalism as a generic approach to counseling. In P. B. Pedersen, (Ed.). Multiculturalism as a fourth force in counseling [Special issue]. *Journal of Counseling and Development, 70,* 6–12.

Rappaport, J. (1987). Terms of empowerment/exemplars of prevention: Toward a theory for community psychology. *American Journal of Community Psychology, 15*(2), 121–147.

Serrano-Garcia, I. (1984). The illusion of empowerment: Community development within a colonial context. In J. Rappaport, C. Swift, & R. Hess (Eds.), *Studies in empowerment: Steps toward understanding and action* (pp. 173–197). New York: Haworth Press.

Singleton, E. G. (1989). Substance use and black youth: Implications of cultural and ethnic differences in adolescent alcohol, cigarette, and illicit drug use. In R. L. Jones (Ed.), *Black adolescents* (pp. 385–401). Berkeley, CA: Cobb & Henry.

Stricker, G., Davis-Russell, E., Bourg, E., Duran, E., Hammond, W. R., McHolland, J., Polite, K., & Vaughn, B. E. (Eds.). (1990). *Toward ethnic diversification in psychology education and training.* Washington DC: American Psychological Association.

Sue, D. W., Arredondo, P., & McDavis, R. J. (1992). Multicultural counseling competencies and standards: A call to the profession. *Journal of Counseling and Development, 70,* 477–486.

Sue, D. W., Ivey, A. E., & Pederson, P. B. (1996). *A theory of multicultural counseling and therapy.* Pacific Grove, CA: Brooks/Cole Publishing Company.

Takaki, R. (1989). *Strangers from a different shore: A History of Asian Americans.* New York: Penguin Books.

Wallerstein, N. (1992). Powerlessness, empowerment, and health: Implications for health promotion programs. *American Journal of Health Promotion, 6*(3), 197–205.

CHAPTER THREE

The Vicissitudes of Cultural Competence

Dealing with Difficult Classroom Dialogue

Gale Young and Elizabeth Davis-Russell

As we have entered the twenty-first century, our discussions in higher education seem to have expanded from a focus on cultural sensitivity to cultural competence. How culturally competent is the faculty member who is confronted with a class of culturally diverse students, or a clinician who enters into a psychotherapy relationship with a culturally different client? In this chapter, we shall provide a definition of cultural competence that includes not only individuals, but systems as well. We will then discuss the components of cultural competence and what is necessary to become culturally competent. We will present a discussion of difficult dialogues; a consequence of movement toward cultural competence, and conclude with some recommendations on how to deal with difficult dialogues in the classroom.

Competence denotes the ability to perform; therefore, the definition of cultural competence that seems most congruent with our perspective is one that is inclusive of attitudes, behaviors, and policies (Cross, Bazron, Dennis, & Isaacs, 1989). This definition specifies that these three must be congruent. On the individual level, the individual must possess a set of congruent attitudes and behaviors that enables him to work effectively in cross-cultural situations. Yet institutions can possess cultural competence, for they can have policies that enable the institution to function effectively in cross-cultural situations.

There are several elements of cultural competence (Cross, et al., 1989). One of these is valuing diversity. The individual or institution has moved beyond the levels of tolerance, acceptance, and respect, to a level of affirmation, solidarity, and critique (Nieto, 1992).

Another element of cultural competence is the capacity of the individual or institution to engage in cultural self-assessment (Cross, et al., 1989). In that self-assessment, the individual engages in an examination of her feelings, attitudes, and perceptions toward her own and other racial, ethnic, cultural, gender, and sexual orientation group. At the California School of Professional Psychology (CSPP), this has occurred in the intercultural labs for students, and in faculty and staff retreats for faculty and staff, respectively. On the institutional level, the Multicultural Education, Research, and Training Institute (MERIT Institute) conducts an audit that assesses the institution's commitment to cultural diversity. The audit is inclusive of the institution's policies and practices.

Culturally competent individuals and institutions have a consciousness of the dynamics inherent when cultures interact (Cross, et al., 1989). They are not only aware of the "dynamics of difference," but also of the dynamics of misinterpretation and misjudgment. These can lead to difficult dialogues, and as we see later in this chapter, the potential for explosive encounters. Culturally competent individuals and institutions are knowledgeable about different communication styles. They understand that one brings culturally prescribed patterns of communication, etiquette, and problem solving to interpersonal interactions, and are aware of the fact that violation of the norms of one another can have serious consequences.

Individuals and institutions possess institutionalized cultural knowledge and also possess developed adaptations to diversity (Cross, et al., 1989). On the institutional level, the latter means moving from rhetoric to establishing policies and practices that convey that diversity is an integral part of the institution. It is a natural part of doing business. On the individual level, it means listening with an open heart, and noticing others feelings and thoughts, as well as one's own. It means responding without judgment and arrogance. It also means allowing oneself to feel and be present in the jagged racial divide, to feel so intensely the differences that divide and simultaneously the commonalties that bind.

Cultural competence is not a luxury. It is a necessity for faculty and clinicians alike. As faculty working to educate and train students from many different cultural backgrounds, imagine this scenario: your class is discussing the day's reading assignments on how families have viewed children differently over the centuries. An European American white student, drawing from her own experience working in a social service agency with people of color, says, "It seemed like those people didn't really care about their children." Several African American students in the class take offense and demand, "What do you mean by 'those people'?" The student who made the comment is puzzled and feels put on the spot. The students who are offended by her comment are not going to be put off; they want to deal directly with her for what they perceive as her racism. Everyone else in the room is waiting to see what happens. Welcome to difficult dialogue!

The possibility that a difficult dialogue will occur is heightened whenever course materials reflect a multicultural perspective, when students are racially or culturally diverse or when the instructor's ethnicity, gender, and sexual orientation are different from the students. This chapter will consider ways to transform these kinds of emotionally charged classroom encounters into opportunities for meaningful dialogues about race, culture, gender, class, and sexual identity. It will explore the dynamics that can make such discussions difficult and present a model of effective strategies for engaging students in cognitive and emotional inquiry and open-minded discussion about multicultural issues.

WHAT IS A DIFFICULT DIALOGUE?

Difficult dialogues, obviously, can occur about any subject, in any situation and between individuals of the same race, culture, gender, and sexual orientation. Many of the dynamics explained in this chapter pertain to the larger scope of difficult dialogues. However, this chapter focuses on the dynamics and patterns that emerge when those difficult dialogues are about and across race, culture, sexual orientation, and gender lines.

Difficult classroom dialogues occur when differences in perspectives are made public, and are challenged or judged to be offensive, often with intense emotions aroused among participants and observers. Such dialogues immediately spotlight the race, gender, culture, and sexual orientation of the participants. The normal classroom conversation stops, and verbal exchanges are no longer student-to-student or faculty-to-student, but White-to-Black, male-to-female, gay-to-heterosexual, and so on. Whether or not a person would normally attach much meaning to these identities, the interaction calls attention to them, and students and faculty alike can find themselves experiencing a strong personal reaction. Confronted with a different cultural perspective, students may experience a variety of responses, from anger at having been "lied to" in the past to disbelief or dismissal of the new information. Instructors may feel threatened by the sudden awareness that some of their students know more about certain subjects than they do, and that their ignorance or biased perspective may become all too apparent to the class.

Difficult dialogues can take different forms. The normal classroom conversation can explode into an intense exchange, which may be characterized by friendly intellectual debate, or veer toward strongly worded disagreement, angry confrontation, or personal attack. From mild to mean, these exchanges have the potential for serious polarization, during which the educational process comes to a standstill. In the worst-case scenario, all attempts at dialogue fail, and verbal (or even physical) violence occurs; some students storm out of the room and go so far as to withdraw from the course. Students descend on the department chair or dean to file a complaint, and the campus paper covers the "incident" and calls you in for an interview. When the class meets again, tension fills the air like fumes that any spark could ignite.

Difficult dialogues can also brew in silence. Ironically one signal that a difficult dialogue is simmering is the absence of visible emotion. Students are quiet, dutiful, and respectful but apparently uninterested in discussion. Feelings are heating up, but there is a lid of polite and deadening silence over them. In this situation, little or nothing is communicated among the students. They leave the class muttering, Man, am I glad this class is over, I hate these PC classes, or I'm not about to say anything and have everyone jump all over me. Day after day, the instructor finds the same silent resistance. It's a long semester, and the teaching evaluations are a disaster.

However, difficult dialogues can also become exciting educational opportunities. In the best-case scenario, a difficult dialogue occurs and the students and instructor move beyond the discomfort, the fear of confrontation, and the tendency to be judgmental. Students demonstrate a willingness to ask questions. The students become energized and curious, taking conversational risks, and inquiring about what others know and feel. The tension in the situation is not only recognized, but it is used as a lightning rod for cognitive inquiry and insight.

An example of this happened in a class of mine, in which the students were discussing stereotypes as learned behavior. A Latino student said, "I don't like this about myself, but when I see a White man driving a Lexus, I say to myself, 'There goes a CEO, a lawyer, a successful person.' But when I see a Black man in a Lexus, I say, 'There goes a drug dealer.' I learned all this from the media."

An African American young woman replied, "I say 'Go Man' and I say to you (the Latino student) 'You're wrong and you should know better.'" She then burst into tears and ran out of the room. An older African American woman followed her, signaling to me that she would comfort her. The bell rang, and class was over. A spontaneous difficult dialogue had presented itself.

Before class convened two days later, I prepared a structure for continuing the discussion that included the students engaging in *mindful listening to self* (which I will discuss in greater detail later in the chapter), followed by a period for reflective writing. Then each student was invited to share one question or feeling they experienced during or after the encounter. The tension and pain that they felt were thus brought out into the open, and the lesson that stereotypes are learned, alive in each of us, and a cause of suffering was more real than any lecture could ever have made it.

Why Are Dialogues About Gender, Race, and Culture So Difficult?

When in a diverse group, people often avoid discussions of race, class, gender, and sexual identity for fear of creating discomfort, embarrassment, or hostility. The avoidance, in the guise of politeness, can take such forms as making light of the topic, shifting topics, or simply ignoring anything said that happens to relate to the topic. This *code of silence* is a reflection of a societal denial that cultural factors matter, and that things such as sexism, racism, and White privilege exists. In the classroom, it can prevent students from gaining experience in difficult dialogues. Because many faculty lack knowledge and awareness beyond their own cultural experience, they feel awkward and timid about discussing—let alone facilitating—student discussions about race, gender, sexual identity, and class issues. In order to avoid feeling that awkwardness or making others uncomfortable, they perpetuate the code of silence.

> Race relations in the U.S. is both an intensely
> intellectual and an extremely emotional issue.

Too many people refer to interracial interactions as walking on eggshells, or walking through a mine field. The racial divide is wide with sharp and jagged edges. Many European Americans feel guilty for the legacy of oppression or defensive over their position of historical privilege. They do not feel race privileged. Even when they acknowledge their White privilege, they do not know what to do about it. Most European Americans believe dearly in the sacred principle of equality and to be called a racist means they are being accused of violating that principle. Being called a racist, for most European Americans, packs the same punch as being called a child molester. For both Whites and people of color, race relations trigger the deeper issues of both identity (Who am I?) and worth (Am I good enough?). Many, if not most, people of color must navigate daily the effects of stereotypes. From subtle to obvious, members of other cultural groups question their worth, judge them to be less qualified, tokens, or a commodity. Many people of color believe they must be twice as good to be perceived as half as much. They get tired of the extra burden of having to navigate the daily tides of racial projections. So, it is understandable why it just seems safer to avoid the topic.

Moreover, because of the inextricable emotional dimension of race relations, most faculty view difficult dialogues as violating academic protocol. The Western academic tradition has typically held emotions to be irrational and not appropriate to the intellectual pursuits of academia. Faculty are trained to emphasize cognitive processes in the classroom, and to treat emotions as private and personal.

Finally, for both students and faculty, difficult dialogues heighten an awareness of personal vulnerability. From a psychological perspective, people craft their identity from the stories they have been told (by family, peers, religious leaders, and society) about what it means to be of a certain race, culture, gender, or sexual identity. Usually, they don't question these identities until others challenge them, which can happen when feeling attacked or spotlighted. Yet, in a classroom with diverse students or a multicultural curriculum, these identity factors (race, culture, gender, class, and sexual identity) can become a point of reference for how students perceive and relate to one another and to the instructor. When instructors deny or ignore the importance of these aspects of identity, they communicate a message to students that the students' feelings in these areas don't belong in the classroom and that perhaps their experiences and knowledge about their ethnicity are not worthy of academic attention. These types of interpretations can contribute to students questioning their overall worth and acceptability to the academic world. And, yet, to acknowledge and discuss them may take instructors outside their academic training and leave them feeling vulnerable.

During difficult dialogues, instructors may feel vulnerable because they don't know when to be the expert and when to let go, when to refer to their own identity and when to refer to the cognitive content. The faculty I work with speak of their lack of intercultural competence. They are embarrassed by how little they really know about the different cultures in the United States. They are often horrified when they realize how few, if any, actual friends they have from a different race or culture, and how few, if any books, movies, plays, and so on, they've read or seen by and about members from a different culture. Faculty report that even when they have friendly intercultural relationships with colleagues, the topic of race or culture rarely arises. As faculty, we are trained to be the experts, to be in charge of a subject matter. Most of us are not experts in race and culture issues. We are out of our element, and when confronted with a lack of knowledge and very different experience we may begin to question our identity and place. No wonder instructors want to defend against this vulnerability by attempting to avoid or contain difficult dialogues. Yet, paradoxically, instructors' awareness and acceptance of their own vulnerability can increase their empathy for their students' vulnerability.

HOW CAN DIFFICULT DIALOGUES HAVE SUCCESSFUL OUTCOMES?

One indication that a difficult dialogue is successful is when students come to integrate cognitive knowledge with emotional responses. Despite the feelings that may be aroused, they become curious about what they don't know or understand, and curious about the feelings as well. As part of this integration, they come to see themselves and their classmates as both emotional and intellectual beings. As they strive to get to know, communicate with, and understand one another, they gain respect for themselves and for their classmates.

Another indication of success is when students begin talking to each other about issues they would normally find threatening. They demonstrate the courage and willingness to ask questions, listen carefully to the responses, and speak honestly about their own perspective. I regularly do a fishbowl exercise after students read McIntosh's (1988) classic essay on White privilege. When White students discuss the essay among themselves, there are two dominant themes: (1) they are truly surprised that not everyone shares the same privileges (for example not being followed in a store, being able to assume you can buy a house, rent an apartment anywhere you can afford, and so on), and (2) they get defensive and try to pick the essay apart. When the students of color discuss the essay, there are three dominate themes: (1) genuine disbelief and mistrust that Whites don't know they have White privilege; (2) anger about White privilege; and (3) appreciation for McIntosh laying it out so clearly. In the end, I put the students together and ask them to re-enact the fishbowl conversations using role-play. After the role-play, the difficult dialogue begins. This difficult dialogue is successful when students begin asking questions that reveal their own vulnerability and true curiosity. Examples of questions and statements that may contribute to a genuine dialogue include: What do you see when you look in the mirror, a woman or a White woman? How do you instruct your children on how to handle racial name-calling? Help me understand what it feels like to be White. How is your life at school different from your life at home? How do you handle always wondering if someone is being friendly to you in a store so they can help you or guard you? Taking a risk might also take the form of self-disclosure such as a story about how the person was oblivious to White privilege or wrongly assumed they were being stereotyped.

A further indication of successful dialogue is when students and instructors begin seeing their vulnerability as a strength. They become aware of the desire to be understood and to understand other human beings across race, culture, and gender lines: this urge to speak genuinely and to understand others becomes stronger than the urge to protect their own perspectives. Paradoxically, successful difficult dialogues often occur when individuals become aware of their defensiveness and have the courage to acknowledge it in the dialogue (for example, Wow, I'm feeling so defensive right now. I wonder why?). Instructors can encourage this practice by giving examples from their own experiences that disclose their own defensiveness and stereotyping.

DEALING WITH DIFFICULT DIALOGUE: A MODEL FOR MULTICULTURAL INQUIRY

The following model for facilitating difficult dialogues is grounded in my twenty years of teaching race-related courses at a racially diverse campus, incorporating ideas from ongoing discussions with many colleagues. It contains four elements:

1. Creating a climate for inquiry
2. Focusing on cognitive inquiry
3. Focusing on emotional inquiry
4. Developing skills for mindful listening

Creating a Climate for Inquiry

In order to prepare students for a difficult dialogue, it is important to create a climate for inquiry within the classroom. This means encouraging students to develop an enthusiasm for seeking, exploring, and loving the questions more than the answers. The following questions can help introduce them to this idea of inquiry:

- What is the goal of inquiry—to find answers or questions or both?
- How are self-reflection and speculation involved?
- What kind of questions do you ask when you are truly interested in inquiry?
- What is involved in an attitude of inquiry?

I offer a perspective from Chodron (1991), who regards the willingness to inquire as "not caring whether the object of our inquisitiveness is bitter or sweet" (p. 3). Rather, genuine inquiry involves the courage to question what we think we already know to be true. Or, put another way, inquiry is finding the questions to our answers. I ask students to consider what it might mean *to not* have a vested interest in whether they liked or didn't like the answer. Would that be possible? What might be the benefits and drawbacks of this attitude?

One way to demonstrate how to transform *answer-driven* statements into *inquiry-driven* questions is for the instructor to put a topic on the board, such as "Therapy and the Single Mother," and then ask the students to generate statements that reflect what they think they know to be true. Students will generally say things like most single mothers are African Americans, or, most are on welfare. After several statements are on the board, the instructor then can ask the students for their sources. Students rarely quote a source; rather, they just assume it's true from the media or have heard it some place. Even when a more accurate answer is given (for example, most single mothers are White), the instructor does not give away the "right answer." At this point, she continues to encourage the students to inquire more specifically into what they truly know and don't know about the topic and particular clients. They can also be asked to consider what they know about different perspectives on the topic. Are there different sources of knowledge that reflect different views on how, for example, men and women, various cultural groups, gays and heterosexuals, and different socioeconomic classes understand this issue? Finally, the instructor can ask students, if they didn't have to worry about "being right, or smart," what questions would they have about the topic?

Focusing on Cognitive Inquiry

Cognitive inquiry in this model means going beyond learning about the theories and research findings that make up a discipline, to investigate the underlying contexts and assumptions that shape its knowledge base. As all of the chapters in this book have pointed out, psychology has not generally taken sociocultural factors into account, in that its theories and research applications have been developed mainly by and about Euro-American males. It is useful to invite students to consider such things as the origin of the concept of whiteness and color that continues to be maintained as a social construct within the United States, and the development and significance of ethnic identity within a color-conscious society. Depending on the course, instructors can guide students toward an understanding of differences in values, attitudes, beliefs, and communication norms among ethnic, national, racial, and gender groups, and an understanding of the effects of economic scarcity or abundance on human development and behavior.

Although most instructors are not experts in the cultural, historical, socioeconomic, and social identity dimensions for each controversial issue, they can model and stimulate inquiry by telling students what they themselves don't know and the questions they want to explore. The goal is to cultivate students' curiosity for discovering knowledge. It would be useful, for example, if during a difficult dialogue on "Therapy and the Single Mother," students would want to explore such questions as: What is the ethnic breakdown of single mothers? Where do single mothers live? What is the breakdown by states and cities? What is the educational achievement level for mothers, fathers, and the children? What support (financial, housing, child-care, and so on) do grandparents and other extended family play in the life of single parents? What community support is available to single mothers and their children? How does a mother's race, culture, socioeconomic background influence the responses to the above questions. How do society's values on marriage affect its policies on single mothers? How does the stress of being a single mother affect her mental health?

Asking such questions involves courage, the courage to reveal what one doesn't know. It takes courage and self-awareness to resist getting caught up in an opinion war or a code of silence. This means noticing feelings—of inadequacy, fear, anger, or guilt—that may come up, and knowing how to consider them in ways that enhance rather than undermine cognitive inquiry.

Focusing Emotional Inquiry

Many people believe that knowledge automatically translates into competent and appropriate attitudes and behavior. Yet, information about other cultural and racial groups can actually increase hostility. Racist and culturally based prejudices can exist along with substantive knowledge to the contrary. The issues of race, culture, and gender are decidedly personal and emotional, and if instructors don't take the emotional dimension into account in the classroom, they may not achieve their cognitive goals. Goleman (1995) has made a very persuasive case that emotional intelligence is in fact interdependent with and as important as cognitive intelligence. If emotional inquiry *is* going to be part of the class, then the topic of feelings should be discussed at the outset. What follows are some basic points I've found helpful when I teach emotional inquiry and some methods for facilitating students' inquiry into their own and other's emotional responses. The foundations for my thinking rely heavily on many of the writings of Welwood, most recently *Toward a Psychology of Awakening* (2000) and Gendlin's *Focusing* (1978).

Feelings are Temporal. Feelings come and then they go. We can talk about our feelings in the past or imagine them in the future, but they occur only in the present moment. In that present moment we may feel many emotions simultaneously or in rapid succession: emotions that may be conflicting, intense, and confusing, or gentle and easily understood. If a feeling is particularly strong, it may feel like a permanent state, leading to the conviction that something must be done to attend to or alleviate it.

Feelings are not Inferences. It is important to help students learn to distinguish between a feeling, such as discomfort, and inferences about the feeling (such as, you are making me uncomfortable, or, I don't want to feel this anymore, so I will do something to stop the feeling). White students who feel remorse or anger about the history and state of racism may begin spinning inferences (for example, that this is a terrible country, that racism is not their fault, that people of color must hate them). What happens is that the feeling becomes translated into a particular inference, which allows them to bypass the actual experience of remorse and anger. If unexamined, this kind of inference can solidify and numb other emotions in the process. Students often need assistance discerning the feeling from the inference.

Feelings are Often Reactive. Feelings are often responses to past experiences, as well as to current stimuli. An emotional reaction to an outspoken classmate may be shaped more by one's cultural background, earlier family dynamics, or previous life experiences than by the actual content of the classmate's utterance. Students need to learn that because feelings are so affected by one's own personal histories, they cannot be trusted as guides for taking rational action in the present.

Emotions and Reactions in Response to Multicultural Material. Sue and Sue (1990) have identified the six most common reactions students experience when working with multicultural curricula. They include

1. Anger, which is often expressed as, Why Blame Me? How dare you? It's your fault.

2. Sadness and remorse, which often translates into, I am bad. I feel so guilty. I don't know what else to do—I feel so sad.

3. Despair often gets communicated as, I can't do anything to change this, and I feel ashamed of being White. I feel like racism will never end.

4. Fear often comes out as, You can't expect me to give up what I've earned, I am scared. They control everything. Why shouldn't they hate me, I'm White, they will just assume I'm like other whites and therefore they will try to hurt me.

5. Intellectualization is a reaction to not wanting to deal with the feelings and comes out in the form of denying the relevancy of feelings and claiming the primacy of the content issues.

6. Withdrawal is another form of not being ready to discuss the feelings and is most often expressed by lowered eyes, silence, and leaving the room.

Noticing and Acknowledging Feelings. Instructors may find it helpful to provide class time to explain the common reactions and feelings and to ask students to add to the list. But, if the instructor stopped here, the discussion about emotional reactions would remain an intellectual issue, so it is important for faculty to give students an opportunity to practice acknowledging their feelings in the moment before they engage in inquiry. They need practice in learning to listen to feelings. To *notice* one's own or another's feelings is to take that moment and check in: What is going on with me right now? What am I sensing is going on with this person right now? Usually what happens here is a jumble of unidentified physical sensations or confused observations, but when given a few moments, the stimuli will settle into a discernible pattern that can be acknowledged, such as, I feel nervous, scattered, hungry, tired, and so on. It is important to tell students that the feelings will change.

Once students have noticed and labeled their feelings, they can then begin to notice the difference between the feelings themselves and the inferences identified with them. For example, a student reported on this process by saying

> At first, I noticed feelings of hunger and weariness, and then resentment and guilt set in. I first began to think about what I wanted to eat and when I might be able to get a rest. Then the resentment came in that you were making me think about race when I was working so hard and didn't even have time to eat. Then I felt guilty for being so self-centered and for all the racial injustices in the world and that I really had it easy.

When the student reported on this experience in class, I was able to assist the class in discerning the differences between her feelings, (hunger, weariness, anger, and guilt) and her inferences (I will eat, rest, blame the instructor for making me think about these things, blame myself for thinking my hunger is more important than racial injustice, and so on).

As the feelings and inferences are identified, the instructor can ask students to explore the emotional content further. Some questions might be: What more is going on underneath this feeling for example anger? What am I angry about, really? Why do I want to blame the instructor? What am I afraid of? Why do I get angry when this issue comes up? Unlike cognitive inquiry, where questions get asked and strategies generated for finding out answers, emotional inquiry encourages the asking and holding of the questions. It involves waiting and listening to the responses.

It is helpful to remind students that they don't need to judge, change, deny, or indulge their feelings. Rather they can continue to acknowledge and inquire, and just notice what emerges. It is essential to provide enough time for students to process the feelings they have acknowledged, as well as to invite students to inquire into the relationship between the cognitive content and their emotions.

Developing Mindful Listening

Listening, once defined by a radio disc jockey as waiting for your turn to interrupt, is better practiced as the full and mindful attention to understanding one's own or another's message. Listening, when engaged mindfully, is the key to establishing an open and inquisitive environment, and is a prerequisite for all the other teaching and learning methods discussed here. Mindfulness, in the Western tradition (Gudykunst & Kim, 1992; Langer, 1989), is the ability to see and transcend the stereotypes, scripts, categories, and automatic reactions that prevent us from responding effectively and appropriately; the assumption is that an act of will is all that's needed to access this ability. In the Eastern tradition, however, mindfulness is a 2,500-year-old practice for cultivating this ability, which allows us to become more open to information and people we might have perceived as different or threatening (Trungpa, 1988).

Mindful listening is a method that is best applied to both listening to self and listening for other. The assumption is that we can best listen to others when we regularly listen to ourselves. Mindful listening to other involves placing the attention on the other and his or her message. The goal is to understand the message from the other person's perspective, not to agree or disagree, win, lose, or make a judgment. The basic instructions for this method include

Focusing on the Other Person. By holding attention on what the other person is saying and feeling, the listener tries to understand the other's message from the other's perspective.

Trying to Be Nonjudgmental. The listener attempts to communicate the desire to understand, which is markedly different than expressing agreement or disagreement.

Paraphrasing. The listener tries to clarify his or her level of understanding, by repeating back in his own words what the other person has said.

Engaging in Gentle Inquiry. The listener asks questions that will allow him to put himself in the other person's shoes. Gentle inquiry isn't interrogation.

Noticing. The listener seeks conscious awareness of his own internal dialogue and external behavior, which brings him back to focusing on the other person. In this sense it is a self-correcting step.

Because even the most skilled listeners forget these principles, interrupt, and offer agreement or disagreement, it is useful to remind students of the guidelines, and to allow them practice time during each difficult dialogue. It is also important for students to engage in mindful listening on their own. Once learned, it can become a useful habit.

Putting the Model into Practice

When a difficult dialogue arises—or when the instructor anticipates that it might—the following systematic approach of combining mindful listening to self with mindful listening to other can be very useful.

Sit Comfortably. Ask students to sit respectfully (whatever that means to them) but comfortably, to put down pens, pencils, drinks, and so on. They can close their eyes or look diffusely at the floor.

Noticing. Ask students to notice their feelings—both physical and emotional—and their thoughts. Invite them to be gentle with themselves and notice the feelings and thoughts they are experiencing. They are likely to become lost in their thoughts, so encourage them to focus on the feeling as well. If they notice that they are lost in thoughts, they should return to breathing (allow two to five minutes).

Breathing. Ask students to notice their breathing, which may allow them to become aware of their thoughts and feelings (allow two to five minutes).

Focusing. Ask students to focus their attention on a potentially difficult question that is derived from an idea presented in a reading, lecture, or class discussion. Ask them to focus on the question. A helpful metaphor is to have the students ask themselves the question (posed by the instructor), and then as if their mind were a movie screen, to watch what shows up without getting caught up in it (allow two to five minutes).

Waiting. Remind students to wait and hold the question and to try not to analyze or search their minds. Rather, the purpose of waiting is to clear a space so that many thoughts and feelings can make themselves known to the individual. You can remind the students that if they are making inferences by judging or arguing with themselves or another, or if they have drifted off into a daydream, that when they notice that, to just acknowledge that they were thinking and to return to their breathing and to the question. If they feel sleepy and distracted, or if intense feelings come up, they are instructed to try to just acknowledge that it is happening and then return to their breathing and the question. Remind them that there is no right answer, no need to fix or change anything. Their only assignment right now is to notice and acknowledge that they are responding to this particular topic (allow two to five minutes).

Emotional Inquiry. At this point, encourage students to engage in gentle inquiry in the same way they would if they were listening to another person. The questions might be: What is going on here? Why am I so angry? Why did I wander off and not want to think about the material? Why did I feel so nervous, tired, and so on? (allow two to five minutes).

Cognitive Inquiry. Here again, encourage students to focus their inquiry toward the cognitive knowledge. The questions might be: What do I know? What troubles me about this concept? What more do I need to know in order to understand this idea? (allow two to five minutes).

Writing. Ask students to write down what they noticed and to describe their experiences with this mode of inquiry (allow two to five minutes).

Discussion. At this point, the instructor can engage in any number of teaching and learning strategies. For example, students can be placed in pairs or groups to discuss the question posed by the instructor, or the instructor can ask for a word, a sentence, or a question from each person that relates to the students' experience with the question. It is helpful to remind students about the principles to practice mindful listening to other (allow ten to thirty minutes).

TAKING THE PLUNGE: AN EXAMPLE

Imagine this scenario: It is early in the course, and you have just barely begun to address the concept of mindful listening. After a brief presentation that touches on a multicultural topic, you ask for questions and comments on the lecture and readings. An African American man who is older than most of the other students consistently responds to your questions; he doesn't really answer them, but instead, uses them to espouse his beliefs and views. His statements invariably begin or end with "the White Man." He says the "White Man" did this, "the White Man" did that, and "the White Man" is responsible for whatever. None of the other students, regardless of ethnicity, want to respond to him or draw his attention for fear of being accused of being "the White Man" or "the White Man's lackey."

What do you do? How might you evoke the spirit of inquiry into this situation? Addressing possible cognitive issues and questions, you might begin by

- Discussing that "the White Man" is a shorthand way of saying institutional racism.
- Establishing a definition for institutional racism.
- Asking all the students: What does "the White Man" mean to them?
- Asking the students: What questions do they have about the phrase "the White Man"?
- Asking students to identify the kind of information they need to know in order to more fully understand what "the White Man" means.
- Inviting emotional inquiry, you might begin by
  — Asking the students to take a moment, and notice and acknowledge what goes on inside of them when they hear "the White Man."
  — Asking them to inquire into their feelings, in the manner discussed earlier.

After students have had a chance to notice and inquire into their emotions, you can then make fruitful use of one of the writing, discussing, or sharing options described above.

The second author closes on a personal note. A while ago, in the Academic Senate, a contentious colleague spoke out about the uselessness of establishing a standing committee for Equity and Diversity. Identifying with my judgments,

I immediately quit listening and began my plan of attack. I spoke not in response to him but in response to all the other people I knew who had similar opinions. In an "academically civil" way I matched his arrogance with my own and lost touch with my own feelings. What would have happened if I had just listened with an open heart, noticed his feelings and thoughts, and my own? How might I have responded? I don't know, but it would have been different and less arrogant. In those rare moments when I allow myself to feel and be present in the jagged racial divide, I feel so intensely the differences that divide, and, simultaneously, the commonalties that bind.

Increasingly, I find that in those moments when I befriend my own prejudice, ignorance, and emotional tides, I am awed, humbled, and often quite sad and sometimes full of wrath, but also I am more honest and compassionate with my students and colleagues, no matter what their attitudes or messages. Situations hurt, anger, and disturb more. Sometimes the feelings scare me but they no longer scare me off, or not for long. My students' feelings are no longer unwanted, ignored, or intellectualized away. Their feelings are a welcome addition to the classroom. Education—to be relevant, as W.E.B. Du Bois (1973) reminds us—must grow out of the life experiences of those being educated. So the more we can practice listening to our own experiences and each others we will see, hear, feel, and understand how different and how similar we are. By bringing the confusions and muddy emotions of race relations into the center of the class, we acknowledge and feel the truth of the racial divide and paradoxically by doing so, we begin to feel more connected to ourselves and to each other.

References

Chodron, Pema. (1991). *The wisdom of no escape and the path of loving-kindness.* Boston & London: Shambhala.

Cross, T. L., Bazron, B. J., Dennis, K. W., & Isaacs, M. R. (1989, March) *A monograph on effective services for minority children who are severely emotionally disturbed* [Monograph]. Washington, DC: National Technical Assistance for Children's Mental Health Center for Child Health and Mental Health, Georgetown University Child Development Center.

Du Bois, W.E.B. (1973). *The education of black people: Ten critiques, 1906–1960.* H. Apthekar (Ed.). New York: Monthly Review Press.

Gendlin, E. T. (1978). *Focusing.* New York: Bantam Books.

Goleman, D. (1995). *Emotional intelligence: Why it can matter more than IQ.* New York: Bantam Books.

Gudykunst, W. B., & Kim, Y. Y. (Eds.). (1992). *Readings on communicating with strangers.* New York: McGraw-Hill.

Langer, E. J. (1989). *Mindfulness.* Reading, MA: Addison-Wesley.

McIntosh, P. (1988). *White privilege: Working paper.* Wellesley College Center for Research on Women, Wellesley, MA.

Nieto, S. (1992). *Affirming diversity: The socialpolitical context of multicultural education.* New York: Longman.

Sue, D. W., Arredondo, P., & McDavis, R. J. (1992). Multicultural organizational development: Implications for the counseling profession. *Journal of Counseling and Development, 70,* 477–486.

Sue, D. W. & Sue D. (1990). *Counseling the culturally different: Theory and practice* (pp. 112–117). New York: John Wiley & Sons.

Trungpa, C. (1988). *Shambhala: The sacred path of the warrior.* Boston: Shambhala.

Welwood, J. (2000). *Toward a psychology of awakening.* Boston: Shambhala.

CHAPTER FOUR

In and Out of the Classroom

A Model for Multicultural Training in Clinical Psychology

Sylvie Taylor, Carlton W. Parks, Kumea Shorter-Gooden, Paula B. Johnson,
Elaine A. Burke, Kimlin Tam Ashing, Richard H. Mendoza,
Judith Holloway, Kenneth Polite, Glenn I. Masuda

This chapter describes the genesis and functioning of the Multicultural Community Clinical Psychology (MCCP) Emphasis Area at the California School of Professional Psychology (CSPP) of Alliant International University, Los Angeles. Since the early 1970s, scholars and providers of clinical services across the United States have emphasized the dearth of multiculturally competent clinicians available to provide services to our ever-diversifying population (American Psychological Association [APA], 1997; Myers, 1992). Despite the APA's recognition of the importance of cultural and individual differences and diversity in the training of psychologists, which has been codified as a domain requirement for accreditation of clinical programs in psychology (APA, 2000), and the subsequent reforms within academic training programs, the training of multiculturally competent psychologists continues to be a significant concern within the field. Some thirty years after the initial discussions of concerns in this area, clinical training programs across the country continue to struggle with these issues in defining how they will structure and implement programs that will "attract and retain students and faculty from differing ethnic, racial, and personal backgrounds . . . ensure a supportive and encouraging learning environment appropriate for the training of diverse individuals and the provision of training opportunities for a broad spectrum of individuals . . . and (implement) a thoughtful and coherent plan to provide students with relevant knowledge and experiences about the role of cultural and individual diversity in psychological phenomena as they relate to the science and practice of professional psychology" (p. 9).

The MCCP Emphasis Area is housed within the APA accredited clinical Ph.D. and Psy.D. programs. The MCCP Emphasis Area has been recognized by the APA Office of Ethnic Minority Affairs as a model strategy for (1) the recruiting, retenting and training of psychologists of color (APA, 1997), and (2) training multiculturally competent psychologists of diverse racial, ethnic, and personal backgrounds. As an institution, CSPP has had a long history of commitment to issues of diversity that have been of particular concern to the Emphasis Area throughout its history. This dedication and passion laid the fertile ground upon which MCCP Emphasis Area grew and flourished.

HISTORICAL ROOTS OF MCCP

In 1985 the faculty at CSPP-LA, with strong support from the administration, created the Ethnic Minority Mental Health Proficiency (EMMHP) within its clinical programs. Its purpose was to train psychologists to understand and serve historically underserved, culturally diverse populations. This nationally recognized model program was merged with the Community-Clinical proficiency in 1990 to form what is now known as the Multicultural Community-Clinical Emphasis Area. This merging of proficiencies arose from the recognition that in order to effectively serve historically underserved ethnic minority populations, it is vital for the clinical psychologist to (1) understand and value cultural differences; (2) have a framework for understanding the diverse communities in which people live; and (3) appreciate how issues of race and ethnicity play themselves out within a wide variety of sociocultural contexts. The joining of the two proficiencies was also influenced by the recognition that diversity extends far beyond race and ethnicity, to include social and psychological communities that have been similarly underserved by traditional psychological models that do not take sociocultural context and the impact of social oppression into consideration. As a result, the MCCP Emphasis Area has broadened its perspective to include race, ethnicity, gender, sexual orientation, religious and spiritual affiliation, ability status, and social class as multicultural issues. In 1997 the MCCP Emphasis Area adopted the following mission:

> Our mission is to nurture the development of clinical psychologists who will work to understand, prevent, and reduce psychological and community distress, as well as enhance the psychological well-being of historically underserved, stigmatized, and oppressed groups. In doing this, we pay special attention to the cultural and sociopolitical context of the individuals, families and communities we serve. We are committed to fostering a climate of inclusion, respect for

differences, and a sense of community both within and outside of CSPP. Ultimately, we strive to empower individuals and communities and to facilitate personal and social healing.

DIVERSITY AND DEMOGRAPHICS OF LOS ANGELES

The MCCP Emphasis Area and CSPP-LA are located in what is arguably the most diverse county within the United States. U.S. Census data for Los Angeles County, which spans an area of 4,083 square miles with a population of 9.9 million, indicates that 9.43 percent of the population are African American, 12.58 percent are Asian or Pacific Islander, 0.28 percent are American Indian, 45.56 percent are Latino, and 32.15 percent are White (County of Los Angeles, 2000). Los Angeles County has the largest population of any county in the United States, exceeding the population of all but eight states (County of Los Angeles, 2000) and boasts the largest urban American Indian population. Approximately 32 percent of adults living in Los Angeles County are foreign born and over 350 languages and dialects are spoken by its residents (Los Angeles Almanac, 2000). This unique demographic situation propels the MCCP Emphasis Area to take a broad view of multiculturalism, striving for diversity within both the faculty and student body.

THEORETICAL FRAMEWORK

Multiculturalism and community psychology provide the framework that guides the professional activities of the emphasis area. Within the multicultural paradigm each ethnic and cultural group is valued; moreover, diversity is viewed as necessary for optimal personal and professional development (Sue & Sue, 1990). Pedersen's model (1988) of how to train multiculturally competent counselors provides a model for our training of multiculturally competent psychologists. We emphasize the students' development of their awareness of themselves as cultural beings and of their awareness of their beliefs and feelings about those who are similar and those who are different. We focus on the students' development of knowledge about different cultures and varying world views. And we train students to develop skills that enable them to effectively assess, intervene, and conduct socially responsible research with diverse individuals and communities.

The other theoretical perspective that is central to MCCP is community psychology. The community psychology framework emphasizes working from an ecological perspective. There is a focus on primary prevention strategies and empowerment, with an emphasis on theories of change that examine problem definition in building theory, research, and action (Duffy & Wong, 1996; Rappaport, 1977; Rappaport & Seidman, 2000; Seidman & Rappaport, 1986). The multicultural, community, and clinical aspects of the program are integrated with each other, and throughout research, field practica, and internship experiences.

THE FACULTY

Since its inception, the MCCP Emphasis Area has sought to maintain a diverse faculty through the active recruitment of core faculty who represent diverse backgrounds on a number of dimensions. The program's national reputation has also contributed to the establishment and maintenance of a critical mass of diverse faculty. The Emphasis Area presently consists of eleven core faculty (four men, seven women). Three faculty members are Anglo, and eight faculty (all of whom are senior faculty) are ethnic minority, including four African Americans (one of whom is biracial-multiethnic), two Latinos, and two Asian Americans. In addition, three faculty are openly gay or lesbian, a dimension of diversity often not made known within academic departments. The diversity of the faculty has led to the creation of a supportive environment for the faculty, and has likely attracted many culturally diverse students to the program.

While each member of the MCCP faculty possesses expertise in some area of human diversity, the faculty also have a wide range of research and applied interests. MCCP faculty interests include, but are not limited to: psychosocial factors affecting cancer and cancer treatment in women of color; pediatric and adult neuropsychology; pediatric health psychology; assessment and culture; the acculturation process in Latinos; identity development in African American women; gay and lesbian identity development; spirituality issues in psychotherapy; nonviolence and peace studies; interpersonal violence; gender roles and power; community psychology models of system interventions; parent-adolescent conflict and psychotherapeutic interventions with immigrant Asian families; psychodynamic psychotherapy with African Americans; and training issues in professional psychology. In addition to research and scholarship, some faculty members are in private clinical practice and others are actively engaged in community consultation projects.

Faculty often work collaboratively on research papers and conference presentations as well as on community consultation projects. On many of these projects, MCCP students are also involved.

STUDENT RECRUITMENT

The MCCP Emphasis Area naturally attracts a highly diverse pool of applicants each year. The faculty have focused on recruitment at the application and interview phases of the admissions process. Recognizing that students from historically oppressed groups and students who have a desire to work with underserved populations often have nontraditional educational histories (for example, protracted undergraduate careers, multiple academic institutions, and so on), the faculty take special care in reviewing written application materials. Applicants whose written materials appear appropriate are then interviewed individually by two MCCP Emphasis Area faculty. An important component of the interview is often seeking greater clarity from the applicant about their educational histories and other issues in their academic or personal histories that may have raised concern about the application. The program also has a commitment to train psychologists who are not people of color to become competent practitioners and scholars with a focus on the disenfranchised.

THE STUDENTS

In 1999 members of the American Psychological Association were 71.1 percent White or Euro-American, 0.4 percent American Indian, 1.6 percent Black, 0.5 percent Other, and 23 percent Unspecified (http://research.apa.org/homepage.html). During the same year, the National Science Foundation reported that recipients of new Ph.D.s in psychology were 84 percent White (Euro-American), 1 percent Native American, 4 percent Asian American, 5 percent Black, and 6 percent Hispanic (Latino) (compiled by the APA Research office, December 2000, http://research.apa.org.homepage.html). While these percentages indicate that people of color continue to be underrepresented among new graduates, there is some evidence that an increasing number of minority students are entering the field. The proportion of students of color amongst graduates with a Ph.D. in clinical psychology was 10.9 percent in 1994, 11.5 percent in 1995, 14.6 percent in 1996, 16.9 percent in 1997, and 16.5 percent in 1998 (based upon the *Summary Report of Doctorate Recipients from United States Universities,* Table compiled by APA Research Office, http://research.apa.org/homepage.html).

These numbers suggest a slow, but positive increase; however, there is certainly a need to examine ways to increase the number of people of color in the field of psychology. Notably, students in the MCCP Emphasis Area are diverse on multiple dimensions, including age, race, ethnicity, nationality, sexual orientation, and social class. Table 4.1 shows the ethnic and gender diversity of students in MCCP over the last decade as well as the percentages of students who have graduated within seven years.

A number of students entering the program each year are pursuing a second career, contributing even further to the richness of the learning environment. Many of our students enter the program with a wealth of community-based experience in working with historically underserved populations and have a strong commitment to return to these communities upon completion of the

Table 4.1. MCCP Students by Entering Year, Ethnicity, Gender, and Completion Rate

Entering Year	Total Number of MCCP Students	Percentage API		Percentage Black		Percentage Hisp.		Percentage Am. Ind.		Percentage As. Ind.		Percentage M/racial		Percentage White		Percentage Other		Percentage Grad.	Percentage Graduated w/in Seven Years
		M	F	M	F	M	F	M	F	M	F	M	F	M	F	M	F		
1991	28	4	14	4	25	7	7	0	4	0	0	0	0	4	21	0	11		79
1992	39	5	13	2	13	0	10	3	3	0	0	0	0	3	33	3	13		77
1993	44	5	5	0	23	2	21	2	2	0	0	2	0	9	21	0	9		82
1994	34	3	15	0	21	3	21	0	0	0	0	0	0	6	26	0	6		88

Entering Year	Total Number of MCCP Students	Percentage API		Percentage Black		Percentage Hisp.		Percentage Am. Ind.		Percentage As. Ind.		Percentage M/racial		Percentage White		Percentage Other		Percentage Grad.	Percentage Cont. Prog.
		M	F	M	F	M	F	M	F	M	F	M	F	M	F	M	F		
1995	28	0	18	0	11	7	14	0	0	0	0	0	0	4	32	4	11	82	11
1996	32	6	25	0	22	0	6	0	6	0	0	0	0	9	16	3	6	69	16
1997	32	3	16	3	28	3	9	3	3	0	6	0	6	3	13	0	3	41	56
1998	36	6	22	3	11	3	17	0	0	6	0	0	0	6	17	3	8	0	83
1999	31	0	19	7	23	3	26	0	0	0	3	0	3	7	3	3	3	0	97
2000	25	4	20	8	4	4	20	0	4	0	12	0	8	0	8	0	8	0	96

Source: Admissions Data CSPP.

Key: API = Asian Pacific Islander   Am. Ind. = American Indian   Percentage Grad. = Percentage who graduated
Hisp. = Hispanic   M/Racial = Multiracial   Percentage Cont. Prog. = Percentage continuing in program as of June 2001
As. Ind. = Asian Indian   Other = Other or Declined to state
As. Ind. = Asian Indian

Note: Percentages have been rounded off so they may not total 100 percent.

program. Following graduation, the majority of MCCP graduates remain actively engaged in providing mental health services to historically underserved populations and working in community-based settings.

For example, an exemplary alumnus from the MCCP-Ph.D. program is a researcher at a major university and is the director of a counseling service for Native American families and children. Additionally, he participates in teaching, consulting and organizational training. He is a Native American who came to CSPP through an unusual route. Growing up on and off a reservation, he began college at sixteen without any career counseling and dropped out at eighteen. He relocated to Los Angeles where he found support. After spending some time in writing, teaching English, and editing for a publishing house, he went back to a local college. There he met a CSPP professor who was teaching undergraduate courses, and, after taking courses in Community Psychology and Peace and Conflict, he found that psychology and social activism could be combined. The professor was impressed with his values and writing skills and encouraged him to apply. He found that the values of MCCP and CSPP were so close to his own that it was his first and only choice. His experience in MCCP validated this and he said it was the first time that he felt he belonged somewhere, and his relationships with his fellow students and faculty provided him with remarkable experiences. He was a very competent student, and he is excelling in his professional career, combining psychology and social justice.

The MCCP Emphasis Area thus creates an environment that promotes professional competence, cultural knowledge and sensitivity, and social harmony. The MCCP ecology fosters an MCCP identity that is respectful and welcoming of diversity among the faculty and students. Our students view MCCP as a home: a place of mentorship and support. As such, MCCP is both an important recruitment and retention resource of culturally and ethnically diverse students for CSPP at Alliant International University.

THE CURRICULUM

The curriculum for MCCP is a combination of what Ridley, Mendoza, and Kanitz (1994) call the separate course design and the integration design. In the separate course design, multicultural training is handled through one or more specific courses. In the integration design, multicultural training is infused throughout the curriculum. The course work of MCCP students includes separate multicultural and community courses, three of which are required of all clinical students and five additional which are specific to MCCP students. At the pre-master's level, MCCP students are required to take two courses: Psychopathology: Etiology and Diagnosis in Sociocultural Context (first year, two semesters), and Community-Clinical Issues in Psychology and Prevention Strategies. As an example, the Psychopathology course teaches students about diagnoses and diagnostic issues. In addition, it provides a historical perspective on people of color and on the research on psychopathology with minority populations. There is an in-depth focus on the influence of racial or ethnic background, economic status, gender, sexual orientation, and disability on diagnostic considerations. Students gain an understanding of the cultural issues and implications in diagnostic categories and they begin to develop skills in formulating culturally sensitive psychodiagnostic formulations.

The above emphasis-area specific courses are in addition to the "separate courses" that all clinical students take. The latter courses are Intercultural Laboratory (first year, one semester) and Multicultural Mental Health (first year, one semester). These courses provide students with a greater awareness of themselves as cultural beings, with a sociocultural and sociopolitical context through which to conceptualize psychopathology, psychological distress, and social problems; and with models, tools, and strategies for working with historically underserved and socially oppressed populations.

At the post-master's level, all clinical students take a one-semester course entitled Sex Roles and Gender. In addition, MCCP students are required to take at least two emphasis-area specific clinical electives. Courses include: Alternative Intervention Strategies, Multicultural Family Therapy, Clinical Interventions with Lesbians and Gay Men, Community Consultation, Belief Systems, Spirituality and Psychotherapy, Advanced Psychodynamic Interventions with Multicultural Populations, Interventions with Victims of Violence, School and Community-Based Interventions with Children and Adolescents, Pediatric Neuropsychology, and Culture, and Understanding Violence and Nonviolence.

While there are specific multicultural and community courses, CSPP-LA's aim is to infuse multicultural content throughout all of its courses—the integration design. CSPP-LA's actual success in integrating multicultural issues into the full range of general psychology, clinical, and research courses has improved over the past decade but is rather variable, depending on the nature of the course and the motivation and multicultural interest and expertise of the faculty instructor. Ridley, Mendoza, and Kanitz (1994) talk of the integration design as the ideal program design. However, they note that it is a difficult design to actualize and to monitor. They add that this design may not provide enough depth in multicultural issues. Thus, MCCP utilizes a combination of the specific course design and the integration design.

The MCCP graduates of the Ph.D. Clinical Psychology Training Program at CSPP-LA are prepared to conduct socially relevant research on applied clinical topics within varied contexts. This model of research is based on the local clinical scientist model espoused by Trierweiler and Stricker (1992) in the National Council of Schools of Professional Psychology's core curriculum in professional psychology. At CSPP-LA, this model has been operationalized behaviorally into a coordinated sequence of research experiences including (1) several research apprenticeship experiences in a faculty's ongoing program of research; (2) a predoctoral research project culminating in a poster session presentation; (3) a year-long research consultation experience in an applied setting resulting in a research product; and (4) the completion of a doctoral dissertation. The research questions emanating from this research training experience are focused primarily on the social problems of marginalized, oppressed, stigmatized, and underserved populations typically inhabiting urban communities.

Some examples of recent MCCP dissertation topics include (1) an examination of the ecological and cultural factors (for example, experiences of racism, racial socialization, and spirituality) on achievement attributions and general achievement motivation among African American youths; (2) an empirical test of the relationship between the experience of racism, belief in an Afrocentric world view, depression, and within-group interpersonal violence in African American men; and (3) an examination of the role of acculturation influences on the development of disordered eating behaviors and body image among Asian American adolescent females.

The MCCP graduates of the Psy.D. Clinical Psychology Training Program at CSPP-LA serve as consultants and clinicians in a wide variety of settings. The Psy.D. Program is based on the practitioner model of graduate education for professional clinical psychologists as set forth in the Vail Conference and further refined by the National Council of Schools of Professional Psychology (Peterson et al., 1992). As a practitioner-oriented program, the Psy.D. program emphasizes applied clinical skills and clinical applications of research knowledge. Students in this program are required to complete an independent doctoral project that usually involves creating a product that will be of service to a particular clinical population or to practitioners. The doctoral projects have included training manuals for mental health practitioners, psychoeducational videos for the lay public, clinical workbooks for clients, psychoeducational books for children, and other tools to enhance the well-being of clinical populations and the professionals who serve them. Some examples of recent MCCP doctoral projects topics are (1) anti-bias education for elementary school children; (2) HIV and AIDS prevention for African American women; and (3) a college course on White racist identity in a multicultural society. The culminating experience of the Psy.D. Program is two year-long in-depth clinical electives that are taught by the clinical leaders amongst the CSPP-LA faculty. Students have choices of courses such as Group Therapy, Couples Therapy, Family Systems Interventions, and Interventions with Multicultural Adolescents.

The curriculum is regularly reviewed and adjusted. Each successive cohort of MCCP students serves as a catalyst for the faculty to refine the educational climate and culture to fit the pressing educational needs of MCCP students in the twenty-first century.

Field Training

CSPP-LA students have the opportunity to obtain clinical training in a wide variety of settings, including community mental health centers, community-based nonprofit organizations, law enforcement agencies (police departments, jails and prisons, probation and diversion programs), hospitals, and so on. Students in the clinical programs participate in practicum placements as well as clinical internships and are consistently in high demand due to the multicultural expertise they develop in the program. Many MCCP students have had the opportunity to assume important roles in serving diverse clients at field training sites due to the knowledge base provided within the MCCP Emphasis Area.

Student Guidance and Mentorship

During the first several years of the program, students are assigned to an MCCP faculty advisor. Later, the doctoral project or dissertation mentor serves as the advisor. Through contact with the advisor, students get advice about the curriculum and courses, and, additionally, they have the opportunity to interface with faculty members around the faculty's research, clinical, and community service. In addition to individual meetings between student and advisor during the first couple of years, advisors meet with a small cohort of advisees on a weekly or biweekly basis. Advisors work to provide students with an orientation to professional development and to training opportunities that highlight the emerging niches available to community-clinical psychologists in the twenty-first century. The advising group meetings provide an important orienting, socialization, and community-building function.

Moreover, for many MCCP students—informal as well as formal, personal as well as professional—guidance, socialization, and mentorship are central to their success. Many students are from cultures that have been marginalized or stigmatized. Many are first-generation college graduates. Few have professional role models in their immediate or extended family. The guidance, socialization, and mentorship process is therefore more complicated. Students are struggling with how to honor their heritage and identity while learning the rules and roles in the psychology profession. They are wrestling with how to apply what they're learning to their particular neighborhood or community when there's limited research or knowledge about their particular group. They're wrestling with how to pay for their education while often supporting a family, financially and emotionally, that, though proud, doesn't fully understand what psychology and professional school is all about. Because of these realities, MCCP faculty put tremendous time and energy into mentoring MCCP students.

Lovitts and Nelson (2000) assert that the successful integration of doctoral students into any department is critical to reducing attrition rates, particularly for ethnic minority students. A critical mass of ethnically and culturally diverse faculty is the most optimal strategy for reducing attrition rates among ethnic minority and culturally diverse students. The MCCP faculty's primary mission is to serve as role models and mentors for students preparing to embark in the field of multicultural community-clinical psychology. The faculty cares about the students' personal as well as professional development; the emphasis is on developing balanced, whole beings. The emphasis on mentoring and guidance is broadened in the attention to developing an MCCP community.

THE MCCP EMPHASIS AREA AS A COMMUNITY

Taken together, the multiple aspects of the program provide a successful model for training clinical psychologists to work in diverse settings with a wide variety of clients. The curriculum, critical mass of diverse faculty and students, combined with the richly textured multicultural landscape of Los Angeles, converge to create a community within the emphasis area that is fertile and supportive for students and faculty to pursue their interests in studying and serving historically oppressed and underserved populations. In addition, the faculty's commitment to a community-psychology perspective leads to substantial efforts toward the development of a sense of community within the emphasis area itself. The belief is that a strong sense of community is essential for students' learning and personal and professional development and that this is especially important in an innovative, nontraditional program with diverse often nontraditional students.

MCCP's sense of community is enhanced by a number of formal and informal opportunities for students to interact with faculty outside of the classroom. The emphasis area sponsors an annual get-together in the fall that brings faculty, students, their families and significant others together for an informal afternoon of socialization, enabling students at various levels of the programs to interact and to get to know each other and the faculty in a more casual setting. This is complemented with informal lunches on campus with students and faculty. The emphasis area also publishes a bi-annual newsletter, The *Community Connection,* which provides students with a forum for exploring issues of interest. Past issues have focused on community and social activism, spirituality, biracial identity development, gay and lesbian issues, and class and classism, among others. Student editors work closely with a sponsoring faculty member in developing and producing the newsletter which is usually eighteen to twenty pages in length and features student submissions, interviews with prominent scholars and practitioners, and faculty and student profiles, as well as news and information about the program, conferences of interest, and more.

The focus on faculty mentoring and guidance of MCCP students and the emphasis on the development of an MCCP community reflect the belief that the learning and development takes place both in and out of the classroom.

MCCP AND BEYOND

As this chapter reveals, the MCCP Emphasis Area provides unique and rich opportunities for students and faculty who share interests in working with historically underserved individuals and communities. Although the program has received national attention as model for multicultural education in clinical psychology, a number of issues remain open for improvement.

The MCCP faculty assume the bulk of responsibility for teaching required diversity related courses to all CSPP-LA students, regardless of emphasis area. This creates a polarization within the emphasis areas, leading some to believe that only faculty within the MCCP Emphasis Area are qualified to teach these courses, or in a more detrimental fashion, that MCCP faculty should bear the full responsibility for diversifying the clinical programs.

In many ways, these problems reflect the dynamic tension that exists around our program design. MCCP exists because we believe that, at this point in time, it is only through a specific and dedicated emphasis area that multicultural community issues will be given serious and in-depth treatment. Yet, there is a larger CSPP-LA Clinical Psychology Program that needs to be more infused with multiculturalism, with respect to faculty, students, and curricular issues. MCCP faculty wrestle with how to apportion our time and expertise so that both the emphasis area thrives and the entire Clinical Psychology Program grows with regard to multiculturalism.

There are a couple of areas where the MCCP faculty are currently working to enhance the learning experience. Strategies are currently under development to provide quality professional socialization experiences to MCCP students seeking to make the successful transition from doctoral student to multicultural community-clinical psychologist. In addition, faculty are working together to find creative, collaborative ways to further develop their own scholarship and to provide a venue for publication and dissemination of their own as well as students', alumni, and alumnae's multicultural-community clinical work.

The hallmark of MCCP has been its responsiveness to the changing needs of diverse, underserved individuals and communities. There's considerable work ahead as we continue to rethink and reconceptualize the training needs of tomorrow's clinical psychology graduate students.

References

American Psychological Association. (1997). *Office of Ethnic Minority Affairs communique, special issue: Psychology and racism.* Washington, DC: Author.

American Psychological Association. (1997). *Visions and transformations: The final report, Commission on Ethnic Minority Recruitment, Retention, and Training in Psychology.* Washington, DC: Author.

American Psychological Association. (2000). *Book 1: Guidelines and principles for accreditation of programs in professional psychology.* Washington, DC: Author.

County of Los Angeles. (2000). County of Los Angeles statistical data. [On-line]. Available: http://www.co.la.ca.us/overview.htm

County of Los Angeles. (2000). About Los Angeles County. [On-line]. Available: http://www.co.la.ca.us/overview.htm

Duffy, K. G., & Wong, F. Y. (1996). *Community psychology.* Boston, MA: Allyn & Bacon.

Los Angeles Almanac. (2000). *Foreign-born persons residing in Los Angeles County; by birthplace, 1990 Census.*[On-line]. Available: http://www.losangelesalmanac.com/topics/Immigration/im06.htm

Lovitts, B. E., & Nelson, C. (2000, November/December). The hidden crisis in graduate education: Attrition from Ph.D. programs. *Academe: Bulletin of the American Association of University Professors,* 44–50.

Myers, H. F. (1992). Overview and historical perspectives on ethnic minority clinical training in psychology. *The Clinical Psychologist, 45*(1), 5–12.

Pedersen, P. (1988). *A handbook for developing multicultural awareness.* Alexandria, VA: American Association for Counseling and Development.

Peterson, R. L., McHolland, J. D., Bent, R. J., Davis-Russell, E., Edwall, G. E., Polite, K., Singer, D. L., & Stricker, G. (1992). (Eds.). *The core curriculum in professional psychology: National Council of Schools of Professional Psychology.* Washington, DC: American Psychological Association.

Rappaport, J. (1977). *Community psychology: Values, research, and action.* New York: Holt, Rinehart, & Winston.

Rappaport, J., & Seidman, E. (2000). *Handbook of community psychology.* New York: Plenum Press.

Ridley, C., Mendoza, D., & Kanitz, B. (1994). Multicultural training: Reexamination, operationalization, and integration. *The Counseling Psychologist, 22*(2), 227–289.

Seidman, E., & Rappaport, J. (Eds.). (1986). *Redefining social problems.* New York: Plenum Press.

Sue, D. W., & Sue, D. (1990). *Counseling the culturally different* (2nd ed.). New York: John Wiley & Sons.

Trierweiler, S., & Stricker, G. (1992). Research and evaluation competency: Training the local clinical scientist. In R. L. Peterson, J. D. McHolland, R. J. Bent, E. Davis-Russell, G. E. Edwall, K. Polite, D. L. Singer, & G. Stricker, (1992). (Eds.). *The core curriculum in professional psychology: National Council of Schools of Professional Psychology* (pp. 103–113). Washington, DC: American Psychological Association.

CHAPTER FIVE

Integrating Diversity Content Across the Curriculum

Evaluation in a Clinical Graduate Program

Sue A. Kuba and Hanya Bluestone

The importance of training graduate students to be sensitive to and knowledgeable about cultural and individual differences has been emphasized in the field of psychology since the 1973 Vail Conference (Allison, Crawford, Echemendia, Robinson, & Knepp, 1994; Atkinson & Hackett, 1988; Atkinson, Morten, & Sue, 1983; Bernal & Padilla, 1982; Lopez et al., 1989; Pedersen & Marsella, 1982; Sue & Zane, 1987). In 1979 the American Psychological Association (APA) codified this commitment to diversity by including Criterion II among the seven criteria for accreditation of doctoral education and training programs. Criterion II specifies that human diversity includes, but is not limited to, "people with handicapping conditions; of differing ages, genders, ethnic and racial backgrounds, religions, and lifestyles; and from differing social and individual backgrounds" (American Psychological Association [APA], 1979, p. 4). In 1995 the APA updated and formalized these criteria, creating Domain D: Cultural and Individual Differences and Diversity.

Domain D requires programs in psychology to address both an affirmative action aspect and an integration aspect of diversity (Altmaier, 1993). At the first level, Domain D emphasizes that the cultural and individual diversity of students and faculty within training programs should reflect the increasingly pluralistic society that professional psychology serves. In fact, statistics suggest that so-called racial and ethnic minority groups will become a *majority* of the United States population within the next twenty years (Sue, 1997). These population trends heighten the need for significant representation of ethnic minorities in the profession.

Whereas focused efforts have been made to improve ethnic minority student and faculty recruitment (Munoz-Dunbar & Stanton, 1999; Ponterotto, 1997), some have noted that initial gains in ethnic minority participation in graduate psychology programs have reached a plateau since 1985 (Bernal, 1994; Bernal & Castro, 1994). There is, however, broad consensus that achieving a "critical mass" of ethnic minority students and faculty is advisable for programs attempting to encourage multicultural competency in their graduates (Bernal, 1994; Guzman, 1991; Munoz-Dunbar & Stanton, 1999; Ponterotto, 1997; Rogers, Hoffman, & Wade, 1998). These ethnic minority faculty and students may promote multicultural competence within their programs by valuing the inclusion of multicultural training (Bernal et al., 1999; Bluestone, Stokes, & Kuba, 1995), establishing a positive campus climate (Ponterotto, 1997), and contributing their unique perspectives within the classroom (Davis-Russell, Forbes, Bascuas, & Duran, 1991; Ponterotto & Casas, 1987).

A growing multicultural literature supports the relationship among a program's faculty ethnic minority representation, its student ethnic minority representation, and its level of multicultural competency. As early as 1987, Ponterotto and Casas found that leading multicultural training programs in counselor education were characterized by student and faculty ethnic minority representation greater than reported national averages. Other investigators have observed that ethnic minority doctoral students are drawn to psychology programs with higher percentages of ethnic minority faculty and students, multicultural courses in the curriculum, and faculty involvement in multicultural research (Bernal & Castro, 1994; Hammond & Yung, 1993; Hills & Strozier, 1992; Munoz-Dunbar & Stanton, 1999; Rogers, Hoffman, & Wade, 1998). Based on this available data, Bernal (1994) proposes "a possible interpretation of these reliable results is that, by increasing the numbers of ethnic minority faculty, training programs can infuse multicultural content into the preparation of all their graduates for work with multicultural populations" (p. 799).

A limitation of this interpretation is its narrow focus on ethnoracial minority groups as the consumers of culturally competent mental health services (Arredondo, 1994; Atkinson, 1994, Pope-Davis, Breaux & Liu, 1997). Training all graduates to think "complexly rather than categorically" (Pope-Davis & Coleman, 1997, p. 84) about race, ethnicity, gender, sexual orientation, age, socioeconomic status, disability, and other dimensions of cultural and individual diversity is a broader imperative (Atkinson & Hackett, 1995) requiring an individualistic and collectivistic orientation (Arredondo, 1994). For this reason, Altmaier (1993) argues that the first level—the affirmative action aspect—of Domain D is often overemphasized. She contends that the diversity of students and faculty is a necessary, but not sufficient, indication of program compliance.

To fully satisfy the requirements of Domain D, programs must also actively "provide students with relevant knowledge and experiences about the role of cultural and individual diversity in psychological phenomena as they relate to the science and practice of professional psychology" (APA, 1995, p. 10).

Most psychology training programs have responded positively to this diversity initiative. Early research documents the efforts of training programs to include a multicultural course or subspecialty within their curricula (Hills & Strozier, 1992; Kanitz, Mendoza, & Ridley, 1992; Rogers, Ponterotto, Conoley, & Wiese, 1992). Subsequent studies report a modest increase in the percentage of counseling psychology programs actually requiring students to complete a multicultural course prior to graduation (Bernal & Castro, 1994; Pontcrotto, 1997). Pope-Davis et al. (1995), however, caution that students in clinical psychology programs have, on average, taken fewer multicultural courses and perceive themselves as somewhat less culturally competent than their peers in counseling psychology. Notwithstanding the progress of numerous programs in implementing a separate-course or area-of-concentration model (cf. Copeland, 1982), specialists now agree that the preferred model for multicultural training is the integrated program design (D'Andrea & Daniels, 1991; Ponterotto, 1997; Pope-Davis & Coleman, 1997; Reynolds, 1997; Rogers, Hoffman, & Wade, 1998; Sue, 1997; Yutrzenka, 1995). Only the integrated program design requires programs to infuse diversity content within and across all training activities. Various authors have outlined models for realizing this integrative approach in curriculum development (Vasquez, 2001), experiential training (Pope-Davis, Breaux, & Liu, 1997), and organizational culture change (Reynolds, 1997).

The development of the Multicultural Competency Checklist (MCC) (Ponterotto et al., 1995) provided one of the first reliable, theoretically derived measures of multicultural training. Composed of 22 self-report items, the MCC evaluates a program's multicultural training in six areas: minority representation, curriculum issues, counseling practice and supervision, research considerations, student and faculty competency evaluation, and physical environment. Ponterotto (1997) proposed that the MCC could "help identify which competencies are being met on a national basis, and which are more resistant to development" (p. 115). This information, in turn, could drive multicultural program development.

In his national survey of APA accredited and non-APA accredited doctoral programs in counseling psychology, Ponterotto (1997) reported that 89 percent of programs had a required multicultural counseling course and 58 percent integrated multicultural content into all course work. More than 80 percent of all programs surveyed actively engaged in multicultural research. Most programs address multicultural issues in clinical supervision (73 percent), despite more limited opportunities across programs for exposure to multicultural clientele during fieldwork (35 percent). These results suggest that, at least in counseling psychology, most programs report that they are actively infusing multicultural issues and exposure across a variety of training experiences for their students.

It remains unclear whether program efforts to move toward an integrated program design are, in fact, resulting in more culturally competent students. As Sue and Sue (1990) have articulated, cultural competence requires a basic awareness of differences, knowledge of the world view of the culturally different client, and skills to intervene appropriately. There is some evidence that multicultural training contributes to students' awareness and knowledge of multicultural issues (Pope-Davis et al., 1995), as well as nonracist White identity development (Neville et al., 1996). One small study of thirty-nine White counseling psychology students, however, found that a single multicultural course had negligible impact on the multicultural sensitivity of some students, whose "intolerant attitudes" were nevertheless accepted by program students and faculty (Steward et al., 1998). Research has not documented a relationship between multicultural training and actual skill acquisition in psychology graduate students. For example, Pope-Davis et al. (1995) identified several training experiences that were related to perceived multicultural awareness and knowledge in counseling and clinical psychology students (for example, multicultural courses and workshops, discussion of multicultural issues in supervision, and contact hours with racially and ethnically diverse clients). None of these educational or clinical variables were significantly associated with students' perceived multicultural skills.

Among doctoral psychology graduates, there is even less evidence that inclusion of diversity content in graduate coursework alone is related to self-reported cultural competence. A relatively recent survey of APA members who received their doctorates in applied psychology, indicated that a majority of respondents did not perceive themselves as highly competent to provide services to racial and ethnic minorities (Allison et al., 1994). These professionals reported only moderate competence with African American, lesbian, gay and bisexual clients and low competence with people with disabilities, Hispanic, Asian American and Native American clients (Allison, Echemendia, Crawford, & Robinson, 1996). The best single predictor of perceived competence in graduates was the number of therapy cases they had during their training with members of a particular diverse group (Allison et al., 1996). When the integration of diversity content in course work was included with other types of exposure to diversity training experiences, however, there was an additive effect, whereby graduates in the high-exposure group reported significantly greater cultural competence than graduates in a low-exposure group.

Several limitations of the extant research complicate the interpretation of these results. In most of the aforementioned investigations, internal training directors were the sole survey respondents, and response rates were low

(Kanitz, Mendoza, & Ridley, 1992). This response pattern may indicate that training directors who responded to the surveys were "positively predisposed to minority issues" (Rogers et al., 1992, p. 612). Moreover, the lack of a consistently used, standardized measure of diversity training limits the comparability of results across studies. In fact, the MCC is one of the few instruments that is gaining as a measure of the integration of multicultural training in programs. When the MCC responses of training directors and students are compared, however, there are notable differences in how multicultural training is perceived, with students (selected by their training directors) reporting less integration of multicultural issues into their coursework than training directors (Constantine et al., 1996). These findings are consistent with earlier research that has noted the sometimes sizeable discrepancies between training directors and clinical psychology graduates in their reports about the inclusion of diversity content within programs' core curricula (Allison et al., 1994; Bernal & Castro, 1994). Whereas research using the MCC has provided some baseline information about multicultural training in programs, there is limited information about the status of training related to other areas of diversity. Consequently, the full impact of Criterion II and Domain D requirements on graduate training in psychology requires further exploration.

This investigation began in 1995 with the goal of developing a reliable and valid instrument to assess training program compliance with the integration aspect of Domain D. The Diversity Rating Form (DRF) (Kuba, 1995)—a measure of the extent to which course lectures and readings address seven diversity dimensions—was the product of this effort. In contrast to the usual training director survey approach, the DRF may be distributed to students and instructors as a standard component of course evaluation. The current study had three objectives: (1) to assess the integration of diversity content in course-work and reading over time; (2) to provide further information about the reliability of the DRF; and (3) to examine whether instructor demographic characteristics were related to ratings of diversity inclusion within courses at a free-standing professional school of psychology. This study also presents a model for how a graduate psychology program can operationally define diversity, measure the inclusion of diversity content in courses, use data to drive continual quality improvement efforts, and tangibly demonstrate a true program commitment to an integrated program design.

PILOT STUDY

Based on the recommendations of previous investigators (Altmaier, 1993; Hills & Strozier, 1992), a pilot study, employing a within-program approach to the assessment of diversity training, was conducted in the spring of 1994. The site for this study was the California School of Professional Psychology in Fresno (CSPP-Fresno), a clinical program that offers proficiency training in cross-cultural psychology, as well as more than ten required courses and electives each year on topics related to human diversity (Kuba, Davis-Russell, & Forbes, 1993). The program's core faculty was 35 percent female, 18 percent ethnic minority, and 18 percent openly gay or lesbian. Integrating diversity training into all courses and clinical practica was an established goal of the CSPP-Fresno faculty and administration. This goal was approached in several ways. These included

1. Providing monthly in-services for one year which explored obstacles to Diversity Inclusion

2. Adopting specific policies regarding faculty recruitment

3. Requiring a service of non-credit experiential courses for students to explore the impact of their own group membership on attitudes and beliefs

4. Discussing ways to evaluate diversity competence without punitive consequences

5. Creating a standing faculty committee on Diversity Issues related to faculty-student education

Therefore, the CSPP-Fresno program was considered representative of graduate psychology programs seeking to make the transition from single course and subspecialty training in diversity to an integrated program design.

Data for the pilot study was obtained from course syllabi, reading lists, and dissertations housed in the library archives at CSPP-Fresno. Data were coded by graduate student research assistants onto an instrument developed specifically for the research project (Stokes & Bluestone, 1994). Each course's topic title, reading title, and dissertation title was assessed for words related to the following diversity dimensions

- Ethnicity
- Gender
- Age
- Sexual orientation
- Socioeconomic status (SES)
- Physical challenge

For example, titles containing the words *minority, racial, ethnic, culture* were coded for ethnicity. Words were counted as indicators of diversity only when their inclusion represented a deviation from expected or normative topics in each of the six dimensions.

The results of the pilot study suggested that CSPP-Fresno had made measurable progress toward meeting Criterion II requirements, as evidenced by a significant increase from 1989 to 1993 in the number of dissertation titles containing diversity terms. Judging from the limited course syllabi and readings lists that were obtained, almost 50 percent of CSPP-Fresno's courses were including multicultural content and 20 percent were addressing gender. Other important diversity dimensions, however, appeared to be receiving less attention from course instructors. In particular, the course syllabi and reading lists analyzed did not reflect the inclusion of training related to people with disabilities. Finally, male and female faculty did not differ in their coverage of gender issues in class. Ethnic minority faculty on the other hand, were significantly more likely to provide multicultural training than their European American colleagues.

Unfortunately the pilot study, though intriguing and less biased than the survey research approach, was plagued by methodological problems. Most significantly, the database was quite unreliable. Course syllabi varied considerably in their content and comprehensiveness across faculty. Similarly, instructors did not consistently submit reading lists and many were incomplete. Although these limitations have been ameliorated by developing a standardized format for course syllabi and reading lists within the program, the problem of between-program comparisons would remain. Finally, the pilot study's goal of assessing the quantity of course diversity content may have obscured the more subtle means by which knowledge and skills related to human diversity were frequently imparted to students.

The pilot study provided direction for the creation of the DRF and its initial findings (Bluestone, Stokes, & Kuba, 1996). It substantiated the need for a standardized measure of diversity training to facilitate comparability of courses within programs and eventually between programs. It led to the development of an instrument geared toward graduate psychology student and faculty respondents rather than program training directors. Finally, the pilot study prompted the decision to de-emphasize the quantity of diversity training in courses and focus instead on the perceived quality of these training opportunities.

METHOD

Faculty and administrative consent was obtained to involve CSPP-Fresno in a longitudinal study of the status of diversity training within its clinical program. At the end of the 1995 spring semester, the DRF (Kuba, 1995), was distributed along with standard course evaluation forms to students and instructors in all courses ($N = 59$). These diversity questionnaires were color coded to distinguish between faculty and student respondents. By June 1995 questionnaires had been collected from thirty-seven out of fifty-nine instructors, constituting a faculty response rate of 63 percent. Of the 1,247 individual student registrations by class for spring courses, 613 questionnaires were returned, yielding a student return rate of approximately 49 percent. In the subsequent five years, an additional 5,539 student ratings were obtained. Faculty ratings were dropped subsequent to the first study's findings that there were no significant differences in the ratings of students and faculty members for the same courses.

Along with demographic information (for example, gender, ethnicity), the DRF assessed the perceived extent to which a particular diversity dimension was addressed within course lectures and discussions, and required reading material. Each DRF item corresponded to one of seven diversity dimensions: (1) ethnicity and culture; (2) gender differences; (3) aging and mature adults; (4) class, SES or poverty; (5) sexual orientation, gay or lesbian issues; (6) religious orientation or spirituality; and (7) physical disability or handicapping conditions. The perceived extent of coverage within each diversity category was rated on a scale from zero (*not at all*) to eight (*thorough integration*). All DRF items were judged to have good face validity by a panel of CSPP-Fresno faculty members from diverse cultural and individual backgrounds.

The anonymity of all responses was assured in order to maximize the participation of students and faculty and to increase the likelihood that respondents would be candid in their ratings of courses. Data on individual courses were not analyzed. Individual faculty members were provided with the opportunity to receive feedback for their own purposes.

Results

Descriptive characteristics for the initial sample of 1,247 and the subsequent sample of 6,786 student responses are presented in Tables 5.1 and 5.2.

Table 5.3 shows the means and standard deviations of DRF items for all student and faculty respondents in the initial sample as well as the means and standard deviations for the subsequent student sample.

Psychometric Properties of the DRF

As Tables 5.4 and 5.5 indicate, the overall intercorrelations of DRF items ranged from 0.39 to 0.77. All Pearson correlations were highly significant ($p < 0.001$). The measure's overall internal consistency, as estimated by coefficient alpha, was 0.96. This value clearly exceeds minimum standards for acceptable reliability (Nunnally, 1978) and establishes a basis for calculating and utilizing a total diversity score in statistical analyses. Preliminary support for the construct validity of the DRF was provided by the highly significant correlation found between course lecture and course reading items ($r = 0.88$; $p < 0.001$), indicating that both of these item sets were related to the same underlying construct.

Table 5.1. Demographic Characteristics of Course Raters for Initial Study

Rater Characteristic	Faculty		Student	
	n	Percent	n	Percent
Gender				
Female	15	40	385	63
Male	22	60	183	30
Not indicated	—	—	45	7
Ethnicity				
European American	34	92	425	69
Persons of color*	3	8	76	13
Not indicated	—	—	112	18
Course type				
Therapy	13	35	326	53
Theory	11	30	149	24
Research	13	35	138	23

*Includes respondents of African, Asian, Latin, Native American, East Indian, and Middle Eastern descent.

Table 5.2. Demographic Characteristics of Course Raters
for Subsequent Analysis

Characteristic	n	Percent
Gender		
Female	3,479	63.2
Male	1,463	26.6
Not indicated	560	10.1
Ethnicity		
European American	3,280	59.6
Persons of color*	704	12.7
Not indicated	1,518	27.6
Course type**		
Therapy	3,187	58.8
Theory	1,213	22.4
Research	1,019	18.8

*Includes respondents of African, Asian, Latin, Native American, East Indian, and Middle Eastern descent.

**Courses in which the primary focus was cultural, were excluded from the analysis so total number of ratings does not equal total n size for the sample.

Table 5.3. Descriptive Statistics for Diversity Rating Form Items for Initial
and Subsequent Analysis

Analysis	Initial		Subsequent	
Diversity Rating Form Item	M	SD	M	SD
Ethnicity				
Course lecture	4.31	2.58	4.24	2.67
Readings	3.65	2.77	3.74	2.82
Gender				
Course lecture	4.35	2.50	4.23	2.58
Readings	3.82	2.68	3.81	2.72
Aging				
Course lecture	3.63	2.68	3.41	2.64
Readings	3.25	2.73	3.11	2.67
Socioeconomic status				
Course lecture	3.82	2.58	3.90	2.68
Readings	3.30	2.66	3.49	2.76
Sexual orientation				
Course lecture	2.60	2.65	2.73	2.74
Readings	2.31	2.66	2.37	2.69
Religious preference				
Course lecture	2.89	2.71	2.85	2.72
Readings	2.53	2.72	2.48	2.69
Physical disability				
Course lecture	2.69	2.64	2.93	2.75
Readings	2.44	2.61	2.66	2.75

Table 5.4. Initial Pearson Correlations Among Diversity Rating Form Items for Course Lectures

Item	1	2	3	4	5	6	7
Ethnicity	—	0.68*	0.58*	0.75*	0.64*	0.65*	0.39*
Gender		—	0.67*	0.68*	0.70*	0.57*	0.40*
Aging			—	0.64*	0.60*	0.52*	0.58*
Socioeconomic status				—	0.64*	0.64*	0.50*
Sexual orientation					—	0.64*	0.45*
Religion						—	0.41*
Physical disability							—

Note: Intercorrelations based on student ratings only.

$df = 575$ for all items.

*$p < 0.001$, one-tailed.

Table 5.5. Subsequent Pearson Correlations Among Diversity Rating Form Items
for Course Lectures

Item	1	2	3	4	5	6	7
Ethnicity	—	0.75*	0.58*	0.77*	0.64*	0.65*	0.47*
Gender		—	0.67*	0.74	0.68*	0.60*	0.50*
Aging			—	0.64*	0.56*	0.56*	0.64*
Socioeconomic status				—	0.64*	0.61*	0.56*
Sexual orientation					—	0.68*	0.50*
Religion						—	0.49*
Physical disability							—

Note: Intercorrelations based on student ratings only.

df = 6615 for all items.

*$p < 0.001$, one-tailed.

To further examine the patterns of interrelationships among items, the fourteen DRF items were submitted to a factor analysis with varimax rotation. A principle components analysis was conducted on the data provided by the student respondents. In the initial analysis, the two factors were extracted with eigenvalues greater than 1.0, collectively accounting for 73 percent of the total variance. Following varimax rotation, these factors were interpreted for items with loadings of 0.50 or higher. One item set, course lectures and course readings related to aging, met inclusion criteria for both factors. This item set was assigned to Factor One due to its slightly higher loading on that factor.

Factor One was labeled Prominent Diversity Topics and consisted of ethnicity, gender, aging, socioeconomic status, sexual orientation, and religion item sets. Factor Two was termed Ancillary Diversity Topics and included the physical disability item set.

When the factor analysis was repeated for the updated data, it yielded a slightly different factor structure, which accounted for 75.7 percent of the variance. Varimax rotation produced two factors based upon item loadings of 0.50 or higher. The item set that corresponded to course readings related to aging continued to be the only item that loaded on both factors. However, in the second analysis, Factor One did not contain the item for aging in class lecture or discussions. Factor Two contained the physical disability and aging item sets (see Table 5.6). Thus, in the new factor structure, aging became a less prominent focus in class discussion or lectures.

These findings, coupled with the instrument's established face validity and internal consistency, support the use of the DRF as a reliable and valid measure of diversity training within programs. The basic consistency of the factor structures over time provides additional support for the construct validity of the instrument.

Table 5.6. Rotated Component Matrix for Subsequent Factor Analysis

Item	Prominent Diversity Topics	Ancillary Diversity Topics
Ethnicity		
Lectures	0.848	0.214
Readings	0.847	0.258
Gender		
Lectures	0.789	0.325
Readings	0.792	0.363
Aging		
Lectures	0.496	0.687
Readings	0.524	0.700
Socioeconomic status		
Lectures	0.775	0.365
Readings	0.782	0.391
Sexual orientation		
Lectures	0.759	0.323
Readings	0.746	0.385
Religious preference		
Lectures	0.749	0.298
Readings	0.740	0.344
Physical disability		
Lectures	0.256	0.900
Readings	0.264	0.903

Note: Rotation converged in three iterations.

Faculty Demographics and Diversity Coverage

In the original publication, Bonferonni-corrected comparisons of total diversity scores by ethnicity and gender of faculty revealed significant differences in diversity coverage. Women instructors ($M = 53.72$) addressed diversity content in their courses significantly more than men ($M = 40.81$; $t(504) = 4.61$; $p < 0.01$, two-tailed). Additionally, faculty of color ($M = 70.33$) were significantly more likely to cover diversity issues in the classroom than their European American colleagues ($M = 41.58$; $t(504) = 6.81$; $p < 0.01$, two-tailed). These differences remained consistent over time and with a larger data set ($n = 4,992$). Women ($M = 50.5$) were much more likely to include diversity content than men ($M = 38.3$, $t(3,470); = 15.07$, $p < 0.01$) and faculty of color maintained a high level of inclusion ($M = 69.4$), while European American faculty increased theirs, but not significantly enough to dispel the difference. ($M = 44.0$; $t(550) = 17.0$, $p < 0.001$).

These global differences were paralleled for almost every diversity dimension, with women and faculty of color earning higher mean scores than men and European American instructors respectively.

Extent of Diversity Coverage at CSPP-Fresno

In the initial study, there was no difference in the total diversity scores of faculty ($M = 40.24$) and students ($M = 48.63$; $t(373) = 1.55$, ns). Among the student raters, no discrepancy was found in ratings of instructors on the basis of student gender or ethnicity.

Multiple t tests with a Bonferonni correction were run to compare multicultural training with training in each of the remaining diversity areas. Due to the highly significant correlation of course lecture and reading content, these analyses were conducted solely on the course lecture items. In the initial analysis, multicultural content was addressed in courses significantly more than content in all of the remaining diversity categories, except gender (see Table 5.7). There was no difference in the perceived extent of coverage of multicultural and gender content in courses.

In regard to diversity coverage by course type, significant variation was found among research, therapy, and theory courses during the analysis. Post-hoc analyses indicated that the least diversity training occurred in research-oriented courses. Theoretical courses appeared to provide the best coverage of diversity topics, with therapy courses somewhere in the middle. This was true in the initial analysis ($F(2,503) = 22.57$, $p < 0.001$), as well as the subsequent one ($F(2,5500) - 115.97$; $p < 0.001$).

Discussion

This study represents a critical step toward understanding how graduate psychology programs have responded to the second level, integration aspect, of the Criterion II and Domain D mandates for training in diversity. Although neither

Table 5.7. Initial Mean Comparisons of Ethnicity Ratings with Other Diversity Ratings for Course Lectures

Diversity Topic	M	df	t
Ethnicity	4.29	—	—
Gender	4.33	595	0.55
Aging	3.65	584	6.27*
Socioeconomic status	3.84	592	5.94*
Sexual orientation	2.58	589	18.35*
Religion	2.91	591	14.87*
Physical disability	2.65	588	13.68*

*$p < 0.005$, two-tailed.

specifies to what extent programs must infuse diversity content into curricula and clinical practica, each does stand as a clear challenge to those who continue to believe that the traditional program design appropriately prepares trainees to serve diverse client populations. The spirit of Criterion II and Domain D acknowledges the need to move graduate training in psychology toward the integrated program design. Proponents of the integrated model for multicultural training have argued that only this program design exposes all students to the requisite training in diversity, encourages faculty to share responsibility for providing this training, and promotes the affirmation of human variability (D'Andrea & Daniels, 1991; Pope, Davis, & Coleman, 1997; Ponterotto, 1997; Reynolds, 1997; Ridley, Mendoza, & Kanitz, 1992; Sue, 1997).

Although this study focused on diversity training within a single clinical psychology program, the results have considerable implications for all programs seeking to make the difficult, yet timely, transition to an integrated program design. The most profound implication of this study emanates from the dramatically superior coverage of diversity content by women and faculty of color. As Hills and Strozier (1992) have suggested, this may, in part, reflect the tendency of newer faculty to be more active in diversity training and research than their more senior colleagues. However, given that women and ethnic minority instructors have been well represented among the more senior faculty at CSPP-Fresno, this interpretation alone does not explain their greater commitment to diversity training. At a time when affirmative action hiring practices have come under such harsh criticism, this finding suggests that women and ethnic minority candidates must be viewed not only in terms of established hiring criteria, but also in terms of the diverse knowledge and skills that they are likely to bring to training programs in psychology. Certainly when a program's primary goal is the enhancement of training in diversity, candidates from diverse cultural and individual backgrounds should be given particular consideration.

A second implication of this study is that multicultural training and training related to other areas of diversity can coexist. In fact, the significant positive correlations found among DRF items suggest that courses with the highest ratings for coverage of multicultural content also obtained high ratings across the remaining diversity dimensions. Of course, some diversity dimensions were more highly related to the multicultural dimension than others were (that is, gender, socioeconomic status, and religion). These findings, however, may potentially quell the fear of some multicultural training advocates that focusing on a broader range of diversity issues will detract from multicultural competence within programs.

Although all the diversity dimensions in this study were interrelated, there was considerable variation in the extent to which each of the seven diversity topics were addressed. Multicultural and gender content were significantly more likely to be included in courses than content related to aging, socioeconomic status, sexual orientation, religion, and physical disability. Instructors in the program earned their lowest ratings for the integration of content regarding sexual orientation and physical disability. This disparity in the extent of coverage of various diversity topics raises interesting questions about how diversity is operationalized and prioritized within programs.

At CSPP-Fresno, it is clear that diversity issues are more likely to be addressed in certain courses. Theory and therapy courses, for instance, contained more diversity content than research courses. These results are best explained by the greater involvement of "diversity advocates" within these course types. Unfortunately, it is not clear from these results whether these diversity advocates were assuming the entire burden of providing diversity training or successfully influencing other faculty who teach similar courses to share this responsibility.

The factor structure produced with the DRF suggests that a core set of diversity topics seems to be included similarly by instructors. These topics include ethnicity and culture, gender, religious preference, socioeconomic status, aging and sexual orientation. The ancillary factor suggests a tendency for those who cover handicapping conditions to also cover aging. These factors may be partially related to curricular emphasis at the CSPP-Fresno campus. The campus actively recruits students and provides special curriculum in neuropsychology. Both aging and physical disability are widely covered in these courses. The stability of the factor structure over a six-year period indicates that most diversity topics are moderately integrated into the curriculum, however handicapping conditions remains on the periphery.

Limitations of the Study

This study's primary limitation was its focus on diversity training at a single graduate psychology training program. Given this within-program design, it is unclear whether results from this study may be generalized to other doctoral programs in psychology. Many graduate programs in psychology may be at a different stage in the process of incorporating diversity training into their curricula. Some may be working toward adding a single course or subspecialty to their program. Others may have already achieved an integrated program design. The goal of this study was merely to propose an alternative approach to the evaluation of program compliance with Criterion II and Domain D in the hope of generating controversy and discussion about how diversity should be operationalized and integrated within graduate psychology training and education.

Whereas studies using traditional survey and descriptive approaches to document diversity training have been limited by their inability to detect the more subtle means by which programs impart this knowledge to students, the current study is limited by its reliance on a self-report measure of diversity training. This study assessed faculty and student perceptions of the quality of diversity training. Although faculty and student perceptions of the status of diversity training at CSPP-Fresno were similar, the study results do not resolve the difficult and extremely interesting question of what respondents considered in forming their judgments about the quality of diversity coverage. Indeed, this study fails to address whether faculty and student opinions about diversity training within a program are related to more objective criterion measures of diversity inclusion.

As Rickard and Clements (1993) have pointed out, there are a number of difficulties inherent in delimiting diversity. This study focused on seven dimensions of diversity described in Criterion II but omitted other dimensions such as nationality, language, and body size, which many would argue are equally important. The priority ascribed to various diversity dimensions may be expected to vary considerably from program to program depending on the program's mission, geographic location, faculty expertise, and student interest. It is also important to acknowledge the underlying assumption of the current investigation. This study was borne from the position that training relevant to traditionally underserved populations should be integrated into all graduate level course work. Some may see this as an unrealistic goal that threatens to impinge upon academic freedom. Others, however, may share this viewpoint and agree that only the integrated program design captures the true intent of Criterion II and Domain D.

FUTURE RESEARCH

There is a clear need for further research on the level of compliance with Domain D in graduate training and education. Survey research and demographic data have been helpful in generating a broad picture of the response to this diversity initiative. However, this body of research has failed to assess how well programs are integrating diversity training into their core curricula through more substantial means. Investigations aimed at this second level of diversity are needed to provide a more accurate measure of the progress that is being made. Whenever possible, these investigations should employ both quantitative and qualitative analyses to obtain the richest and most accurate yield of information.

Previous studies have focused primarily on multicultural competence within training programs. While this research is critically important, it does not reflect the larger definition of diversity as outlined in Domain D. As a result, there is limited information available regarding the inclusion of other diversity dimensions in graduate education. Additional studies on the status of training related to gender, aging, sexual orientation, socioeconomic status, and handicapping conditions, as well as other important diversity dimensions would help training directors to set reasonable goals for integrating various aspects of diversity into their programs.

Finally, this study presents a strong case for the use of the DRF as an alternative to the traditional survey research approach. The longitudinal data collected using the DRF continue to allow CSPP-Fresno to monitor its level of inclusion of diversity training as the clinical faculty work toward an integrated program design. Presently, they are searching for a method of objectively evaluating diversity competency across all courses in the curriculum. Such objective measures may provide further evidence in support of diversity integration and direction for enhanced training.

Additional steps that would extend the scope of this study might include the development of multisite studies of diversity training to compare the strengths and limitations of graduate psychology programs in various settings (for example, professional schools and university programs) and disciplines (for example, school psychology, counseling psychology, and clinical psychology). Many undergraduate and graduate departments have requested use of the DRF since the original publication (Bluestone, Stokes, & Kuba, 1996). The instrument affords investigators a means by which to conduct in-depth, comparative research on program compliance with Criterion II. Such research is likely to make an enlightening and significant contribution to the extant literature.

Endnote

The APA requires doctoral training programs in psychology to address diversity by virtue of Domain D: Cultural and Individual Differences and Diversity of its accreditation guidelines (APA, 1995). Often programs address only the composition of faculty and students in their attempts to document diversity. Most authors agree that an integration of diversity topics across course offerings is preferable, but difficult to measure (Pope-Davis & Coleman, 1997; Sue, 1997). The study in this chapter has three purposes: (1) continuing application of the DRF (Kuba, 1995) to assess the integration of diversity content in course work and reading over time; (2) to provide additional information regarding the reliability of the DRF; and (3) to examine whether instructor demographic characteristics were related to ratings of diversity inclusion within courses at a free-standing professional school of psychology. The DRF was completed initially by 613 students and 37 faculty members. Data was gathered over a five-year period for an additional 5,502 responses. The DRF demonstrated high reliability ($\alpha = 0.96$) and construct validity ($r = 0.88$; $p < 0.001$). Women ($p < 0.01$) and faculty of color ($p < 0.01$) were significantly more likely to include diversity dimensions in course content than men and European American faculty in both the initial data and the longitudinal sample. The authors discuss implications for the assessment and integration of diversity in doctoral programs.

References

Allison, K. W., Crawford, I., Echemendia, R., Robinson, L., & Knepp, D. (1994). Human diversity and professional competence: Training in clinical and counseling psychology revisited. *American Psychologists, 49*, 792–796.

Allison, K. W., Echemendia, R., Crawford, I., & Robinson, L. (1996) Predicting cultural competence: Implications for practice and training. *Professional Psychology: Research and Practice, 27*, 386–393.

Altmaier, E. M. (1993). Role of Criterion II in accreditation. *Professional Psychology: Research and Practice, 24*, 127–129.

American Psychological Association. (1979). *Criteria for accreditation of doctoral training programs and internships in professional psychology.* Washington, DC: American Psychological Association.

American Psychological Association. (1995). *Guidelines and principles for accreditation of programs in professional psychology.* Washington, DC: American Psychological Association.

Arredondo, P. (1994). Multicultural training: A response. *The Counseling Psychologist, 22*, 308–314.

Atkinson, D. R. (1994). Multicultural training: A call for standards. *The Counseling Psychologist, 22*, 300–307.

Atkinson, D. R., & Hackett, G. (1988). *Counseling non-ethnic American minorities.* Springfield, IL: Charles C. Thomas.

Atkinson, D. R., & Hackett, G. (1995). *Counseling diverse populations.* Madison, WI: William C. Brown.

Atkinson, D. R., Morten, G., & Sue, D. W. (1983). *Counseling American minorities: A cross-cultural perspective.* Dubuque, IA: William C. Brown.

Bernal, M. (1994). Some issues and content missed by survey studies. *American Journal of Community Psychology, 22*, 799–801.

Bernal, M. E., & Castro, F. G. (1994). Are clinical psychologists prepared for service and research with ethnic minorities? Report of a decade of progress. *American Psychologist, 49*, 797–805.

Bernal, M. E., & Padilla, A. (1982). Status of minority curricula and training in clinical psychology. *American Psychologist, 37*, 780–787.

Bernal, M. E., Sirolli, A. A., Weisser, S. K., Ruiz, J. A., Chamberlain, V. J., & Knight, G. P. (1999). Relevance of multicultural training to student's applications to clinical psychology programs. *Cultural Diversity and Ethnic Minority Psychology, 5*, 43–55.

Bluestone, H.H., Stokes, A., & Kuba, S. A. (1996) Toward an integrated program design: Evaluating the status of diversity training in a graduate school curriculum. *Professional Psychology: Research and Practice, 27*, 394–400.

Constantine, M. G., Ladany, N., Inman, A. G., & Ponterotto, J. G. (1996). Students' perceptions of multicultural training in counseling psychology programs. *Journal of Multicultural Counseling and Development, 24*, 241–253.

Copeland, E. J. (1982). Minority populations and traditional counseling programs: Some alternatives. *Counselor Education and Supervision, 21,* 187–193.

D'Andrea, M., & Daniels, J. (1991). Exploring the different levels of multicultural counseling training in counselor education. *Journal of Counseling and Development, 70,* 78–85.

Davis-Russell, E. (1990). Incorporating ethnic minority issues into curriculum: Myths and realities. In G. Stricker, E. Davis-Russell, E. Bourg, E. Duran, W. R. Hammond, J. D. McHolland, K. Polite, & B. E. Vaughn (Eds.), *Toward ethnic diversification in psychology education and training* (pp. 171–177). Washington, DC: American Psychological Association.

Davis-Russell, E., Forbes, W. T., Bascuas, J., & Duran, E. (1991). Ethnic diversity and the core curriculum. In R. L. Peterson, J. D. McHolland, R. J. Bent, E. Davis-Russell, G. E. Edwall, K. Polite, D. L. Singer, & G. Stricker (Eds.), *The core curriculum in professional psychology* (pp. 147–151). Washington, DC: American Psychological Association.

Guzman, L. P. (1991). Incorporating cultural diversity into psychology training programmes. In H. F. Myers, P. Wohlford, L. P. Guzman, & R. J. Echemendia (Eds.), *Ethnic minority perspectives on clinical training and services in psychology* (pp. 67–70). Washington, DC: American Psychological Association.

Hammond, W. R., Yung, B. (1993). Minority student recruitment and retention practices among schools of professional psychology: A national survey and analysis. *Professional Psychology: Research and Practice, 24,* 3–12.

Hills, H. I., & Strozier, A. L. (1992). Multicultural training in APA-approved counseling psychology programs: A survey. *Professional Psychology: Research and Practice, 23,* 43–51.

Kanitz, B. E., Mendoza, D. W., & Ridley, C. R. (1992). Multicultural training in religiosity-oriented counselor education programs: A survey. *Journal of Psychology and Christianity, 11,* 337–344.

Kuba, S. A. (1995). [Diversity Rating Form]. (Available from the author at California School of Professional Psychology, 5130 E. Clinton Way, Fresno, CA 93727).

Kuba, S. A., Davis-Russell, E., & Forbes, W. (1993). *Psy. D. self study: Section Four response.* Fresno, CA: California School of Professional Psychology.

Lopez, S. R., Grover, K. P., Holland, D., Johnson, M. J., Kain, C. D., Kanel, K., Mellins, C. A., & Rhyne, M. C. (1989). Development of culturally sensitive psychotherapists. *Professional Psychology: Research and Practice, 20,* 369–376.

Munoz-Dunbar, R., & Stanton, A. L. (1999). Ethnic diversity in clinical psychology: Recruitment and admission practices among doctoral programs. *Teaching of Psychology, 26,* 259–263.

Neville, H. A., Heppner, M. J., Louie, C. E., Thompson, C. E., Brooks, L., & Baker, C. E. (1996). The impact of multicultural training on white racial identity attitudes and therapy competencies. *Professional Psychology: Research and Practice, 27,* 83–89.

Nunnally, J. C. (1978). *Psychometric theory* (2nd edition). New York: McGraw-Hill.

Pedersen, P. B., & Marsella, A. J. (1982). The ethical crisis for cross-cultural counseling and therapy. *Professional Psychology, 13,* 492–500.

Ponterotto, J. G. (1997) Multicultural counseling training: A competency model and national survey. In C. B. Pope-Davis, H. L. K. Coleman, et al. (Eds.), *Multicultural counseling competencies: Assessment, education and training, and supervision* (pp. 111–130). Thousand Oaks, CA: Sage.

Ponterotto, J. G., Alexander, C. M., & Grieger, I. (1995). A multicultural competency checklist for counseling training programs. *Journal of Multicultural Counseling and Development, 23,* 11–20.

Ponterotto, J. G., & Casas, J. M. (1987). In search of multicultural competence within counselor education programs. *Journal of Counseling and Development, 65,* 430–434.

Pope-Davis, D. B., Breaux, C., & Liu, W. M. (1997). A multicultural immersion experience: Filling a void in multicultural training. In D. B. Pope-Davis, H. L. K. Coleman, et al. (Eds.), *Multicultural counseling competencies: Assessment, education and training, and supervision* (pp. 271–241). Thousand Oaks, CA: Sage.

Pope-Davis, D. B., Coleman, H. L. K., et al. (Eds.) (1997). *Multicultural counseling competencies: Assessment, education and training, and supervision.* Thousand Oaks, CA: Sage.

Pope-Davis, D. B., Reynolds, A., Dings, J. G., & Nielson, D. (1995). Examining multicultural counseling competencies of graduate students in psychology. *Professional Psychology: Research and Practice, 26,* 322–329.

Reynolds, A. L. (1997). Using the multicultural change intervention matrix (MCIM) as a multicultural counseling training model. In D. B. Pope-Davis, H. L. K. Coleman, et al. (Eds.), *Multicultural counseling competencies: Assessment, education and training, and supervision* (pp. 209–225). Thousand Oaks, CA: Sage.

Rickard, H. C., & Clements, C. B. (1993). Critique of APA accreditation Criterion II: Cultural and individual differences. *Professional Psychology: Research and Practice, 24,* 123–126.

Ridley, C. R., Mendoza, D. W., & Kanitz, B. E. (1992). Program designs for multicultural training. *Journal of Psychology and Christianity, 11,* 326–336.

Rogers, M. R., Hoffman, M. A., & Wade, J. (1998). Notable multicultural training in APA-approved counseling psychology and school psychology programs. *Cultural Diversity and Ethnic Minority Psychology, 4,* 212–226.

Rogers, M. R., Ponterotto, J. G., Conoley, J. C., & Wiese, M. J. (1992). Multicultural training in school psychology: A national survey. *School Psychology Review, 21,* 603–616.

Steward, R. J., Morales, P. C., Bartell, P. A., Miller, M., & Weeks, D. (1998). *Journal of Multicultural Counseling and Development, 26,* 13–27.

Stokes, A., & Bluestone, H. H. (1994). [Diversity Record Sheet]. (Available from Annemarie Stokes, California School of Professional Psychology, 5130 E. Clinton Way, Fresno, CA 93727).

Sue, D. (1997). Multicultural training. *International Journal of Intercultural Relations, 21*, 175–193.

Sue, D. W., & Sue, D. (1990). *Counseling the culturally different: Theory and practice* (2nd edition). New York: John Wiley.

Sue, S., & Zane, N. (1987). The role of culture and cultural technique in psychotherapy: A critique and reformulation. *American Psychologist, 42*,37–45.

Vasquez, M. J. T. (2001). Advancing the study of Chicana/o psychology. *Counseling Psychologist, 29*, 118–127.

Yutrzenka, B. A. (1995). Making a case for training in ethnic and cultural diversity in increasing treatment efficacy. *Journal of Consulting and Clinical Psychology, 63*, 197–206.

CHAPTER SIX

Lesbians, Gays, and Family Psychology

Resources for Teaching and Practice

Robert-Jay Green

Having participated in and led various kinds of diversity training on the topics of race relations, gender, and sexual orientation (Green, 1998a,b,c), I believe that five overlapping elements are important for learning to work with a given cultural group: (1) *sensitization* (developing a comfortable awareness of "not knowing everything" and an enthusiasm for learning more); (2) *didactic training* (acquiring information through lectures and readings); (3) *personal contact* (reducing phobic and prejudicial responses through cooperative interactions with members of the cultural group); (4) *supervised clinical experience* (acquiring intervention skills that are culturally attuned under the guidance of professionals who specialize in working with members of the cultural group); and (5) *seeking consultation* (developing the self-awareness and comfort to seek future case consultation from such experts). This chapter will describe resources for facilitating the first three of these training components (sensitization, didactic training, and personal contact) with an emphasis on learning to work with lesbian women and gay men in couples and families. These materials were originally developed for a family psychology doctoral-level course, but the interview questions and treatment-planning guidelines are geared for practicing therapists as well. Instructors also can use these materials to create course modules or short workshops on lesbian and gay issues in couples therapy, family therapy, cultural diversity, human sexuality, or human development. Most of the videotapes recommended can be used in talks given to nonprofessionals as well. Before presenting these teaching and practice resources, however, I will describe the status of lesbian, gay, and bisexual issues in the field of family psychology and demonstrate why training in these issues has become so crucial.

LESBIANS, GAYS, AND THE FIELD OF FAMILY PSYCHOLOGY

The *official* U.S. government policy on lesbians and gays in the armed forces (Don't ask, don't tell) now parallels what has been, historically, the *unofficial* policy in many families and in the field of family psychology: don't ask, don't tell, don't teach much about it, don't write about it!

During the years 1990–1995, a total of 718 articles were submitted for publication to the *Journal of Marital and Family Therapy* (Sprenkle & Bailey, 1995). Of these, only seven (or approximately 1 percent) were on the topic of homosexuality. A similar picture emerged in terms of manuscripts submitted to *Family Process* during this period.

Given the overall rejection rates for all types of manuscripts, the result is that only a minuscule number of articles on lesbians and gays have been published in these two leading family therapy journals (Laird & Green, 1996a). Not only is there a dearth of articles explicitly addressing this theme, but even books and articles on other popular subjects in the field of family psychology (for example, couples therapy, eating disorders, substance abuse, depression, and stepfamilies) almost never use case examples with lesbian or gay family members.

It is believed the low visibility of this topic in print has lead to the false impression that family psychologists and other family therapists rarely see lesbian and gay clients in their practices. Therefore, it is important to examine two growing myths: (1) the idea that heterosexual family therapists seldom work with lesbian and gay clients (2) and the related idea that such clients almost exclusively seek the services of lesbian and gay mental health professionals.

Recently, Green and Bobele (1994) surveyed a random sample of clinical members (four hundred fifty-four therapists) of the American Association for Marriage and Family Therapy (AAMFT), the vast majority of whom are, presumably, heterosexual. Among their current caseloads, *"72 percent . . . of these family therapists reported that approximately one-tenth of their practice involved gays and/or lesbians . . ."* [italics added] (p. 357). If we estimate the average family therapist's caseload at twenty clients per week, then these therapists are seeing two cases every week that involve gays or lesbians. Another 8 percent of the AAMFT sample reported that some proportion of their current caseload (but less than one-tenth) involved lesbian or gay clients. Most likely, these findings are underestimates in that some lesbian, gay, and bisexual clients (particularly adolescents, married persons, some parents who fear loss of child custody, and elderly clients who grew up in more repressive times) never reveal their homosexual or bisexual orientations to their therapists.

Although many lesbian women and gay men prefer to see openly lesbian or gay therapists, such matching does not feel essential to a plurality of these clients. In a survey of 128 lesbian female or gay male individuals who were currently in couple relationships, 47 percent stated that a therapist's sexual orientation would *not* be a factor in their selection of whom to see for couple problems; and 40 percent would prefer seeing a lesbian or gay professional (Modrcin & Wyers, 1990). Among lesbians and gays who had sought therapy for couple problems in the past, 41 percent never knew the sexual orientation of their therapist.

Openly lesbian and gay couples seem to be more willing to participate in therapy than are heterosexual couples. In various large national surveys, about half (44–54 percent) of the lesbian female respondents and about one-third (27–32 percent) of gay male respondents indicate that they had sought professional help for couple problems (Bradford, Ryan, & Rothblum, 1994; Bryant & Demian, 1994; Modrcin & Wyers, 1990). When asked whether they would seek therapy in the future if they had a serious relationship difficulty, 86 percent of lesbians and 60 percent of gay men who were currently in couple relationships answered unequivocally, "yes" (Modrcin & Wyers, 1990). More than half of these respondents (53 percent) said they would prefer couples therapy than individual therapy.

Taken together, findings from the various surveys indicate clearly that most family therapists during their careers—whether they are heterosexual, bisexual, lesbian, or gay—will be working with substantial numbers of lesbian and gay clients. Given that most family therapists are heterosexual, one wonders why so very little has been written about cross-cultural issues for straight therapists working with lesbian and gay couples and families (for a notable exception, see Siegel & Walker, 1996). One might also ask why so little has been written on how family therapy teachers and supervisors can prepare trainees, and themselves, for this work. Most disturbing, in light of the practice patterns detailed above, is that Doherty and Simmons (1996) recently found that almost half of all family therapists in the AAMFT reported that they do not feel competent treating lesbian women or gay men. Clearly, there is an urgent need for more training on lesbian and gay issues in the field of family psychology and family therapy. In extrapolating from the above surveys, it seems that many professionals are working with lesbian and gay couples and families even though they do not feel competent doing so. Therefore, the following will describe some resources for teaching and learning about lesbians and gays in couples and families.

READINGS

Instructors and students first need a basic introduction to the lives of lesbian and gay persons in families, couples, and family therapy. Until recently, there was no adequate collection of readings in this area. In an attempt to fill this void,

Laird (Smith College) and the author, edited a new volume, *Lesbians and Gays in Couples and Families: A Handbook for Therapists* (Laird & Green, 1996b). This book was designed to provide family therapists with a comprehensive overview of lesbian and gay therapy issues in four domains:

- Family of origin relationships
- Couple relationships
- Lesbian or gay parents and their children
- The social contexts of lesbian or gay families and their therapists

The book also contains chapters specifically focused on ethnic minority issues, including African American lesbians (Greene & Boyd-Franklin, 1996); Asian American lesbians, gays, and bisexuals (Liu & Chan, 1996); and Latino gay or bisexual men (Morales, 1996).

Because the literature on lesbian and gay issues is vast and growing rapidly, listed in Appendix A (by topics) are some selected readings that are most up-to-date, comprehensive, and relevant to family therapists.

There also are many excellent books on coming out and parenting that can be used for bibliotherapy with lesbian and gay clients and their family members (Borhek, 1993; Clark, 1987; Fairchild & Hayward, 1989; Martin, 1993; Siegel & Lowe, 1994). An annotated bibliography of self-help readings and a list of local support groups for all family members are available from Parents, Families, and Friends of Lesbians and Gays (PFLAG, 1996). A new magazine edited by Laura Markowitz, *In the Family*, is an excellent source of personal essays on lesbian and gay family life. A fun and challenging way to teach heterosexual students about lesbian and gay stereotypes is to use Rochlin's (1992) "The Heterosexual Questionnaire" (a one-page parody of myths about lesbians and gay men), having classmates pair-off and interview each other using Rochlin's questions.

VIDEOTAPES

For the majority of students who have had little or no personal contact with lesbian and gay people, videotapes are essential for conveying the texture of family life. Although instructors can automatically assume that students are familiar with the lives of ordinary, well-functioning heterosexual families, the same assumption can't be made about students' familiarity with ordinary lesbians and gays in families. As one might imagine, if students' only lifetime exposure to heterosexuals occurred through viewing tapes of dysfunctional families in treatment, then students would develop a rather negatively skewed image of the "heterosexual lifestyle."

Therefore, it is crucial for instructors to show some videos of ordinary and nonclinical lesbian and gay couples and families, rather than only tapes of lesbians and gays in treatment. Nontherapy videotapes that I have screened with much positive feedback from students are listed by topical area in Appendix B at the end of this chapter.

If instructors have limited time and resources to order only one videotape, it is highly recommend the documentary *Gay Youth* (Walton, 1992), for its insightful treatment of coming out, parental support versus rejection, peer harassment at school, and suicidality among lesbian and gay youths from various ethnic groups. Regarding youth suicide, Gibson (1989) presented harrowing evidence that lesbian and gay youths are two to three times more likely to attempt suicide than heterosexual youths and that lesbian and gay youths comprise 30 percent of all completed youth suicides (Savin-Williams, 1994; 1996). This elevated suicide rate is a consequence of disapproval from families, peers, and teachers, and of the youths' internalization of society's prejudice (*internalized homophobia*, a form of self-hatred).

In this context, the Governor of Massachusetts and the state's Board of Education recently endorsed an exemplary set of guidelines for *Making Schools Safe for Gay and Lesbian Youth* (Governor's Commission on Gay and Lesbian Youth, 1993). These guidelines include (1) developing policies to protect students from harassment, violence, and discrimination; (2) offering training to school personnel in violence and suicide prevention; (3) offering school-based support groups on lesbian and gay issues for all students and for the formation of "gay/heterosexual student alliances"; and (4) providing school-based counseling for family members of lesbian and gay students. Similar programs are starting up in other localities and in some private high schools (Woog, 1995).

The videotape, *Gay Youth* (Walton, 1992), does a superb job of educating professionals about the relevant issues for adolescents and young adults. Lesbian- and gay-affirmative community presentations, consultation to high schools, and support groups for lesbian and gay youths and their families have the potential to save many lives. Trainees can participate as co-leaders and co-facilitators in such community outreach projects.

PERSONAL CONTACT: INTERVIEWS

The research on homophobia (antigay prejudice) shows that heterosexuals who have more contact with lesbians and gay men express more positive attitudes toward these groups (Herek, 1994). For example, in research on family therapists' attitudes, less prejudice is related to more personal contact with lesbians and gays, either as clients, friends, or relatives (Green & Bobele, 1994). Thus, it seems likely that greater contact between heterosexual trainees and lesbian and gay persons (especially if it's positive in tone and requires a cooperative effort toward shared goals) leads to a reduction in trainees' homophobia.

The obvious implication of these findings is that training programs should increase opportunities for positive, cooperative contact between heterosexual students and lesbian and gay persons, both within and outside of the therapy context. This requires making sure that lesbian and gay instructors and students are admitted into the program and the creation of a safe environment for their open participation. In the field of family therapy training, the Commission on Accreditation for Marriage and Family Therapy Education finally voted (in November, 1995) to add sexual orientation to its antidiscrimination clause. Strict enforcement of this standard will help ensure that lesbian and gay students and faculty members are protected against the most blatant forms of discrimination in admissions, hiring, retention, evaluation, and promotion. However, no amount of legislation can protect lesbians and gays from the more subtle bigotry and ignorance that sometimes appear. Personal contact and education are the only routes to countering prejudicial attitudes.

As a way to increase students' comfort with and knowledge about lesbians and gays in families, I have assigned students in my classes the task of interviewing ordinary (nonclient) lesbian and gay individuals and couples from the community. The complete interviewing instructions are presented in Appendix C at the end of this chapter. Note that the interview topics and most of the questions in Appendix C can also be used by experienced therapists as a framework for exploring the couple and family issues of lesbian and gay clients in treatment.

In terms of students' learning on both an affective and cognitive level, this interview assignment has proven to be uniformly positive, and it ranks as the single most enlightening and rewarding learning activity. For some heterosexual students, it is their first sustained personal contact with an openly lesbian or gay person and provides at least minimal preparation for later seeing lesbian and gay clients in therapy. Even for lesbian and gay students with years of such contact, the interviews provide an unusual opportunity to reflect on commonalities and diversity within the community.

In the San Francisco Bay Area where I teach, every student has been able to locate an interviewee on his or her own. In smaller or more conservative communities, it may be necessary for the instructor to visit a local lesbian/gay organization to ask for volunteer interviewees and to prepare volunteers for the possible naïveté of the therapists-in-training.

TREATMENT PLANNING

For an in-class exercise or an exam on treatment planning, the "Family Treatment Plan" is used, which is presented in Appendix D. For this assignment, the instructor shows any of the commercial videotapes listed in Appendix B that depict couples or families undergoing intense conflict over discovery or disclosure of a family member's lesbian or gay identity. Alternatively, instructors can use videos of actual therapy sessions with lesbian and gay family members or couples. After viewing the tape, students are asked to write (in class) a treatment plan based on the case material they have just seen. This can be followed by class discussion of students' responses; or, if used as an exam, the instructor can provide written comments and evaluations of each student's treatment plan. In addition, practicing professionals may use this framework for developing actual treatment plans for their cases.

The study of lesbian and gay couple and family relationships provides new perspectives on heterosexual family patterns and challenges the universality of many assumptions built into family systems theories (Green, 2000b; Green, Bettinger, & Zacks, 1996). It also highlights how psychological and social support services for lesbian, gay, bisexual, and transgender couples and families have to be different from couple and family services for heterosexuals. For example, at the Alternative Family Institute—the lesbian, gay, bisexual, and transgender clinical and research center that I direct at the California School of Professional Psychology (see website: http://www.altfamily.org)—the most popular support groups are on "Considering Parenthood." Such groups focus on issues that are unique to this population (special legal contracts for lesbian and gay co-parents and for second parent adoptions, dealing with prejudice from adoption or alternative insemination agencies, and preparing psychologically for the kind of discriminatory "microaggressions" that lesbian and gay parents must endure in the community and sometimes in their own families of origin). By contrast, heterosexuals almost never so painstakingly consider the personal and relational consequences of parenthood before becoming parents, and it's unlikely they would even be motivated to attend such support groups.

Research on lesbian and gay issues also highlights the need for a Multiplex Gender theory to replace dichotomous thinking about supposedly invariant male and female gender roles across all social classes and ethnic and racial groups (Green, Bettinger, & Zacks, 1996). Lesbians, gay men, and heterosexual women and men live in partially overlapping but partially separate cultures, and their gender-role development often follows distinctive trajectories culminating in unique patterns of couple and family relationships. In the past, this nonconformity of lesbian women and gay men has been used to pathologize them or to exclude them from consideration as bona fide family members, as if lesbians and gays live a "nonfamily" lifestyle or an "antifamily" lifestyle simply because their couple relationships don't follow the traditional gender prescriptions.

In this vein, not very long ago, I witnessed one of the leading national figures in the field of family therapy taunt the "father" in a family role-play by sarcastically and derisively asking him if he was "a queer," and then asking the adolescent son and daughter in the role-play whether they thought their father might be "a queer" because he was not "standing up" to their mother.

I happened to be role-playing the part of the son, and I argued (in role) with the therapist over these remarks.

In the discussion period afterwards, several audience members commented that they were quite moved that the son stood up for his father so vehemently, "modeling" for father "how to be a man." Everyone who spoke was very complimentary toward the therapist. Nobody in this audience of over three hundred persons commented on the therapist's implied contempt toward gay persons, or his use of the word *queer* as an epithet to shame the parents into conforming to a traditional gender hierarchy.

Did anybody else perceive the antigay hostility in the therapist's behavior? Did anyone consider that the adolescent son (or the person role-playing the son) was gay? Were all three hundred of these family therapists too intimidated by the leader's reputation to comment publicly on his behavior? Were they afraid of being perceived as "impolite" or labeled "queer" for even raising the issue? Did their muteness under such circumstances tacitly encourage other family therapists in the audience to make antigay comments in therapy?

Don't ask, don't tell. . . . In a culture with widespread antipathy toward lesbian and gay relationships, what messages do silence, "neutrality," and omission of lesbian and gay topics convey to students in our classes, workshops, and supervision groups?

APPENDIX A: SOME RECOMMENDED READINGS ON LESBIAN AND GAY ISSUES

1. Families and Couples—Chapter on "Lesbian and gay families" in *Normal family processes* (2nd ed.) (Laird, 1993); *Lesbians and gays in couples and families: A handbook for therapists* (Laird & Green, 1996b); special section of *Journal of Marital and Family Therapy* on "Gay, lesbian, and bisexual issues in family therapy" (Green, 2000a); *Mom, dad, I'm gay: How families negotiate coming out* (Savin-Williams, 2001).

2. Lifespan Developmental Psychology—*Lesbian, gay, and bisexual identities over the lifespan: Psychological perspectives* (D'Augelli & Patterson, 1995); *The lives of lesbians, gays, and bisexuals: Children to adults* (Savin-Williams & Cohen, 1996).

3. Clinical, Personality, and Social Psychology—*Homosexuality: Research implications for public policy* (Gonsiorek & Weinrich, 1991); and *Lesbian and gay psychology: Theory, research, and clinical applications* (Greene & Herek, 1994); *Stigma and sexual orientation: Understanding prejudice against lesbians, gay men, and bisexuals* (Herek, 1998).

4. Lesbians/Gays/Bisexuals of Color—*Ethnic and cultural diversity among lesbians and gay men* (Greene, 1997); chapters by Greene & Boyd-Franklin (1996), Liu & Chan (1996), and Morales (1996) in *Lesbians and gays in couples and families: A handbook for therapists; the spirit and the flesh: Sexual diversity in American Indian culture* (Williams, 1992).

5. HIV/AIDS and Gay Men—*In the midst of winter: Counseling families, couples, and individuals with AIDS infection* (Walker, 1995); *AIDS, identity, and community: The HIV epidemic and lesbians and gay men* (Herek & Greene, 1995).

6. Recent Empirical Research—special issues of the journals *Developmental Psychology* (Patterson, 1995); and *Journal of Consulting and Clinical Psychology* (Rothblum, 1994).

7. Cultural Anthropology—*Families we choose: Lesbians, gays, kinship* (Weston, 1991); *Gay culture in America: Essays from the field* (Herdt, 1992); *The spirit and the flesh: Sexual diversity in American Indian culture* (Williams, 1992); *Women crossing boundaries: A psychology of immigration and transformations of sexuality* (Espin, 1999).

APPENDIX B: LESBIAN, GAY, AND BISEXUAL FAMILY TOPICS AND RELATED VIDEOTAPES FOR TEACHING

For documentaries, complete ordering information appears in the reference list to this article. Commercial videos are listed below without reference information as these can be obtained through local video stores.

1. Lesbian and Gay Youths: *Gay youth* (Walton, 1992); *From a secret place.* (Heller, 1993); *Homoteens* (Jubela, 1993).

2. Initial Coming Out and Family Conflict: *Oranges are not the only fruit; Doing time on Maple Drive; Consenting adult.*

3. Parents' Long-term Coping with Son or Daughter's Coming Out: *Parents come out* (Cooper, 1985); *Straight from the heart* (Mosbacher & Reid, 1994); *Coming out, coming home: Asian American and Pacific Islander family stories* (Hima, 1995); *Family values: An American tragedy* (Walton, 1996).

4. Transitions of Heterosexually Married Couple as Husband Comes Out: *Making love.*

5. Lesbian Couples: *Serving in silence: The Margarethe Cammermeyer story* (a 1995 NBC movie); *The incredibly true adventure of two girls in love.*

6. Gay Male Couples: *The wedding banquet*; segments on gay male couple in *For better or worse: Five long-term couples* (Collier, 1993).

7. Lesbian and Gay Parents: *Not all parents are straight* (White & Faro, 1986).

8. Children of Lesbian and Gay Parents: *Both of my moms' names are Judy* (Lesbian & Gay Parents Association, 1994).

9. Ethnic Minority Lesbians and Gays: *Coming out, coming home: Asian American and Pacific Islander family stories* (Hima, 1995); *Psychotherapy with gay & lesbian clients: Program 4—diversity* (Buendía Productions, 1995); *Homoteens* (Jubela, 1993); *The wedding banquet* (interracial Chinese/White male couple, dealing with family of origin issues).

10. Older Lesbians and Gays: *Silent pioneers: Gay and lesbian elders* (Snyder, Winer, & Marks, 1984).

11. HIV/AIDS and Gay Male Couples: *Silverlake life: The view from here*; *Longtime Companion*; *Philadelphia.*

12. Legal Issues for Lesbian and Gay Couples: *Lifetime commitment: A portrait of Karen Thompson* (Zeldes, 1987).

APPENDIX C: FAMILY ORIENTED INTERVIEWS OF LESBIAN WOMEN AND GAY MEN

Instructions

Your task is to interview a lesbian or gay male couple or an individual (over age eighteen) around the topic: Lesbian and gay couple and family relationships. In a subsequent class meeting, you will be discussing with your classmates the results of your interview.

The interviews should last one to two hours each. Specific interview questions could cover the topics below, but you should freely edit or omit certain questions to fit the circumstances, language, and comfort level of both the person(s) you are interviewing and yourself.

Do *not* enlist interviewees from among your clients or from colleagues' clients. Choose friends, friends of friends, acquaintances, neighbors, relatives, and so on. All interviewees must sign two copies of the "Consent Form to be

Interviewed for a Graduate Psychology Class," and one copy is for them to keep. You should inform the interviewee that you are doing this interview as an assignment for a lesbian- and gay-affirmative graduate class on family and couple relationships. Inform them that your course instructor's name, phone number, and address appear on the consent form in case they have any questions or concerns later. You must inform the interviewees in advance that they may freely decline to participate and can decline to answer any question or topic during the interview. Also, inform the interviewees that their names and other identifying information (such as occupation) will be omitted or disguised in your summary for the class discussion.

With the interviewees' permission, you may take notes during the interview so that you can recall what was said and summarize it for purposes of discussion in class. Keep in mind that you are not doing "therapy" or "formal research" in these interviews, but are simply gathering some information for a class assignment. You can ask simple clarifying questions in order to understand the overt content of the interviewee's first response to your questions, but do *not* probe for "unconscious" or unspoken feelings beyond the overt content that the interviewee spontaneously offers. Also, do *not* give interpretations, analysis, or commentary on the material. You are there to learn, not teach or do therapy. Just try to get the story from the interviewees' perspectives and in their own words.

Interview Topics and Questions

I. Families of Origin:
  A. When did you first become aware that you might be lesbian or gay?
  B. How do you think this "different-ness" may have affected your relationships with family members as you were growing up?
  C. If you have *not* come out to certain family members, what factors led to this decision?
  D. If you have come out to certain family members, describe the process, including what preceded, happened during, and has followed the disclosure up to the present time?

II. Lesbian and Gay Couple Relationships
  A. How do you define being "a couple" (what does it mean to you that you are a "couple")?
  B. What has been the history of your becoming a couple?
  C. How did your becoming a couple affect your relationships with other family members, friends, the lesbian and gay community, and the straight community?
  D. Using your own experience as an example, how do you think lesbian and gay couple relationships are similar to and different from heterosexual couple relationships?

E. What are the challenges that lesbian and gay couples face in a predominantly heterosexual and homophobic society, and how have you dealt with these challenges?

III. Lesbian and Gay Parents:

A. What has been the history of your becoming a parent?

B. If your children did not always know you were lesbian or gay, how did you handle coming out to them? How have they reacted?

C. How has being a lesbian or gay parent affected your relationships with former or current partners (if any), with family members, friends, the lesbian and gay community, and the straight community?

D. Using your own experience as an example, what are the challenges that lesbian or gay *parents* face in a predominantly heterosexual and homophobic society?

E. What are the challenges that *children* of lesbian or gay parents face in a predominantly heterosexual and homophobic society?

F. How does your child relate with you (and your partner, if any) on the issue of having a lesbian or gay parent(s)?

G. How does your child deal with her or his friends, teachers, and others around the issue of your being lesbian or gay?

H. Based on your experience, how can lesbian and gay parents prepare or help children deal with these challenges?

IV. Families of Choice:

A. Who are the people in your closest social support network (including relatives, friends, coworkers, neighbors, and so on)?

B. How closely do the persons in this network relate to one another?

C. Describe the activities and any rituals (birthdays, holidays, couple anniversaries, regular get-togethers for meals) that you participate in with your closest network members?

D. What sorts of mutual emotional support and practical assistance do you and these persons provide for each other?

E. Some lesbian and gay people consider their closest friends to be "family," and some authors have used the term "families of choice" to describe these relationships. Does this term fit your experience with your closest friends, that they have become a family?

V. Advice to Professionals:

A. What do you think therapists most need to keep in mind when trying to understand and help lesbians and gay men in couples and families?

B. Are there new kinds of support groups, counseling services, or community organizations that you think need to be developed to help lesbian and gay couples and families?

APPENDIX D: TREATMENT PLANNING GUIDELINES

This exercise is based on the videotape shown in class. You should follow the outline below exactly, using the outline format to organize your answers. After the videotape is shown, you will have approximately one hour to write your answers. Print or write clearly, every other line.

I. Clinical Hypotheses (formulation):

List hypotheses that describe the possible relationship between the presenting problem(s) and characteristics of the client's significant interpersonal systems (including family, friends, and community).

    A. Hypothesis #1:

    B. Hypothesis #2:

    C. Hypothesis #3:

    D. Other:

II. Goals:

What goals would you set for the client? Give behavioral examples of the kinds of things the client would be *doing or saying differently at the end of treatment* so that you would know whether each of your stated goals had been reached. Use the following format to answer this question:

    A. Goal Statement #1:

        1. Behavioral examples:

    B. Goal Statement #2:

        2. Behavioral examples:

    C. Goal Statement #3:

        3. Behavioral examples:

    and so on.

III. Structure of Treatment

    A. Would you include other significant system members in sessions? If so, who and when? Give rationale.

    B. How frequently would you schedule sessions and how long do you think therapy would last?

    C. Would you use any "adjunctive" treatments or referrals (for example, hospitalization; vocational testing; medication; addiction treatment programs such as AA, NA, OA, Al-Anon; therapeutic, psychoeducational, or support groups; lesbian, gay, bisexual and transgender community organizations; and so on.)? Give rationale for each referral.

IV. Therapeutic Relationship

    A. How would you expect this client to relate to you (for example, cooperation, open defiance, passive resistance, excessive dependency, aggression, avoidance, denial, control, intellectualization, humor as resistance, other forms of resistance, and so on)?

B. How would you expect to feel and relate to this client?

1. How would go about joining with this client? Use of self?
2. Any difficulties you anticipate around taking sides in family conflicts, getting frustrated, maintaining the therapeutic frame, setting limits, forming a therapeutic alliance, "counter-transference," cultural ethnocentrism.

V. Specific Interventions and Rationale

Based on the ideas presented in this course, *write exactly what you might say or do with this client (as if you were writing a script for a play) to attain each of the goals you established in item II above.* You may use techniques from any therapy approach if they are consistent with and would facilitate reaching your stated goals. Use the following format:

A. Techniques for reaching Goal #1:
B. Techniques for reaching Goal #2:
C. Techniques for reaching Goal #3:
D. Other:

References

Borhek, M. V. (1993). *Coming out to parents: A two-way survival guide for lesbians and gay men and their parents* (2nd ed.). Cleveland, OH: Pilgrim.

Bradford, J., Ryan, C., & Rothblum, E. D. (1994). National lesbian health care survey: Implications for mental health care. *Journal of Consulting and Clinical Psychology, 62,* 228–242.

Bryant, A. S., & Demian. (1994). Relationship characteristics of American gay and lesbian couples: Findings from a national survey. *Journal of Gay and Lesbian Social Services, 1,* 101–117.

Buendía Productions. (1995). *Psychotherapy with gay and lesbian clients: Program 4 Diversity* [Videotape]. (Available from Buendía Productions, P.O. Box 1896, Santa Ana, CA 92702, Tel.: 800-513-1092)

Clark, D. K. (1987). *Loving someone gay* (2nd ed.). Berkeley, CA. Celestial Arts.

Collier, D. (Director). (1993). *For better or for worse: Five long-term couples* [Film] (Available from Videofinders, Public Broadcasting Corporation, New York, Tel.: 800-842-2298)

Cooper, A. (Director). (1985). *Parents come out* [Videotape]. (Available from Parents, Families, and Friends of Lesbians and Gays—PFLAG, 1101 14th St., NW, Suite 1030, Washington, DC, 20005-3406, Tel.: 202-638-4200, Fax: 202-638-0243, E-mail: pflagntl@aol.com; Website: www.pflag.org)

D'Augelli, A. R., & Patterson, C. J. (Eds.). (1995). *Lesbian, gay, and bisexual identities over the lifespan: Psychological perspectives.* New York: Oxford University Press.

Doherty, W. J., & Simmons, D. S. (1996). Clinical practice patterns of marriage and family therapists: A national survey of therapists and their clients. *Journal of Marital and Family Therapy, 22,* 9–25.

Espin, O. (1999). *Women crossing boundaries: A psychology of immigration and transformations of sexuality.* New York: Routledge.

Fairchild, B., & Hayward, N. (1989). *Now that you know: What every parent should know about homosexuality.* San Diego, CA: Harcourt, Brace, & Jovanovich.

Gibson, P. (1989). Gay male and lesbian youth suicide. In *Report of the Secretary's task force on youth suicide, Vol. 3: Prevention and interventions in youth suicide.* U.S. Department of Health and Human Services: Rockville, MD.

Gonsiorek, J. C., & Weinrich, J. D. (Eds.), (1991). *Homosexuality: Research implications for public policy.* Thousand Oaks, CA: Sage.

Governor's Commission on Gay and Lesbian Youth. (1993). *Making schools safe for gay and lesbian youth: Breaking the silence in schools and in families.* (Publication No. 17296-60-500-2/93-C.R.) [Available from: Commonwealth of Massachusetts, State House, Room 111, Boston, MA 02133, Tel.: 617-727-3600 ext. 312]

Green, R.-J. (1998a). Race and the field of family therapy. In M. McGoldrick (Ed.), *Revisioning family therapy: Race, culture, and gender in clinical practice* (pp. 93–110). New York: Guilford Press.

Green, R.-J. (1998b). Traditional norms of masculinity. *Journal of Feminist Family Therapy, 10,* 81–83.

Green, R.-J. (1998c). Training programs: Guidelines for multicultural transformation. In M. McGoldrick (Ed.), *Revisioning family therapy: Race, culture, and gender in clinical practice* (pp. 111–117). New York: Guilford Press.

Green, R.-J. (2000a). Lesbians, gay men, and their parents: A critique of LaSala and the prevailing clinical "wisdom." *Family Process, 39,* 257–266.

Green, R.-J. (Ed.). (2000b). Special Section: Gay, lesbian, and bisexual issues in family therapy. *Journal of Marital and Family Therapy, 26,* 407–468.

Green, R.-J., Bettinger, M., & Zacks, E. (1996). Are lesbian couples fused and gay male couples disengaged? Questioning gender straightjackets. In J. Laird & R.-J. Green (Eds.), *Lesbians and gays in couples and families: A handbook for therapists* (pp. 185–230). San Francisco: Jossey-Bass.

Green, S. K., & Bobele, M. (1994). Family therapists' response to AIDS: An examination of attitudes, knowledge, and contact. *Journal of Marital and Family Therapy, 20,* 349–367.

Greene, B. (Ed.). (1997). *Ethnic and cultural diversity among lesbians and gay men.* Thousand Oaks, CA: Sage.

Greene, B., & Boyd-Franklin, N. (1996). African American lesbians: Issues in couples therapy. In J. Laird & R.-J. Green (Eds.), *Lesbians and gays in couples and families: A handbook for therapists* (pp. 251–271). San Francisco: Jossey-Bass.

Greene, B., & Herek, G. (Eds.). (1994). *Lesbian and gay psychology: Theory, research, and clinical applications.* Thousand Oaks, CA: Sage.

Heller, K. (Director). (1993). *From a secret place: America's families cope with the coming out process of gay and lesbian youth* [Videotape]. (Available from Guilford Publications, 72 Spring St., New York, NY 10012, Tel.: 1-800-365-7006; Catalog #0264)

Herdt, G. (Ed.). (1992). *Gay culture in America: Essays from the field.* Boston, MA: Beacon Press.

Herek, G. (1994). Assessing heterosexuals' attitudes toward lesbians and gay men: A review of empirical research with the ATLG Scale. In B. Greene & G. Herek (Eds.), *Lesbian and gay psychology: Theory, research, and clinical applications* (pp. 206–228). Thousand Oaks, CA: Sage.

Herek, G. (Ed.). (1998). *Stigma and sexual orientation: Understanding prejudice against lesbians, gay men, and bisexuals.* Thousand Oaks, CA: Sage.

Herek, G., & Greene, B. (1995). *AIDS, identity, and community: The HIV epidemic and lesbians and gay men.* Thousand Oaks, CA: Sage.

Hima, B. (Director), & A/PI-PFLAG Family Project (Producer). (1995). *Coming out, coming home: Asian American and Pacific Islander family stories* [Videotape]. (Available from A/PI-PFLAG Family Project, P.O. Box 640223, San Francisco, CA 94164; Tel.: 415-921-8859 ext. 2; E-mail: VisCamp@aol.com)

Jubela, J. (Director). *Homoteens* [Videotape]. (Available from Frameline Distribution, 346 Ninth St., San Francisco, CA 94103; Tel.: 415-703-8654 or 415-703-8655; Fax: 415-861-1404, E-mail: info@frameline.org, Website-www.frameline.org)

Laird, J. (1993). Lesbian and gay families. In F. Walsh (Ed.), *Normal family processes* (2nd ed.), (pp. 282–328). New York: Guilford Press.

Laird, J., & Green, R.-J. (1996a). Lesbians and gays in couple and family relationships: Central issues. In J. Laird & R.-J. Green (Eds.), *Lesbians and gays in couples and families: A handbook for therapists* (pp. 1–12). San Francisco: Jossey-Bass.

Laird, J., & Green, R.-J. (Eds.). (1996b). *Lesbians and gays in couples and families: A handbook for therapists.* San Francisco: Jossey-Bass.

Lesbian & Gay Parents Association. (Producer). (1994). *Both of my mom's names are Judy* [Videotape]. (Available from Gay and Lesbian Parents Coalition International, Box 50360, Washington, DC, 20091; Tel.: 202 583 8029)

Liu, P., & Chan, C. (1996). Lesbian, gay, and bisexual Asian Americans and their families. In J. Laird & R.-J. Green (Eds.), *Lesbians and gays in couples and families: A handbook for therapists* (pp. 137–152). San Francisco: Jossey-Bass.

Martin, A. (1993). *The lesbian and gay parenting handbook.* New York: HarperCollins.

Modrcin, M. J., & Wyers, N. L. (1990). Lesbian and gay couples: Where they turn when help is needed. *Journal of Gay & Lesbian Psychotherapy, 1,* 89–104.

Morales, E. (1996). Gender roles among Latino gay/bisexual men: Implications for family and couple relationships. In J. Laird & R.-J. Green (Eds.), *Lesbians and gays in couples and families: A handbook for therapists* (pp. 272–297). San Francisco: Jossey-Bass.

Mosbacher, D., & Reid, F. (Directors). (1994). *Straight from the heart* [Videotape]. (Available from The Cinema Guild, 1697 Broadway, Suite 506, New York, NY, 10019-5904; Tel.: 800-723-5522)

Patterson, C. J. (Ed.). (1995). Sexual orientation and human development [Special issue]. *Developmental Psychology, 31*(1).

PFLAG (1996). *Recommended readings.* (Available free from Parents, Families, and Friends of Lesbians and Gays—PFLAG, 1101 14th St., NW, Suite 1030, Washington, DC, 20005-3406; Tel.: 202-638-4200; Fax: 202-638-0243, E-mail: pflagntl@aol.com, Website: www.pflag.org)

Rochlin, M. (1992). The heterosexual questionnaire. In M. S. Kimmel & M. A. Messner (Eds.), *Men's lives* (2nd ed., pp. 482–483). New York: Macmillan.

Rothblum, E. (Ed.). (1994). Mental health of lesbians and gay men [Special section]. *Journal of Consulting and Clinical Psychology, 63*(2), 211–261.

Savin-Williams, R. C. (1994). Verbal and physical abuse as stressors in the lives of lesbian, gay male, and bisexual youths: Associations with school problems, running away, substance abuse, prostitution, and suicide. *Journal of Consulting and Clinical Psychology, 62*, 261–269.

Savin-Williams, R. C. (1996). Self-labeling and disclosure among gay, lesbian, and bisexual youths. In J. Laird & R.-J. Green (Eds.), *Lesbians and gays in couples and families: A handbook for therapists* (pp. 153–182). San Francisco: Jossey-Bass.

Savin-Williams, R. C. (2001). *Mom, Dad. I'm gay: How families negotiate coming out.* Washington, DC: American Psychological Association.

Savin-Williams, R. C., & Cohen, K. M. (Eds.). (1996). *The lives of lesbians, gays, and bisexuals: Children to adults.* Fort Worth, TX: Harcourt Brace.

Siegel, S., & Lowe, E., Jr. (1994). *Uncharted lives: Understanding the life passages of gay men.* New York: Dutton.

Siegel, S., & Walker, G. (1996). Connections: Conversation between a straight therapist and a gay therapist. In J. Laird & R.-J. Green (Eds.), *Lesbians and gays in couples and families: A handbook for therapists* (pp. 28–68). San Francisco: Jossey-Bass.

Snyder, P., Winer, L, & Marks, H. (Directors/Producers). (1984). *Silent pioneers: Gay and lesbian elders* [Videotape]. (Available from The Filmakers Library, 124 East 40th St., Suite 901, New York, NY 10016; Tel.: 212-808-4980)

Sprenkle, D., & Bailey, C. E. (1995, October). *JMFT advisory editor newsletter, 6*(1).

Walker, G. (1995). *In the midst of winter: Counseling families, couples, and individuals with AIDS infection.* New York: W.W. Norton.

Walton, P. (Producer/Director). (1992). *Gay youth* [Videotape]. (Available for purchase by individuals and high schools from Pam Walton Productions, P.O. Box 391025, Mountain View, CA 94039; Tel.: 415-960-3414) (Available for rental or purchase by colleges and libraries from The Filmakers Library, 124 East 40th St., Suite 901, New York, NY 10016; Tel.: 212-808-4980)

Walton, P. (Producer/Director). (1996). *Family values: An American tragedy* [Videotape]. (Available from Pam Walton Productions, P.O. Box 391025, Mountain View, CA 94039; Tel.: 415-960-3414)

Weston, K. (1991). *Families we choose: Lesbians, gays, kinship.* New York: Columbia University Press.

White, K, & Faro, A. (Producers). (1986). *Not all parents are straight* [Videotape]. (Available from The Cinema Guild, 1697 Broadway, Suite 506, New York, NY, 10019-5904; Tel.: 800-723-5522)

Williams, W. L. (1992). *The spirit and the flesh: Sexual diversity in American Indian culture.* (Rev. ed.). Boston: Beacon Press.

Woog, D. (1995). *School's out: The impact of gay and lesbian issues on America's schools.* Boston: Alyson.

Zeldes, K. (Director), & Media Action (Producer). (1987). *Lifetime commitment: A portrait of Karen Thompson* [Videotape]. (Available from Women Make Movies, Inc., Distribution Service, 462 Broadway, Suite 500D, New York, NY 10013; Tel.: 212-925-0606)

PART TWO

RESEARCH

A Professional Psychology School Model for the Research Training of Psychologists

Carlton W. Parks and Judith Holloway

The core curriculum in professional psychology focusing on research and evaluation competencies, developed by the National Council of Schools of Professional Psychology (CSPP) (Trierweiler & Stricker, 1992), served as the framework for the research training experiences provided to clinical psychology students at CSPP-LA of Alliant University. This model prepares the professional psychologist to become a "local clinical scientist" within the context of applied settings conducting socially relevant research with marginalized, stigmatized, and oppressed populations. This is a shift in focus from more traditional research training approaches since the research questions that the local clinical scientist examines typically originate in the community. The local scientist serves as a facilitator of this research process in an applied setting in the community rather than as an administrator at the apex of a hierarchical structure. Therefore, training experiences should provide professional psychology students with a varied array of consultation and organizational skills to conduct culturally informed community-based research.

The major skills that professional psychology students need to acquire include the ability to (1) access efficiently up-to-date information about multicultural issues concerning racially and culturally diverse populations; (2) effectively communicate orally and in written communications that will reach and influence racially and culturally diverse populations in the community; (3) apply one's knowledge of research design and data analysis techniques to applied research questions; (4) utilize interpersonal skills in making connections to and increasing one's awareness of issues facing the local community that they are serving; (5) make the best fit possible between the research question and the research methodology employed that will yield ecologically valid data; (6) facilitate efficiently the research process within the context of applied settings from the inception of a study until those findings have been communicated to various facets of the local and regional community; and (7) incorporate scientific thinking in the execution of clinical activities based on the underlying assumption that research can inform clinical practice (Barlow, 1981; Trierweiler & Stricker, 1991).

At the cornerstone of these skills or competencies is a value-laden perspective to research training (Rappaport, 1977). The focus is on how to be an effective change agent within urban community settings as a professional psychologist conducting socially relevant research with oppressed and underserved populations (Jackson, 2000; Mays, 2000; Strickland, 2000). These values need to be communicated through an educational institution's mission statement, core curriculum, professional field training experiences, administration, and faculty.

Specifically, core faculty need to serve as accessible role models for students on how to conduct socially relevant research with marginalized, stigmatized, and oppressed populations (Parks, Cutts, & Robinson, 1998; Parks, Norrington-Sands, Woodson, & Chana, 2000). Moreover, core faculty need to embrace and be comfortable with the process wherein ambiguity and conflicts will arise as professional psychology students and faculty separately begin to grapple with their world views as they begin to embrace more intensely a multicultural community-clinical psychology perspective to research. This shift in focus has direct ramifications on professional psychology students' and their faculty's conceptualization(s) about issues of race, culture, minority perspectives, power, and being a professional psychology researcher in the twenty-first Century (Ani, 1994; hooks, 1994).

A coordinated sequence of research experiences should transmit these values and skills (both orally and through written products) to the professional psychology student. These experiences can include (1) participation in ongoing research in research teams with faculty members; (2) conducting small-scale studies (for example, pre-doctoral research projects or as a paid research assistant) in research teams under faculty supervision; (3) conducting applied clinical research for an academic year, in an applied clinical setting in consultation with the clinical staff of the agency; (4) the completion of large scale research projects with minimal faculty supervision and consultation; (5) the presentation of findings, at local, regional, national, and international conferences; (6) the collaboration on manuscripts designed to communicate findings to relevant constituency groups that influences social policy; and (7) serving as an advocate on a variety of levels in the community for the population served to positively influence changes on the local and regional levels (Nelson, 1995).

A systematic review of the topic areas of multicultural research conducted by doctoral psychology programs have yielded a rather diverse array of methodologies used to conduct research with diverse populations in diverse settings (Trickett, Watts, & Birman, 1994). The goal of professional psychology research training is to empower students with research design and data analytic skills based on theoretical models for multicultural research to address problems related to the human condition within the community (Trierweiler & Stricker, 1992). No one theoretical model is superior to another one with each theoretical model having its strengths and limitations. The goal is to be able to make the best fit between the research question(s) and the methodology being used to facilitate the generation of ecologically valid data (Bronfenbrenner, 1979). The following five theoretical models of human diversity are frequently used by professional psychologists.

1. Clinical research based on the medical model
2. Population-specific research
3. Cross-cultural research
4. Applied community psychology research and ecological constructs
5. Multicultural feminist research

CLINICAL RESEARCH BASED ON THE MEDICAL MODEL

Kazdin (1998) discusses clinical research based on the scientific method as research that focuses on the diagnosis, assessment, and therapeutic treatment of psychiatric diagnoses based primarily on the medical model (that is, focus on symptom constellations (clusters) that comprise psychiatric disorders that can be treated with pharmacological or psychotherapeutic treatments). Clinical researchers typically specialize in one diagnostic category (for example, affective disorders, substance abuse, and eating disorders), and attempt to capture this phenomenon in diverse populations and contexts. The objective is to draw inferences based on the theory, research design, and statistics employed toward the resolution of research questions. Hersen and Bellack (1984) assert that clinical psychology research involves three primary aims: (1) to order and classify behavior (that is, psychiatric diagnostic categories) based on the medical model (the Diagnostic and Statistical Manual of Psychiatric Disorders, DSM-IVTR, 2000), and the methodologies for making these psychiatric diagnoses, such as interviews, scales, and observational strategies, and inventories; (2) the study of personality and issues of stability versus change across time, settings, and interpersonal contexts; and (3) the modification of behavior through psychotherapeutic intervention modalities implemented under specific circumstances (that is, therapist characteristics, patient characteristics, and the specifics of the treatment). Most projects will fit entirely or in part under these three categories.

Clearly, the strength of clinical research is the balance between theory, methodology, and the empirical findings that are programmatic in nature and make contributions to the current state of our knowledge (Hersen & Bellack, 1984). Increasingly, clinical research endeavors are incorporating a multidisciplinary focus that provides invaluable insights into the phenomena associated with the human condition (Hersen & Bellack). The strengths and resilience of ethnically and culturally diverse individuals living in challenging environments are being incorporated into the designs of clinical research endeavors (Cicchetti & Cohen, 1995).

There is a pressing need for clinical researchers to focus more intensely on the impact of sociocultural influences (for example, race, SES, and culture) on the expression of atypical behavior among diverse populations (Forgays, 1991; Jenkins & Ramsey, 1991; Monroe & Roberts, 1991). The training of local clinical scientists in professional psychology programs would benefit from exposure and immersion into the literature in community and social psychiatry that is the cornerstone of training in psychiatric epidemiology in schools of public health. This perspective for clinical research has served as a catalyst for the development of population-specific research endeavors. Two examples of CSPP-LA Ph.D. dissertations that were based on the medical model include (1) a descriptive study of the Minnesota Multiphasic Personality Inventory-2 (MMPI) profiles of Anglo heterosexual male and female sex addicts, utilizing Carnes' (1983) three levels of sexual addiction (Bradford, 1997); and (2) a descriptive study of the ethnic differences among African American and Latino sexually abused boys based on standardized psychological assessments (for example, Children's Depression Inventory, and the State-Trait Anger Expression Inventory) (Moisan, 1995).

POPULATION-SPECIFIC RESEARCH APPROACHES

The primary focus of this approach is on the intensive examination of a single population as compared to a comparative analysis of two or more populations. Documentation of the population's world view (for example, historical legacy, hereditary predisposition, cultural values, beliefs, behaviors, and traditions) is at the center of the research process and the researcher's firsthand knowledge, awareness of the world view, and culture based on her frame of reference can be invaluable (Watts, 1994). The world view of a population is a primary determinant of human behavior (Nobles, 1986; Ramirez, 1983; Sue & Sue, 1990). The identification of distinctive patterns of cultural values and behavior (for example, strengths and competencies, value and behavioral preferences, shortcoming and failings, adaptations to oppression, and internalized oppression) is a critical feature of population-specific approaches with an emphasis on competencies rather than deficiencies. For instance, Jones (1986) identified time perception, rhythm, improvisation, oral tradition, and spirituality as patterns and themes of African American personality.

Culture is not the byproduct of oppression. Rather, culture is mediated by environmental circumstances; for example, demands, constraints (oppression), opportunities, and resources (Sue & Okazaki, 1990). According to Watts (1994), environmental circumstances (that is, demands, constraints (oppression), opportunities and resources) can have a significant impact on a population, and it's the responsibility of the researcher to uncover and document these empirically (Sue & Okazaki). These data can be generated through the implementation of alternative sources and methodologies (that is, the creative arts, qualitative approaches, and case studies) that reflect the explicit world view(s) of the population and their distinctive patterns of cultural values and behavior (Watts). Local clinical scientists in training benefit from exposure to these alternative sources and methodologies in their attempts to examine sociocultural influences as mediators of mental health, and adjustment with specific racial and cultural groups within community settings. Two examples of CSPP-LA Ph.D. dissertations based on population-specific approaches include (1) an exploratory study focusing on the development of the Biracial Identity Development Inventory (BIDI) to examine the relationship between stages of biracial identity development and perceived alienation in a sample of eighty-three biracial (African American and Caucasian) adults (Aikins, 1995); and (2) a descriptive study of the relationship between self-esteem, acculturation, socioeconomic status, and lesbian identity formation with a sample of ninety-two Latina lesbians (Alquijay, 1993).

CROSS-CULTURAL RESEARCH APPROACHES

The cross-cultural research approaches afford researchers the opportunity to compare and contrast two or more cultures. Cross-cultural constructs provide researchers with the opportunity to gain a better understanding of the impact on ethnocentrism on our perceptions of reality. Berry, Poortinga, Segall, and Dasen (1992) have asserted that U.S. psychological research tends to be ethnocentric at the levels of (1) selection of items and test stimuli; (2) selection of instruments and procedures; (3) operationalization of constructs; and (4) selection of research topics for investigation. Thus, cross-cultural researchers need to reconceptualize the research process and begin a shift in focus, if the goal is to yield ecologically valid findings (Bronfenbrenner, 1979). Typically, cross-cultural researchers seek (1) to empirically document universal cultural attributes (etic) as well as distinctions between cultures (emic); (2) to reveal how these universals impact the psychological functioning of individuals in diverse cultures based on a comparative analysis; and (3) to better understand, relate to, and intervene in diverse cultures (Watts, 1994). The world views of cross-cultural researchers are often left unstated in the research process, and presumed to be objective. Berry et al. (1992) defined cross-cultural psychology "as the study of similarities and difference in individual psychological functioning in various cultural and ethnic groups; of the relationships between psychological, sociocultural, ecological, and biological variables; and of current changes in these variables" (p. 2).

From the inception of the research questions and hypotheses to the operationalization of constructs and measurement strategies to data collection and analysis and interpretation, there needs to be peer collaboration with the indigenous populations in order to obtain ecologically valid findings. The term indigenous means it is native to the region and not transported from the outside, and it's developed for the natives of that region, and not for outsiders (Sinha, 1997, p. 133). Indigenous psychology has four underlying themes associated with it: (1) psychological knowledge is not externally imposed; instead, cultural traditions should give rise to it; (2) true psychology is not experimentally contrived but exists in the daily, mundane activities of people; (3) behavior is to be understood and interpreted in terms of indigenous and local frames of reference; and (4) indigenous psychology embodies psychological knowledge that is relevant and is designed for its people (Berry, Poortinga, Segall, & Dasen, 1992, pp. 380–381). The importance of these assertions cannot be overemphasized since they are major obstacles to the attainment of ecologically valid findings by cross-cultural researchers (Bronfenbrenner, 1979).

The one major underlying assumption of the cross-cultural research approach is the interdependence of culture and the self, which suggests the need for "multifaceted, and culturally grounded views of the self" (Miller, 1997, p. 107). This is one illustration of the hurdles that need to be transcended with respect to construct validity and measurement strategies when conducting culturally informed cross-cultural research endeavors. Research training in conducting ethnographies within the community (Jessor, Colby, & Shweder, 1996) can be invaluable in heightening the awareness and perceptions of local clinical scientists in professional psychology training concerning the interdependence of culture and the self. Two examples of CSPP-LA Ph.D. dissertations focusing on cross-cultural topics include (1) an examination of the clinical symptoms of grief associated with the culturally prescribed mourning rituals, types of loss, immigration history of the bereaved, religious affiliation (Islamic and Hindu), cultural self-identification, perceived social support and the role(s) of ritual specialists in a sample of fifty-nine Asian Indian women (Girglani, 1999); and

(2) an investigation of the depictions of Arabs and Muslims as compared to Western Europeans and Israelis in the U.S. news media (Madani, 2000).

APPLIED COMMUNITY PSYCHOLOGY RESEARCH AND ECOLOGICAL CONSTRUCTS

The systematic study of individuals and their social interactions from an ecological perspective has been the cornerstone of community psychology (Linney, 2000). This ecological perspective strongly asserts that behavior and context are intertwined, and that persons affect contexts, and contexts affect persons (Bronfenbrenner, 1979, 1995; Lewin, 1935; Rappaport, 1977). The interrelationships between social structures and social processes influence the psychological well-being of individuals, couples, small groups, and families (Taylor, 1992; Nelson, 1995; Jackson & Neighbors, 1996; Neighbors & Jackson, 1996; De La Cancela, Chin & Jenkins, 1998). Community researchers interested in primary prevention for example, Bloom (1996) and Albee & Gullotta (1997) have paid considerable attention to the assessment of contextual influences as necessary to health promotion for at-risk populations. Although community-clinical researchers have primarily been interested in small groups, family, and friendship networks, recent work has incorporated local neighborhoods, organizations, and social policy issues as important units of analysis of the relationship of oppression to physical and mental health (Harrell 2000; Harrell, LaFromboise, Masuda, & Seymour, 2000) because these areas are overlapping (De La Cancela, Chin, & Jenkins, 1998; Nelson, 1995).

The goal of the community psychology researcher is the collection of "authentic findings" through facilitating the creation of a collaborative relationship with research participant (that is, the research process is "empowering rather that disempowering" (Rappaport, 1994, p. 370). Rappaport asserts that empowerment is a multidimensional process construct wherein individuals influence, and are influenced by societal structures such as the family, school, neighborhood, church, voluntary organizations, self- and mutual-help groups, and organizations. The focus of this approach is to build upon the existing strengths and competencies of the underserved rather than accentuating weaknesses. This necessitates the reliance on local neighborhood resources for support and remediation. This interdependence between contextual meaning and understanding what works, results in data from qualitative evaluative research rather than quantitative research efforts in naturalistic settings. Community psychology researchers engaged in empowerment theory research strive to establish a long-term relationship with the populations of interest and communities of interest that is based on mutual respect. This research endeavor needs to "represent the social reality of the people researched, that involvement be informed, and that feedback, and collaboration be continuous, in order to give a 'voice for the voiceless'" (p. 370). Empowerment is therefore an important foundation in the training of community-clinical psychologists, in order to produce effective local clinical scientists within the community (Nelson, 1995). Two examples of CSPP-LA Ph.D. dissertations focusing on applied community psychology topics include (1) a study that examined client data at two clinics in Southern California. One clinic was considered a culturally specific clinic utilizing culturally responsive strategies, and one was a nonculturally specific clinic. The goal of this study was to determine if the culturally specific clinic provided more effective clinical services than the nonculturally specific clinic (Gonzalez, 1999); and (2) the application of a community psychology empowerment perspective to parent education among African American and Latino families by reframing the problem to focus on the values and assumptions of parent education rather than the "deficits" of these culturally diverse parents (Atkinson, 1994).

MULTICULTURAL FEMINIST RESEARCH

Brown (1995) coined the term *multicultural feminism* as "the development of a multicultural, non-White, and non-Western feminist database" (p. 152). It is becoming increasingly apparent that feminism is applicable to culturally and ethnically diverse populations (Collins, 1990; Digby, 1998; hooks, 2000; Hurtado, 1996; Parks & Cutts, 1999). A multicultural feminist consciousness guides the questions posed, data collected, and how they are interpreted (Landrine, Klonoff, & Brown-Collins, 1995).

Cammaert and Larsen (1988) reviewed a number of feminist values that influence multicultural feminist research efforts: (1) the "personal is political" where phenomenological experiences that reflect the realities of marginalized and stigmatized populations with respect to oppression are validated, respected, and incorporated into the research questions posed and the designs selected to study those questions; (2) "choice"—the constraints that result in limited life choices for varied facets of our contemporary society that result in the internalization of dysfunctional beliefs and attitudes that inhibit self-actualization and empowerment; (3) "equalization of power"—power needs to be shared, and hierarchical relationships need to be discouraged whenever they appear on the scene; (4) "androgyny"—men and women embark on a journey wherein the masculinity and femininity constructs are reformulated to be more inclusive of a diverse range of male and female characteristics; (5) "social action"—to be committed to change the status quo with respect to discrimination and oppression, particularly with respect to institutionalized racism, sexism, and heterosexism;

and (6) "ethical considerations"—when conducting multicultural feminist research endeavors.

Landrine, Klonoff, and Brown-Collins (1995) argue that the language used in traditional research practices are embedded in a patriarchal system where terms like *subjects* and *graduate students* and the *principal investigator* tend to reinforce racist, classist, and ethnocentric stratification that maintains the status quo and are inappropriate in multicultural feminist research endeavors. Additionally, what questions are "worthy" of scientific attention and which "subcultures" are worthy of systematic empirical attention, and inclusion into the current state of our knowledge also tends to reinforce the "traditional" practice of social science research. Finally, the utilization of alternative methodologies (for example, phenomenological approaches) (Elliott, Fischer, & Rennie, 2000; Kimmel & Garko, 1995; Urban, 1991) that can potentially assist researchers engaged in contextually based programs of research (Landrine, 1995) are critically devalued within the scientific community. The utilization of literary works (hooks, 1981, 1984, 1989, 1990, 1992, 1996, 1997, 1999) can be an effective strategy to train local clinical scientists to capture ethnic diversity in feminism in naturalistic settings using phenomenological approaches (Kimmel & Garko, 1995). These are some of the challenges facing multicultural feminist researchers in the twenty-first Century. Two examples of CSPP-LA Ph.D. dissertations focusing on multicultural feminist topics include (1) an examination of how African American and Euro-American women conceptualize the concept of feminism (Schultz, 1995); and (2) a demonstration of the contributions of community and feminist psychology to the operationalization of the construct of nonviolence (Bommersbach, 2000).

This is an exciting time to be involved in the training of professional psychologists working with diverse ethnic and cultural populations. The authors strongly recommend that training programs incorporate diverse theoretical models that encompass a wide variety of theoretical orientations and theories that can inform the research process of professional psychology students. The five theoretical models discussed in this chapter, as a group, are not mutually exclusive or orthogonal to one another, and there consists considerable overlap between them. Students need to be keenly aware of this reality. These five theoretical models can inform the training of local clinical scientists engaging in multicultural research. These authors also strongly suggest the development of a structured research practicum experience within the context of an applied clinical setting, which results in the completion of a research project in consultation with the clinical staff.

Finally, it is essential for faculty to be role models of the values inherent in the training of culturally informed professional psychologists who are effective local clinical scientists and advocate for their community in the twenty-first Century (hooks, 1994; Nelson, 1995; Rappaport, 1977, 1994).

References

Aikins, A. L. (1995). Biracial identity development and alienation in racially mixed adults (Doctoral dissertation, California School of Professional Psychology, Los Angeles, 1995). *Dissertation Abstracts International, 56*(5), 2851.

Albee, G. W., & Gullotta, T. P. (Eds.). (1997). *Primary prevention works: Issues in children's and families' lives, volume 6.* Thousand Oaks, CA: Sage.

Aliquijay, M. A. (1993). The relationship among self-esteem, acculturation, and lesbian identity formation (Doctoral dissertation, California School of Professional Psychology, Los Angeles, 1993). *Dissertation Abstracts International, 54*(4), 2269.

American Psychiatric Association. (2000). *Diagnostic and statistical manual of mental disorders* (4th ed., TR). Washington, DC: Author.

Ani, M. (1994). *Yurugu: An African-centered critique of european cultural thought and behavior.* Trenton, NJ: Africa World Press.

Atkinson, J. (1994). A multicultural community empowerment approach to parent education: African American and Latino families (Doctoral dissertation, California School of Professional Psychology, Los Angeles, 1994). *Dissertation Abstracts International, 55*(6), 1504.

Barlow, D. H. (1981). On the relation of clinical research to clinical practice: Current issues, new directions. *Journal of Consulting and Clinical Psychology, 49*(2), 147–155.

Berry, J. W., Poortinga, Y. H., Segall, M. H., & Dasen, P. R. (1992). *Cross-cultural psychology: Research and application.* Cambridge, England: Cambridge University Press.

Bloom, M. (1996). *Primary prevention practices: Issues in children's and families' lives, volume 5.* Thousand Oaks, CA: Sage.

Bommersbach, M. L. (2000). *Nonviolence: Definition and integration with community and feminist psychology.* Unpublished doctoral dissertation, California School of Professional Psychology, Los Angeles.

Bradford, V. J. (1997). Personality profiles of Anglo heterosexual male and female sex addicts (Doctoral dissertation, California School of Professional Psychology, Los Angeles, 1996). *Dissertation Abstracts International, 58*(3), 1520.

Bronfenbrenner, U. (1979). *The ecology of human development.* Cambridge, MA: Harvard University Press.

Bronfenbrenner, U. (1995). Developmental ecology through space and time: A future perspective. In P. Moen, & G. Elder (Eds.), *Examining lives in context: Perspectives in the ecology of human development* (pp. 619–647). Washington, DC: American Psychological Association.

Brown, L. S. (1995). Cultural diversity in feminist therapy: Theory and practice. In H. Landrine (Ed.), *Bringing cultural diversity to feminist psychology: Theory, research, and practice* (pp. 143–161). Washington, DC: American Psychological Association.

Cammaert, L. P., & Larsen, C. C. (1988). Feminist frameworks of psychotherapy. In M. A. Dutton-Douglas, & L.E.A. Walker (Eds.), *Feminist psychotherapies: Integration of therapeutic and feminist systems* (pp. 12–36). Norwood, NJ: Ablex Publishing.

Carnes, P. (1983). *Out of the shadows: Understanding sexual addiction.* Minneapolis, MN: Compcare Publishers.

Cicchetti, D., & Cohen, D. J. (Eds.). (1995). *Developmental psychopathology: Risk, disorder, and adaptation, volume 2.* New York: John Wiley & Sons.

Collins, P. H. (1990). *Black feminist thought: Knowledge, consciousness, and the politics of empowerment.* New York: Routledge.

De La Cancela, V., Chin, J. L., & Jenkins, Y. M. (1998). *Community health psychology: Empowerment for diverse communities.* New York: Routledge.

Digby, T. (Ed.). (1998). *Men doing feminism.* New York: Routledge.

Elliott, R., Fischer, C. T., & Rennie, D. L. (2000). Also against methodolatry: Reply to Reicher. *British Journal of Clinical Psychology, 39*(1), 7–10.

Forgays, D. G. (1991). Primary prevention of psychopathology. In M. Hersen, A. E. Kazdin, & A. S. Bellack (Eds.), *The clinical psychology handbook* (2nd ed., pp. 743–761). Elmsford, NY: Pergamon Press.

Girglani, H. S. (1999). Experiences of grief and mourning among Asian-Indian women: Clinical and cultural contexts (Doctoral dissertation, California School of Professional Psychology, Los Angeles, 1998). *Dissertation Abstracts International, 60*(1), 365.

Gonzalez, M. A. (1999). Patterns of mental health service utilization and treatment outcome in a community sample of Hispanic adults (Doctoral dissertation, California School of Professional Psychology, Los Angeles, 1999). *Dissertation Abstracts International, 60*(5), 2339.

Harrell, S. P. (2000). A multidimensional conceptualization of racism-related stress: Implications for the well being of people of color. *American Journal of Orthopsychiatry, 70*(1), 42–57.

Harrell, S. P. (Symposium Chair), LaFromboise, T., Masuda, G. I., & Seymour, G. (2000, March). *Reaching the intersection of race and gender: Implications for finding the next level.* Presented at the Presidential Mini-Convention's Taking Diversity to the Next Level at the annual proceedings of the California Psychological Association, San Jose, CA.

Hersen, M., & Bellack, A. S. (1984). Research in clinical psychology. In A. S. Bellack & M. Hersen (Eds.), *Research methods in clinical psychology* (pp. 1–23). Elmsford, NY: Pergamon Press.

hooks, b. (1981). *Ain't I a woman: Black women and feminism.* Boston: South End Press.

hooks, b. (1984). *Feminist theory: From margin to center.* Boston: South End Press.

hooks, b. (1989). *Talking back: Thinking feminist, thinking black.* Boston: South End Press.

hooks, b. (1990). *Yearning: Race, gender, and cultural politics.* Boston: South End Press.

hooks, b. (1992). *Black looks: Race and representation.* Boston: South End Press.

hooks, b. (1994). *Teaching to transgress: Education as the practice of freedom.* NY: Routledge.

hooks, b. (1996). *Bone Black: Memories of childhood.* Henry Holt.

hooks, b. (1997). *Wounds of passion: A writing life.* NY: Henry Holt.

hooks, b. (1999). *Remembered rapture: The writer at work.* NY: Henry Holt.

hooks, b. (2000). *Feminism is for everybody: Passionate politics.* Cambridge, MA: South End Press.

Hurtado, A. (1996). *The color of privilege: Three blasphemies on race and feminism.* Ann Arbor: University of Michigan Press.

Jackson, J., & Neighbors, H. W. (1996). Changes in African-American resources and mental health: 1979 to 1992. In H. Neighbors, & J. S. Jackson (Eds.), *Mental health in Black America* (pp. 189–212). Thousand Oaks, CA: Sage.

Jackson, J. (2000). What *ought* psychology to do? *American Psychologist, 55*(3), 328–330.

Jenkins, J. O., & Ramsey, G. A. (1991). Minorities. In M. Hersen, A. E. Kazdin, & A. S. Bellack (Eds.), *The clinical psychology handbook* (2nd ed., pp. 724–740). Elmsford, NY: Pergamon Press.

Jessor, R., Colby, A. & Shweder, R. A. (Eds.). (1996). *Ethnography and human development: Context and meaning in social inquiry.* Chicago, IL: University of Chicago Press.

Jones, J. M. (1986). Racism: A cultural analysis of the problem. In J. F. Dividio, & S. L. Gaertner (Eds.), *Prejudice, discrimination, and racism* (pp. 279–314). New York: Academic Press.

Kazdin, A. E. (Ed.). (1998). *Methodological issues and strategies in clinical research* (2nd ed.). Washington, DC: American Psychological Association.

Kimmel, E. B., & Garko, M. G. (1995). Ethnic diversity in the experience of feminism: An existential-phenomenological approach. In H. Landrine (Ed.), *Bringing cultural diversity to feminist psychology: Theory, research, and practice* (pp. 27–53). Washington, DC: American Psychological Association.

Landrine, H. (1995). Introduction: Cultural diversity, contextualism, and feminist psychology. In H. Landrine (Ed.), *Bringing cultural diversity to feminist psychology: Theory, research, and practice* (pp. 1–20). Washington, DC: American Psychological Association.

Landrine, H., Klonoff, E. A., & Brown-Collins, A. (1995). Cultural diversity and methodology in feminist psychology: Critique, proposal, empirical example. In H. Landrine (Ed.), *Bringing cultural diversity to feminist psychology: Theory, research, and practice* (pp. 55–75). Washington, DC: American Psychological Association.

Lewin, K. (1935). *A dynamic theory of personality.* NY: McGraw-Hill.

Linney, J. A. (2000). Assessing ecological constructs and community context. In J. Rappaport, & E. Seidman (Eds.), *Handbook of community psychology* (pp. 647–668). New York: Kluwer Academic/Plenum.

Madani, A. O. (2000). Depictions of Arabs and Muslims in the U.S. news media (Doctoral dissertation, California School of Professional Psychology, Los Angeles, 1999). *Dissertation Abstracts International, 60*(9), 4965.

Mays, V. M. (2000). A social justice agenda. *American Psychologist, 55*(3), 326–327.

Miller, J. G. (1997). Theoretical issues in cultural psychology. In J. W. Berry, Y. H. Poortinga, & J. Pandey (Eds.), *Handbook of cross-cultural psychology: Vol. 1— Theory and method* (2nd ed., pp. 85–128). Boston: Allyn & Bacon.

Moisan, P. A. (1995). Psychological outcome of sexually abused Black and Latino boys (Doctoral dissertation, California School of Professional Psychology, Los Angeles, 1994). *Dissertation Abstracts International, 55*(11), 5080.

Monroe, S. M., & Roberts, J. E. (1991). Psychopathology research. In M. Hersen, A. E. Kazdin, & A. S. Bellack (Eds.), *The clinical psychology handbook* (2nd ed., pp. 276–292). Elmsford, NY: Pergamon Press.

Nelson, J. (1995). Working with inner-city tribes. Collaborating with the enemy or finding opportunities for building community? In L. Combrinck-Graham (Ed.), *Children in families at risk: Maintaining the connections* (pp. 3–31). New York: Guilford Press.

Nobles, W. (1986). *African psychology.* Oakland, CA: Black Family Institute.

Parks, C. W., Cutts, R. N., & Robinson, J. D. (1998). The preparation of graduate students for multicultural community research with sexually oppressed populations. *California Psychologist, 31*(7), 17.

Parks, C. W., & Cutts, R. N. (1999). Feminist therapy empowers coming out in African American men. *California Psychologist, 32*(7), 24–25.

Parks, C. W., Norrington-Sands, K., Woodson, K. M., & Chana, S. (2000). Multiculturally community-oriented research with African-Americans in adulthood. *California Psychologist, 33*(6), 30–31.

Ramirez, M. (1983). *Psychology of the Americas: Mestizo perspectives on personality and mental health.* Elmsford, NY: Pergamon Press.

Rappaport, J. (1977). *Community psychology: Values, research, and action.* NY: Holt, Rinehart, & Winston.

Rappaport, J. (1994). Empowerment as a guide to doing research: Diversity as a positive value. In E. J. Trickett, R. J. Watts, & D. Birman (Eds.), *Human diversity: Perspectives on people in context* (pp. 359–382). San Francisco, CA: Jossey-Bass.

Schultz, M. L. (1995). Gender-based and multicultural attitudes towards feminism: An exploratory study among African American and Caucasian women (Doctoral dissertation, California School of Professional Psychology, Los Angeles, 1994). *Dissertation Abstracts International, 55*(11), 5086.

Sinha, D. (1997). Indigenizing psychology. In J. W. Berry, Y. H. Poortinga, & J. Pandey (Eds.), *Handbook of cross-cultural psychology: Vol. 1—Theory and method* (2nd ed., pp. 129–169). Boston: Allyn & Bacon.

Strickland, B. R. (2000). Misassumptions, misadventures, and the misuse of psychology. *American Psychologist, 55*(3), 331–338.

Sue, S., & Sue, D. W. (1990). *Counseling the culturally different: Theory and practice* (2nd ed.). New York: John Wiley & Sons.

Sue, S., & Okazaki, S. (1990). Asian-American educational achievements: A phenomenon in search of an explanation. *American Psychologist, 45*, 913–920.

Taylor, S. E. (1992). The mental health status of Black Americans: An overview. In R. L. Braithwaite, & S. E. Taylor (Eds.), *Health issues in the Black community* (pp. 20–34). San Francisco: Jossey-Bass.

Trierweiler, S. J., & Stricker, G. (1991). Research and evaluation competency: Training the local clinical scientist. In R. L. Peterson, J. D. McHolland, R. J. Bent, E. Davis-Russell, G. E. Edwall, K. Polite, D. L. Singer, & G. Stricker (Eds.), *The core curriculum in professional psychology of the National Council of Schools of Professional Psychology* (pp.103–113). Washington, DC: American Psychological Association.

Trickett, E. J., Watts, R. J., & Birman, D. (Eds.). (1994). *Human diversity: Perspectives on people in context*. San Francisco: Jossey-Bass.

Urban, H. B. (1991). Humanistic, phenomenological, and existential approaches. In M. Hersen, A. E. Kazdin, & A. S. Bellack (Eds.), *The clinical psychology handbook* (2nd ed., pp. 200–219). Elmsford, NY: Pergamon Press.

Watts, R. J. (1994). Paradigms of diversity. In E. J. Trickett, R. J. Watts, & D. Birman (Eds.), *Human diversity: Perspectives on people in context* (pp. 49–80). San Francisco: Jossey-Bass.

CHAPTER EIGHT

Qualitative Methods

An Essential Tool for Multicultural Psychology

Kumea Shorter-Gooden

W
e are in the midst of a multicultural movement in psychology, the development of a psychology that is not eurocentric, but which is sensitive and responsive to the lives and needs of people of a variety of cultural, racial, ethnic, gender, class, religious, age, ability, and sexual orientation backgrounds (American Psychological Association [APA], 1990; Pedersen, 1991a; Sue, Arredondo, & McDavis, 1992). Multicultural psychology stands on the shoulders of psychologies that focus on specific oppressed populations; for example, Black psychology and Latino(a) psychology. The demands of various disenfranchised groups have led to the evolution of multicultural psychology. Those demands have called for a psychology that does not assert that the norm is an Anglo heterosexual middle-class man, for a psychology that does not see being different as being deficient, for a psychology that is responsive to and sensitive to the humanity of all persons.

The focus of multicultural psychology is often on people of color, but many psychologists look more broadly at all those who are marginalized, oppressed, and underserved by mainstream society. In its broadest sense, multicultural psychology goes even further and asserts that culture is an important aspect of all humans and that psychology should incorporate the notion of culture in all of its research and in its interventions. In this regard, in multicultural psychology, a cultural perspective is important in understanding the Latina lesbian as well as the Anglo heterosexual male.

Over the past three decades, research emanating from a traditional eurocentric psychology, that is, a non-, and oftentimes, antimulticultural perspective, has been criticized for not being sensitive to the needs and concerns of people of color, for using Anglo norms as a basis for understanding people of color, for focusing on comparisons across races while ignoring intra-group variation, and for using a deficit model as a way of constructing a psychology of people of color (Akbar, 1991; Boykin, 1979; Jones & Korchin, 1982; Myers, 1992; Nobles, 1985; Ponterotto & Casas, 1991; Zane & Sue, 1986). Accordingly, culturally sensitive psychologists have often critiqued the findings of eurocentric psychology. While less attention has been paid to the research methods that undergird eurocentric psychology, a number of scholars have called for the use of alternatives to traditional positivist quantitative methods, specifically, for the use of qualitative methods in studying people of color or multicultural issues (Bennett et al., 1994; Boykin, 1979; Jones & Thorne, 1987; Landrine, Klonoff, & Brown-Collins, 1992; Ponterotto & Casas, 1991). However, the actual utilization of qualitative methods in multicultural psychology has been quite limited.

To get a sense of how much of the current multicultural research is qualitative, this author conducted an analysis of multicultural empirical articles in selected journals from 1996 through 2000. For the purpose of this analysis, *multicultural research* was defined narrowly as research that included a focus on race, culture, or ethnicity in populations living within the United States. The journals that were included were five major psychology-related journals that focus on people of color within the United States. They were *American Indian and Alaska Native Mental Health Research, Cultural Diversity and Ethnic Minority Psychology* (which from 1996 through 1998 was *Cultural Diversity and Mental Health*), *Hispanic Journal of Behavioral Sciences, Journal of Black Psychology,* and *Journal of Multicultural Counseling and Development.* For the years 1996 through 2000, of 386 total multicultural empirical articles, 15 percent were qualitative or of mixed qualitative and quantitative design. Eighty-five percent were of strictly quantitative design. This analysis suggests that qualitative methods are far from being integral to multicultural psychology.

While the reasons that qualitative methods have not become more central to the field of psychology are complex, the author's contention is that the lack of specific attention to the interface between multicultural psychology and qualitative methods contributes to this problem. Although a few scholars have addressed particular benefits of qualitative methods for multicultural psychology (Bennett et al., 1994; Howard, 1991; Jones & Thorne 1987; Landrine et al., 1992), there has not been a systematic elucidation of the multiple advantages of qualitative methods for advancing multicultural psychology. The aim of this chapter is to do just that. To this end, after a brief description of qualitative methods, six core values of multicultural psychology are proposed and delineated, and the specific advantages of qualitative methods in addressing each of these values are detailed. The chapter concludes with an illustration of a particular area of research within the multicultural arena—Black racial identity—wherein a qualitative research strategy could deepen our understanding.

A BRIEF DESCRIPTION OF QUALITATIVE METHODS

Qualitative methods are not new to psychology. Freud and Piaget used qualitative approaches to generate and test theories. However, qualitative approaches to research inquiry were eventually supplanted by quantitative approaches, - characterized by controlled experimentation and based on models from the biological and physical sciences. Over the past three decades, concurrent with (but seemingly separate from) the multicultural movement in psychology, there has been a rising chorus of voices asserting the value of qualitative methods in psychological research and the need for research strategies that go beyond psychology's traditional "hard science" approach which stem from a positivist paradigm (Hoshmand, 1989; Jones & Thorne, 1987; Landrine et al., 1992, Matthews & Paradise, 1988; Ponterotto & Casas, 1991). In the positivist, sometimes referred to as the objectivist, paradigm, knowledge generation is seen as an objective process and learning about humans is seen as similar to learning about nature (Guba, 1990). Quantification is seen as critical to knowledge generation, and experimental and quasi-experimental research are the norm.

In contrast, the growing interest in qualitative methods is linked with the development of social constructionism within psychology (Gergen, 1985). In the constructionist, sometimes called constructivist, interpretive, or alternate, paradigm, the focus is on learning about people in their natural settings and learning about how people make sense of their own world (Guba, 1990). Qualitative methods encompass a variety of models and theories, and these methods utilize a variety of data collection strategies, including individual interviews, focus groups, participant-observation, life histories, case studies, narratives, biographies, and archival data (Patton, 1990). These methods emphasize a naturalistic, holistic, and phenomenological approach to inquiry.

Though qualitative methods are experiencing a reawakening in psychology, our colleagues in anthropology, sociology, education, and nursing have long traditions of utilizing qualitative approaches to understand people and communities. Within the field of psychology, organizational psychologists (Berg & Smith, 1988), counseling psychologists (Hoshmand, 1989; Ponterotto & Casas, 1991), and feminist psychologists (Landrine et al., 1992) have been in the forefront of exploring alternate paradigms and developing qualitative research methods.

POINTS OF CONVERGENCE OF MULTICULTURAL PSYCHOLOGY AND QUALITATIVE METHODS

Based on a review of the literature in multicultural psychology as well as a review of related literature that preceded the formal multicultural movement in psychology, six core values of multiculturalism are proposed:

1. Diversity as normative
2. The creation of new models and understandings
3. The illumination of cultural meanings
4. An ecological view of the person
5. A diversity of ways of knowing
6. Culturally sensitive and empathic relationships

Following, the rationale for each proposed value is given, the problems that quantitative methods have in meeting these values are explored, and the points of convergence between qualitative methods and these values are detailed.

Diversity as Normative

It goes without saying that in multicultural psychology there must be room for diversity. Watts (1992) says that a psychology of human diversity, in other words, multicultural psychology, assumes multiple realities and multiple truths. Zane and Sue (1986) and Pedersen (1991b) believe that multiculturalism acknowledges the existence of both culture-general (universal) truths and culture-specific truths. In other words, the belief is that there are important areas of difference as well as commonalties across cultures. Multicultural psychology requires research methods that don't contribute to the pathologizing of differences, but instead, support the notion that diversity is expected and normative.

One of the challenges with the application of the positivist quantitative paradigm to multicultural psychology is that in the positivist paradigm there is often an implicit assumption that diversity, or being different, is problematic. The null hypothesis assumption is that there are no differences between groups. When differences are found, the explicit or implicit notion is that one group's performance or score or characteristic is superior to the other group's. Are Anglos more intelligent than African Americans? Are late adolescent men more individuated than late adolescent women? Are Japanese American women more advanced in ethnic identity development than Japanese American men? These are the sorts of questions that the traditional paradigm is best suited to answer. And in the answers to these questions, "being different" generally means "being deviant" or "being less than." Hierarchical distinctions and distinctions between what's considered "normal" and "abnormal" are rife in this paradigm. And the focus, even statistically, is on the central tendencies, the means, and what is deemed "normal."

In the positivist paradigm, the focus is on the etic, universal truths, rather than the emic, culture-specific truths. In fact, because of the biases toward the experiences of the mainstream group, what has been believed to be the etic has actually been a pseudo-etic, to use Triandis's (1972) term, in other words, the imposition of mainstream norms and standards, as if they are universal, on other groups (Marin & Marin, 1991).

In contrast, in qualitative research, there tends to be a focus on the emic (Patton, 1990). Diversity is assumed; it is not seen as error or as a problem. The goal in qualitative research is not to establish the mean score of a population on some variable of interest, but rather to learn about the different ways that people make sense of their experience. The range and variation in human experience is important. Thus, qualitative methods and multicultural psychology share an appreciation and respect for diversity.

The Creation of New Models and Understandings

Multiculturalism represents a relatively new approach to psychological study. Multicultural psychology is not a subspecialty of psychology, like clinical or social. Instead, it has been called a *fourth force* in psychology, comparable and complementary to psychodynamic, behavioral, and humanistic understandings of human behavior (Pedersen, 1991b). Multiculturalism is a different approach to psychology—an approach that is sensitive to race, gender, class, age, and so on; an approach that does not make use of an imposed etic. To develop this new approach, multicultural psychology is in need of innovation, new models, and creativity. Simply adhering to the traditional models and theories is not enough.

The methodology of positivism emphasizes a careful step-by-step process of research advancement. Verification of existing theories and verification of preconceived hypotheses are seen as critical to any study. Because of this, the positivist approach is inherently conservative. The development of a new canon of knowledge is slow and painstaking if the research process is based on incremental advances in theory verification (Bennett et al., 1994). And since the existing Eurocentric canon is biased in its understanding of certain groups, the inherent conservatism is even more troublesome.

In contrast to the methodology of positivist empiricism, qualitative research encourages the "discovery" of theory from data (Patton, 1990). An inductive rather than a deductive approach is often used and the investigator is not limited to the verification of theories through hypothesis testing. Investigators often, though not always, explore a problem of concern without a theoretical framework, and then allow the data to help them generate a working theory. Thus, there is more room for creativity, hunches, intuition, and for breaking out of established—and often biased—ways of understanding phenomena. Consequently, qualitative approaches offer the possibility of developing new models and understandings through their emphasis on the importance of "discovery."

The Illumination of Cultural Meanings

A basic tenet of multicultural psychology is that culture is an important element of each person's being; in fact, people generally belong to multiple cultures that may have an impact on their psychological makeup (Pedersen, 1988). *Culture* is defined as "the set of attitudes, values, beliefs, and behaviors, shared by a group of people, communicated from one generation to the next via language or some other means of communication" (Barnouw, 1985 cited in Matsumoto, 1994, p. 4). Culture is not coincident with race and nationality but is often related to these characteristics. *Objective culture* refers to the visible artifacts and behaviors of a group (Pedersen); however, a psychology of culture must pay attention to *subjective culture,* a term coined by Triandis (1972), which refers to the "internalized feelings, attitudes, opinions, and assumptions members of a culture hold that, although profoundly important to the culture, are difficult to verify" (Pedersen, p. 4).

Thus, "culture is as much an individual psychological construct as it is a macro, social construct" (Matsumoto, 1994, p. 4), and what is important about culture is how the culture is represented internally in the person's sense of self (Gehrie, 1979). When the focus is on the inner meaning of experience, the relevant question is no longer: Is the self-esteem of Anglo adolescents higher than that of Native American adolescents? Instead, the question might be: What is it about the cultural identity(ies) and experiences of Native American adolescents (or Anglo adolescents) that influences their self-esteem? Thus, a multicultural perspective means a focus on the inner cultural experience of the person, how the person's membership in various cultures influences his sense of self and his relationship to the world. From this viewpoint, simply knowing the research participants' races or nationalities is not sufficient for cultural understanding.

Psychologists have not been very effective in getting at the inner experience of culture. Pedersen (1991c) and Matsumoto (1994) believe that multicultural research is difficult because there is no adequate way to "measure" culture. Quantification of inner cultural experience is difficult. Others point to problems with the common strategy of applying concepts and measures derived from a eurocentric perspective to people from other cultures (Jones & Thorne, 1987; Marin & Marin, 1991; Matsumoto). When concepts and instruments derived from one group are automatically applied to another group (without ascertaining construct and measurement equivalence), the latter group's experience is obscured; the inner experience of culture is lost.

Qualitative methods, however, are particularly useful in answering questions about the meaning of experience, about how people construe their lives, and about the ways in which people understand their own cultural connections and identities (Patton, 1990). In qualitative research, the focus is on enlisting the help of participants in understanding their experience and their world. The inner meaning of participants' identities and life experiences are often garnered through dialogue and interaction. Qualitative researchers rely on the participants' own words and voices. This approach allows for depth, complexity, and a focus on the inner meaning of experience, or, in other words, a focus on the illumination of cultural meanings.

An Ecological View of the Person

Multicultural psychology requires an ecological view of the person, in other words, a view of the person in the context of their environment (Hughes, Seidman, & Williams, 1993; Watts, 1992). Culturally sensitive psychologists have critiqued the individually oriented, person-blame ethos of traditional psychology, where the socioeconomic-political context, and particularly the reality of oppression, is ignored (Akbar, 1991; Ryan, 1976). Moreover, there is a growing body of evidence that for many people of color (Myers, 1988; Sue & Sue, 1990) and for many women (Miller, 1991), being in relationship with others and being connected to others, is central to their sense of self. Thus, what is required in multicultural psychology is attention to the individual in the context of their social system, in the context of the family, relationships, the neighborhood, local institutions as well as the larger socioeconomic-political system.

In the positivist paradigm, individuals, as isolated beings, are usually the focus of study, while families, groups, and communities sometimes seem too complex and messy to allow for rigorous study. One of the problems is that the research questions that quantitative methods are suited for require a limited number of variables and a limited degree of complexity. To factor in the impact of multiple layers of phenomena on a person or on a community is challenging, quantitatively or qualitatively. But the quantitative requirements for a limited number of clearly specified variables makes this particularly difficult.

Moreover, the tendency in the positivist paradigm is to remove the individual from their environment and manipulate them in order to discern truth. The laboratory experiment is the hallmark of this strategy. The assumption is that the person in this isolated, separated situation can teach us about the person who typically lives in a family, in relationships, in communities. This research strategy may be particularly problematic in studying people of color and women, many of whom, as mentioned, may have an identity that is more centered around the family or the community than around their individuality.

In contrast, in the qualitative paradigm there is an emphasis on context; on a naturalistic and holistic approach (Patton, 1990). Qualitative researchers often collect data in the field, sometimes through interviews, sometimes through participant-observation. The belief is that these data collection strategies allow one to get a picture of the person in their environment. Variables are not restricted in advance and there is openness to unexpected and unpredictable factors that influence the person. The person is not stripped of context in order to be understood; the focus is on getting a picture of the whole person in the context of their world. Thus, in the qualitative approach, context and environment are important, and the assumption is that knowledge about isolated people or isolated variables is a very limited brand of knowledge.

A Diversity of Ways of Knowing

Increasingly, culturally sensitive scholars are exploring cultural differences in what different groups constitute as knowledge and truth, that is their ontology, and in their beliefs about how one gains knowledge, that is their epistemology. We are learning that the way Anglo males in the United States construe and gain knowledge is not necessarily the way that other groups do it. For example, Belenky, Clinchy, Goldberger, and Tarule (1986) have found that women have "ways of knowing" that include both "separate knowing," which speaks to traditional analytic and impersonal approaches, as well as "connected knowing," which addresses learning through experience and through connection with others. Similarly, a number of scholars believe that the epistemology of many people of African, Asian, Latino, and Native American descent is based on the notion that science involves values and subjectivity, and that to gain knowledge means to involve oneself (Jackson & Meadows, 1991; Myers, 1992). Thus, experiential knowledge and self-knowledge are vital; both internal and external sources of knowledge are important. Multicultural psychology would seem to require recognition of the diversity of epistemologies, a diversity of ways of knowing.

The epistemology of the positivist paradigm, from which quantitative methods derive, is objectivist (Guba, 1990). The notion is that if the researcher does not interfere with the phenomenon of interest; if the researcher can stand back as if "behind a thick wall of one-way glass" (p. 19), then reality can be ascertained. Research, when done well, is deemed to be a completely neutral process. The distance and detachment of the researcher is designed to control for the potential impact of the investigator on what's being studied.

The epistemology in the constructionist paradigm, from which qualitative methods derive, is subjectivist (Guba, 1990). The process of knowing is seen as requiring involvement with that which is to be known—with the humans who are being studied. Distance and manipulation are thought to get in the way of knowing the reality of the other. Inquiry is not thought to be value free; thus, multiple constructions or multiple realities are possible (Guba). Moreover, because alternate ways of knowing are acknowledged, alternate models of knowing are also considered.

An example is the notion of life as narrative, the idea that people organize and make sense of their lives through stories, which is a developing view amongst some qualitatively oriented psychologists (Howard, 1991; Sarbin, 1986). The metaphor of story provides us with a different way of knowing people and a different way of understanding how people know themselves. It is an alternative to traditional psychology models that emphasize abstractions and theoretical concepts.

Narrative is a term that has been borrowed from literature and storytelling. In fact, qualitative approaches tend to be somewhat multidisciplinary in spirit, borrowing from the humanities and the arts, in particular. Scientists are not seen as the only professionals who have access to the tools for garnering knowledge. Novelists, poets, biographers, and artists are viewed as having important and useful insights into the human condition. Thus, the emphasis in qualitative research on multiple ways of knowing and multiple realities converges with the multicultural notion that different cultures have different ways of knowing.

Culturally Sensitive and Empathic Relationships

A cornerstone of multicultural psychology is the importance of psychologists developing culturally sensitive and empathic relationships not only with clients (APA, 1990, Sue, Ito, & Bradshaw, 1982), but with research participants (Sue et al., 1992), and with the community at large. Communities of color have rarely been included as active participants in the research process, and have often been exploited by researchers (Sue et al.). The research agenda of psychologists has often been at odds with the research needs of the communities they study. Multicultural psychology calls for a correction of these historic problems.

In traditional research, the relationship between the researcher and the subject highlights the issues of power, control, and manipulation, and often "recapitulate(s) racist, classist, and ethnocentric forms of relation" (Landrine et al., 1992, p. 147). Our subjects are subject to us; they are generally not viewed as participants with us in the inquiry process. We are considered the experts; they are not.

In qualitative research, subjects are often called "participants" and are often seen as co-researchers or collaborators in the inquiry process (Patton, 1990). Since the participants are seen as the holders of knowledge, involving them actively in the process of understanding their particular reality is critical. The task of the investigator is to meet the participant in such a way that the pair are able to jointly construct a view of reality (Mishler, 1986). In this kind of research, participants often feel empowered because they have the opportunity to give voice to their experiences and to be heard. Moreover, collaboration between researchers and participants often contributes to more useful and practical understandings (Matthews & Paradise, 1988; Ponterotto & Casas, 1991).

The generation of research that is useful is one important sign of cultural sensitivity and empathy with the community that is being studied. Thus, qualitative research seems well suited to the task of developing productive, nonexploitative relationships with research participants and their communities.

Implications of These Points of Convergence

In sum, the assumptions underlying qualitative research strategies fit well with each of the six proposed core values of multicultural psychology. The author's argument is not that qualitative methods ought to be used exclusively and in lieu of quantitative approaches in multicultural psychology. There are indeed strengths and limitations to both qualitative and quantitative research. For example, in qualitative research, there are challenges around issues of reliability when the analysis of results depends largely on the researcher's interpretation, and around external validity, when sample sizes are small (Marshall & Rossman, 1989). It's also important to note that using a qualitative approach does not automatically ensure culturally sensitive research. Although qualitative methods provide a framework that shares some assumptions with multicultural psychology, they do not provide a panacea for the challenge of multicultural sensitivity.

Moreover, it's important to acknowledge that in sketching out the differences between quantitative and qualitative methods and between the positivist and constructionist paradigm, I have oversimplified the differences, glossed over tremendous variation within each approach, and not addressed the reality of blurred boundaries between these approaches. Quantitative methods don't all fit neatly within the positivist paradigm, nor do all qualitative methods fit perfectly in the constructionist paradigm. For example, some interview studies are inductive, open-ended, and exploratory in approach, whereas others are more structured, closed, and deductive in strategy. Thus, there may be significant variation within what appears to be a similar data collection strategy.

While some researchers feel that quantitative and qualitative approaches are fundamentally philosophically incompatible and thus cannot be combined, a growing number advocate for the combined use of qualitative and quantitative methods (Polkinghorne, 1991). Many believe, as does this author, that the use of multiple and diverse methods for understanding human phenomena can deepen and expand our understanding (Bennett et al., 1994; Matthews & Paradise, 1988; Patton, 1990). Qualitative methods and quantitative methods answer different kinds of questions. Thus in combining these approaches, we gain different, but complementary lenses on a particular issue or phenomenon. Moreover, the notion of methodological diversity resonates with the constructionist notion of diverse ways of knowing. There is no one-way or single path to knowledge or understanding.

The author is concerned, however, that the calls for utilizing qualitative strategies and for combining qualitative and quantitative approaches, seem not to have had much impact on the kind of research that's being conducted and published. Multicultural psychology continues to be dominated by quantitative approaches, even though, as argued earlier, a quantitative approach is limited when it comes to making sense of cultural issues and understandings.

There are undoubtedly complex reasons why qualitative research has not caught on and revolutionized multicultural psychology. The reward system in academia, including publication and promotion opportunities, is often tied to the execution of quantitative research (Marshall & Rossman, 1989). Moreover, as Kuhn (1962) has taught us, paradigms tend to have a life of their own; they are inherently unyielding to discrepant information and divergent ways of doing things. Breaking away from the positivist paradigm, even when it is not adequate, is difficult.

In order to advance the dialogue about and consideration of qualitative research in multicultural psychology, I offer as an illustration research on racial identity in African Americans; a major area of research within the field of multicultural psychology that has spawned theories and empiricism on identity in other groups.

AN ILLUSTRATION: RESEARCH ON BLACK RACIAL IDENTITY

Working independently, Thomas (1971) and Cross (Hall, Cross, & Freedle, 1972) developed theories about the Negro-to-Black conversion experience. Cross's richly descriptive theory of *psychological nigrescence* became the springboard for the work of many others on Black racial identity development. He proposed a five-stage theory (later amended to four stages) to explain the development of a Black identity from the Pre-encounter stage, which characterizes a Black person who has pro-White and anti-Black attitudes, through the Internalization stage, where the person has developed positive feelings about being Black, but is not rigid, and sees positive aspects of other cultures as well. Cross and colleagues utilized a Q-sort, a somewhat flexible and open-ended research tool, to test the validity of this model and found substantial support (Hall et al., 1972).

Ten years later, the Racial Identity Attitude Scale (RIAS), a paper-and-pencil measure of Black racial identity, was developed by Parham and Helms (1981) based on Cross's original Q-sort items. Using this measure, numerous investigators have studied associations between the four stages of racial identity and other variables; for example, preferences for counselor's race (Parham & Helms), depression (Munford, 1994), and locus of control and attitudes toward feminism (Martin & Hall, 1992).

The RIAS has been used widely, and this line of research has clearly added to our understanding of Black racial identity development and its salience for African Americans. However, the almost sole reliance on the RIAS and a few other self-report measures, as the way to collect data on Black identity, really limits what we can learn. Much of the richness of Cross's theoretical descriptions of Black identity get lost in the operationalization into questionnaire format. Significant questions have in fact, been raised about the utility of the RIAS in studying Black racial identity (Ponterotto, 1989). More recently, Sellers and colleagues (Sellers, Smith, Shelton, Rowley, & Chavous, 1998) have developed a more differentiated and complex model and measure of Black racial identity. While this model, the Multidimensional Model of Racial Identity (MMRI), has promise, the measurement tool still reflects the traditional positivist format. This author's concern is about the value of relying on any paper-and-pencil measure as a way of understanding identity.

We know very little about the inner meaning of identity to African Americans, how African Americans construct and make sense of their own racial identity. We don't know how Blacks talk about their identity, what labels and terms they use; we only know whether they agreed or not with preconceived statements about identity on self-report inventories.

We know a fair amount about racial identity as a *variable* and whether it is related to other variables; for example, depression, but we know very little about the African American *person,* in a holistic sense, for whom racial identity is one important characteristic. We know how many Blacks have scored on racial identity measures, but we do not know much about how, for any one person, racial identity is woven into the sense of self.

We know almost nothing about how racial identity intersects with other aspects of identity, for example, gender, sexual orientation, spirituality; we know very little about the interconnectedness of various aspects of identity (Shorter-Gooden & Washington, 1996). How does one's identity as a woman intersect with one's Black identity? How is one's Black identity interwoven with one's identity as a gay Christian? For the most part, racial identity has been studied in isolation as if it exists completely separate from other aspects of identity.

Even though the stated focus of racial identity scholars has been on the *process* of change in identity over time, the strategy for data collection has generally been to ask participants at one point in time to agree or disagree with attitude statements. Process has nearly always been inferred rather than directly studied or inquired about.

These limitations could be addressed in part through a qualitative research strategy. With open-ended interviews, we could learn about what being Black means to people; we could learn about the inner meaning of Black racial identity. We could gain an ecological perspective on racial identity; we could learn about the relationship between the person's environment (the situational context, the local environment, as well as the broader sociopolitical context) and their sense of Blackness. We could gain a sense of how a person's racial identity is connected with other aspects of their identity and other aspects of their life; in other words, we could get a more holistic picture of how racial identity is woven into the person's life.

With a qualitative approach, we might develop a better sense of how to intervene with children, adolescents, and adults in order to facilitate healthy identity development. For example, we could gain insight into whether and how racial identity influences adolescents' academic achievement, career motivation, and prosocial behavior. Exploratory qualitative studies—using interviews and focus groups—could pave the way for longitudinal studies of mixed qualitative and quantitative design, which could help us to learn about how racial identity is constructed and changes over time, and the impact of these shifts on adolescents' attitudes, beliefs, and behaviors. Qualitative approaches in studying racial identity might yield findings that guide us in developing prevention programs and other interventions. In addition, qualitative approaches can help us to explore new models for understanding and conceptualizing racial identity in African Americans. We can take a more inductive, open-ended stance, and listen to people talk about their identity as a way of arriving at hunches about appropriate models for conceptualizing Black racial identity. The emphasis in African American culture is on the collective self, on a sense of self based on one's connection to the group, and on the importance of "we-ness" not just "I-ness" (Nobles, 1985). We might interview people in kinship groups or conduct focus groups in order to learn more about the collective process and content of identity formation.

While some researchers have called for the use of qualitative approaches in studying Black racial identity (Helms, 1989; Parham, 1989; Ponterotto, 1989), little has developed in this direction. One qualitative study of identity in late adolescent African American women provides a step in this direction (Shorter-Gooden & Washington, 1996). In this interview study, the emphasis was on learning how women construe racial, gender, religious, and other aspects of their identity, how these identity domains intersect, and what these women see as central to their sense of identity. Additional qualitative studies of identity could contribute to a fuller, richer understanding of Black racial identity and to insights that allow us to better utilize racial identity theory to enhance the well-being of the African American community.

References

Akbar, N. (1991). Paradigms of African American research. In R. L. Jones (Ed.), *Black psychology* (3rd ed., pp. 709–725). Berkeley, CA: Cobb & Henry.

American Psychological Association. (1990). *Guidelines for providers of psychological services to ethnic, linguistic, and culturally diverse populations*. Washington, DC: Author.

Belenky, M. J., Clinchy, B. M., Goldberger, N. R., & Tarule, J. M. (1986). *Women's ways of knowing.* NY: Basic Books.

Bennett, S. E., et al. (1994). *Methodological diversity for cultural diversity: Integrating qualitative and quantitative approaches.* Symposium presented at the annual convention of the American Psychological Association, Los Angeles, CA.

Berg, D. N., & Smith, K. K. (1988). *The self in social inquiry.* Newbury Park, CA: Sage.

Boykin, A. W. (1979). Black psychology and the research process: Keeping the baby but throwing out the bath water. In A. W. Boykin, A. J. Franklin, & J. F. Yates (Eds.), *Research directions of Black psychologists* (pp. 85–103). NY: Russell Sage Foundation.

Gehrie, M. J. (1979). Culture as internal representation. *Psychiatry, 42*(5), 165–170.

Gergen, K. (1985). The social constructionist movement in modern psychology. *American Psychologist, 40*(3), 266–275.

Guba, E. G. (1990). The alternative paradigm dialog. In E. G. Guba (Ed.), *The paradigm dialog* (pp. 17–27). Newbury Park, CA: Sage.

Hall, W. S., Cross, W. D., Jr., & Freedle, R. (1972). *Stages in the development of a Black identity.* Iowa City, IA: The American College Testing Program.

Helms, J. E. (1989). Considering some methodological issues in racial identity counseling research. *The Counseling Psychologist, 17*(2), 227–252.

Hoshmand, L. T. (1989). Alternate research paradigms: A review and teaching proposal. *The Counseling Psychologist, 17*(1), 3–79.

Howard, G. S. (1991). Culture tales: A narrative approach to thinking, cross-cultural psychology, and psychotherapy. *American Psychologist, 46*(3), 187–197.

Hughes, D., Seidman, E., & Williams, N. (1993). Cultural phenomena and the research enterprise. *American Journal Community Psychology, 21*(6), 687–703.

Jackson, A. P., & Meadows, F. B. (1991). Getting to the bottom to understand the top. *Journal of Counseling and Development, 70,* 72–76.

Jones, E. E., & Korchin, S. J. (1982). Minority mental health: Perspectives. In E. E. Jones, & S. J. Korchin (Eds.), *Minority mental health* (pp. 3–36). NY: Praeger.

Jones, E. E., & Thorne, A. (1987). Rediscovery of the subject: Intercultural approaches to clinical assessment. *Journal of Consulting and Clinical Psychology, 55*(4), 488–495.

Kuhn, T. S. (1962). *The structure of scientific revolutions.* Chicago: Chicago University Press.

Landrine, H., Klonoff, E. A., & Brown-Collins, A. (1992). Cultural diversity and methodology in feminist psychology: Critique, proposal, empirical example. *Psychology of Women Quarterly, 16,* 145–163.

Marin, G., & Marin, B. V. (1991). *Research with Hispanic populations.* Newbury Park, CA: Sage.

Marshall, C., & Rossman, G. B. (1989). *Designing qualitative research.* Thousand Oaks, CA: Sage.

Martin, J. K., & Hall, G.C.N. (1992). Thinking Black, thinking internal, thinking feminist. *Journal of Counseling Psychology, 39*(4), 509–514.

Matsumoto, D. (1994). *Cultural influences on research methods and statistics.* Pacific Grove, CA: Brooks/Cole.

Matthews, B., & Paradise, L. V. (1988). Toward methodological diversity: Qualitative research approaches. *Journal of Mental Health Counseling, 10*(4), 225–234.

Miller, J. B. (1991). The development of women's sense of self. In J. V. Jordan, A. G. Kaplan, J. B. Miller, I. P. Stiver, & J. L. Surrey (Eds.), *Women's growth in connection: Writings from the Stone Center* (pp. 11–26). NY: Guilford Press.

Mishler, E. G. (1986). *Research interviewing: Context and narrative.* Cambridge, MA: Harvard University Press.

Munford, M. B. (1994). Relationship of gender, self-esteem, social class, and racial identity to depression in Blacks. *Journal of Black Psychology, 20*(2), 157–174.

Myers, L. J. (1988). *Understanding an Afrocentric worldview: Introduction to an optimal psychology.* Dubuque, IA: Kendall/Hunt.

Myers, L. J. (1992). Transpersonal psychology: The role of the Afrocentric paradigm. In A.K.H. Burlew, W. C. Banks, H. P. McAdoo, & D. A. Azibo (Eds.), *African American psychology: Theory, research, and practice* (pp. 5–17). Newbury Park, CA: Sage.

Nobles, W. W. (1985). *Africanity and the Black family: The development of a theoretical model* Oakland, CA: Black Family Institute.

Parham, T. A. (1989). Cycles of psychological nigrescence. *The Counseling Psychologist, 17*(2), 187–226.

Parham, T. A., & Helms, J. E. (1981). The influence of Black students' racial identity attitudes on preferences for counselor's race. *Journal of Counseling Psychology, 28*, 250–257.

Patton, M. Q. (1990). *Qualitative evaluation and research methods* (2nd ed.). Newbury Park, CA: Sage.

Pedersen, P. P. (1988). *A handbook for developing multicultural awareness.* Alexandria, VA: American Association for Counseling and Development.

Pedersen, P. P. (1991a). Introduction to the special issue on multiculturalism as a fourth force in counseling. *Journal of Counseling and Development, 70,* 4.

Pedersen, P. P. (1991b). Multiculturalism as a generic approach to counseling. *Journal of Counseling and Development, 70,* 6–12.

Pedersen, P. P. (1991c). Introduction to Part 3: Research opportunities. *Journal of Counseling and Development, 70,* 142.

Polkinghorne, D. E. (1991). Two conflicting calls for methodological reform. *The Counseling Psychologist, 19*(1), 103–114.

Ponterotto, J. G. (1989). Expanding directions for racial identity research. *The Counseling Psychologist, 17*(2), 264–272.

Ponterotto, J. G., & Casas, J. M. (1991). *Handbook of racial/ethnic minority counseling research*. Springfield, IL: Chas. C. Thomas.

Ryan, W. (1976). *Blaming the victim*. NY: Vintage Books.

Sarbin, T. R. (1986). The narrative as a root metaphor for psychology. In T. R. Sarbin (Ed.), *Narrative psychology: The storied nature of human conduct* (pp. 3–21). NY: Praeger.

Sellers, R. M., Smith, M. A., Shelton, J. N., Rowley, S.A.J., Chavous, T. M. (1998). Multidimensional model of racial identity: A reconceptualization of African American racial identity. *Personality and Social Psychology Review, 2*(1), 18–39.

Shorter-Gooden, K., & Washington, N. C. (1996). Young, Black, and female: The challenge of weaving an identity. *Journal of Adolescence, 19*, 465–475.

Sue, D. W., Arredondo, P., & McDavis, R. J. (1992). Multicultural counseling competencies and standards: A call to the profession. *Journal of Counseling and Development, 70*, 477–486.

Sue, D. W., & Sue, D. (1990). *Counseling the culturally different: Theory and practice*. (2nd ed.). NY: John Wiley & Sons.

Sue, S., Ito, J., & Bradshaw, C. (1982). Ethnic minority research: Trends and directions. In E. E. Jones & S. J. Korchin (Eds.), *Minority mental health* (pp. 37–58). NY: Praeger.

Thomas, C. W. (1971). *Boys no more*. Beverly Hills: Glencoe Press.

Triandis, H. C. (1972). *The analysis of subjective culture*. NY: John Wiley & Sons.

Watts, R. J. (1992). Elements of a psychology of human diversity. *Journal of Community Psychology, 20*, 116–131.

Zane, N., & Sue, S. (1986). Reappraisal of ethnic minority issues: Research alternatives. In E. Seidman & J. Rappaport (Eds.), *Redefining social problems* (pp. 289–304). NY: Plenum Press.

CHAPTER NINE

A Multicultural Awareness in Research Practices: A Self-Reflective Process

Debra M. Kawahara

Multicultural awareness is one of the key competencies expected in a culturally competent psychologist (Pedersen, 2000). This area of skill has not been emphasized in research practices as much as in direct counseling interactions. Yet, the researcher clearly brings his own world views, values, biases, prejudices, and stereotypes to the research arena, which permeates all levels. This can ultimately have an enormous impact on the decisions made about the theoretical perspective, research methodology, and research procedures utilized in a study. Without this awareness, the researcher is blinded by his own cultural encapsulation and does not account for the many ways that culture influences his perception and research practices.

This is important because the social implications of the researcher's conclusions can lead to insensitive, discriminatory, and unintentionally or intentionally harmful beliefs and behaviors. The classic book by Guthrie (1976), *Even the Rat Was White,* provides numerous historical examples of how research studies were used to support the belief that African Americans were inferior, inadequate, and deviant using intelligence testing. Unfortunately, these types of research conclusions are still being published today. For example, Jensen (1998) utilized scientific methodology and psychometrics to draw conclusions about racial differences of intelligence, and then infer the difference to population genetics and evolutionary theory (Buckhalt, 1999).

This chapter is an example of a researcher's process to examine the influences of her own cultural assumptions, biases, and prejudices on a previously conducted research study and its impact on the decisions made during the research process. The chapter is divided into three segments. First, the previously conducted study is presented. Second, the researcher's own reflections about the study are discussed. Last, the researcher concludes with her thoughts on how she would conduct the study differently with this new awareness. By highlighting this process, readers will hopefully gain insight into examining their own cultural framework while conducting research and be able to engage in more culturally competent research.

THE RESEARCH STUDY

My journey begins as a young, enthusiastic graduate student starting work on my dissertation. I became interested in the psychological consequences of the Japanese Internment as it touched something deep within me. I felt to more fully understand the impact of the Internment that I could contribute to society on multiple levels: professionally, personally, communally, and educationally. A systematic framework was provided to conduct the research study. Given my unawareness, I followed the steps in the framework. The first step of the process was to review the literature related to the psychological consequences of the Japanese Internment. Various areas were searched like the Holocaust and other traumatic experiences, coping, adaptation, ethnic identity, and acculturation.

I finally decided to focus specifically on the psychological adjustment of the children of the internees. Two factors led to this decision based on the literature. First, few empirical studies had been done to date. What had been found was that communication about the Internment was rare and brief between parent and child, and the children felt that it was not a topic to be discussed (Miyoshi, 1978; Nagata, 1989, 1990, 1998). However, it also led to a feeling that a part of their identity was missing. The other major factor was the literature on the Holocaust presented conflicting results. Clinical observations and case studies found effects being transmitted from parent to child; but more controlled experimental studies found no significant differences in mental health, psychological adjustment, and defensive strategies (Albeck, 1994; Rose & Garske, 1987; Steinberg, 1989; Zlotogorski, 1983). In the end, I decided to study psychological adjustment because the literature on both the Japanese Internment and Holocaust suggested generational transmission occurred due to the trauma of incarceration of one or both parents.

Once I narrowed the focus, a theoretical model to guide the study was found. McCann, Sakheim, and Abrahamson's model (1988) of the complex relations among common responses to traumatic events, cognitive schemas, and psychological adjustment was adopted. The model emphasized the self as an active agent in construing reality based upon a cognitive-constructive theoretical perspective. This led to the formation of my research questions.

From this point, the rest of the study seemed to fall naturally into place. I found standardized measurements to tap the constructs and developed procedures to carry out the study. I collected the data and then analyzed them. This is when I was hit with a big surprise. The study found no significant differences in the various cognitive schemas or psychological adjustment variables based on the participant's parental internment. It showed no evidence that there was a generational transmission of the effects of the Japanese Internment on subsequent generations.

I experienced a wide array of emotions from disappointment to shock and confusion and What happened? was the only question that entered my mind. It could be argued that there was no effect and that the nonsignificance is the true outcome, but this went against my own heuristic understanding and observations of the community and its members. The absence of significant findings only stirred more questions in me and actually made me examine myself and my study more closely in order to understand what might have possibly gone wrong.

When I returned back to the study years later, it triggered my thinking about it again. Both my development and growth had undergone significant changes as well as the field matured and expanded the definitions of culturally competent behaviors in education, research, and therapy practices. I realized that the framework that I followed had cultural values, assumptions, and biases embedded deep within it. By utilizing this framework without intentionally asking what cultural assumptions were being reinforced by following it, I abdicated much of my critical analysis and decision-making power of the research study. In essence, I conformed to the power and privilege of the patriarchical, Western, middle-upper class world view that heavily influenced and influences American psychology. So, what was the impact of this action?

A Self-Reflection on the Study

In this section, I shall take a retrospective look at some factors that influenced my study.

Bias Toward Quantitative Research. First, although my graduate program was considered progressive in multicultural competency training in clinical psychology at the time, research methodology within the program still adhered to the experimental approach of the past. Research courses were empirical and quantitative and multivariate statistical courses were mandatory. No other research methodological approaches were offered nor were any faculty known to be proficient in these areas. Further, the institution required that dissertations be either experimental or theoretical in nature. Based on these conditions and the framework given to me, only one research methodology was deemed appropriate and I adhered to it unquestioningly.

I now recognize that both the institution and my bias toward quantitative research were influenced by the past. According to Cahan and White (1992), psychology as a field had a desire to be part of the broad reorganization of society at the turn of the century. Within American universities, psychology wanted to be included in the rise of research universities and to be recognized as a legitimate discipline among the physical sciences. In order to be accepted and integrated into this complex system, those holding positions of power in psychology and in universities developed an infrastructure that reinforced and rewarded the research methodologies of the physical sciences, particularly physics (Cahan & White). The end result is a widely held assumption that reductionistic, quantitative, experimental research is the single standard to determine whether research is valuable and worthy (Casas & Mann, 1996).

Presently, I am more cognizant about different research methodologies utilized in other social sciences that are beginning to gain acceptance and implementation within psychology. For example, the use of qualitative research methods is becoming more frequently published in prestigious psychological journals. Unlike quantitative research methodologies, these appear to lend themselves more to the inquiry about the social construction of reality, the intimate relationship of the phenomenon of the study and the researcher, and the situational factors that shape inquiry (Espin, 1998). Thus, there is more focus on the subjective experience of a phenomenon and the person is allowed to give the experience its meaning, instead of the researcher interpreting it. As a result of this new information, I would place greater importance and value on the decision of research methodology. I would ask questions such as How much is truly known about this phenomenon? and What methodology would best illuminate the phenomenon and the research questions posed?

Bias Towards Behaviorism. The investigation of the phenomenon was heavily influenced by behaviorism. The model developed by McCann, Sakheim, and Abrahamson (1988) was heavily based on behavioral components: schemas and psychological adjustment variables. These were based on cognitions or thoughts and exhibited behavioral symptoms. Unknowingly, I defined the phenomenon in behavioral terms because that was how others defined and used it in previous research. However, I failed to respect the fact that previous studies on the generational transmission of the Internment were related to ethnic identity and affiliation preferences and not traditional psychological symptoms per se. Thus, the mistake may have been in deciding to measure the phenomenon based on specific Western behavioral concept of psychological symptomatology and measured by standardized instruments on White middle-class individuals.

Again, reflecting back on the history of American psychology, the influence of the past can be seen. In the 1930s, psychology as a field was still struggling to gain respectability within research universities and hoped that a solid scientific grounding and unifying theory around behaviorism could facilitate this agenda (Cahan & White, 1992). Psychology embraced methodological behaviorism consisting of the use of laboratory studies of conditioning and learning. Also, in the politics of psychology departments, older researchers of sensation and perception formed coalitions with younger psychologists of conditioning and learning. This power base within university psychology departments then held the norms of departments close to the values, standards, and procedures of the natural sciences. These defined the domain of experimental psychology. This eventually led to the widely held assumption that "science" and "scientific research" consisted of behaviorism, treatment-group comparison, and statistics. These norms are still widely used throughout the field.

Ethnocultural Transference and Countertransference. The possible interactional dynamics between the researcher, the research participants, and the research topic are not often considered, but could have profound impact on the data collected. By utilizing the empirical, quantitative research methodology, the influence of the researcher is assumed to be nullified. However, one of the areas where reactions could have taken place is within and between the researcher and the research participants.

Comas-Diaz and Jacobsen (1991) have discussed the issues of ethnocultural transference and counter-transference in the therapeutic dyad that can be transformed to the research setting. These dynamics can emerge in both the researcher and the participants. The researcher needs to be able to recognize and manage these reactions, because the reactions can influence the development of the research study, the data collected, and the analysis and interpretation of the data.

In terms of intra-ethnic transference and counter-transference issues of overidentification, distancing, ambivalence, anger, ethnocentrism, guilt, or despair can emerge. For example, in my study, the researcher and the research participants were of the same ethnic background and this may have caused the participants to feel an obligation and loyalty to participate due to my ethnic background being the same. However, participants' ambivalent feelings about showing the community in a bad light and shame around disclosing personal information could result in influencing their responses to the research instruments. On the other hand, inter-ethnic research dyads can evoke other reactions such as overcompliance, friendliness, pity, anger, aggression, denial, mistrust, and suspicion. These reactions can be based on various sources, including the individual's personal experiences with the researcher's racial or ethnic group; race relations between the ethnicities, and the sociopolitical history of the ethnic groups within the United States. Given the potential impact of transferential and counter-transferential reactions, researchers need to understand and examine the complex dynamics of ethnicity in the research context so these can be considered in the development and outcome of the study.

Bias Towards Survey Data. In terms of the procedures, the bias in psychology is toward statistically interpreting group data using a sampling philosophy. The underlying assumption and value in this research approach is that there are universal principles that can be found with experimental methodologies and a single standard to understand humans and their behavior. As such, survey research is widely used with a large number of participants. I, again, conformed to this norm by using a paper-and-pencil survey, which was completed and then mailed back to me. However, questions about how I approached the community, how the research participants were recruited, and the indirect manner in which data are collected were never asked. I assumed that the procedures based on experimental methods were to be used if I were to conduct worthy research. Yet, reflecting back on this, this seems to be the most important phase of the study because the researcher and the research participants actually interact and are highly influenced by the cultural norms, values, and expectations of the cultural situation during the interaction.

Changes in the Research Study Based on Awareness

Given these revelations and awareness, I know that I would develop a much different study today. First and foremost, I would ask two very intentional questions about the research methodology: (1) what different research methodological approaches could be used to examine the phenomenon? and (2) which methodology is best suited to illuminate understanding of the phenomenon? Undeniably, qualitative research methods would have to be considered.

The generational transmission of the effects of the Japanese Internment is still relatively in its infancy. Although more than fifty years has passed since the Internment, it has only been in the last twenty years that people have been discussing their experiences more. Furthermore, the complicated process of transmission is not well understood in itself. Given that the essence of this phenomenon is not completely understood, qualitative methods would be a better approach because of its exploratory and emergent nature. This would allow the true essence of the phenomenon to be understood, instead of assuming that it is the same with other similar phenomenon. Further, the nature of how qualitative research information is gathered appears to be more personal and intimate, actually lending itself more to the details and nuances that would not be detectable from quantifiable measures.

Various qualitative tools could be used for a future study. One very appropriate approach would be life narratives. This would allow a person to show their lifelong ordeal of dealing with the experience. An example of the importance of this can be seen in the artwork of Hisako Hibi. She was a first-generation

Japanese American woman who expressed herself through paintings over a period of sixty years. One can see in her paintings that a dramatic change in perspective occurred. Her paintings during the years of her internment contained more dark colors, desolate places, and solitary individuals. However, later in her life, the transformation of her vision is seen in her paintings, as the paintings were vibrant, playful, and integrated. Thus, a life narrative could show the developmental process of dealing with group incarceration over a lifetime.

Second, interviews allow the participant to interact with the researcher in a more direct and personable manner. Through this process, the researcher can develop a theory based on the information that transpires while the study is in process. I believe that this tool lends itself readily to the internees themselves. The barrier to discussing the Japanese Internment has been a challenging and painful one for many former internees. However, much of the silence is related to the cultural values of being strong by not revealing distress to others as well as not burdening others with one's problems because that would be inconsiderate on the part of the distressed person. However, if the person felt safe, comfortable, and trusting that discussing the Japanese Internment was good for the community and subsequent generations, a rapport could probably be developed with a discussion following.

Further, the interview process could lend itself to looking at the parent-child dyad. This would allow the examination of the specific patterns of how the effects are transmitted as well as the themes of what is transmitted. This information would be powerful because there are other communities who are undergoing traumatic experiences based on group identification such as political prisoners or refugees.

Last, focus groups could be another powerful tool to examine the phenomenon. An example of a focus group can be seen in the work of Dr. Satsuki Ina (1999). She recently made a video of her weekend retreats with former internees who **were** children when they were incarcerated. The video shows the emotionally painful experience and how that affected the way that they saw themselves. In addition, the video captures the sense of belonging and commonalities that these people were able to gain through the group process. By the end of the video, each seemed to understand how the experience affects their lives today and events that happen in the past, and they seemed to be able to let go of some pain they had been carrying for years by themselves.

Regarding the procedures, there are several aspects where thoughtful consideration to cultural appropriateness could have taken place. First, more thought about the recruitment of research participants could have been given. Psychologists are often seen as authority figures and experts. This creates a power dynamic within the researcher and participant dyad. I believe that the power differential in the relationship is not often considered and the psychologist often takes for granted the position of power held. Second, the respect and dignity of the participant is not often given the utmost concern and care by the researcher.

Cultural knowledge related to the appropriate ways and steps to engage communities into research projects and whether research procedures are culturally respectful or culturally imposing should be obtained and utilized. Last, the manner in which data are collected needs to be examined. The preference of communication may be different for the research participant and the researcher. Which mode of communication is used could very much influence the data collected as well as the way these data are interpreted.

CONCLUSION

The goal of this chapter was to examine my own cultural assumptions, values, and biases in my research practices. It is hoped that by reflecting back on my own research and critically analyzing my actions from a past research study that others could learn to conduct more culturally competent research.

As shown throughout the chapter, a failure to ask the right questions had significant implications to the entire research process. By not asking these questions, the research study was clearly influenced by my own assumptions, biases, and prejudices, which were operating and permeating the study unconsciously. This ultimately influenced the structure and outcome of the entire study. Clearly, it illustrates the need for explicitly questioning one's own world view, beliefs, and assumptions so the researcher can consciously be attuned to its potential influence throughout a research study. In conclusion, the following questions are posed to assist the researcher in assessing his own cultural competency in their research skills:

1. Do I have the necessary awareness, knowledge, and skills to conduct research with this community? If not, have cultural or ethnic experts been consulted?

2. What assumptions, biases, prejudices, and stereotypes do I bring to the study?

3. What different research methodologies can be used to examine the phenomenon?

4. What potential transference and counter-transference issues may arise due to myself, the research participants, and the research topic?

References

Albeck, H. J. (1994). *Intergenerational consequences of trauma: reframing traps in treatment theory . . . a second generation perspective.* Westport, CT: Greenwood.

Buckhalt, J. A. (1999). Defending the science of mental ability and its central dogma: A book review of Jensen on Intelligence-g-Factor. *Psycoloquy, 10.*

Cahan, E. D., & White, S. H. (1992). Proposals for a second psychology. *American Psychologist, 47*(2), 224–235.

Casas, J. M., & Mann, D. (1996). MCT theory and implications for research. In D. W. Sue, A. E. Ivey, & P. B. Pedersen, *A theory of multicultural counseling and therapy* (pp. 139–154). Pacific Grove, CA: Brooks/Cole.

Comas-Diaz, L., & Jacobsen, F. M. (1991). Ethnocultural transference and countertransference in the therapeutic dyad. *American Journal of Orthopsychiatry, 61*(3), 392–402.

Espin, O. M. (1998). *Qualitative research methods in psychology.* Continuing education workshop presented at the California School of Professional Psychology, San Diego, CA.

Guthrie, R. (1976). *Even the rat was white.* New York: Harper & Row.

Ina, S. (1999). The children of the camps project [On-line]. Available: Kimina@children-of-the-camps.org

Jensen, A. (1998). *The G factor: The science of mental ability.* New York: Praeger.

McCann, I. L., Sakheim, D. K., & Abrahamson, D. J. (1988). Trauma and victimization: A model of psychological adaptation. *Counseling Psychologist, 16*(4), 531–594.

Miyoshi, N. (1978). *Identity crisis of the Sansei and the concentration camp.* (Grant No. 1 R13 H 25655-01).

Nagata, D. K. (1989). Long-term effects of the Japanese American internment camps: Impact upon the children of the internees. *Asian American Psychological Association Journal, 13*(1), 48–55.

Nagata, D. K. (1990). The Japanese American internment: Exploring the transgenerational consequences of traumatic stress. *Journal of Traumatic Stress, 3*(1), 47–69.

Nagata, D. K. (1998). *Legacy of injustice: Exploring the cross-generational impact of the Japanese American internment.* New York: Plenum Press.

Pedersen, P. (2000). *A handbook for developing multicultural awareness* (3rd ed.). Alexandria, VA: American Counseling Association.

Rose, S. L., & Garske, J. (1987). Family environment, adjustment, and coping among children of Holocaust survivors: A comparative investigation. *American Journal of Orthopsychiatry, 57,* 332–344.

Steinberg, A. (1989). Holocaust survivors and their children: A review of the clinical literature. In P. Marcus, & A. Rosenberg (Eds.), *Healing their wounds: Psychotherapy with Holocaust survivors and their families.* New York: Praeger.

Zlotogorski, Z. (1983). Offspring of concentration camp survivors: The relationship of perceptions of family cohesion and adaptability of levels of ego functioning. *Comprehensive Psychiatry, 24,* 354–354.

PART THREE

INTERVENTION

CHAPTER TEN

Latinos' Perceptions of the Rorschach Inkblots

An Examination of the Popular Response

Mary A. Bachran

We live in a pluralistic society, embedded in a pluralistic world. That there exists a multitude of ways to survive and thrive is no longer a question that is seriously open to discussion. What still is debated, however, is the impact of these various ways of being on a person's perception of the world, and whether that perception is similar enough with other frames of reference to be seen and accurately measured in the same manner. This debate surrounds and embroils the field of psychological testing, both objective and projective. It is the aim of this chapter to examine the basis of one such technique, the Rorschach Inkblot Test, to determine if a Latino sample perceives the ambiguous stimuli in fundamentally the same manner as the major cultural "norm."

The Rorschach Inkblot Test has been a standard in psychological assessment since its inception by Herman Rorschach in 1921 (Exner, 1993). In spite of the controversies that raged during the middle of this century surrounding its validity and usefulness, the Rorschach is still one of the most frequently used assessment instruments by clinicians (Archer, Imhof, Marvish, & Piotrowski, 1991; Lubin, Larsen, Matarazzo, & Seever, 1985; Piotrowski & Keller, 1989).

The Rorschach has been conceptualized as a test of perception from its inception (Draguns, Haley, & Phillips, 1968; Exner, 1980, 1993; Rorschach, 1942). In this case, the first step to creating norms for Latinos is to determine if they perceive the stimulus in the same manner as those upon whom the test was normed. Of all the Rorschach variables, the "Popular" response is the most analogous to the functioning of perception (Hallowell, 1956). Therefore, this chapter compared Latinos' perceptions of the Rorschach inkblots to Exner's normative samples (Exner, 1993) through an examination of their Popular responses.

There is an assumption in psychology that a "projective test developed and standardized in one society can be used elsewhere with only minor modifications in content, scoring or application" (Bock, 1988, p. 100). This is termed the projective assumption and, as a general practice, it is invalid (Bock). In order to use a psychological instrument on a population other than the one it was normed upon, we must first understand if or how much another population differs from the norm. While differences in Rorschach performance have been found between Latinos living in the United States and the majority culture, no normative data have ever been collected on this population. Without baseline data from which to interpret the Rorschach protocols of Latinos, or even the foundation to begin to collect these data, psychologists are hampered in serving the needs of this community (Esquirel, 1992).

Cross-culturally, the Rorschach has been utilized for many years to study personality differences as well as for assessment purposes. Only nine studies since 1949, however, have investigated Latinos' performance on the Rorschach (Johnson & Sikes, 1965; Kluckholn & Strodbeck, 1961; Rodriguez-Sutil, Ortiz, Carrovas, & Moreno Garcia, 1994; Tulchin & Levy, 1945; Velasquez & Callahan, 1992) and only two of these focused on Latinos living in the United States (Johnson & Sikes; Kluckholn & Strodbeck). These studies have found differences in Latinos' Rorschach performance which would indicate the Latino subculture is essentially different from the White majority culture (Kaplan, 1955).

Research done with Latinos has found significant differences between Latino subjects and majority culture subjects. Tulchin and Levy (1945) compared the protocols of Spanish and English refugee children. The English children had a mean Popular score of 6.1 while the Spanish children's score was 4.5. They determined that the higher incidence of Popular responding in the English children was due to cultural norms.

Johnson and Sikes (1965) compared the Rorschach protocols of African American, Latino and White psychiatric patients. There was a significant difference between the groups on the Popular response. While all the patients' scores were greater than one standard deviation below Exner's norms, the White patients' scores were closest (4.16), followed by the Latinos (3.36), followed by the African Americans (2.48). In this study the Latinos were tested by Latino examiners in their native tongue.

While many studies have been performed on diverse populations around the world, little work has been done with the Rorschach on Latinos living in the United States (Frank, 1993). Results obtained from the studies available point to differences in Rorschach responding which may be indicative of the need to establish Latino norms. Nothing has been done, however, to attempt to understand whether Latinos perceive the inkblots in the same manner as majority culture subjects.

METHOD

The study for this chapter investigated Latinos' perceptions of the Rorschach Ink Blots by examining their Popular responses. It was hypothesized that while differences would be found between the number of Popular responses produced by the Latinos' as compared to Exner's norms, the differences would not be significant.

Participants

Subjects were 152 clients from the Psychological Services Center (PSC) of a free-standing professional school of psychology. Ages of the subjects ranged from twelve years old upward and included both sexes. Ethnicity was determined by self-identification on the information forms.

Instruments

The Rorschach Ink Blot Test was used in this study. The Rorschach is a well-known instrument that has been shown to be reliable and valid. Exner's scoring system was used to score the protocols at the time of administration, and his norms were used as the comparison group.

Design and Procedure

Protocols were taken from the testing records at the PSC. Those files identified as Latino were given a code number and the number of Popular responses recorded. Age and sex were also noted. Descriptive statistics were generated on the Latino sample. Then the Latino sample was compared with Exner's norms by means of an independent t-test. The 0.05 level of probability was considered as significant.

RESULTS

The number of Popular responses was collected from the Rorschach records of 152 subjects. All subjects' records were taken from the PSC and were self-identified as Latino. Of the subjects, 63.8 percent were male and 36.2 percent were female. Ages ranged from thirteen years old to fifty-eight years old, with a mean of 23.34.

To compute the t-tests, the subjects were divided by age into five groups. These groups corresponded in age to the groups as outlined in Exner's normative data. The groups consisted of thirteen year olds ($N = 13$), fourteen year olds ($N = 14$), fifteen year olds ($N = 19$), sixteen year olds ($N = 23$), and those seventeen years of age or older ($N = 83$). Sample t-tests were then computed for each of the groups with the appropriate normative data. Because nine t-tests were used to analyze the data, the level of significance was changed to 0.034 to account for the increase in alpha error generated by the use of repeated measures.

The first analysis was performed to determine whether the Latino sample ages seventeen and older, deviated significantly from Exner's normative sample in regard to age. Only this sample was analyzed because the other samples were homogeneous in age. The results indicated that the sample was the same as Exner's normative sample, $t_{850.05} = 1.48; p > 0.05$.

Next, the samples were compared with the number of Popular responses given by each. In all the groups, highly significant differences were found between the number of Popular responses given by the Latino sample, as compared to Exner's normative data (see Table 10.1). The Latinos consistently produced fewer Popular responses than the norm, as shown in Figure 10.1. These results don't support the hypothesis proposed.

Because the sample was obtained from a clinical population, it was then hypothesized that the differences obtained in the analysis were due to the possible existence of pathology in the sample. If this was the case, then there should have been no significant difference between the number of Populars produced by the sample of Latinos and Exner's norms for schizophrenic, depressive, and personality disorder groups.

To test this hypothesis, the age group, seventeen and older, was compared to Exner's norms for populations of schizophrenics, personality disorders, and depressives. The oldest age group was utilized because Exner's norms are based on an adult population over the age of seventeen years. Normative data is not provided in these categories for persons under the age of seventeen years.

Three subsequent t-tests were performed as indicated above. All the tests found that there were highly significant differences between the sample and Exner's norms (see Table 10.2). Again, the Latinos in the sample consistently

Table 10.1. Popular Responses of Latinos as Compared to Exner's Norms

Age	Mean	Standard Deviation	t-Value	DF	Probability
17+	3.84	1.92	14.44	82	<0.001
16	3.96	1.43	8.40	22	<0.001
15	3.53	1.84	6.65	18	<0.001
14	5.00	1.57	2.43	13	0.030
13	3.38	2.18	4.64	12	0.001

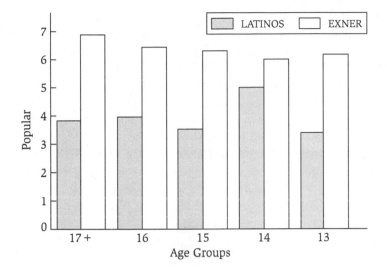

Figure 10.1. Mean number of Popular responses.

Table 10.2. Popular Responses of Latinos as Compared to Schizophrenics, Depressives, and Personality Disorders

Population	t-Value	DF	Probability
Schizophrenics	3.92	82	<0.001
Depressives	0.52	82	<0.001
Personality disorders	5.15	82	<0.001

reported fewer Popular responses than the norm group. Thus, the subsequent hypothesis was also not supported. There are significant differences between the number of Popular responses given by the Latino sample and Exner's normative data on "normals," schizophrenics, depressives, and personality disordered persons.

DISCUSSION

In the original hypothesis, it was proposed that the sample of Latinos would not produce a significantly different number of Popular responses than Exner's normative sample. This hypothesis wasn't confirmed. Instead, the Latinos in the sample produced significantly fewer Populars. According to the original premise, this would indicate that the Latinos in the sample aren't perceiving the blots in the same manner as Exner's normative population, and that the manner in which they see the blots is, in fact, significantly different.

These results confirm the findings of other researchers who have used the Rorschach with Latinos. Tulchin and Levy (1945) found that Spanish children produced significantly fewer Popular responses than English children, and attributed differences in common social evaluations as the underlying cause. These social evaluations can be seen as perceptions of social situations. Johnson and Sikes (1965) also found significant differences in Popular responses in the Rorschach records of Mexican American and Anglo psychiatric patients. These differences were evident even when the patients were tested by a culturally similar examiner in their own language. This situation should have helped ameliorate any cross-cultural examiner or language effects. The fact that the Mexican Americans in this study still produced far fewer Populars is a strong indication that some perceptual differences are involved. It is interesting to note that the mean number of Popular responses produced by Johnson and Sikes' sample of inpatient Mexican Americans (3.36) is close to the average number of Populars produced by the sample in this study (3.84). This may be a function of pathology in both samples, a matter which will be addressed next.

The results of this study, however, do not coincide with Kraneau's (1983) investigation of Hispanics and Rorschach responding. Kraneau found that the Popular responses of his sample of Hispanics from the southwestern United States was not significantly different from a similar sample of Anglo Americans. The number of Populars produced by both groups was less than Exner's normative values (Anglos = 5.33, Hispanics = 5.50). However, these means were not compared to Exner's norms, so no statement about a significant difference with these norms can be made. It is interesting though, that in this nonclinical sample, the average educational level of the subjects generally included some college, and the Hispanics produced more Populars than the Anglos. The higher number of Populars may actually be a function of educational level. Schachtel (1945) stated that "the attitudes—definitions of the Rorschach situation— discussed are products of Western civilization and many of them develop fully and become a deeply ingrained personality pattern in connection with the competitive life of school or school-like experiences" (p. 447). Consequently, experience in the Western educational system may determine how the Rorschach blots are perceived. In Kraneau's study, increased involvement in the educational system may be partially responsible for a higher degree of Popular responding. While the educational level of the Latinos in this study was not addressed, this, too, may be a factor in their low numbers of Populars.

Exner (1993), himself, concedes that his list of Popular responses does not unilaterally translate cross-culturally. Internationally, only eleven of his thirteen Popular responses meet the criterion of one in every three records for inclusion in his system. The other two Populars were only found in 31 percent and 26 percent of the records collected from around the world. No mention was made of the average number of Popular responses produced in these records, however, and it may well be that they don't correspond with Exner's norms either, and may, in fact, be far below these norms.

Cross-culturally, there are a certain number of percepts which seem to appear in every culture. The fact that most people can perceive at least part of the Rorschach in similar ways doesn't mean that they perceive enough of the test in the same manner so as to draw universal conclusions from their responses. In fact, studies done on Arabs, Saulteaux Indians, Samoan young men, Laplanders, Haitians, and Navajo children, just to name a few, have consistently found a low number of Popular responses (Bourguignon, Nett, & Emily, 1955; Boyer, Miller, & DeVos, 1984; DeVos & Miner, 1989; Hallowell, 1941; Kendell, 1988; Leighton & Kluckholn, 1948; Siegman, 1956). It would appear, therefore, that the premise that everyone perceives the Rorschach in the same manner is as yet to be substantiated and, in fact, appears to be fallacious.

In this study, it was assumed that there would be no difference between the sample and Exner because of the effects of acculturation. This was not the case. Unfortunately, there was no way to assess the level of acculturation from the records obtained. It is possible that the sample was from a predominantly unacculturated population, and this resulted in the lower number of Popular responses. Many other studies have found that the more a cultural group becomes acculturated to "Western" ways, the greater the number of Popular responses produced. This was found to be true of Arabs, Laplanders, Navajos, Zunis, Spanish Americans, and Mormons (Boyer et al., 1984; DeVos & Miner, 1989; Kaplan, 1955). Kraneau (1983), however, found that acculturation factors did not affect the number of Popular responses produced in his Hispanic American sample. His sample was primarily bicultural, which may have increased the number of their Populars. This is, obviously, an area that warrants further research. It would be valuable to discover whether a Latino's perception of the blots changes with his level of acculturation, and at what point the difference in perceptions makes the test invalid for that person.

One of the limitations of this study was that the population was obtained from the clients of a psychological clinic. It might be inferred, therefore, that the sample contained pathology severe enough to produce significantly fewer Populars. In fact, a low number of Populars has been found in populations that display some degree of pathology (Beck & Molish, 1967; Howes & DeBlassie, 1989; Molish, 1951; Piotrowski, 1957). It was also interesting that the mean number of Populars in this sample did nearly match those of a population of inpatient Latinos (Johnson & Sikes, 1965). The number of Populars, however, is still significantly below the number provided by Exner for his populations of depressives, character disorders, and schizophrenics. This, then, may not necessarily reflect an extremely high degree of pathology in the sample, but rather, may be the combination of some degree of pathology combined with a sufficiently different basic perception. These two factors may together produce such a low

mean. This, too, is an area for further investigation. Will a nonclinical population of Latinos produce significantly lower Popular responding than Exner's
norms? Until this question is answered, it is an unwarranted assumption that
pathology is the only deciding factor in the results of this study.

Another consideration is the validity of the normative data as published by
Exner. Are his norms accurate for the population overall? In an ongoing study
presented by Haroian, Erdberg, and Shaffer (1995), a sample of 128 people who
scored within normal limits on the Minnesota Multiphasic Personality Inventory, 2, and the Wechsler Adult Intelligence scale, Revised, only produced an
average of 4.78 (SD = 2.09) Popular responses. This is far below Exner's figure
of 6.89, but within one standard deviation of the number of Populars produced
by the Latino sample in this study. Hamel (1996), as well, examined a group of
100 predominantly White parochial school students, ages six to twelve, and
found an average of 3.81 (SD = 1.95) Popular responses. Again, this number is
far below Exner's norms, but nearly identical with the data of the Latinos.

Combined, these studies indicate that the normative data produced by Exner
may not be correct. If this is the case, then the significantly lower number of
Populars produced by the Latino sample may actually be much closer to the
number of Populars produced by the population as a whole than is readily
apparent. This would indicate that the Latinos in this study were actually perceiving the blots in the same manner as the rest of the population. Obviously,
this is an area of great confusion and concern. Much more research is needed
to confirm Exner's normative data, or provide new norms for the Rorschach.

The question then arises considering the above information, are the
Rorschach results of Latinos valid, and can their protocols be interpreted?
The answer to the first question appears to be no, if one is using Exner's
norms. The fundamental perceptions of the Latinos in this study are so far from
those outlined by Exner that it would appear to invalidate the results. If other
normative data were to be compiled which was approximately the same as the
Haroian et al. (1995) study, then it could be assumed that the basic perceptions
of both groups were similar enough to allow comparison. However, more data
need to be obtained from Latinos outside a clinical setting before a validity statement can be made with more certainty about the Latino population as a whole.

In light of the data presented in the study for this chapter, it would appear that
the Rorschachs of Latinos can be interpreted only cautiously, at best, and not with
the Exner norms. This would correspond with the observations of many other
researchers who have used the Rorschach cross-culturally (Cook, 1942; Frank,
1993; Hallowell, 1945; Kraneau, 1983; Mattlar, Carlsson, & Forsander, 1993; Molish, 1951; Schachtel, 1945; Spindler & Spindler, 1967, to name only a few), and
who have urged the compilation of culturally appropriate norms. How can assessments be made about personality functioning in an individual when it is uncertain if the differences found in the individual's record may be due to cultural

factors, or perception differences, or invalid normative data? At this point in time, it is uncertain which of these factors, or combination of these factors, and many others, are at play in the Rorschach records of Latinos. Much more data are needed before it is reasonable to claim that the differences in the records are due to pathology, rather than on other factors. Until these data are collected, it appears that only limited interpretation can be made about the Rorschach results of Latinos, and even fewer when using Exner's normative data.

Endnote

Past research with ethnic populations on the Rorschach has indicated that, because of cultural differences, the test may need to be normed for specific populations. Only limited research has been performed with Latinos on the Rorschach, and none investigating if they perceive the blots in the same manner as the Euro-American culture. The purpose of the study presented in this chapter was to examine this question. Because the Popular response is the most analogous to basic perception, it was chosen as the variable to be examined. The number of Popular responses was recorded from protocols of self-identified Latino subjects tested by the Psychological Service Center at the California School of Professional Psychology. Results indicated that all groups differed significantly from Exner's published normative data. These results indicate that Latinos may not perceive the blots in the same manner as the normed population. If so, new norms will need to be established for Latinos. Future research should focus on obtaining results from a nonclinical population.

References

Archer, R. P., Imhof, E. A., Marvish, M., & Piotrowski, C. (1991). Psychological test usage with adolescent clients: 1990 survey findings. *Professional Psychology: Research and Practice, 22*, 247–252.

Beck, S. J., & Molish, H. B. (1967). *Rorschach's test* (Vol. 2). New York: Grune & Stratton.

Bock, P. K. (1988). *Rethinking psychological anthropology: Continuity and change in the study of human action.* New York: W. H. Freeman.

Bourguignon, E., Nett, E., & Emily, W. (1955). Rorschach Populars in a sample of Haitian protocols, *Journal of Projective Techniques, 19*, 117–124.

Boyer, L. B., Miller, C. M., & DeVos, G. A. (1984). A comparison of Rorschach protocols obtained from two groups of Laplanders from Northern Finland. *Journal of Psychoanalytic Anthropology, 7*(4), 379–396.

Cook, P. H. (1942). The application of the Rorschach test to a Samoan group. *Rorschach Research Exchange, 6*, 51–70.

DeVos, G. A., & Miner, H. (1989). Oasis and Casbah: Acculturative stress. In G. A. DeVos & L. B. Boyer (Eds.), *Symbolic analysis cross-culturally: The Rorschach Test* (pp. 210–245). Berkeley, CA: University of California Press.

Draguns, J. G., Haley, E. M., & Phillips, L. (1968). Studies of Rorschach content: A review of research literature. Part III: Theoretical formulations. *Journal of Projective Techniques and Personality Assessment, 32*(1), 16–32.

Esquirel, G. B. (1992). Some needed research on the assessment of Hispanics in clinical settings. In K. F. Geisinger (Ed.), *Psychological Testing of Hispanics* (pp. 267–269). Washington, DC: American Psychological Association.

Exner, J. E. (1980). But it's only an inkblot. *Journal of Personality Assessment, 44*(6), 563–577.

Exner, J. E. (1993). *The Rorschach: A comprehensive system: Volume I. Basic foundations* (3rd ed.). New York: John Wiley & Sons.

Frank, G. (1993). The use of the Rorschach with Hispanic Americans. *Psychological Reports, 72*, 276–278.

Hallowell, A. I. (1941). The Rorschach method as an aid in the study of personalities in primitive societies. *Character and Personality, 9*, 235–245.

Hallowell, A. I. (1945). The Rorschach technique in the study of personality and culture. *American Anthropologist, 47*, 195–210.

Hallowell, I. (1956). The Rorschach technique in personality and culture studies. In B. Klopfer (Ed.), *Developments in the Rorschach Technique: Vol. 2* (pp. 458–544). New York: Harcourt, Brace & World.

Hamel, M. (1996). *A normative study of cooperative movement responses among preadolescent Rorschach protocols*. Unpublished doctoral dissertation, California School of Professional Psychology, Fresno, CA.

Haroian, J., Erdberg, P., & Shaffer, T. (1995, March). *Contemporary psychological test findings: A Rorschach normative study*. Paper presented at the midwinter meeting of the Society for Personality Assessment, Atlanta, GA.

Howes, R. D., & DeBlassie, R. R. (1989). Modal errors in the cross-cultural use of the Rorschach. *Journal of Multicultural Counseling and Development, 17*, 79–84.

Johnson, D. L., & Sikes, M. P. (1965). Rorschach and TAT responses of Negro, Mexican-American and Anglo psychiatric patients. *Journal of Projective Techniques and Personality Assessment, 29*, 183–188.

Kaplan, B. (1955). Reflections of the acculturation process in the Rorschach test. *Journal of Projective Techniques, 19*, 30–35.

Kendell, G. S. (1988). The Rorschach Ink Blot Experiment: Consideration of the popular response. (Doctoral dissertation, California School of Professional Psychology, 1985). *Dissertation Abstracts International, 49/07B*, 2860.

Kluckholn, F. R., & Strodbeck, F. L. (1961). *Variations in value orientations*. Westport, CT: Greenwood Press.

Kraneau, E. J. (1983). Level of acculturation/biculturation and Rorschach protocols of Hispanic Americans and Anglo Americans. (Doctoral dissertation, Oklahoma State University, 1983). *Dissertations Abstracts International, 44/10B*, 3200.

Leighton, D., & Kluckholn, C. (1948). *Children of the people: The Navajo individual and his development.* Cambridge, MA: Harvard University Press.

Lubin, B., Larsen, R. M., Matarazzo, J. D., & Seever, M. (1985). Psychological test usage in five professional settings. *American Psychologist, 40,* 857–861.

Mattlar, C. E., Carlsson, A., & Forsander, C. (1993). The issue of the Popular response: Definition and universal versus culture-specific Popular responses. *British Journal of Projective Psychology, 38,* 53–62.

Molish, H. B. (1951). The Popular response in Rorschach records of normals, neurotics and schizophrenics. *American Journal of Orthopsychiatry, 21,* 523–531.

Piotrowski, C. & Keller, J. W. (1989). Psychological testing in outpatient mental health facilities: A national study. *Professional Psychology: Research & Practice, 20,* 423–425.

Piotrowski, Z. A. (1957). *Perceptanalysis.* New York: Macmillan.

Rodriguez-Sutil, C., Ortiz, P., Carrovas, C. P., & Moreno Garcia, M. C. (1994). Perceptual accuracy as measured by the Rorschach: Are American norm applicable for cross-cultural assessment? *Perceptual and Motor Skills, 78,* 1287–1290.

Rorschach, H. (1942). *Psychodiagnostics.* Berne, Switzerland: Verlang Hans Huber.

Schachtel, E. G. (1945). Subjective definitions of the Rorschach test situation and their effect on test performance. *Psychiatry, 8,* 419–448.

Siegman, A. W. (1956). A "culture and personality" study based on a comparison of Rorschach performance. *Journal of Social Psychology, 44,* 173–178.

Spindler, L., & Spindler, G. (1967). Male and female adaptation in culture change: Menomini. In R. Hurt (Ed.), *Personalities and Cultures: Readings in Psychological Anthropology* (pp. 56–78). Austin, TX: University of Texas Press.

Tulchin, S. H., & Levy, D. M. (1945). Rorschach test differences in a group of Spanish and English refugee children. *American Journal of Orthopsychiatry, 15,* 361–368.

Velasquez, R. J., & Callahan, W. J. (1992). Psychological testing of Hispanic Americans in clinical settings: Overview and issues. In K. F. Geisinger (Ed.), *Psychological Testing of Hispanics,* (pp. 253–265). Washington, DC: American Psychological Association.

CHAPTER ELEVEN

Is The Sociocultural Background of the Psychologist Important?

Elizabeth Davis-Russell

In this chapter, the importance of the sociocultural context to the clinical enterprise will be discussed with a specific look at how we as psychologists are influenced by our own sociocultural context. In order to frame comments related to these questions, I would like to begin with a definition of culture borrowed from Hughes (1976) as cited in Gaw (1993). Many have been offered, but I find this one particularly valuable.

CULTURE

Culture is a learned configuration of images and other symbolic elements, such as language, widely shared among members of a given society or social group, which, for individuals, functions as an orientational framework for behavior, and for the group, serves as the communicational matrix which tends to coordinate and sanction behavior (p. 13).

If we look at that definition we see that there are several points that can be gleaned. One is that culture is pervasive and "not a compressed set of empirical variables" (p. 15). If culture is pervasive, the question posed in this title is one that probably doesn't need to be asked, but having been asked, we will attempt to show its importance.

Hughes (1993) goes on to elucidate about the concept of culture. He states that it is a field concept. As such, he suggests that a "number of factors or variables may be selected and conceptualized for a given analysis" (p.15). Since concepts have their origin and data, what are the data of culture? According to Hughes, there are two sets of data that we can look at when we think about culture; one is behavior, that is, what people do, what they say, and what they think. The other set of data is artifacts, what people have made in the form of art, artifacts, architecture, and technology (p.15). Our focus is on the former; that is, behavior, what people do, what they say, what they think. As we think about what we do as psychologists, and specifically, as I turn to my own frame of reference, what is it from my own sociocultural context that influences the way I frame questions, the way I understand the clinical enterprise, and so on? There are a number of factors of culture that are important. There are twelve factors that can be seen as influences on my behavior as I function as a psychologist whose sociocultural context may be different from others.

TWELVE FACTORS OF CULTURE

The first is values. It is said that there are shared values among members of a group. I grew up in a culture, my context being Liberia, West Africa, and would therefore hold some of the shared values of that cultural group. What are some of the shared values that influence some of the beliefs that I hold and the way in which I function? One is valuing living, valuing being. Given those values, I think one of the difficult issues for me as a psychologist would be, what do I do then, with someone who does not value living? Here, then, we see a clash of values from different sociocultural contexts. If I have someone who says, I no longer want to live, what do I do with that?

Another shared value is family. Family is preeminent. Family, as we will discuss later, takes precedence over the individual. That influences, then, my conception of family; what family means, the individual's responsibility to family, and so on. Given this frame of reference, it keeps me always vigilant about not contaminating my clients' concept of family. If I have a client whose values clearly emphasize the nuclear family as being preeminent, who has a different sense of family, as a psychologist, I need to be extremely vigilant that there is not a contamination by me.

Another factor with sociocultural influences is the underlying assumptions of a culture. The nature of the human person is one of the underlying assumptions that are shared by members of a given cultural group. Do we see the human person as being all evil, a mixture of both good and evil, or as all good? Within my own sociocultural context there is a dualism of good and evil. Therefore, the human person must be guided throughout childhood so that the evil is not overshadowing the good. Working with clients whose cultural perspectives are different means keeping in check my assumptions and working with theirs.

Another factor for consideration is what is believed to be normal behavior for members of the cultural group. This is one of the critical issues for clinical psychologists. How do we deal with that? What is its influence on the psychologist? For me, coming from a different sociocultural context means exploring what is normal within each group's context and not assuming a universal sense of normality. Rather, a more relativistic stance should be taken.

Each culture defines what is permissible, and what is forbidden. Each culture has its taboos. What is forbidden? Within my culture of origin, an example of what is forbidden is a discussion of family issues outside of the family. This is contradictory to what is expected in psychotherapy. There is a saying that there are things one talks about within the family, and there are things one talks about outside of the family. Those things that are kept within the family are never discussed outside of the family. This causes conflict between what is a family and sociocultural value, and the values underlying my training as a clinical psychologist. Further examples of what is forbidden and what is permissible are the roles of persons in the society and the rules of interaction. Roles are very formal within Liberian society. This particular influence of my culture of origin makes it easy for me to stay within the therapeutic frame. I have had a difficult time, and to some extent still do, with the informality evidenced in formal situations.

Another area of cultural influence is patterns of interpersonal etiquette and demeanor; how one conducts oneself. In my country of origin, the rules about how one conducts oneself are very prescriptive. Briefly, one is expected to conduct oneself at all times with dignity so that one does not bring shame to oneself or bring shame to the family. There is always the family that one has to think about, so one's behavior and demeanor must always be beyond reproach.

Ways of conveying affection; so critical to the issues presented in therapy, show tremendous differences among cultures. In my culture of origin, there is not an emphasis on outward displays of affection or on the use of words to convey affection. Affection, instead, is demonstrated in behaviors, in doing. If a parent comes in, it is easy for one outside of that sociocultural context to assume that there is not much loving within the family if one is looking for the overt signs, such as hugging, kissing, and so on. However, the affection is demonstrated in other ways of caring for family members.

What are ideas of disease and causation? Within my sociocultural context, diseases are seen not only according to the typical medical explanations, but there are also metaphysical explanations that are acceptable. What that does for me as a psychologist is to make me suspend judgment, rather than immediately assuming that a patient or client is delusional when they start talking about other-worldly things, and instead to search to understand the specific context and meaning of what the client is presenting. The influences, then, make me more open to the varied ways of conception of a client's problem.

A conception of kinship is one of the other influences. Here, the conception of kinship is not limited. It is much more extensive, so that family involves parents, uncles and aunts, and cousins. Cousins are very much part of the family, and not just first cousins, but first, second, and third cousins. If you can think that there is some connection, then that person is part of the family. Often, people will ask, which cousin is this? Well, it might be the fifteenth cousin, but they are still part of the family. So, the conception of kinship is quite broad. This is important, because as we begin to work with multicultural families where the conception of kinship is not limited to the nuclear family, that becomes essential. Also, people can become incorporated into the family and become kin, not necessarily by blood. Within Liberia, for example, as I talk about my brothers and sisters, there're my biological brothers and sisters, but also there're my brothers and sisters who have been brought into my family by my parents. These siblings have lived with us over the years without formal adoption processes, but they are still my brothers and sisters. So you can see a different conception of kinship.

Another cultural factor with which I struggle is personal autonomy versus group. The more acculturated I've become, the more intense I think the struggle has become, because the sociocultural context in which I grew up was that the group took precedence over personal autonomy. I, therefore, am empathic to my clients who struggle closely with those same issues. This means then, that I have to closely monitor my feelings so that I don't over identify with their issues, and don't contaminate the clinical endeavor.

Problem conceptualization and expression is another issue. We often try to create dichotomies to talk about whether one sees one's problem from a psychologically introspective point of view, or an externalization. When one looks at cultures such as the one in which I grew up, where forces outside of one's self are very powerful forces, then the problem always does not reside within one. The spirits can be responsible for some of what ails the individual. If you have a client, then, who frames the problems in this way, I think it is easy for one from a different perspective to say that this person consistently externalizes the problem and does not accept responsibility for the problem. What it requires from us, then, is an understanding of that broader context and an understanding of how the individual frames that. For me, it enables me to be able to understand the psychological introspective point of view, but to also look with the client at the external factors that the client sees as important in shaping the issues for him.

Since this society places much emphasis on race, a conception of race becomes important. Growing up in a mono-racial society makes me see race very differently from people who grew up in this society. Race is not a salient factor for me. It has not been part of my experience to look in the mirror in the morning and say, I am a Black person. I grew up as a Black person, and that was never an issue. Therefore, coming into a culture where race is an issue has forced me to look at the next point, which is reaction to racial oppression. Even there, distinctions are framed by my own cultural context. My reactions are not to see myself as limited, but to, in essence, see myself as limitless, with all of the advantages that non-Black persons have within this society. I assume that I belong, and others have to prove that I don't belong. I assume that I have all of the rights and privileges that others have, and those who think differently have to prove me wrong. Racial barriers become obstacles that challenge me to overcome them. That perspective influences my approach to events and to life generally. Within the cultural context in which I was raised, it is your responsibility to the group that propels you. You are expected to enhance the family and group, whether it is the family, the clan, and so on. So that becomes your motivation, and excuses such as racial oppression are not acceptable. When I talk with my friends who are African Americans, born and raised in this country, those differences are often highlighted. This is one area in which those earlier cultural influences have remained strong. Therefore, I have to be careful in therapy that I do not assume that my African American clients have the same perspective about race as I do, or to blame them because they may see themselves as victims of racial oppression.

SUMMARY

By discussing some of the influences of my culture of origin, I have alluded to a couple of questions; what are others' perceptions of our own group, and what are some of the resources upon which we can draw as members of a particular group? What I have demonstrated is that our thinking, feeling, and ways of behaving are influenced by our cultural experiences. These may be very different from the clients with whom we work. Some of those clients may hold stereotypic views of our group. Yet, some of these early influences serve as resources upon which we draw in our work with clients. Rather than assume no differences, or deny these differences, we are better served by embracing them while recognizing them and monitoring their impacts on the therapeutic endeavor.

References

Gaw, Albert C. (Ed.). (1993). *Culture, ethnicity, and mental illness.* Washington, DC: American Psychiatric Press.

Hughes, Charles C. (Ed.). (1976). *Custom-made: Introductory readings for cultural anthropology.* Chicago, IL: Rand McNally.

Hughes, Charles C. (1993). Culture in Clinical Psychiatry. In *Culture, ethnicity, and mental illness.* Washington, DC: American Psychiatric Press.

CHAPTER TWELVE

The Culturally Different Patient in Psychoanalytic Psychotherapy

Renae K. Chung and Shelley J. Stokes

More than at any time in history, American society is becoming more multilingual, multiethnic, and multicultural than ever and will continue so in the future (Aponte & Clifford, 1993; U.S. Bureau of the Census, 2000). While 71 percent of the U.S. population is currently composed of European Americans, by the year 2050 this figure is expected to decline to 53 percent with Latinos representing 25 percent, African Americans 13 percent, Asian Americans and Asian Pacific Americans 9 percent, and American Indians 1 percent (U.S. Bureau of the Census). During the turn of the new millennium in some states such as California, no one ethnic group represented a statistical majority, that is, none comprising more than 50 percent of the population (U.S. Bureau of the Census, 2000). Furthermore, by the year 2020 it is anticipated that the District of Columbia will have 72.6 percent "minority" representation, New Mexico 67.8 percent, Hawaii 64.6 percent, California 62.3 percent, and Texas 53.9 percent (U.S. Bureau of the Census).

This demographic shift presents a substantial challenge for therapists who conduct relevant and ethical practice with culturally diverse clients whose norms, values, and world views may differ from their own (Arredondo, 1996; Cheung & Snowden, 1990; Kiselica, 1998; Korman, 1973; Pedersen, 1997; Sue & Sue, 1999). Unfortunately, despite rapid and ongoing demographic change, psychological understanding of how ethnic, cultural, linguistic, and individual factors dynamically interact (Piker, 1998; Shweder, 1991) remains woefully insufficient.

Learning about the culture of every foreign and ethnic patient is not a viable solution. Such would be an impossible task, and more importantly, research has shown that therapists' knowledge about their patients' cultural backgrounds has no bearing on patients' therapeutic progress (Sue & Zane, 1987; Seeley, 2000). At best, our general knowledge of culture, and perhaps, more limited knowledge of specific cultures, provides us with templates for understanding potential meanings. Such templates may increase the range of possible interpretations of meaning, but do not in any a priori fashion determine any *specific* meaning. Even in 1958 Devereux suggested that obtaining a more general familiarity with general characteristics, categories, and functions of culture per se may be more relevant than learning about the stereotypical characteristics of particular cultures.

There is, however, a clear necessity for us as therapists to develop an understanding of the rich and specific individual, family, and cultural context, which each patient traverses. When cultural, racial, linguistic, and other differences between the patient and therapist exist, the patient and therapist may, indeed, not share culturally shaped world views, assumptions, habits, or patterns of thought (Seeley, 2000, p. 14). As a result, the patient and therapist may experience difficulties in creating shared meanings. However, even when patients come from "similar" cultural backgrounds as their therapists, shared meanings are not guaranteed, and the therapist must be cautious not to automatically (or often unconsciously) assume the patient has similar experiences, values, norms, and world views as her own (Griffith, 1977; Lorion, 1978; Parloff, Waskow, & Wolfe, 1978; Poussaint, 1980; Sue & Sue, 1990; Thompson, 1989). This becomes an even more complex conundrum for those patients who have a complex personal identity and may be continually faced with questions about where they belong (cf. De Nicola, 1997). How people interact with culture is complex and the process of enculturation affects seemingly similar individuals in a different manner (cf. Ho, 1995, p. 16).

To understand the patient in her complexity, the therapist must walk the fine line between embracing the patient's subjective experience, while still embracing a broader understanding of human dynamics. From this middle ground, the therapist discerns not only the meanings of the patient's experience, but she must also be able to discern the patient's maladaptive strategies, including the patient's potential use of cultural factors as defense against examination of her own material and associated painful affects.

In addressing the issue of cultural variations between patient and psychotherapist, particular focus has been directed toward the traditional psychodynamic models generally, and psychoanalytic paradigms specifically. Such models of psychological understanding and treatment frequently have been criticized as being eurocentric in origin and in scope, and thus, of limited usefulness in treating clients from non-Western backgrounds (cf. Lichtman, 1998; Mattei, 1999).

Contrastingly, we will argue that the assertion that psychoanalytically based models assume specific invariances which render us incapable of incorporating cultural dimensions of patients' experiences, implies that the practice of psychoanalysis or psychoanalytic psychotherapy is aculturally rigid in a way that it need not be. In our view, the essential problem when working in intercultural contexts is not a stultification of thinking the problem is less located in the paradigm, per se, than in the nonuse or misuse of its basic percepts by the practitioner.

In a broad sense, psychotherapists and psychoanalysts who work from any theoretic orientation must ground their analysis in the patient's enculturated senses of self, of others, and of relationships. The question is one of whether the wide spectrum of the patient's unconscious impulses, motivations, wishes, fantasies, identifications, and histories, which are culturally imbued, are adequately understood by the psychotherapist.

The Map is Not the Territory
(Korzybski, 1933, *Science and Sanity*)

As psychotherapists actively engaged with our patients, we strive to understand unique meanings through empathic connection. To some extent, we locate the patient's experience within our own, keeping in mind that "the map is not the territory," that is, recognizing that our empathy or resonance is not the same thing as the patient's own experience (De Nicola, 1997). We clarify, question, and reflect proximate understandings and provide a context for patients to tell their own story in their own way. If things go well in this process, the therapist and patient begin the attempt to build a bridge of communication. The patient communicates his predicament and experience in explanations anchored in words of distress. He faces the difficult tasks: to reveal intimate personal material, to recount family histories, to express emotional reactions, and to air interpersonal conflicts in ways that his indigenous culture may prohibit (Draguns, 1985; Seeley, 2000; Varma, 1988) or the patient's defenses may not easily allow. However, in attempting such tasks, an opportunity is provided for the patient to explore painful material that he previously may have found impossible to discuss.

In this process, the therapist attempts to bridge communication through words anchored in an understanding of the patient and of the process of psychotherapy, utilizing the metaphors of the patient. In order for these bridges to meet, continual translation must occur. To the extent to which the patient feels we "get it," a potential for therapeutic alliance can begin to be forged. For the therapist and patient involved in this process, exploration becomes more useful and edifying than assumptiveness. Form and syntax of questions, timing, and attunement come to bear, but such considerations should not smother the process of exploration. To the contrary, a more daunting problem arises when the therapist feels that some questions should not be asked because he or she may not like the answers (that is, counter-transferentially based *selective attunement*). In this sense, what the therapist chooses to ignore in the conduct of therapy is just as important as what he chooses to explore with the patients.

The therapist responds to the patient's material with authenticity, humanity, and empathy. The therapist, in classical jargon, becomes a *servant of the patient's process,* creating a context in which the patient is free to explore any conflictual areas of her life. Questions naturally emerge in the context of the patient's story as the therapist works to understand the culturally specific aspects of the patient's experience, rather than employing stereotypic categories regarding the patient's cultural group(s). Furthermore, because it is the experience of the patient that truly matters, rather than the molding of his patient's experience to fit theoretical assumptions; the therapist strives to understand the existential perspective of the patient, that is, world view, values, and cultural factors as these come to bear on the internal conflicts uncovered and explored during the therapeutic interaction.

We, in effect, work to create a safe space for patients to investigate their lives and problems. We attempt to assist patients in their efforts to accomplish what they may have thought was impossible, to integrate the past in a way that does not kill the present; to suture fragmented areas of their lives, to face feelings of being out of tune, or of being a stranger to one's roots; to new understandings and coping strategies; to reconstruct their stories while being ready for this progressive telling to impact everything, and to take advantage of being "a stranger" to the therapist and to themselves (cf. Di Nicola, 1997).

In the active dialectic process between the therapist and the patient, ideally, the therapist (1) responds with appropriate affect, mirroring, probes, silence, interpretation, clarification, processing and summarization; (2) is appropriate and comfortable in attending behaviors as reflected in body language, eye contact, facial expression, and other nonverbal behavior; (3) is able to track the patient's conscious and unconscious material; (4) uses good judgment in timing and use of reflections; (5) maintains a nonjudgmental attitude; (6) actively listens and provides empathic responses; and (7) engages in the ongoing management of counter-transferential issues as these arise. For all patients, difficult assessments must be made in the face of the therapist's discoveries and understandings, however, with culturally different patients the processes of recognition, recall, inference, analysis, cause and effect, integration, and synthesis may become quite challenging and complex.

In the case of one former patient (of another therapist) interviewed by Seeley (2000, p. 97–111), we see breakdowns at many levels of the therapeutic process. This patient was a thirty-year-old graduate student, born and raised in Calcutta, a Brahmin by birth who had disavowed his caste and grew up in a middle-class household in India. During his doctoral studies in the United States, he began to experience difficulties in his hearing and underwent surgery, only to find that his ear had suffered permanent damage. He found himself "in pain, unable to work, short of funds, and completely demoralized," and unable to concentrate on his studies. He blamed himself for his problems and considered quitting academic studies. He also considered committing suicide, but realized that he would be unable to kill himself.

Although he felt that his problem was not a psychological one, and he believed that mental health treatment was only another manifestation of European imperialism, he reluctantly accepted a referral to a Euro-American therapist. He experienced a highly negative transference to this therapist as he saw the therapist as a representative of a country that had oppressed and dominated his native home country. He, therefore, devalued the therapy itself, and negated nearly every aspect of treatment. In his therapy, he felt that he learned little about himself. Though he felt his life was "in a terrible mess," he used his psychotherapy only as "English conversation practice." Not surprisingly, he felt disempowered, oppressed, misjudged, and misunderstood.

This transference, which persisted throughout treatment, was never explored in the therapy, though that patient's feelings were easily accessible in response to a simple question asked by the interviewer. She directly asked how it felt never to be sure of whether his psychotherapist was getting what he was saying or not. His perception that his therapist not only misunderstood, but that she also misjudged and devalued his family practices, and his culture remained unexplored in the psychotherapy, ignored or unnoticed by the therapist. It is surprising that the therapist would have no conscious or unconscious sense that the therapy was not going well, or, if she did, that he would leave this issue unaddressed.

How then do we understand this patient's reality, his dilemma, and how do we come to understand what has happened in the course of his treatment given the limited data provided? Perhaps one can begin with the recognition that we all know what it means to sacrifice dreams, to face the loss of achieving our deepest aspirations, to not know where to turn next in our lives, to face the shame of "failure" and of "disappointment" of self, of family, of others. Perhaps we haven't faced the specific challenges and traumas of this patient's childhood in a native India reeling from the aftermath of Western colonization, but from our own experiences and identifications we know what it means to feel disempowered, oppressed, misjudged, and misunderstood. The therapeutic task, in essence, is to understand what these meanings hold for him, and to understand that, yes, he was "in a terrible mess."

Finding a common language for mutual understanding and exploration of the patient's experience requires the use of metaphor to open space for such communication. Such potential for communication is aptly illustrated by Seeley (2000) in her interview:

> I asked Prakesh to tell me the Bengali term that described how he had felt . . .
> and he offered the word *mushkil*. He translated *mushkil* as "I'm in trouble," or

"I'm in a terrible mess." I then asked Prakesh to tell me about other situations to which *mushkil* might refer, and he provided the examples of boarding a bus without money for the fare or of being in debt. The differences between *mushkil*, as Prakesh defined it, and the English *depression* are striking; *mushkil* refers to an external rather than an internal state of affairs, is devoid of psychological and emotional content, and lacks connotations of illness and incapacity. Yet Prakesh maintained that this word accurately portrayed his suicidality and despair (pp. 101–102).

The word *mushkil* was used by this patient to describe his state of affairs. It needed no translation for this patient into the Western idiom of depression. He was, indeed, in trouble in a way that medication would not fix, though it might (or might not) alter his mood. Thus, even in the face of cultural difference between he and the interviewer, real communication *was* possible.

THE CULTURALLY DIFFERENT PATIENT
AND OBJECT RELATIONS THEORY

Object relations theory can make a unique contribution to our understanding of the relationship between culture and personality at the *micro* level as it provides us with an understanding of intrapsychic processes that influence adult interpersonal behavior. In essence, object relations theories represent attempts to conceptualize how, from the time we are born, we evolve feelings and images and beliefs and experiences that become definitional for us about our relationships, our attempt to organize human phenomena, and our feelings, thoughts, and beliefs about people and self.

Most directly put, this body of theories (as well as classical psychoanalytic theory preceding it) must assert that to the degree to which culture is expressed in care-taking behavior of infants is the degree to which the culture influences the internalized representations of the individual. Thus, contrary to popular belief that "Freud didn't care about culture," his psychoanalytic work implicitly acknowledged its importance (Piker, 1998). His emphasis on culture derived primarily from his theory of mental symbolism (Breur & Freud, 1955), which stressed the lifelong importance of the experiences of infancy and early childhood and the psychosymbolic processes embedded in the individual and in her culture (Piker).

One might trace the emergence of psychoanalytic object relations theory from Freud's work, specifically from his structural theory (Freud, 1923), in which he asserts that the first identifications in early childhood will be profound and lasting. The origins of both the ego and the superego are linked with the precipitates of past object relations (Kernberg, 1984a). In their break from drive theory to a more relational model of human functioning, early object relations theorists began to move away from understanding object relations in terms of drive derivatives and increasingly toward the position that the relational posture, in and of itself, is essential to normal human development. They also supported the view that early object relationships, which were internalized, mediated ongoing external realities, coloring, and frequently distorting, new interpersonal experiences.

Object relations theory suggests that humans are motivated from birth by the need for significant relationships with objects (Fairbairn, 1952). This central concept of object relations theory deviates from classical psychoanalytic theory in that the formation and maintenance of object relationships, rather than drives, becomes the primary motivator for human behavior. The earliest significant object relationships form enduring psychological "templates" for all future relationships, as well as being instrumental in psychic development and structuralization.

During infancy, the child is entirely dependent upon the caretaker for need gratification. Healthy emotional development is a product of consistent empathic attunement given by the primary caretaker and of the caretaker's efforts at repairing of the ruptures in this attunement. Internalized representations of self and others are laid down based on the earliest introjects from the primary caretaking relationship. The infant's ego structure is immature and must rely on auxiliary ego functions provided by the mother or family that serves as a basis for all subsequent attachment and stimulates the structuralization of the infant's mind. Care-taking ministrations serve the purpose of soothing and organizing for the child until these functions are interiorized through maturation and the continuous internalization of self- and other-representations. Prior to the achievement of object constancy, splitting is used to keep the "all good" and "all bad" spheres polarized. This is necessary in order to preserve the all good parts from destruction by the all bad.

The capacity for dependency, trust, and intimacy as adults is determined by the level of trust and nurturance in the encoded internalized object relations from the earliest period. Adult relationships are sought and formed based on early models. Internal object relations and intrapsychic conflicts are defended against, repeated, lived through, or mastered in interpersonal intimate relationships.

Primary caretakers must facilitate the infant's indulgence of primary narcissism, act as a container for their aggression, and allow optimal frustration to foster a sense of safety and continuity in the development of self. If the infant consistently experiences empathic attunement, an abundance of positive experiences are internalized into the representational world, allowing for the development of a basically positive stable and coherent sense of self. With such experiences, the growing child (and later the mature adult) comes to manifest broader and broader capacities for spontaneity, aliveness of affect, self-entitlement, self-activation, self-esteem, self-soothing, commitment, creativity, and intimacy (Masterson, 1985).

To achieve adequate emotional health as an adult, several outcomes must be attained from the first few years of life. The infant's primary narcissism must be gratified in a consistent manner so that a sense of trust and security is fostered. There is a growing differentiation between infant and caretaker. If the caretaker has supplied "good enough mothering" (Winnicott, 1950, 1965), the anxiety of separation can be managed on a gradual basis since the caretaker does not abruptly threaten the infant's dependency. The infant gradually develops differentiated boundaries between self and other, and becomes able to relate to others as separate whole objects, rather than as part objects split into the good and the bad. The infant begins to maintain a sense of positive self-esteem, becomes able to regulate internal tension states, develops increasing ability to experience a wide range of emotions, and is able to internalize a sense of confidence in his own competence.

For individuals who do not receive empathically attuned nurturance during critical developmental periods, enduring deficits occur. Having lacked appropriate nurturance and having few positive internalized self and object representations, such adults find it difficult to self-soothe during times of anxiety or stress. As the young child encounters persecutory and rejecting interactions from the primary caretaker, the child must internalize the aspects of the critical, yet loved, parent in order to control the object in the internal psychic world. The child internalizes the persecutory interactions which become repressed and retained as an introject for self-representations. Lack of positive introjects leaves the child with little ability to self-soothe, and when the child is unable to extract soothing from others, this is felt as a core injury.

Under such circumstances, it becomes difficult to maintain a stable sense of positive well-being. Dependency needs unmet in childhood continue to operate on a primitive level as an adult. A pervasive sense of rage may develop that these needs have gone unmet, and the adult may consequently search to fulfill dependency needs in a desperate and demanding manner, based in an impoverished sense of self.

Life situations are unconsciously interpreted in the light of the inner world, resulting in distorted expectations of other people, and unconscious attempts are made to force and change close relationships into fitting the internal construction. An abundance of negative internalized experiences from childhood crystallizes in the adult as her basic "template" for the world, significant objects, and for the self, and distort or "spoil" all subsequent adult relationships (based on previous negative internal working models).

The continued hunger to have unresolved dependency needs met, and the tendencies to look to others to supply emotional regulation often contribute to relationship difficulties. Boundary diffusion and looking to objects to fulfill primitive needs becomes a predominant characteristic. This often results in the individual trying to restore a sense of soothing from external objects, such as a partner. When the partner is unable to supply self-regulating functions, this is felt as a core injury. Such an experience may result in narcissistic rage.

At the same time, when the person seeks merger with a partner, he or she becomes intensely afraid of engulfment and has difficulty regulating intimacy and distance within the relationship. Although there is an intense desire for intimacy, the regressive qualities of dependency and vulnerability inherent in intimacy come to involve intense anxieties. Acting-out behaviors may be initiated to reduce the level of intimacy, and may also cause anxiety by threatening loss of an attachment. The need for intimacy may then reemerge within this cycle of intense emotions (Zosky, 1999, p. 61). Without achievement of a Kleinian depressive position or a Mahlerian stage of self and object constancy, anger is experienced intensely (Siegel, 1992). Due to splitting, modulation of anger becomes difficult, and judgment and reality-testing become prone to distortion.

Borderline, schizoid, narcissistic, and other personality disorders are thought to emerge in the pre-oedipal phase due to empathic failures of the primary caretaking matrix (Masterson, 1972, 1976, 1980, 1981, 1988, 1993, 2000; Masterson & Klein, 1989, 1995). Lack of adequate nurturing impedes the child from developing a sense of object constancy and the ability to integrate good and bad self and object representations into the whole, integrated representation (Kernberg, 1975; Mahler, 1971; Masterson, 1972). Adults with such resultant borderline personality organization (Kernberg), including borderlines, schizoids, narcissists, and other, manifest impoverishment of ego functioning, use of primitive defenses (for example, splitting, projection, and projective identification), and distorted and affect-laden self and object representations. Early primitive needs continue to motivate behavior in adult intimate relationships.

Interestingly, while some (Kakar, 1985) have agreed that the more relational approaches in psychoanalytic theory are quite useful in intercultural psychotherapy, others (Lichtman, 1998; Seeley, 2000) believe that object relations theory's representation of objects is incomplete by virtue of its omission of culture, and its acceptance of Western and universalizing conceptions of objects, of the self, and of relationships which would limit its application in the treatment of non-Western patients. As Seeley asserts, "For although object relations theory conceives of internalized objects as embedded in a relational matrix, it fails to situate objects in their cultural worlds" (p. 49).

The question, perhaps, is how can such embedding be done without resorting to cultural stereotype, or resorting to a circular and impotence-inducing stance of extreme cultural relativism (that is, that every cultural group is distinct and must be understood on its terms, as explained by its own people)? We assert that one locates the meaning of "objects" in the meaning attributed to them *by the individual.*

Thus, it is unclear why it would be necessary to infer that "objects" must refer only to universal, decontextualized experience. While some universal objects likely do exist, in fact, it can't be a functional requirement that all internalized objects be, by definition, "universal" in an absolute sense. Rather by definition, "objects" must reference individual experiences and associated affect states. Thus, the content of intrapsychic objects vary extensively across cultural settings and within individual minds, and must by definition evolve from the culturally laden experiences, meanings, and associated affects particular to the individual. Individual development does not occur in a culture-free, decontextualized, a-familial vacuum. In this sense, the work of clinical psychoanalysis, particularly object relations is preoccupied with the emergence into thought of early subjective, context-laden memories of being and relating (cf. Bollas, 1987).

Contrary to the argument that object relations theories overlook the variation which exists across cultures in defining what composes objects (that is, whether external or internal, real or imagined) and excluding "ancestral spirits, objects that lack fixed identities, cosmic forces, and supernatural beings" (Landrine, 1992; Seeley, 2000), it seems curious that one would, perforce, be confined to conceiving the notion of "objects" in any limited way. Even Melanie Klein, the essential founder of the British School of Object Relations, conceived of a wide range of objects populating the infant's phantasy world including not only part (human) objects, but also activities and things. From this point of reference no elements of human experience would, a priori, be excluded from being an internal object representation, including supernatural beings, cosmic forces, and ancestral spirits. Freud also allowed that an object is the mental representation of an external things *not necessarily a person* which is invested with energy by the psyche.

In actuality, the notion of "objects" in object relations theories has been evolving continually over time. The clinical concept of the "object" began as one of the most incidental features within Freud's formulations concerning the nature of the drives. It was the term originally chosen by Freud to designate the target of instinctual drives, "other," real or imaginary, toward whom the drive is directed. In the early phases of development, the object comes under the aegis of the pleasure principle, that is, what is pleasurable is at first treated as part of the self. The world of the infant (à la Anna Freud) becomes split into "good" need satisfying objects and "bad" need frustrating objects, and only later in development are these fused into mental representations vested with memories of pleasure as well as pain.

Melanie Klein extended such conceptions in her stress on the importance of very early internalized object relations in determining the vicissitudes of intrapsychic conflict and psychic structures, linking psychoanalytic instinct theory with early object relations and early constellations of defensive operations, and stressing the importance of pregenital aggression in determining phantasic primitive internal objects and the basic structure of the superego.

In her early papers, Klein described very complex *phantasies* in young children involving objects (or unconscious images) that she considered created out of the (Freudian) drives themselves, independent of real others in the external world, and "wholly phantastic" (Klein, 1930). She saw these phantastic images of breasts, penises, the womb, babies, poison explosions, conflagrations, and so on, as constituting the child's early object relations world. The child lives in dread of his objects, destroying, burning, mutilating, and poisoning him, because these activities dominate his own phantasies toward them, and therefore, constitute the substance of his projections onto them. Pleasurable sensations, on the other hand, such as comfort and security, are "felt to come from good forces" (Klein, 1952), and help to neutralize danger and aggression. Real others in the infant's external world are constantly internalized, established as internal objects, and projected out onto external figures once again as a mode of relating to the outside world. However, not just people, but all experiences and situations are internalized. Thus, for Klein, the content and nature of relations with objects, both real people in the outside world and phantasized images of others as internal presences, were the crucial determinant of psychical processes, both normal and pathological, and form the basis of one's behavior, moods, and sense of self. In fact, for Klein, relations with internal objects constitute the very fabric of the self.

Without attempting an extensive historical review of the range and development of object relations theories, it will suffice for our present purposes to briefly observe how Fairbairn (1952) revised and extended Klein's work by contributing further to the understanding of primitive object relations by addressing in greater detail schizoid defensive operations, particularly splitting. Guntrip went further into the realm of what we now know to be the schizoid personality disorder proper, elaborating the nature of the "final split." Winnicott (1965) introduced the notion of the developing "false self," contrasting it with a true, authentic self. Mahler (1971) traced the development of increasing differentiation of the self through the twin processes of separation-individuation in which the infant becomes a unique person in his own right. Masterson (1985, 1988, 1993) further extended Mahler's work in explication of the various disorders of the self resulting from developmental arrests during the process of separation individuation, resulting in impairments in the "real" self, impairments in relational capacities, ego deficits, and primitive defenses.

Much of this work is frequently mischaracterized and misunderstood, because of its evocations of the terms "self," "separation," "individuation," and the like. For example, Lichtman (1998) suggests that

> In all human societies, infants learn to distinguish themselves from others.
> There are no societies in which people cannot identify themselves as distinct
> human beings. So, in this sense all human beings become separate individuals.

> But it is certainly not the case that they become individuals in the same way. There is a profound difference between the concept of "the individual" and the concept of "individuality." The kind of individual self that prevails in Western capitalist society is radically different from those selves which are indigenous to other societies. That is why the anthropologist, Clifford Geertz, can rightly assert that "Western conception of the person as a bounded, unique, more or less integrated motivational and cognitive universe . . . set contrastingly both against other such wholes and against its social and natural background, is . . . a rather peculiar idea within the context of the world's cultures" (Geertz—1998, cited in Lichtman, p. 119).

Lichtman (1998) seems, however, to confuse the psychological concept of individuation with sociopolitical concepts of "individuality" and "separateness from others." On the contrary, "individuation" must also be distinguished from a "Westernized individuality" and from a "lack of relatedness." By definition, lack of individuation is manifested in an inability or difficulty to tolerate differences. The less individuated individual would indeed, recognize that others are distinct from the self, but would have extreme difficulty in tolerating others' opinions or experience when these differ from his or her own. The less individuated individual (reference the narcissistic disordered patient described variously by Masterson (1981, 1988, 1993), Kernberg (1975, 1984b), Kohut (1977), and others) demands a psychological fusion between self and other in which the other can only be tolerated if the other remains on the same emotional, ideological, or volitional page (that is, remains in "like-mindedness" or psychological fusion).

When Mahler (1971) writes of the "psychological birth of the human infant," she is referring to an infant who is becoming a unique person in his or her own right (which can be conceived as becoming a self in the contexts of others: a group, a culture, a family, and so on). Human beings are never interchangeable cogs in a wheel. If self-other differentiation is not attained by the infant by five or six months of age (differentiation of "I" and "not I"), we must wonder about severe disturbance. We distinguish our selves from others, and others from each other based on "who we are" defined on whatever cultural template the definition takes place.

Lichtman (1998) seems to use a purely social and cultural construction of individuation as an argument against object relations and against other psychoanalytically derived views. He asserts that they all are grounded in a point of view in which the self, understood as "a separate, autonomous, boundaried, independent, private initiator of its own agency" (p. 118), and he contrasts this with a less-Westernized self that might be a more "contextualized being whose fundamental relations to its society are an intrinsic aspect of its nature" (p. 119). Here we will argue, again, that the deeply "relational" concepts of self are highly understandable (in health or in pathology) from a psychoanalytically based, object relations point of view.

More to the point, politicization of psychological constructs seems a rather useless enterprise. As Masterson (1985) notes:

> Sociocultural values can either potentiate and reinforce or impair and inhibit real self expression and fulfillment. Contemporary sociocultural forces do not have as powerful an influence as the parents during the vulnerable developmental years of formation of the self; nevertheless, in later years they do affect the functioning of the self!
>
> The sociocultural forces would influence those who have an autonomous, fully developed real self differently than those with a disorder of the self. In the case of the former, the positive forces would reinforce and potentiate self-expression and the negative forces would probably be met by the real self with sustained and often effective resistance. The effects on those with a disordered self would be quite different. The narcissistic disordered self would exploit the values of freedom and independence to gain narcissistic, not real self-gratification and would fiercely battle the infringement of the negative forces on the individual's sense of entitlement.
>
> The borderline disordered self would react to the positive forces not with greater real self-expression but with greater anxiety about real self-expression. It would react to the negative forces as a reinforcement of its pathological defense (pp. 104–105).

The clinical material presented below illustrates the successful integration of subjective cultural issues into the paradigm of an ego-psychological and object relations based psychoanalytically oriented psychotherapy. These vignettes will each illustrate that the development of an idiographic understanding (Allport, 1955) of the rich and specific individual, family, and cultural context which each patient develops is a basic requirement of all psychotherapies, regardless of heterogeneity or homogeneity between patient and therapist. This process, perforce, involves the therapist's highly concerted attempt to understand the patient's experience of the internal and external world from the patient's perspective. As mentioned earlier, this becomes an even more complex conundrum with patients who have a complex personal identity who may be continually faced with questions of how to forge a coherent account of who they are.

VIGNETTES

The work of psychoanalytic psychotherapy, generally, and object relations therapy, specifically, involves a joint effort of exploration; an examination, as it were, of the personal conflicts, struggles, symptoms, and adaptations of a given individual. Through this exploration, individuals are provided the opportunity to find a different way of conducting themselves that they, themselves, find more gratifying and less conflictual. Properly conducted, this work is nondirective, involves no imposition of the therapist's personal point of view, no projection of the therapist's values onto the patient, nor the imposition of any a priori solution, direction, or goal. The work of the psychotherapy is to explore internal conflicts. If there is no internal conflict, then no basis for psychotherapy exists. The job of the therapist is not to promote a theory of psychological health, nor to dictate what should or should not be, but rather to explore what patients are in internal conflict about.

Illustrations of these principles in intercultural psychoanalytic psychotherapy are presented below of psychotherapies between a fifty-eight-year-old male, ethnically Jewish psychoanalytic ego psychologist and a first-generation Japanese couple divided over how the wife should respond to the mother-in-law's insistence that she behave as a dutiful daughter (Case 1), a fifty-year-old female, Mennonite psychoanalytically oriented psychologist and Roman Catholic male patient in conflict about his adherence to his religious values and belief and his pending marriage choice (Case 2), and a Hispanic female patient upset over her husband's infidelity branded as typical behavior of Hispanic men and a fifty-four-year-old Afro American psychologist trained in psychoanalytic object relations psychotherapy (Case 3).

Case 1

A first-generation Japanese American couple (Mr. and Ms. S.) came to psychotherapy because they were on the verge of divorce. The conflict between the couple stemmed from the husband's desire for his wife to continually tolerate his mother's dominance when she was in their home, in effect, wanting her to behave as a "dutiful daughter." Ms. S. asserted that this was unacceptable to her, in that she was now a Japanese American and would not put up with what she described as her mother-in-law's "old cultural value system." She insisted that her husband tell his mother to back down when she disliked or disagreed with what she did in her home, or otherwise simply keep her mouth shut or stay away. Because it would be easier and less conflictual for him, Mr. S. wanted his wife to accept his mother's demands, to remain silent when his mother told her how she should and should not cook, clean house, treat him, and raise the children. The conflict between Mr. and Ms. S. was also manifested itself in their sexual relations as Mr. S. expected her to "unreasonably respond" to his every sexual need. This couple had been married for ten years. They had two children, a six-year-old son and a four-year-old daughter.

Mr. S. had been raised in a highly child-centered environment. His mother had indulged him and rewarded his childish self-centeredness until he was approximately seven years of age, after which things began to change, and she began to painfully shame him in order to control his burgeoning infantile grandiosity and narcissism which could, then, not be expressed directly, but could only find expression through the "other" (the perfect wife, the perfect mother, the perfect family in which no conflict or shame existed). He continued to rely on others to relieve his own internal distress, demanding like-mindedness and emotional fusion. He unconsciously sacrificed himself (and his wife) through attempting to gratify his mother's needs with the unconscious hope that she would love and adore him as the perfect and dutiful son. Basing much of his esteem on his sense of perceptiveness and ability to intuitively respond to the needs of the other, he remained deeply distressed that he could not adequately respond to the needs of *both* his mother and his wife, yet he seemed to have little emotional involvement with either of them. Both partners, however, remained adamant that they "loved each other."

Mr. S. presented with a narcissistic personality structure. His conflicts reflected characteristic deficits frequently attributable to such structure, for example, he had the capacity for sexual excitement but was without capacity for deep investment in the love object. He experienced extreme frustration when the desired sexual object (his wife) would not become immediately available to him. His idealization of his wife centered around physical beauty and her strength of her convictions, as attributes he admired, and unconsciously incorporated as part of the self. He used sexual activity as a means of tension release from pressures at work, and his "right" as a husband. During orgasm he described feelings of being "loved, secure, and at peace," and was highly dependent on sexual activity for his sense of belonging and worth. When rebuffed, Mr. S. reported feeling "alone, unloved, and abandoned." As a defense against feeling fragmented, he would then become enraged.

Mr. S. had difficulty describing his relationship with his mother, but stated that she was a woman he "put on a pedestal" and that she was "always there for (him)," "attended to (his) needs," and only shamed him "when he deserved it." He felt indulged by both his mother and his father, but felt no "warmth" from either of them. In particular, he unconsciously needed and longed for a warm and caring mother, and, at the same time, unconsciously needed to take revenge against her. This paralleled the unconscious idealization and devaluation of his wife, with the consequent experiences of estrangement from her and abandonment by her when she is not on the same emotional page or in total consonance with him. The concomitant feelings were ones of deprivation, depression, and rage.

Although Mr. S. appeared to be assertive with his wife, this was actually a pseudo-assertion. In his personal life, he presented as compliant to his mother, and when she was in conflict with his wife, he became unsure of what was the "right thing to do" and "the right way to feel," but resorted to the use of "culture" to shame his wife into complying. He was invariably concerned about what others would say about him. His insecurity resulted in the expectation that his wife would obey his requests and act accordingly. When this did not occur, Mr. S. experienced himself as inadequate, fragmented, and alone; on the edge of abandonment.

Ms. S. presented with a borderline personality structure. She demonstrated a primitive, unrealistic, idealization of the love object, whom she did not perceive in any depth. The internal representation of her paternal part-object, offered approval for regressive and clinging behavior, which made her part self-representation feel unique, special and taken care of. However, in the face of external assault (from her mother-in-law or husband) the constellation of a healthy, though impaired, part of the real self, became angry and felt belittled and annihilated. Her attempts at asserting herself were limited to her relationship with her husband, rather than with her mother-in-law or with others. Her efforts at assertion then became acts of aggression and retaliation. Ms. S. had not experienced validation for being an individual and negotiated her interactions to be sure that someone would take care of her.

In addition, Ms. S. demonstrated little capacity for empathy, or insight, into her actions or the motivations for her actions. She readily agreed with the therapist's interventions without emotional resonance. When the experience in therapy would become at all painful, Ms. S. would move to anger and attack of her husband, herself, or the therapist, as a distancing defense where relatedness was not possible.

Ms. S.'s distancing defense had been crucial in her maintaining a sense of psychological equilibrium, and when those few opportunities for closeness materialized, it activated an impaired real self, which lacked the capacity to make the relationship work. In attempting to give up the distancing defense, she would resort to clinging dependency as a form of self-protection, moving ultimately to hopelessness, and helplessness which dominated her entire life (including her feelings about her relationships with her husband, mother-in-law, and others).

Both Mr. and Ms. S. focused on the "other" in order to get their needs met. They expected the other to understand and to acquiesce to their desires, existing in an angry but sometimes symbiotic and fused relationship in which they could not see the other person as having separate feelings, wishes, desires, and thoughts. What, then, was the work of psychotherapy?

Clearly the work of psychoanalytic psychotherapy was not to tell Mr. and Ms. S. who was correct or not correct. Instead, it was to highlight the differences they were experiencing, to explore where these differences came from, what was idiosyncratic to them, how they talked or did not with each other about these problems, and ultimately, to explore with them whether, or to what degree, they each (or mutually) would decide to accommodate to the other. The focus was on their making their own decisions, on their working them out, and on their living with the consequences of their decisions. Employing the principles of therapeutic neutrality and empathic resonance, the psychotherapist had no investment in a specific outcome. The psychotherapist facilitated the exploration process but had no particular answer or solution to their problems. The management of their problems mirrored their intrapsychic conflicts and struggles as these were manifested in their attempts to get the other to conform. Together, the couple was able to reach some satisfactory, but not complete, resolution of their problems.

Case 2

Dr. C., a thirty-six-year-old male university professor who was raised in an orthodox Roman Catholic tradition, came to therapy because he wanted to marry a woman outside of his religion. He was conflicted over whether or not he "should" pursue this desire and admitted that he did have some strong family centered and religiously based inhibitions against marrying the woman whom he loved. Despite severe anxiety, Dr. C. found himself still "functional" but experiencing "a lot of guilt" over his ambivalence and worried about what this ambivalence was doing to his relationship with his possible future wife. He now faced the acrimony and derision of his parents as well as his own sense of ambivalence and guilt over his desire to marry a non-Catholic woman. He was stuck, unable to activate himself for fear of being abandoned by his parents, his fiancée, his community of friends, and by God. He found himself experiencing increasing difficulty in controlling his anger, which resulted in continual emotional outbursts toward his fiancée, his coworkers, and around his community of friends.

Dr. C. was the third of six children. He was his mother's "favorite" son until age five when his sister was born, followed by the birth of a brother two years later. He idealized the good mother who made him feel wanted, and gave him "a sense of continuity." He expressed discomfort, however, over his mother's use of him as a recipient and confidant of her disappointment and anger at his father. Such times would fill him with "nervousness, frustration, and anxiety." His mother would then, subsequently respond by "isolating herself" which left Dr. C., as a child, feeling "not connected," and "icky," and no longer feeling what he described as "mom and me." He would cope with this feeling of isolation by becoming "absorbed in playing" which he described as "disconnecting."

After the birth of his sister, the patient became supplanted as his mother's favorite. He was repeatedly told that he was "stupid" and asked, "What is wrong with you?" Clarification by the therapist of his anger, jealously, and his need to be comforted, held, and reassured were initially met with tears. This was followed by recriminations of "I was always attention-seeking, acting-out."

Information about Dr. C.'s father elicited much anger, sarcasm, and tears. He was described as a patriarch who "ruled" the home. According to his father, Dr. C. couldn't do anything right. "It all had to be his way, the right way." Dr. C. noted that as a teenager, when he tried to negotiate with his father regarding how he was to clean the garage or to do any other chores, he was ordered to comply with the father's directions or leave the family. Dr. C. also recalled that as an undergraduate in college, he made an effort to discuss sexuality with his father who had stated, "Women could get pregnant from sweat." His disagreement with this statement caused his father to "explode," yelling, "I'll tell YOU about sex." He found himself subsequently evicted from the house and did not return for seven days. Throughout his childhood and adolescence, his mother's threatening words, "I'll tell your father when he gets home," instilled great fear and compliance in him at the expense of any expression of his real self.

The therapist concluded that Dr. C. presented with a borderline intrapsychic personality structure, seeking to find anyone who cares, and adjusting his life to guarantee that someone will care about him. His interactions were negotiated to gain attachment and to avoid the anxieties and danger of nonattachment. This pattern was most clearly evidenced in his relationship with his parents, whom he experienced as hurtful, and negating of himself. Any attempts at asserting his own ideas were met with disdain or derision. This pattern also extended to his object representation of God as a kind of archetypal parental object who could be critical, hurtful, and negating of him. To contemplate marrying someone who was non-Catholic, was risking not only the loss of his parents, but also the loss of God, and eternal damnation.

At the beginning of treatment, Dr. C. presented defensively with laughter, even when addressing serious and depressing issues. The demand from him during the initial sessions seemed to be for the therapist to give him specific instructions on how to avoid, or change, his feelings or to join him in his self-recriminations which were accompanied by uncontrolled sobbing. This weeping appeared to be a defense against underlying feelings of fear, rage, and hopelessness. An examination of the wailing produced a sheepish smile, with the subsequent revelation that he was hoping that God would see his despair and "have pity on (him)."

As Dr. C. described his experiences of childhood, as well as his present conflicts with his parents, mirroring interventions by the therapist were met with mixed responses such as "Oh no, it wasn't that horrible," as well as expressions of his loneliness and despair. As the treatment progressed, he no longer used laughter as a defense against his emotions. His anger with the therapist began to surface as expressed in his forgetting sessions or arriving late. When confronted with his absentee behavior as a self-destructive acting out of his anger, Dr. C. was able to acknowledge and examine this. He also began to examine, in a deeper fashion, the personal internal conflicts he was experiencing while containing impulses to act-out.

The therapist and Dr. C. began to explore his attachment to his parents and to his religious beliefs. While part of him rationally said it was ridiculous to limit who he could or could not love, another part of him was emotionally unable to integrate this concept. He had, in essence, an intrapsychic conflict between superego and id. He struggled with whether he should adhere to his beliefs and what he saw as his traditional values, or reject them, and with whether there might be a more complex answer, that is, finding a way to bridge differences. As Dr. C. worked through the issues of separation and individuation from his parental objects, he also began to separate his parents from his images of God. His parents became less divine and more human, while his image of God became less contaminated with distortions. Dr. C. then decided more actively to discuss these issues with clergy at his church and decided not to include his parents in his process of decision making.

Case 3

A young, recently married, Hispanic woman (Ms. E.) came to therapy with a complaint that her husband drank and continued to have sexual relations with other women. She felt powerless to do anything about this and was highly resentful, depressed, and upset. Her husband and her mother insisted that this is the nature of Hispanic men, and that women have to accommodate to this fact.

Ms. E. met her husband while employed as a secretary in a college department. He was a graduate student at the time and was considerably older than she was. Following his graduation, they dated for two years before marrying. Though they tried, and eventually sought medical advice, the couple found that they were unable to have children. This was a profound source of disappointment for them both, "a horrible punishment from God."

Although the facts of her personal history were global and somewhat sketchy, Ms. E. revealed that she was the younger child in a family of two girls. She had little to say of her relationship with her sister (two years older) except that they were very competitive. Her most difficult period was during adolescence, particularly her high school years. She "wore glasses, felt fat and ugly, and wasn't sociable" like her sister. At times, she experienced extreme despair. Her mother prayed that she would have a happy life. Her father continued to be oblivious, denying any problems within the family.

In spite of these problems, Ms. E. did well academically throughout her school years, though she described herself as feeling bored, and basically, unchallenged. It seemed that, at times, "things would get better and then they (inevitably) would get worse." She would simply "try and try again" to no real avail, leaving her feeling alone in her struggle.

In many ways Ms. E. saw herself as a martyr. She defended against the disappointments she felt in her life through detachment or rage. She felt entitled to a better life, which she tragically feared she would never have. Ms. E. felt neglected, inadequate, and depressed. The fact that her mother and her husband insisted that her husband's behavior was culturally sanctioned exacerbated her conflict, anger, and despair.

Ms. E. was seen once a week in individual psychotherapy for a little more than six months. During the early sessions, Ms. E. seemed to have great difficulty in organizing herself, feeling that the therapist placed undue and unfair pressure on her to talk about her feelings and about her self. She responded angrily without reflection or deepening and when this was interpreted to her, as her defense against her vulnerability, she replied that she felt guilty when she shared her feelings with others, and expressed resentment at having to respond to everyone's "whim."

Interventions with Ms. E. began to characteristically take the form of mirroring interpretations of her underlying vulnerability. The therapist would interpret, "I think what happened just now is that you started to focus on your feelings about not sticking up for yourself and that scared you and made you uncomfortable. When this happens, you then shift away from yourself and focus on others or on other things—in this instance focusing on me—as a way to stop these uncomfortable feelings."

Slowly Ms. E. began to explore her feelings in greater depth, saying, "I don't know what to do with my husband or my life. I always want somebody else to make me feel better about myself. I feel like I don't have a purpose in life. . . . I had a scary thought this week that maybe I married the wrong person. It's not easy to talk about this. I haven't been able to fix the problem by myself and that hurts."

To her credit, Ms. E. was able to make some progress in her six months of treatment. She left therapy feeling a little better about her life and with a resolve that she couldn't solve all of her problems completely but was working on improving things in her life. She was cautiously hopeful that she could persuade her husband to discontinue his affairs and to engage in couples work with a therapist of their mutual choice. She came to the conclusion that her husband's affairs were not acceptable to her in spite of her husband's and her mother's assertions. She saw herself as a strong Hispanic woman who embraced her culture and who was to be valued.

It is important to note that in working with this patient, the job of the therapist was not to tell the patient that she should accept what she is unhappy about. Nor was the therapist there to tell the patient that she should reject her husband's behavior. The psychotherapy here focused on exploration of what the patient was unhappy about and on what kept her from doing what she would like to do. The work of the therapy was to facilitate resolution within her and not on how she *should* respond.

In these three vignettes we see the importance of culture and beliefs as these are manifest in the individuals experience and subjective reality. This subjective reality along with the unique conflicts it engenders is the realm of foremost clinical concern. They represent the work of a psychoanalytic psychotherapy of an exploratory nature which examines the personal conflicts, struggles, symptoms, and adaptations of a given individual, couple, or family. In a culturally sensitive manner, this type of work helps patients to examine their experiences, their reactions, and their unhappiness in order for them to find ways of conducting themselves that they find gratifying and less conflictual.

Just as humans are evolving and dynamic, our theories must continue to evolve dynamically as well. We continue to work in the context of newly evolving understanding of human dynamics and the unfolding of these dynamics in the psychotherapeutic process. The work of psychotherapy in the twentieth and twenty-first century has constituted a "heroic" effort, operating under the guiding assumption that a psychotherapist should be able to treat any patient who walked in the door (Wachtel, 2000). We assumed that as long as we, as therapists, related effectively, with empathy, adequately analyzed our countertransference, and took into account different characteristics between the patient and psychotherapist, we would provide effective psychotherapy to anyone. It seems, however, that we have overestimated our abilities, and psychoanalytically oriented psychotherapies are currently undergoing a soul-searching process which will inevitably lead to modification in its theories and practice (Sanville, 2000; Wachtel).

Indeed, one might muse that this is an exciting enterprise in which through concepts, metaphors, symbols, dreams, images, and so on, we create a shared process between therapist and patient. We may, in effect, create a space that "allows us to imagine and think about polarities without collapsing the tension between them, or worse yet, reducing one to the other" (Benjamin, 1988). It is not necessary to choose between "psychological" and the "cultural," the "internal" and the "external" to tell a meaningful story (Mattei, 1999).

This movement is already underway as evidenced by increasing number of analytic journals that address the importance of issues such as the nonpathologizing of cultures and the investigation of how cultural differences influence diagnosis, intervention, and treatment. In addition, others have argued (Patterson, 1996) that by placing increasing emphasis on the interpersonal nature of the therapeutic relationship, we are coming to increasingly value the importance of individual cultural differences as well. Part of the rebirth of the practice of psychoanalytic psychotherapy in the new millennium is to continue to build new bridges in order to provide the most optimal service for patients (Sanville, 2000).

As psychotherapists and educators, we have responded to this move forward by incorporating culture sensitive training into our new curricula. In fact, early efforts to recognize and address cultural diversity in training by the American Psychology Association (APA) date back to the Vail conference in 1973. In the summary statement from this conference, cultural competence was defined as a "matter of ethical practice" and recommendations were made for cultural diversity to be included in education and training of psychologists (Abreu & Atkinson, 2000). In response, by 1980, 41 percent of clinical psychology training programs implemented at least one course in cultural diversity, although only 9 percent of the programs actually required completion of the course to graduate. A decade later the proportion of clinical psychology programs offering required courses in cultural diversity and in multiculturalism had increased to 62 percent and 26 percent respectively (Bernal & Castro, 1994, cited in Abreu & Atkinson, 2000). A similar survey, limited to APA-approved counseling psychology programs, revealed that 87 percent of its institutions offered at least one multicultural class and 59 percent mandated at least one cultural diversity class (Hills & Strozier, 1992, cited in Abreu & Atkinson, 2000).

Still, in spite of notable improvements over the past decade, graduate-level training programs have been criticized on the pragmatic basis that graduate-level counselors or therapists are no more effective than paraprofessionals with relatively little training (Christensen & Jacobson, 1994; Dawes, 1994; Humphreys, 1996; Peterson, 1995, all cited in Hanna, Bemak, & Chung, 1999). Clearly, greater specification of how cultural "templates" are to be incorporated in actual clinical work is needed. Part of the success of our success will depend on whether we choose to maintain dialogue in spite of divergent voices and differences in culture and worldviews. It is, indeed, in the appreciation of the complexity of the human psyche that we can begin to respect our uniquenesses and commonalities within the psychotherapeutic encounter.

References

Abreu, J. M., & Atkinson, D. R. (2000). Multicultural counseling training: Past, present, and future directions. *Counseling Psychologist, 28*(5), 641–656.

Allport, G. W. (1955). *Becoming, basic considerations for a psychology of personality.* New Haven, CT, London: Yale University Press.

Aponte, J.F.E., & Clifford, J. P. (1993). Incorporating ethnically diverse content and training into predominately White graduate and professional programs: Dealing with inertia and resistance. New York; Columbia University Teacher's College. (Eric Document Reproduction Service No. ED 376 235). Cited in C. C. Holcomb-McCoy, & J. E. Myers. (1999). Multicultural competence and counselor training: A national survey. *Journal of Counseling and Development, 77*(3), 294–302.

Arredondo, P. (1996). *Successful diversity management initiatives.* Thousand Oaks, CA: Sage.

Benjamin, J. (1988). Bonds of love: Psychoanalysis, feminism, and the problem of domination. New York: Pantheon. Cited in M. de Lourdes Mattei. (1999). A latina space: Ethnicity as an intersubjective third. *Smith College Studies in Social Work; Norhampton, 69*(2), 225

Bollas, C. (1987). *The shadow of the object: Psychoanalysis of the unthought known.* London: Free Association Books.

Breuer, J., & Freud, S. (1955). Studies on hysteria. London: Hogarth. Cited in Steven Piker. (1998). Contributions of psychological anthropology. *Journal of Cross-Cultural Psychology, 29*(1), 9–31.

Cheung, F. K., & Snowden, L. R. (1990). Community mental health and ethnic minority populations. *Community Mental Health Journal, 26,* 277–291. Cited in J. M. Abreu, & D. R. Atkinson. (2000). Multicultural counseling training: Past, present, and future directions. *Counseling Psychologist; College Park, 28*(5), 641–656.

Christensen, A., & Jacobson, N. S. (1994). Who (or what) can do psychotherapy: The status and challenge of nonprofessional therapies. *Psychological Sciences, 5,* 8–14.

Devereux, G. (1958). Cultural factors in psychoanalytic therapy. *Journal of the American Psychoanalytic Association, 1,* 629–655.

Di Nicola, V. (1997). *A stranger in the family: Culture, families, and therapy.* WW Norton.

Draguns, J. (1985). Psychological disorders across cultures. In P. Pedersen (Ed.), *Handbook of cross-cultural counseling and therapy* (pp. 55–62). Westport, CT: Greenwood.

Fairbairn, W.R.D. (1952). *An object relations theory of personality.* London: Tavistock.

Freud, S. (1923). *The Ego and the Id.* In Standard Edition 19: 13–66.

Geertz, C. (1998). *Local knowledge.* New York: Basic Books. Cited in Lichtman, (1998). The illusion of the true self: A critique of contemporary bourgeois psychoanalysis. *Capitalism, Nature, Socialism, 9,* 113–132.

Griffith, M. S. (1977). The influence of race on the psychotherapeutic relationship. *Psychiatry, 40*(1) 27–40.

Guntrip, H. (1968). *Schizad phenomena, object relations, and the self.* London: Hogarth Press.

Hanna, F. J., Bemak, G., & Chung, R. C. (1999). Toward a new paradigm for multicultural counseling. *Journal of Counseling and Development, 77*(2), 125–134

Ho, D.Y.F. (1995). Internalized culture, culturocentrism, and transcendence. *The Counseling Psychologist, 23*(1), 4–24. Cited in Jody L. Swartz-Kulstad & William E. Martin, Jr. (1999). Impact of culture and context on psychosocial adaptation: The cultural and contextual guide process. *Journal of Counseling and Development, 77*(3), 281–293.

Kakar, S. (1985). Psychoanalysis and non-Western cultures. *International Review of Psycho-Analysis, 12,* 441–448.

Kernberg, O. (1975). *Borderline conditions and pathological narcissism.* Northvale, NJ: Jason Aronson.

Kernberg, O. (1984a). *Object relations theory and clinical psychoanalysis.* Northvale, NJ: Jason Aronson.

Kernberg, O. (1984b). *Severe personality disorders, psychotherapeutic strategies.* New Haven, CT: Yale University Press.

Kiselica, M. S. (1998). Preparing Anglos for the challenges and joys of multiculturalism. *The Counseling Psychologist, 26,* 5–21.

Klein, M. (1930). The importance of symbol-formation in the development of the child. Cited in *Contributions to psychoanalysis 1921–1945 (The writings of Melanie Klein, vol. 2).* (1964) New York: McGraw-Hill.

Klein, M. (1952). The mutual influences in the development of ego and id. Cited in *Envy and gratitude and other works 1946–1963 (The writings of Melanie Klein, vol. 3).* (1977). New York: Delacourt Press.

Kohut, H. (1977). *The restoration of the self.* Madison, WI: International Universities Press

Korman, M. (1973). *Levels and patterns of professional training of professional training in psychology.* Paper presented at the annual meeting of the American Psychological Association, Washington, DC. Cited in J. M. Abreu & D. R. Atkinson. (2000). Multicultural counseling training: Past, present, and future directions. *Counseling Psychologist; College Park, 28*(5), 641–656.

Korzybski, A. (1933). *Science and sanity.* Chicago: International Non-Aristotelian Library.

Landrine, H. (1992). Clinical implications of cultural differences: The referential versus the indexical self. *Clinical Psychology Review, 12,* 401–415.

Lichtman, R. (1998). The illusion of the true self: A critique of contemporary bourgeois psychoanalysis. *Capitalism, Nature, Socialism 9*(3), 113–132.

Lorion, R. (1978). Research on psychotherapy and behavior change with the disadvantaged: Past, present, and future directions. In S. Garfield & A. Bergin (Eds.), *Handbook of psychotherapy and behavior change.* New York: John Wiley & Sons.

Mahler, M. S. (1971). A study of the separation-individuation process and its possible application to borderline phenomena in the psychoanalytic situation. *Psychoanalytic Study of the Child, 26,* 403–424.

Masterson, J. F. (1972). *Treatment of the borderline adolescent, a developmental approach.* New York: John Wiley & Sons.

Masterson, J. F. (1976). *Psychotherapy of the borderline adult.* New York: Brunner/Mazel.

Masterson, J. F. (1980). *From borderline adolescent to functioning adult, the test of time.* New York: Brunner/Mazel.

Masterson, J. F. (1981). *The narcissistic and borderline disorders, an integrated developmental approach.* New York: Brunner/Mazel.

Masterson, J. F. (1985). *The real self, a developmental, self, and object relations approach.* New York: Brunner/Mazel.

Masterson, J. F. (1988). *The search for the real self.* New York: The Free Press.

Masterson, J. F. (1993). *The emerging self.* New York: Brunner/Mazel.

Masterson, J. F. (2000). *The personality disorders.* Phoenix, AZ: Zeig, Tucker & Theisen.

Masterson, J. F., & Klein, R. (1989). *Psychotherapy of the disorders of the self, the Masterson approach.* New York: Brunner/Mazel.

Masterson, J. F., & Klein, R. (1995). *Disorders of the self, new therapeutic horizons.* New York: Brunner/Mazel.

Mattei, M. (1999). A Latina space: Ethnicity as an intersubjective third. *Smith College Studies in Social Work; Norhampton, 69*(2), 225.

Parloff, M., Waskow, L., & Wolfe, B. (1978). Research on therapist variables in relation to process and outcome. In S. Garfield & A. Bergin (Eds.), *Handbook of psychotherapy and behavior change.* New York: John Wiley and Sons.

Patterson, C. H. (1996). Multicultural counseling: From diversity to universality. *Journal of Counseling and Development, 74,* 227–231.

Pedersen, P. B. (1997). The cultural context of the American Counseling Association code of ethics. *Journal of Counseling and Development, 76*(1), 23–28.

Piker, S. (1998). Contributions of psychological anthropology. *Journal of Cross-Cultural Psychology, 29*(1), 9–31.

Poussaint, A. (1980). Inter racial relations and prejudice. In H. Kaplin, A. Freeman, & B. Sadock (Eds.), *Comprehensive textbook of psychiatry: Volume III.* Baltimore: Willins.

Sanville, J. B. (2000). Intracultural and intercultural dialogue in psychoanalytic psychotherapy and psychoanalysis. *Clinical Social Work, 28*(4), 417–429.

Seeley, K. M. (2000). *Cultural psychotherapy: Working with culture in the clinical encounter.* Northvale, NJ: Jason Aronson.

Shweder, R. (1991) *Thinking through cultures: Expeditions in cultural psychology.* Cambridge, MA: Harvard University Press.

Siegel, J. S. (1992). *Repairing intimacy: An object relations approach to couples therapy.* Northvale, NJ: Jason Aronson.

Sue, D. W., & Sue, D (1990). *Counseling the culturally different: Theory and practice.* New York: John Wiley & Sons. In F. J. Hanna, F. Bemak & R. Chi-Ying Chung (Eds.), *Journal of Counseling and Development, 77*(2), 125–134.

Sue, D. W., & Sue, D. (1999). *Counseling the culturally different* (3rd ed.). New York: John Wiley & Sons.

Sue, S., & Zane, N. (1987). The role of culture and cultural techniques in psychotherapy. *American Psychologist, 42*(1), 37–45.

Thompson, C. (1989) Psychoanalytic psychotherapy with inner-city patients. *Journal of Contemporary Psychotherapy, 19,* 137–148.

U. S. Bureau of the Census. (2000). Washington, DC.

Varma, V. K. (1988). Culture, personality and psychotherapy. *International Journal of Social Psychiatry, 34*(2), 142–149.

Wachtel, P. L. (2000). Psychotherapy in the twenty-first century. *American Journal of Psychotherapy, 54*(4), 441–450.

Winnicott, D. W. (1950). *Collected papers, through paediatrics to psycho-analysis.* New York: Basic Books.

Winnicott, D. W. (1965). *The maturational processes and the facilitating environment.* Madison, CT: International Universities Press.

Zosky, D. L. (1999). The application of object relations theory to domestic violence. *Clinical Social Work Journal, 27*(1), 55–69.

CHAPTER THIRTEEN

The Application of Psychoanalytic Theory and Practice to African Americans

Harriet Curtis-Boles

The importance of considering sociocultural and historical factors in understanding human nature has assumed central importance in contemporary psychological discourse. This discourse appears to be perpetuated and fueled by at least two distinct, but complementary, perspectives. The first evolves from the writings of minority psychologists and social scientists who have appreciated for many years the limitations of traditional psychological theories when applied to people of color. From the early 1900s, pioneers in this field (Billingsley, 1968; DuBois, 1903; Frazier, 1939, 1968; Hill, 1972) emphasized the importance of cultural values, socioeconomic factors and the realities of discrimination and racism in understanding the psychology and life experience of minority group peoples. In recent years with the growing diversity of our nation, this perspective has coalesced into the field of multicultural psychology represented by a range of professionals of varying ethnic backgrounds (Comas-Diaz & Griffith, 1988; Pedersen, 1985; Pinderhughes, 1989; Sue & Sue, 1990). On a separate track, there has been increasing dialogue in psychological circles on the importance of historicizing and contextualizing theory. This perspective is represented by "modern" or philosophical hermeneutics (Chessick, 1990; Cushman, 1995; Gadamer, 1975) often referred to as postmodernism and poststructuralism (Gergen, 1985). Poststructuralists admonish psychologists to consider theory in the social, cultural, and historical context in which it was created. Proponents argue that how we interpret and "see" our world is predicated upon the "customs, institutions, and language of a given culture" (Chessick) and our particular position in the social structure. Context determines experience: "reality" can vary tremendously depending upon the vantage point from which one experiences it.

Freudian theory has come under particular scrutiny from both camps because of its assumed "universal" application suggesting that it is a theory that transcends both time and circumstance, history and sociocultural conditions (Cushman, 1994; Grey, 1993; Jackson, 2000; Sue & Sue, 1990; Toews, 1991). Post-Freudian psychoanalytic theories have been equally guilty of assuming a "privileged epistemological position that transcends the exigencies of culture and politics" (Cushman, p. 802). As an African American professional I believe that there is much of value in psychoanalytic theories that can be applied across cultures and ethnicities. However, in order to remain viable and functional in a continually changing and increasingly diverse society, psychodynamic thinkers must respond to the cultural and political critique presented by minority and poststructuralist psychologists and find ways of productively addressing the issues they raise.

This chapter will address what I see as major limitations of Freudian theory and contemporary psychoanalytic thought in representing and understanding the psyche and life experience of African Americans. Framed in a White, eurocentric perspective, these theories fail to integrate into their understanding of healthy development and psychopathology an acknowledgment and appreciation for the sociocultural challenges most African Americans face, including racism and discrimination, poverty, and violence. Key African American cultural values that conflict with the Western world view and their implications for healthy functioning are ignored, resulting in a tendency to overpathologize, minimize strengths, and misinterpret the behavior and motivations of African American families and individuals.

I will begin my critique by contextualizing Freudian theory within the social and historical climate of the time, paying particular attention to Freud's position on race and ethnicity. Historians have noted that as a Jew in German Austria, Freud's life was significantly influenced by anti-Semitism, yet his theories are conspicuously lacking any direct reference to the psychological costs of minority status. Though contemporary psychoanalytic theories have departed in many ways from classical psychoanalytic thought consistent with Freudian theory, attention to ethnicity and cultural variance are missing. The result is a body of knowledge that is at best, incomplete, and at worse remiss in its treatment of African Americans.

FREUDIAN THEORY: SOCIAL AND CULTURAL CONTEXT

Freud was a revolutionary thinker in his time, departing from traditional Victorian and Darwinian notions of psychiatry to identify psychological sources and cures for "nervous disorders." Psychoanalytic theory established innovative explanations for the etiology and operation of pathological processes using the concepts of biological and psychic determinism, sexual and aggressive drives, fixation, repression, and the unconscious mind. Though clearly not a conformist (his theories of sexuality shocked the Viennese medical society), Freud viewed and interpreted the thoughts and behaviors of his clients through a lens reflecting the values and biases of his culture, historical era, and social status.

It has been written that Freud was his own, most closely studied analytic subject (Gay, 1978, 1988). By inference, it must be assumed that his theories also reflect aspects of his personal experience, both as a man and a Jew (Toews, 1991). Though a staunch assimilationist, Freud's social position and political view did not protect him from the strong anti-Semitism of German Austria. He, like other German Jews, felt the sting of racial prejudice and the stigma of being a feared and detested social minority. There are many sources of evidence of this from Freud's personal life. As an adult, Freud spoke frequently of the negative impact being Jewish had on his academic and professional career. In a quote found in Blatt (1988), Freud spoke of the disappointment he felt when he first joined the university in 1873: "I found that I was expected to feel myself inferior or an alien because I was a Jew. I refused absolutely to do the first of those things. I have never been able to see why I should feel ashamed of my descent" (pp. 646–647).

Though perhaps not ashamed of his descent, Freud was clearly concerned about the impact of his ethnicity on the acceptance of psychoanalysis. In 1908 he communicated with Jung the "indispensability" of the Aryan to the survival of his theories (Blatt, 1988). In Freud's statement was an implied recognition of the lack of power and influence of the Jewish people and himself in turn, as a member of this ethnic group. Freud feared alienating this group could result in the death of psychoanalysis or reducing it to a "Jewish affair," neither of which were acceptable to him (Gilman, 1991). On a deeper psychological level, Freud's battle to have the universality of psychoanalytic concepts recognized and accepted may have also been an attempt to defeat the racism of his times by placing all men on equal footing, driven by the same powerful instinctual drives and urges.

In a parallel existence on a different continent, as Freud was developing psychoanalytic theory, DuBois (1903) wrote about the double consciousness and duality of the American Negro. The American Negro's plight living in a world of social degradation, systematic humiliation, and active racism, was not unlike that of the German Jew. As the American Negro was "looking at himself through the eyes of others and measuring his soul by the tape of a world that held him in contempt and pity" (p. 49), many German Jews were succumbing to self-hatred and internalized racism as a result of anti-Semitism. In an atmosphere of hatred and oppression, it is not unusual for the "victim" to reject his own culture and embrace the standards and values of those in power.

The focus on the father and son relationship and identification with the aggressor in Freud's theory of the Oedipal complex, and his position on accommodating to civilization could clearly be transferred to an assimilationist view of managing racial prejudice and discrimination. Identifying with and becoming like those in authority while repressing what is innate or perhaps "instinctual" may be one way of being accepted in a racially hostile world. Becoming "German" and putting aside what was Jewish could result in acceptance and avoiding annihilation in German Vienna, as identifying with father and turning away from mother secured survival for the male child of Freud's Oedipal theory. It should be noted here that annihilation and genocide have been critical themes in the history of the Jews. From the days of the religious wars through the pogroms of the twentieth century, loss of life has closely followed upon the heels of persecution. The themes of annihilation and identification with the aggressor represented in the Oedipal complex may have sources in Freud's "ethnic unconscious" and remnants of memories of these events. Herron (1995) defines the ethnic unconscious as "repressed material shared by each generation with the next and with most people of that ethnic group" (p. 521). Repressed fears and age-old feelings of vulnerability may have played a part in Freud's authoritarian solution to the Oedipal complex. The father has the capacity to destroy but can also protect. Wish-fulfilling fantasies of safety may be found in identification and conformity. Though, interestingly enough, no references are made in Freudian psychoanalysis to the psychological consequences of the ethnic minority experience, Freud's living of this experience may have influenced both the centrality of and his choice of healthy response to the Oedipal dilemma.

PSYCHOANALYTIC THEORY AND THE AFRICAN AMERICAN EXPERIENCE

This section will explore the relevance of the Oedipal Complex to African Americans.

African Americans and The Oedipal Complex

Though biological determinism plays a critical role in classical psychoanalytic thought, Freud was one of the first to recognize and articulate the importance of relationships in early childhood to psychological health and development. The Oedipus complex integrates Freudian drive theory with the concepts of attachment and identification. Its general relevance lies in the significance it places upon the parent and child relationship to the developing self as an emotional, psychological, and gendered being as well as in its characterization of the

Errata

Figure 21.1 was omitted and inadvertently referred to as Table 21.1 on page 309. Figure 21.1 (below) depicts the sequence of events that influence White ethnic American students' emotional reactions to the mandatory race relations course. (See second paragraph on page 309.)

Figure 21.1 A Heuristic Model of the Consequences of Different Emotion Management Strategies in Responses to Mandatory Diversity Training.

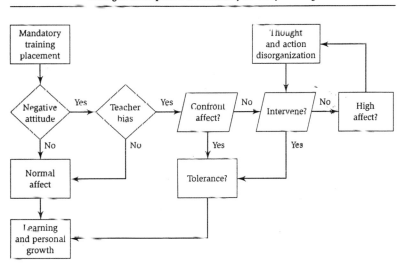

intense and ambivalent nature of these early attachments. Among its limitations is the exclusive focus on the traditional, nuclear family that makes no allowance for alternative concepts of family and how healthy individuals can develop from these familial structures. As a result, African Americans whose families do not fit the traditional model have frequently been pathologized or regarded as deviant by contemporary psychoanalytic thinkers.

The extended family is an important African American cultural tradition operating from the values of interdependence and interconnectedness. These values evolve from fundamental African-based beliefs such as "I am because we are" and "it takes a whole village to raise a child" and have significant philosophical and practical implications. Among these are: self is defined in connection to others and child-rearing occurs in an intimately woven multigenerational and community system. This means that for many African American children, whether in two-parent or single-parent homes, grandparents, aunts, uncles, and fictive kin play significant roles in their upbringing. The normative nature of this family structure in the African American community requires a reconceptualization of Freud's Oedipal complex to identify ways in which extended family influence normal child development.

Recent years have seen a rapid increase in single-parent families. According to the 2000 U.S. Census, 45.1 percent of African American children under the age of eighteen live in female-headed, single-parent households. Reactions to this matrifocal family pattern has ranged from alarm, as evidenced in Moynihan's (1965) depiction of the Black female headed household as emasculating, disorganized, and unstable; to studied concern with psychologists in recent years seeking to identify protective factors in the family and community which support positive growth (Bowman & Howard, 1985; Hill, 1999; Taylor, Chatters, Tucker, & Lewis, 1990). Supportive involvement of extended kin has been one of the most consistent protective factors identified in the research literature. In fact this cultural pattern has been repeatedly lauded as a key contributor to the resilience of African American families from slavery to present times (Boyd-Franklin & Franklin, 2000; Genero, 1998; McAdoo, 1998). A traditional psychoanalytic interpretation of the consequences of being raised in a single-parent family would likely include concerns about the identity development, relational skills, and self-regulating abilities of the developing child. The Oedipal complex as scripted by Freud, renders the male child particularly vulnerable to negative psychological consequences when the father is absent.

For children across cultures, the first and primary attachment is to mothering figures who nurture and provide for the infant's dependency needs. In African American culture though the task of mothering may be shared, by the time a child is entering the Oedipal period (three- or four-years-old), a primary maternal figure has typically been identified through a combination of distinct emotional and psychological experiences and social traditions. Unless the biological mother has been absent or sporadically present during the pre-Oedipal years (due for example, to illness or substance abuse), she becomes the cathectic object of the Oedipal struggle. In redefining the role of the Oedipal complex in female development, feminist psychoanalysts (Chodorow, 1989) have normalized the girls' continuing attachment and dependence on the mother, but it is still generally assumed that in order for healthy development to occur for boys, the attachment to mother must be modified with an accompanying shift in primary identification to the father. African American social scientists have emphasized that the active involvement of a positive father figure is particularly critical for the identity and personality development of African American boys given negative societal projections, discrimination, and racism (Boyd-Franklin & Franklin, 2000; Kunjufu, 1995). How then does this important shift to a significant male figure occur for African American boys raised in single, female parent homes? African American mothers are very aware that they need male involvement in raising their sons. In many instances the extended family structure affords significant interactions with males—grandfathers, uncles, an older brother, and play dads—throughout the child's life that form "father" relationships. In other instances, mothers will seek out and cultivate relationships with male figures for their sons at significant marker points in their development. It is through identification and attachment to these significant males and the socialization process that many African American boys learn what it means to be "a man." A case example illustrates these points: Mr. M., a forty-five-year-old African American man came into treatment following the death of his mother. He described his mother as a "pillar of strength" and someone who was always there for him. Her death had resulted in profound feelings of loss and sadness and rekindled unresolved anger at his father for his "peripheral involvement" in his life. Mr. M. was raised for most of his life by his mother. His mother and father divorced when he was two-years-old. Between the ages of three and nine years, he lived with his mother and younger sister in an extended household with his grandparents. His father was consistently, though distantly, involved in his life through weekly visits spent at the paternal grandmother's home. He described his mother as a determined and strong woman who after completing her nursing degree established a separate home for him and his younger sister. She instilled the importance of an education, a "fighting spirit" and strong belief in God as keys to success in life. As a child he had regular household chores and was given the task of watching over his sister, which he felt taught him responsibility at an early age. He had a special relationship with his grandfather who took him to baseball games, came to his track meets and "kept him in line" as a teenager. He stated it was his grandfather and not his father who he looked to as the "kind of man" he wanted to be when he grew up. Mr. M. worked as a successful lawyer and was a good father and husband with two daughters in college. This man was a healthy and successful product of a female, single-parent family supported by extended kin. In addition to the values instilled in him by his mother, he was able to draw upon his relationship with his grandfather in establishing a stable self identity, internalizing the masculine role and establishing socially appropriate mechanisms of self-regulation and control.

Negative consequences may result when there are no extended family supports to assist the single African American mother in raising her male child. A case was reported in a group consultation of a nine-year-old African American boy who was brought into treatment by his mother because of problems in school. J. was described as aggressive and disruptive, getting into frequent fights with peers. In contrast, his mother reported that although he occasionally misbehaved, he was not a problem at home. J.'s parents never married and he had had very little contact with his father since birth. There was a short period in his life when his father called and would promise to come visit him but never followed through. His mother asked that he stop calling if he was going to continue to disappoint J., and the father rarely called after this request. Though J.'s mother had lived in California for thirteen years, she reported having no friends and had not been in a relationship with a man since J.'s birth. J. and his mother lacked extended family support since all of her family lived in Florida. Though she described her relationship with her family as "close," she and J. had not seen them for four years. She left Florida at the age of twenty-three to escape a "traumatic relationship" with a man she was engaged to marry. His mother volunteered at the school daily, while J. was a kindergartner, because of his difficulties with separation. After this first year his problems at school escalated. J. isolated himself from peers with his aggressive behavior and was alternately "charming and manipulative" and disrespectful to his teachers, cursing them when he did not get what he wanted. The therapist reported that the mother alternated between treating J. like an adult or "spouse" and a child. In her isolation, the child was the mother's sole source of companionship and she relied inappropriately on him to meet her emotional needs. Her dependence on his emotional availability resulted in inconsistent discipline and limit setting. Throughout his life, J. and his mother had operated as an isolated unit, threatened by intrusion from the outside world.

J.'s emotional investment in one love object combined with fear of abandonment introduced by the early "loss" of his father and his mother's inappropriate emeshment with him, produced a child with blurred interpersonal boundaries, poor social skills and impulse control, and an idiosyncratic sense of good and bad. The outside world was treated as an unwanted intrusion on his relationship with his mother at the same time that this exclusiveness threatened his natural need for individuation and separate identity development. The absence of J.'s father or other caring male parenting figures during the Oedipal phase of his life resulted in the internalization of a distorted and limited understanding of what it meant to be male, heavily influenced by J.'s unhealthy relationship with his mother. The involvement of an extended family in this child's life could have provided the needed support and emotional supplies that both J. *and* his mother lacked and a male role model for J., allowing for healthier development. For many African American males from the inner cities, the absence of such supports results in negative role models being drawn from the streets; gang members or drug dealers whose power and sense of masculinity spring from a culture of violence and victimization. Without a strong intervening influence, many of these boys grow up to be like the males they emulate; angry, and violent, physically and psychologically at risk.

Oedipal themes and dynamics frequently appear in their more traditional form in two-parent African American families, but an active and involved extended family will still have an important influence. It is not atypical for an African American child in this type of family structure to spend intensive and extended time in the homes of their grandparents or "aunties" with these family members having the parent's explicit approval to "parent" the child in their absence. This approval involves permission to teach, love, and discipline this child as they would their own. At six-years-old my daughter would frequently say she had "three homes"; ours, her grandparents' and her aunt's. Children raised in this manner have significant attachments to multiple family members and can draw upon all these individuals for nurturance, identification, and modeling. Feminist psychoanalytic writers (Chodorow, 1989; Jordan, Surrey, & Kaplan, 1991) have suggested that because fathers are more involved in work and other activities out of the home, a child's identification and relationship with the father must be mediated by abstract or role-defined behaviors. The African American child whose relationship with his or her father is supplemented by close and involved male relatives will have other real-life attachments to model and practice appropriate gender behavior and as significant supports and love objects. Other extended family members are similarly available to provide emotional supplies and to cushion losses or psychological wounds incurred in the primary parent and child relationship.

Contemporary Psychoanalysis

Contemporary psychoanalytic theories are numerous and varied and include the interpersonal psychoanalysis of Sullivan (1953); the work of Klein (1953); ego psychology (Hartmann, 1958; Jacobson, 1964; Mahler, 1975); object relations theories (Fairbairn, 1962; Kernberg, 1975; Winnicott, 1965); and self-psychology (Kohut, 1971, 1977). Most of these theories have abandoned the classical Freudian drive model with its emphasis on "biology as destiny" and emphasize relational, environmental factors in understanding healthy development and psychopathology focusing on the mother and child bond. Given the diversity of contemporary psychoanalytic thought, this critique will focus on some strengths and weaknesses of object relations theories as a psychology for African Americans.

Object relations theory addresses how the self is constructed and reconstructed through relational experience over the lifetime. From a developmental perspective, though the focus is on early object relations and pre-Oedipal experience, in principle this theory allows for the consideration of not only interpersonal histories but also interactions with social and cultural institutions as they are internalized in the construction of the self. Because development is not strictly scripted as in the Oedipal complex of Freudian theory, but grounded in historical, individual experience; gender, ethnic, and cultural variations in the content of self stories are expected (Chodorow, 1989). Though autonomy and self-boundedness remain significant markers of the mature individual, the emphasis on human connection renders this theory more compatible with the African American cultural world view that values interdependence and "we-ness" over the traditional Western values of individuality, competition, and separateness. Unfortunately in its traditional presentation, the narrow scope of experience explicitly addressed in object relations theory, invites pathologizing critical aspects of the African American experience and missing the larger sociocultural context. I will address two implied assumptions in object relations theories that are problematic in representing African American development.

Object relations theories identify the central function of the mother or primary parenting figure in the early childhood years as protecting the child from noxious and potentially traumatic experiences that could derail the developmental process. The mother accomplishes this by accurately and consistently providing for the physical and psychological needs of the child. It is assumed that failures to do so are a result of parental pathology or inadequacy and that the mother has the ability to control and manage the child's environment. This position fails to take into account real life circumstances that impinge upon African American families that the parent often can't control. Many authors (Kotlowitz, 1998; McAdoo, 1998) have described the plight of Black families living under poverty conditions. Substandard housing, poor nutrition, and inadequate health care render the children in these families vulnerable to health problems that can interfere with their emotional and psychological development. Inner-city violence and the struggles of daily survival can maximize stress and overtax parental resources. Genero (1998) commented that amidst these negative realities simply attending to the tasks of daily living is "an extraordinary achievement" (p. 32). An individual who is a model of psychological health and fully capable of responding emotionally to the needs of their child might falter under such circumstances. A theory that focuses on the individual pathology of the parent as the source of childhood, and, consequently adult dysfunction, while overlooking the contribution of external obstacles and institutional failures, serves to perpetuate the victimization and oppression of African

American people. An integrated approach taking into consideration the impact on development of both parental characteristics and broader environmental challenges is necessary to understand and effectively intervene with African American families and individuals suffering psychological distress. A theory of healthy development for African Americans must also consider the central role of survival and adaptation and parents' responsibility to prepare their children to live with racism and discrimination. This requires skills in flexibility, anger management, social attunement and self-preservation that are typically unnecessary for individuals in the majority culture. Some of these skills may even be regarded as dysfunctional by majority culture standards and the tactics that parents utilize to instill these skills, harsh and punitive. For example, African Americans parents often require strict obedience from children and demonstrate limited tolerance for open disagreement and "discussion" of parenting demands. Many African American parents believe that this instills "proper respect for authority" which is an important survival tool in a society that has demonstrated historical hostility and intolerance of its members. It is important that the appropriateness and value of these types of skills and parenting behaviors be recognized, understood within a cultural context, and integrated into theories of healthy development.

There is also an assumption in object relations theories that healthy parenting in the formative years is sufficient to instill the child with internal stability, self-esteem and goal directedness that will be carried into adulthood. I support the foundational importance of healthy parenting in the development of all children. What is not addressed here, are the far-reaching and destructive consequences of chronic and unrelenting racism on mental health and well-being. Too many African Americans, loved and cherished in their families, face insults and injuries in the world that can cripple them emotionally and extinguish hopes and dreams. Institutional racism, manifest in such things as inequality in education, employment, and the legal justice system can be more injurious than individual racist attacks on personal worth and integrity. Children often observe the effects of racism in their parents' lives before they experience it themselves. Combined these experiences can result in individuals who are bitter, angry, depressed and hopeless and reject the American dream as a false bag of goods.

Racism and Discrimination

It is an acknowledged fact that racism and discrimination are crucial factors in shaping the lives of African Americans. Statistics on unemployment and underemployment, rates of incarceration, poverty, and special education tracking bear witness to the impact of these factors in the African American community. The psychological effects of the legacy of slavery and the distinctive history of African

Americans in the United States are not as visible, but no less profound. Growing up Black in the United States is different from growing up White in the United States, a difference that crosses educational and socioeconomic boundaries. From the perspective of personal history and contemporary circumstances, racism is part of the everyday present and past experiences of the African American. Discussions of racism in ethnically mixed settings are often stimulated by precipitating events like the Million Man March, the O. J. Simpson trial, a racial slur or insensitive, oppressive comment. For African Americans these single events often trigger a string of memories and recollections, all punctuated by vivid images and painful emotions. These recollections typically include concrete examples of when our humanity and personhood were diminished and devalued by experiences like being called "nigger," instances of our opinions being dismissed or met with suspicion or being made invisible or alternately an example because of our race. At the same time ancestral history resonates with lived insults. There is a place in the African American consciousness, whether immediate or more distantly present, that recalls the enslavement of our forefathers, the lynching of innocent Black men and women, the Black Codes of the late 1800s and the "separate, but equal" of Jim Crowism. Other memories too painful to recall remain locked in our unconscious and may leave permanent wounds on our psyche.

Until recent years psychoanalytic theories and practice have been virtually silent on issues of race and racism. As previously indicated, Freud was no stranger to racism, but for reasons not fully understood, he chose not to integrate an examination of the psychological effects of racial prejudice, victimization, and oppression into psychoanalytic theory. Power dynamics, issues of authority and competition were examined from an individualistic perspective, principally within the context of family and societal strictures without consideration to ethnicity. Contemporary psychoanalytic thinkers (Dimen, 2000; Leary, 2000) have acknowledged that attention to race and racism has historically been missing from psychoanalytic dialogues and some have begun to address this void by writing about the impact of these factors on their clinical practice. Acknowledging that the clinical relationship in the United States is embedded in a history of racial atrocities and a social structure that supports racial inequities, many of these writings have focused on transference and counter-transference dynamics (Altman, 2000; Elliot, 1996; Leary, 2000). Directives regarding the management of racial elements in the treatment that have appeared in the writings of social scientists of color for many years (Greene, 1985; Ridley, 1995; Sue & Sue, 1990, 1999) are now being given voice by psychoanalysts. These directives include the importance of acknowledging that racism exists, understanding that racial elements are pre-scripted into the therapy relationship because of the history of race relations in this country and that the therapist must examine and attend to her own racism and how it operates in the treatment. As previously addressed concerns have indicated, attention to racial dynamics in the relational aspects of treatment is an important, but insufficient step in making psychoanalytic theory and practice viable for African Americans.

Religion

One final point about psychoanalysis and its application to African Americans concerns its position on religion. Freud was an avowed atheist and saw religion as an illusion used in the service of civilization to contain the natural instincts of man. The anti-Semitic oppression from which he suffered (approved by the state and the church), the consequent ethnic group identity conflicts with which he struggled, and his general ignorance of Jewish tradition, probably contributed to this ideological position. In his essay "The Future of an Illusion," Freud identified the church and God with the protective and punishing father and asserted that religion was used to distract man from the pain inherent in living and the helplessness of the human condition. Religion is a significant and integral part of the cultural terrain of many African Americans. Research has shown that faith, religious belief, and prayer are primary sources of coping with life problems for many Black people, and that being a part of a "church family" serves multiple supportive and practical functions (Boyd-Franklin, 1989; Ramseur, 1991; Taylor, Mattis, & Chatters, 1999). A clinician trained in a traditional psychodynamic perspective might tend to place religion and religious practice in the category of defense and see it as a maladaptive and ineffective method of dealing with problems that are intrapsychic in nature. Even those with an appreciation for faith and religion are not trained to know how to "talk about" and help the client to utilize this belief system to their advantage. African American clients whose relationship with God is a primary and focal aspect of their lives will be quickly alienated by a therapist who is unable to "hear" and take in this aspect of their life experience. These clients would be even more distanced by a therapist who attempts to interpret or "categorize" their faith in the context of such dynamics as avoidance, externalization, and denial. The therapist must appreciate and accept clients within the context of their cultural worlds and belief systems. An awareness and respect for the client's religious beliefs and practices can be communicated in multiply ways. During history taking the client could be asked about religious and spiritual influences in their upbringing including whether they attended church, what were the religious practices of their family and what role, if any, religion plays in their current life. It is also important to determine if and under what circumstances the client uses her faith practices to manage life problems. Inquiring about these issues both invites and grants permission to the client to discuss spiritual concerns in treatment.

CLINICAL IMPLICATIONS

Since its inception, psychoanalytic theory has been used to develop and inform treatment strategies to relieve psychological pain. It has too often happened in practice that psychoanalytically oriented therapists avoid seeing and understanding the myriad consequences of racism and discrimination for the African American client and fail to situate the client within his cultural context. These omissions are typically shaped not only by theoretical orientation, but also by the particular world view and life experience of the therapist. A clinical example will illustrate this point. A white female therapist sought my consultation in working with a ten-year-old African American boy and his mother who was a single parent. This therapist described herself as psychodynamically oriented and worked in play therapy with the child with collateral sessions with the mother. Though she reported the sessions with the child as going well, she found it very difficult to work with the mother. She described the mother as angry, impulsive, and too preoccupied with her own problems to be sensitive to her son's needs. In speaking independently with staff at the child's school, the therapist had determined that the mother was sabotaging her son's hopes of success at his new school by her "aggressive and out of control behavior" with school officials. When encouraged to explore this mother's history and current experience further, the therapist, knowing that the family lived in a neighborhood wrought with violence, discovered that this mother drove her children everywhere and never let them leave their building without being accompanied by her, that the mother was actively struggling with the housing authority to get more suitable housing for herself and her four children, and that as a child this mother had to "fight off" the attentions of her step-father who tried to molest her. This mother's experience of life was that it is often unsafe and threatening and that you had to "fight" to survive. When the therapist shared with me that an Individual Educational Planning meeting (IEP) had been scheduled for her ten-year-old client at his school, I suggested she speak with the mother about attending with her to provide support and advocacy for the child. The therapist returned from this meeting appalled at the manner in which this group of White teachers and administrators dealt with this mother describing a situation where the mother's attempts to speak for her child were either ignored or discredited. In contrast, her voice as a White professional was heard where the mother's was not. The therapist reported that this meeting clued her in to the "insensitivity and bias" with which this institution responded to this mother. Prior to this firsthand experience, the therapist had attributed the mother's ineffectiveness with the school solely to her "angry and unreasonable" nature.

It is essential in understanding and clinically intervening with African Americans that the impact of racism, discrimination and color prejudice be addressed. A theoretical or clinical orientation that does not take these factors into account risks distortion and misinterpretation by minimizing the ways in which social, political and economic factors impinge upon the mental health, psychological well-being and coping styles of Black people. Freud's "laboratory" did not give him access to these observations and few contemporary psycho-dynamic thinkers have paid attention to the particular life experiences that shape the psyche of the African American.

It is not uncommon for African American clients to find themselves in treatment with well-meaning, caring, and bright therapists who view and evaluate their lives within a rigid, stereotypically applied perspective that does not take into account the client's everyday experiences. This everyday reality can include racism, poverty, intrusion by multiple bureaucracies, anger, helplessness, and powerlessness. Intrapsychic explanations for these feelings minimize the political and social plight of African American people. Being ignorant to the importance of race in the development and daily life of African Americans is an invalidation of who we are as a people. Rigid adherence to a theoretical orientation without taking into consideration a client's cultural context and real life experiences can result in "missing" the big picture. Theory strongly influences how psychotherapists interpret the world. If therapists are not aware of the biases and limitations inherent in these theories, they risk seeing only what they expect and want to see. Freud cannot be severely faulted for the limitations of psychoanalytic theory when applied to African Americans because as was mentioned earlier, his observations were neither based on or directed to people of African descent. But those who live in a world where manifestations of racism and prejudice are readily visible are clearly remiss and responsible when these factors are not accounted for in our understanding of and work with people of color.

CONCLUSIONS

To be a legitimate paradigm for African American development, psychoanalytic theory must transcend the cocoon of the middle-class White world and acknowledge, study, and integrate other realities. Today's psychologist and practitioner must consider cultural variations in values, world view, history, and life experience. Particularly salient in working with Minority clients is an acknowledgment and understanding of the operation of prejudice and racism. Such an understanding requires a shift from an exclusively intrapsychic and individual focus to include an understanding of institutional and systemic factors. These factors have the potential of both enhancing and impeding an individual's development and successful functioning.

References

Altman, N. (2000). Black and white thinking: A psychoanalyst reconsiders race. *Psychoanalytic Dialogues, 10*(4), 589–605.

Billingsley, A. (1968). *Black families in white America.* Englewood Cliffs, NJ: Prentice Hall.

Blatt, D. S. (1988). The development of the hero: Sigmund Freud and the reformation of the Jewish tradition. *Psychoanalysis and Contemporary Thought, 11*(4), 639–704.

Boyd-Franklin, N. (1989). *Black families in therapy: A multisystems approach.* New York: Guilford Press.

Boyd-Franklin, N., & Franklin, A. J. (2000). *Boys into men: Raising our African American teenage sons.* New York: Penguin Books.

Bowman, P. J., & Howard, C. (1985). Race socialization, motivation and academic achievement: A study of black youths in three-generation families. *Journal of the American Academy of Child Psychiatry, 24,* 134–141.

Chessick, R. (1990). Hermeneutics for psychologists. *American Journal of Psychotherapy, 64*(2), 256–273.

Chodorow, N. (1989). *Feminism and psychoanalytic theory.* New Haven, CT: Yale University Press.

Comas-Diaz, L., & Griffith, E. (1988). *Clinical guideline in cross-cultural mental health.* New York: John Wiley & Sons.

Cushman, P. (1994). Confronting Sullivan's spider: Hermeneutics and the politics of therapy. *Contemporary Psychoanalysis, 30*(4), 800–844.

Cushman, P. (1995). *Constructing the self, constructing America.* Reading, MA: Addison-Wesley.

Dimen, M. (2000). Introduction. *Psychoanalytic Dialogues, 10*(4), 569–578.

DuBois, W.E.B. (1903). *The souls of Black folk.* Chicago: McClurg Press.

DuBois, W.E.B. (1908). *The Negro American family.* Chicago: McClurg Press.

Elliot, P. (1996). Working through racism: Confronting the strangely familiar. *Journal of Psychoanalytic Culture and Society, 1,* 63–72.

Fairbairn, W. (1962). *An object relations theory of the personality.* New York: Basic Books.

Frazier, F. (1939). *The Negro family in the United States.* Chicago: University of Chicago Press.

Frazier, F. (1968). *On race relations.* Chicago: University of Chicago Press.

Freud, S. (1927). The future of an illusion. In P. Gay (Ed.), *The Freud reader, 1989* (pp. 685–721). New York: Norton.

Gadamer, H. (1975). *Truth and method.* New York: Continuum.

Gay, P. (1978). *Freud, Jews and other Germans: Masters and victims in modernist culture.* New York: Norton.

Gay, P. (1988). *Freud: A life for our time.* New York: Norton.

Genero, N. (1998). Culture, resiliency and mutual psychological development. In H. Mc Cubbin, E. Thompson, A. Thompson, & J. Futrell (Eds.), *Resiliency in African-American families* (pp. 31–48). Thousand Oaks, CA: Sage.

Gergen, K. J. (1985). The social constructionist movement in modern psychology. *American Psychologist, 40*(3), 266–273.

Gilman, S. L. (1991). *The Jew's body.* New York: Routledge.

Greene, B. A. (1985). Considerations in the treatment of Black patients by White therapists. *Psychotherapy, 22,* 389–393.

Grey, C. C. (1993). Culture, character and the analytic engagement: Toward a subversive psychoanalysis. *Contemporary Psychoanalysis, 29*(3), 487–502.

Hartmann, H. (1958). *Ego psychology and the problem of adaptation.* New York: International University Press.

Herron, W. (1995). Development of the ethnic unconscious. *Psychoanalytic Psychology, 12*(4), 521–532.

Hill, R. (1972). *The strengths of Black families.* New York: Emerson-Hill.

Hill, S. A. (1999). *African American children: Socialization and development in families.* Thousand Oaks, CA: Sage.

Jackson, L. (2000). The new multiculturalism and psychodynamic theory: Psychodynamic psychotherapy and African-American women. In L. Jackson & B. Greene (Eds.), *Psychotherapy with African-American women: Innovations in psychodynamic perspectives and practice* (pp. 1–14). New York: Guilford Press.

Jacobson, E. (1964). *The self and the object world.* New York: International Universities Press.

Jordan, J., Surrey, J., & Kaplan, A. (1991). Women and empathy: Implications for psychological development and psychotherapy. In J. Jordan, A. Kaplan, J. B. Miller, I. Stiver, & J. Surrey (Eds.), *Women's growth in connection* (pp. 27–51). New York: Guilford Press.

Kernberg, O. F. (1975). *Borderline conditions and pathological narcissism.* New York: Aronson.

Klein, M. (1953). *Love, hate and reparation with Joan Riviere.* London: Hogarth.

Kohut, H. (1971). *The analysis of the self.* New York: International Universities Press.

Kohut, H. (1977). *The restoration of the self.* New York: International Universities Press.

Kotlowitz, A. (1998). Breaking the silence: Growing up in today's inner city. In H. Mc Cubbin, E. Thompson, A. Thompson, & J. Futrell (Eds.), *Resiliency in African-American families* (pp. 3–16). Thousand Oaks, CA: Sage.

Kunjufu, J. (1995). *Countering the conspiracy to destroy Black boys* (Vol. 4). Chicago: African-American Images.

Leary, K. (2000). Racial enactments in dynamic treatment. *Psychoanalytic Dialogues, 10*(4), 639–653.

Mahler, M. (1975). *The psychological birth of the human infant.* New York: Basic Books.

McAdoo, H. P. (1998). African-American families: Strengths and realities. In H. Mc Cubbin, E. Thompson, A. Thompson, & J. Futrell (Eds.), *Resiliency in African-American families* (pp. 17–30). Thousand Oaks, CA: Sage.

Moynihan, D. P. (1965). Employment, income and the ordeal of the Negro family. *Daedalus,* 745–770.

Pedersen, P. (Ed.). (1985). *Handbook of cross-cultural counseling and therapy.* New York: Praeger.

Pinderhughes, E. (1989). *Understanding race, ethnicity and power: The key to efficacy in clinical practice.* Ontario: Free Press.

Ramseur, H. P. (1991). Psychologically healthy Black adults. In R. Jones (Ed.), *Black psychology.* Berkeley, CA: Cobb & Henry.

Ridley, C. R. (1995). Overcoming unintentional racism in counseling and therapy: A practitioner's guide to intentional intervention. Thousand Oaks, CA: Sage.

Sue, D. W., & Sue, D. (1990). *Counseling the culturally different: Theory and practice* (2nd ed.). New York: John Wiley & Sons.

Sue, D. W., & Sue, D. (1999). *Counseling the culturally different: Theory and practice* (3rd ed.). New York: John Wiley & Sons.

Sullivan, H. S. (1953). *The interpersonal theory of psychiatry.* New York: Norton.

Taylor, R. J., Chatters, L. M., Tucker, M. B., & Lewis, E. (1990). Developments in research on black families: A decade review. *Journal of Marriage and Family, 52,* 993–1014.

Taylor, R. J., Mattis, J., & Chatters, L. (1999). Subjective religiosity among African-Americans: A synthesis of findings from five national samples. *Journal of Black Psychology, 25*(4), 524–543.

Toews, J. (1991). Historicizing psychoanalysis: Freud in his time for our time. *Journal of Modern History, 63,* 504–545.

U. S. Bureau of the Census. (2000). Washington, DC.

Winnicott, D. (1965). *The maturational process and the facilitating environment.* New York: International Universities Press.

CHAPTER FOURTEEN

Caught Between Cultures

The Young Asian American in Therapy

William W. Chien and Leena Banerjee

There is a generation of young Asian Americans today who may be foreign born or American born, who may be the only ones over fourteen in their families who speak English well and have thus negotiated a life between the ethnic language culture and linguistic isolation of their families on the one hand, and their English speaking, Euro-American educational and work environments on the other. The U.S. Surgeon General (2001) reports that there are 35 percent Asian American households that live in linguistic isolation, a percentage that rises to 52 percent for Laotian Americans and 61 percent for Hmong Americans. Insofar as language is a key vehicle of culture, there are still others who live or have grown up in bilingual families who are experiencing the conflicts inherent between the culture of the home, family, and ethnic group and the culture of the larger community and media. In many cases, they are the first generation within their families to be dealing with the task of integrating two cultures within their identities and their families (Panat & Banerjee, 1994). In addition to these intergenerational and intercultural stresses, there are those associated with experiences of racism, which in turn, can impact their identity development (Alvarez & Helms, 2001).

At the societal level, the passage of multiculturalism to the mainstream remains slow and so long as the mainstream is not struggling to own and integrate its diversity beyond the level of appearance at the deeper level of values, these psychological and cultural conflicts remain the special burdens of subgroups like young Asian Americans and their families (Banerjee, 2001). This group—who has spent most, if not all, of childhood in the United States—is made up of Asian Americans who have faced multifaceted cultural conflicts, which produce risks for their mental health and well-being. These risks are the focus of this chapter. This group may also be the most likely consumer of psychotherapy or be instrumental in introducing their families to psychotherapy. Thus, it is assumed that their primary clinical concerns will extend beyond the conflicts and challenges inherent in immigrant or refugee experiences and conditions such as posttraumatic stress disorder, adjustment disorders, and poverty resulting from them. Some of the more common presenting problems for this group of focus in this chapter include: parent-child conflicts with frequent complaints of parents being too overbearing or controlling; guilt and shame over career choices that don't correspond to parental expectations, embarrassment and misunderstanding regarding sexual or social behavior, and somatization of emotional conflicts. Clinical suggestions will be geared primarily toward individual therapy with some discussion of issues pertinent in family therapy.

Conceptual schemas have been used to categorize the different ways in which individuals in this group deal with this risk factor of cultural conflict. The traditionalist (Sue & Sue, 1971) is similar to the dissociator (Hutnik, 1991; Panat & Banerjee, 1994) who identifies strongly with the ethnic group and minimally with the majority group. The over-westernized (Sue & Sue) is similar to the assimilator (Hutnik; Panat & Banerjee) who strongly identifies with the majority group and rejects ties to the ethnic group. The marginal (Hutnik; Panat & Banerjee) chooses a low identification with both the ethnic and the majority cultures. The acculturator (Hutnik; Panat & Banerjee) seeks to strike a balance between ethnic and majority culture identifications and may choose the label Asian American; whereas the radical (Sue & Sue), a more militant relative of the acculturator, may go further and make concerns of poverty, unemployment, racism, and juvenile delinquency a focus of their life with the aim of exposing and changing discrimination towards Asian Americans. The family of acculturative stances has generally been recognized to be those most often associated with overall well-being. New research (Tsai, Ying, & Lee, 2001) with Chinese Americans indicates that orientation to ethnic culture significantly predicts self-esteem above and beyond the contributions of age, gender, grade point average, and socioeconomic status. Further, there appear to be gender differences such as the emotional domain of pride in culture being associated with self-esteem in females and the nonemotional domain of cultural orientation and bilingual proficiency being associated with self-esteem in males.

THE LARGER CULTURAL CONTEXT

Asian Americans comprise a diverse and fast-growing group of ten-million strong who are from about forty-three different ethnicities and presently comprise 4 percent of the U.S. population (U.S. Census Bureau, 2000). The communities share ties and common philosophical influences such as those of the Confucius doctrine, the Vedas, and others, as well as collectivist orientation to human development and social functioning. They also share resiliencies in the form of family cohesion, educational achievement, motivation for upward mobility, and the willingness for hard work (U.S. Surgeon General's Report, 2001). At the same time there are over one hundred different languages and dialects, distinct premigration national histories and identities, and migration motives that range from fleeing political persecution and mass traumatization to seeking economic and professional betterment. Add to these intra-ethnic differences, levels of acculturation, generational status, religious affiliation, socioeconomic status, and sexual identity and one begins to appreciate how diverse this group really is.

The "model minority" (Chan, 1991) myth is easily challenged by even a casual glance at subgroup differences for Asian Americans, which are pronounced on virtually every dimension. Average family size for Asian Americans is 3.8, slightly higher than the size for all Americans which is 3.2 although the fertility rates of Chinese and Japanese American women are falling below the replacement level of 2.1 (U.S. Census Bureau, 1990). The Surgeon General (2001) reports that 75 percent of Asian Americans live in "family households" with the rate of female-headed households ranging from 13 percent for Indian, Chinese, and Korean Americans to 18 percent for Southeast Asians. Forty-four percent of Asian Americans receive college educations as compared to 28 percent Euro-Americans. However, within the group this ranges from 58 percent for South Asians to 32 percent for Hmong Americans, and 26 percent for Laotian Americans (U.S. Census Bureau, 2001). Family income for Asian Americans tends to be higher than the national average, but the income distribution is bimodal with 33 percent Asian Americans enjoying incomes above $75,000 compared to 29 percent nonHispanic White Americans, 43 percent Cambodian Americans, and 64 percent Hmong Americans suffering from poverty (U.S. Surgeon General's Report).

The freshly released supplement to Surgeon General's Report (2001) indicates that our knowledge of Asian American mental health needs is very limited. At the same time, Asian Americans as a group are rapidly increasing in size due to immigration. It is projected that by the year 2020, there will be twenty million Asian Americans who will comprise 6 percent of the population. The knowledge that we do have comes from research on Chinese, Japanese, and Southeast Asian groups to the neglect of other subgroups. Available information indicates prevalence rates for mental illness to be no different from other Americans, though the distribution of specific syndromes may be different, such as, elevated levels of depression (Miu, 1996; Patel & Gaw, 1996; Takeuchi, Chung, Lin, Shen, Kurasaki, Chun, & Sue, 1998) and neurasthenia (Yamamoto, 1992; Zheng, Lin, Takeuchi, Kurasaki, Wang, & Cheung, 1997), and may vary with the level of acculturation. At the same time the rates of utilization of mental health services are lowest of any ethnic group, regardless of gender, age and location. The majority of Asian American clients seek services when the severity levels of symptoms are high, suggesting a delay in seeking help. The cultural barriers to seeking mental health services are identified to be shame, stigma, lack of financial resources, different conceptions of health and treatment underlying western mental health services, and lack of same ethnicity and same language mental health providers (U. S. Surgeon General's Report, 2001). Moreover, well-meaning but culturally insensitive mental health provisions can maintain the barriers that prevent those seeking help to adequately benefit.

CLINICAL IMPLICATIONS

Values have been described to be at the heart and essence of culture (Kroeber & Kluckhohn, 1952) and, in point of fact, make a useful starting point for considering in some detail the differences between Asian American values and Euro-American values that carry over into the practice of psychotherapy (see Table 14.1). By identifying and contrasting major cultural values common to the largest Asian American ethnic groups and values reflected in Western approaches to psychotherapy, striking differences emerge. The young Asian

Table 14.1. Contrasting Values and Clinical Implications

Asian American Values	Common Western Psychotherapy Values
Focus on extended family and multiple caregivers	Focus on nuclear family and nuclear parenting
Primary relationship parent-child bond	Primary relationship-marital bond
Emphasis on interpersonal "connection and maintaining harmony"	Emphasis on the individual, self "honesty above all else"
Role hierarchy	Collegial, democratic, egalitarian
Self-restraint	Catharsis, self disclosure

Source: Kroeber and Kluckholn, 1952.

American clients who have been dealing with the conflicts between cultures in their own lives and identities, face the risk of exacerbation of this conflict in the therapy context and climate in the absence of awareness of the same, and skills to handle this with sensitivity and competence.

Focus on Extended Family and Multiple Caregivers Versus Nuclear Family Parenting

Asian culture is group oriented compared to Euro-Western culture, which places high regard for individuality and autonomy. Encouraging clients to attain personal goals, and self-actualization may be appropriate for more acculturated Asian Americans, but more traditional Asian Americans consider such goals difficult to justify because of the value placed on living in the context of one's perceived roles and responsibilities within the group. One's actions are commonly weighed in relation to the impact they have on others in one's life. For clinicians, inquiry into the implications of "self" development, or "self-actualization" requires particular attention to discussing the client's perception of the impact such pursuits will have on their reference group, for example, family, community, and so on. Indeed, the constructs self-actualization and self-development may, in fact, be less useful descriptors than interpersonal actualization and collective betterment on the level of family, extended family, or community group. Individuation may similarly be less meaningful than differentiation, which involves seeking an optimal intrapsychic balance between being driven by emotions and reason and an interpersonal balance between the search for individual and interpersonal well-being, with the nature, pace, and timing of the differentiation being culturally determined.

From a therapeutic perspective that values the influence of early childhood experiences on clients, inquiring into the clients relationship with "parental" figures necessitates inquiring into the role and experiences with extended family members as well such as aunts, uncles, grandparents, and cousins who may have had an equal or more significant impact on the clients developing self than the client's own parents.

The influence of this value on Asian American clients can be a profound sense of confusion, guilt, anxiety, and sense of helplessness for those who desire what can be experienced as "selfish" pursuits over the interests of others. The first author has found that validating and contextualing these feelings and discussing the client's concerns regarding the impact one's pursuit may have on others is particularly helpful.

Primary Relationship Parent Child Versus Marital Bond

In Euro-Western culture, the quality of the marital relationship is highly regarded and seen to be of primary importance as reflected in the values espoused by marital couple's therapy and structural, strategic, and other family therapies

(Minuchin & Fishman, 1994; Haley, 1987). In Asian families, the quality of the relationship between parents is also highly regarded, but it is considered to be of less importance and secondary to the parent-child bond, typically meant to connote the mother-child bond. The elevation of this bond ensures continuity with the family of origin (Hsu, 1971) bond. Mothers confiding their woes and frustrations to their children, including those frustrations toward their spouse, may be viewed as boundary violations and inappropriate triangulation through the lens of traditional mainstream family therapies. Yet, in Asian cultures, such activities can be commonplace and to alter the communication patterns and quality of communications between parent and child may leave mother and child feeling isolated, detached, and alienated from the fabric of their culture. This isn't to imply that parent-child bonds should supercede marital bonds in all cases in Asian American households, or that the absence of a primary bond between parent and child is suggestive of dysfunction. Instead, the issue is the common occurrence of a primary bond between parent and child is not assumed to be pathological. Falicov (1998) recounts a story about Milton Erickson instructing a woman to throw up on the floor when her parents-in-law visited without warning, in order to dramatically drive home the point that she needed them to respect her privacy and needs. It is unlikely, as Falicov pointed out, that this kind of strategy would have a chance of achieving beneficial, intended effects in an Asian American family because of the absence of the cultural assumption that the marital relationship is the most important family relationship and its privacy is necessary to protect at all costs and by most means.

Emphasis on Interpersonal Harmony Versus Emphasis on Honesty

With great emphasis placed on one's role and identity within the group context, it comes as no surprise that for Asian Americans there is great emphasis on interpersonal relationships. Exciting multicultural research on attachment theory is bringing to light that there are significant differences in the meaning and manner in which sensitivity, competence, and a secure base are fostered in early parenting relationships by Euro American parents and Japanese parents (Rothbaum, Weisz, Pott, Miyake, & Morelli, 2000). For example, Euro-American parents valuing independence show sensitivity in response to a child expressing a need. This gives the child the opportunity to act independently and have that act as well as their bonding needs reinforced. Japanese parents valuing interdependence show sensitivity by anticipating their child's needs and model sensitivity and attunement to others and reinforce bonding needs. The familial self (Roland, 1988), important for Asian Americans, involves connectedness and emotional investment in the family of origin, and extended family and strong identification with its honor and reputation (Falicov, 1998). Similar sentiments are also emphasized in the context of filial piety or the attitude of the child or younger family members towards the parents or older family members. The Asian American client, when in therapy, is likely to be very responsive to an emotionally invested relationship context in which there is subtle, intuitive understanding of communication and attention to verbal as well as nonverbal modes of communication and respect for close, interdependent ties within the larger family. Also forms of address such as "Auntie Y" or "Uncle X," suggesting the familiarity of pseudo-kin, have been suggested for some Chinese American families (Tseng & Hsu, 1991).

Maintaining harmony in the interpersonal network of relationships assumes great significance. This is reflected in such phenomena as choosing not to publicly disagree with one another. Adages such as the "nail that stands up gets hammered down" and Asian Americans reporting that they often feel uncomfortable speaking their mind in public, illustrate this reality. The need to maintain interpersonal harmony is so profound that in Asian cultural groups, maintaining interpersonal harmony is more important than "honesty." Therefore, publicly agreeing by nodding or verbalizing agreement, while privately disagreeing, is not uncommon. "White lies" are tolerated and understood as attempts to maintain this harmony.

For clinicians, understanding that the client's actions may not be consistent with their words can prevent pathologizing behavior and labeling them as passive aggressiveness, defensiveness, or antisocial traits and be understood in terms of its social objective to maintain interpersonal harmony and cohesiveness. Clinicians should consider the possibility of interpersonal conflicts, therapeutic ruptures, contextualizing the meaning of such discrepancies, and sensitively inquire or respond in a manner that is more congruent to the clients wishes and needs. For example, a clinician working with an Asian American client who is experiencing roommate conflicts might encourage assertiveness training, including direct, honest and "nonthreatening" verbal communication between client and roommate. The Asian American client may publicly agree that such an approach would be helpful, but may find such goals a tremendous stretch that participation in therapy may drop or cease. Clinically, taking more time and perhaps "baby steps" toward helping the client communicate verbally or nonverbally her concerns in a respectful, caring way and to the extent that their cultural narrative allows, may be more beneficial. Additionally, indirect modes of communication might be more helpful, such as, leaving a note, speaking with a trusted third party; again a conscious and appropriate use of triangulation.

Role Hierarchy Versus Collegial, Democratic, Egalitarian Values

Asian cultures have long been socially organized in a hierarchical manner, which espoused a world view in a top-down fashion. Individuals who exist in such a culture come to hold conscious and unconscious expectations of one another's roles in society. Power differentials, various social responsibilities, and roles to be fulfilled, result from such a world view.

Amae (Kobayashi, Banerjee, & Ichinotsubo-Ezzi, 2001) is a term used to describe an implicit yet powerful social dimension found in Japanese culture that describes dependency expectations of being nurtured and being the nurturer in a way that has been analogous to the mother-infant bond. Yi (1995) similarly discusses a "benevolent transference" that develops between Asian Americans and their therapist whereby the Asian client unconsciously agrees to be the "good, diligent" client with the expectation the therapist will address the dependency needs of the client in an unspoken arrangement. Lack of awareness of such expectations can lead to confusion, frustration, and a sense of failure on the part of both provider and recipient.

For clinicians it is important to recognize that Asian American clients, particularly more traditional in culture may see you as an "expert" who will nurture, care, and provide for them. To fulfill the social hierarchical expectations, therapists could introduce themselves formally as Ms., Mrs., Mr., or Dr. _____ while giving clients the option of calling them Ms., Mrs., Mr., or Dr. _____, or by their first name. To greet the Asian client by their first name may, in fact, create confusion, disappointment, and loss of confidence in the ascribed credibility of the clinician. By the time Asian clients have come to therapy, they have overcome great psychological and social stigmas and are frequently seeking an "expert" who will "cure" them, not a peer who will befriend them. In the first author's own experience working with Asian American young adults, clients have preferred to address him as Dr. Chien as opposed to Bill or William. To further fulfill the social obligation of an "expert" who will provide a "cure," the first author has found it helpful to carefully and thoroughly introduce and explain the process of therapy along with providing it.

Self-Restraint or Self-Disclosure?

There is an inherent paradox between the Asian preference for restraint, silence, meditative reflection, and verbal self-expression entailed in the process of western psychotherapy. However, with the Asian American in therapy, the quality of an invested and attuned relationship, in which there is awareness and respect for the emotional significance of the family or group, may be key to facilitating discussions of personal feelings, thoughts, or wishes. In the first author's clinical experience, the question, How does that make you feel? to an Asian American client may not produce its intended effect. An alternative, shared with the first author by a former supervisor with extensive experience working with Asian American clients and psychology interns (M. A. Takemoto, personal communication, September 21, 1996), is to ask the question differently, What do you *think* about that? Client affect can often be distilled from clients' descriptions of their thoughts and experiences by attending to nonverbal communication, when gingerly reflected back can be validated or refuted. Clinical sensitivity to the readiness for self-disclosure and the extent of self-disclosure conveying acceptance of the same are likely to be facilitative of the therapeutic process, whereas direct well-intentioned encouragement of greater self-expression may lead to therapeutic impasses.

Due to the fact that psychotherapy itself is a particularly exotic and culturally unfamiliar tool for Asian Americans, clients can benefit from thorough explanations and education of what psychotherapy involves, along with ample opportunities to ask questions and a slowing down of the process. The first author recalls a mentor in graduate school describing the process of psychotherapy as involving "training the client to be a client." Clinical experience has shown this to be helpful with nonAsian American clients, and essential with Asian American clients. Chao (1992) provides refreshing examples of some of the ways in which she trains by translating the Chinese characters for psychologist to mean "expert of the inner heart," or the Vietnamese, which mean "expert of the heart and soul," or "the bull's eye or center of things." Therapy can also be introduced as a relationship that can provide "gifts" (Sue & Zane, 1987) in the form of encouragement, structure, and explanation.

For the young Asian American client who is traditional or dissociative, close attention and sensitivity to Asian values will be key to retaining and progressing in therapy. In addition, same ethnicity and bilingual ability in the therapist may be particularly valuable. For the over-Westernized or assimilative Asian Americans and the marginal Asian Americans, issues of racism, internalized racism, and their influence on ethnic identity development will be clinically pertinent. Further, Asian American clinicians with mature and healthy ethnic and racial identity schemas themselves can be influential in the way their clients come to regard themselves ethnically and racially and be sources of their empowerment and validation (Alvarez & Helms, 2001). Acculturative Asian Americans may be most inclined and prepared to explore the ongoing processes of divergent cultural influences, value conflicts, and their integration in various aspects of their lives and may become willing to bring in their families to work collaboratively with them to achieve integration at a larger, familial level. Finally, awareness, understanding, and respect for ancient Asian traditions of alternative healing and medicine that clients in this group may also be utilizing can be of benefit in building the therapeutic alliance and in coordinating care.

References

Alvarez, A. N., & Helms, J. E. (2001). Racial identity and reflected appraisals as influences on Asian American's racial adjustment. *Cultural Diversity and Ethnic Minority Psychology, 7*(3), 217–231.

Banerjee, L. (2001). *Psychology and the reach of multiculturalism in American Culture.* Manuscript in preparation.

Chan, S. (1991). *Asian-Americans: An interpretive history.* Boston: Twayne.

Chao, C. M. (1992). The inner heart: Therapy with South East Asian families. In L. A. Vargas & J. D. Koss-Chioino (Eds.), *Working with culture, psychotherapeutic interventions with ethnic minority children and adolescents.* San Francisco: Jossey Bass.

Falicov, C. (1998). The cultural meaning of family triangles. In M. McGoldrick (Ed.), *Revisioning family therapy, race, culture and gender in clinical practice.* New York: Guilford Press.

Haley, J. (1987). *Problem solving therapy.* San Francisco: Jossey Bass.

Hsu, F. K. (Ed.). (1971). *Kinship and culture.* Chicago: Aldine.

Hutnik, N. (1991). *Ethnic minority identity: A social psychological perspective.* Oxford: Clarendon Press.

Kobayashi, K., Banerjee, L., & Ichinotsubo-Ezzi, T. (2001). *Amae in graduate classes and clinical supervision.* Manuscript submitted for publication.

Kroeber, A. L., & Kluckholn, C. (1952). *Culture: A critical review of concepts and definitions.* New York: Vintage Books.

Minuchin, S., & Fishman, H. C. (1994). *Family therapy techniques.* Cambridge, MA: Harvard University Press.

Minuchin, S., & Nichols, M. (1993). *Family healing: Strategies for hope and understanding.* New York: Simon & Schuster.

Miu, A. C. (1996). Depression among elderly Chinese immigrants: An exploratory study. *Social Work, 41,* 633–645.

Panat, S., & Banerjee, L. (1994, October). *Conflicting allegiances: Indian womens' struggle to bridge generations and reaching a common identity.* Paper presented at the UCLA South Asian Womens' Conference: Forging New Identities in America, Los Angeles, CA.

Patel, S. P., & Gaw, A. C. (1996). Suicide among immigrants from the Indian sub-continent: A review. *Psychiatric Services, 47,* 517–521.

Roland, A. (1988). *In search of self in India and Japan: Toward a cross-cultural psychology.* Princeton, NJ: Princeton University Press.

Rothbaum, F., Weisz, J., Pott, M., Miyake, K., & Morelli, G. (2000). Attachment and culture: Security in the United States and Japan. *American Psychologist, 55*(10), 1093–1104.

Sue, S. & Zane, N. (1987). The role of culture and cultural techniques in psychotherapy: A critique and reformulation. *American Psychologist, 42*(1), 37–45.

Sue, D.W., & Sue, D. (1990). *Counseling the culturally different, theory and practice.* New York: John Wiley & Sons.

Sue, S. & Sue, S. W. (1971). Chinese American personality and mental health. *Amerasia Journal, 1,* 36–49.

Takeuchi, D. T., Chung, R. C., Lin, K. M., Shen, H., Kurasaki, K., Chun, C., & Sue, S.(1998). Lifetime and twelve month prevalence rates of major depression episodes and dysthymia among Chinese Americans in Los Angeles. *American Journal of Psychiatry, 155,* 1407–1414.

Tsai, J. L., Ying, Yu-Wen, & Lee, P. E. (2001). Cultural predictors of self-esteem: A study of Chinese-American female and male young adults. *Cultural Diversity and Ethnic Minority Psychology, 7*(3), 284–297.

Tseng, W. S., & Hsu, J. (1991). *Culture and family, problems and therapy.* New York: Haworth Press.

Uba, L. (1994). *Asian Americans: Personality patterns, identity and mental health.* New York: Guilford Press.

U.S. Census Bureau (1990). Profiles of Asians and Pacific Islanders: Selected characteristics. (CPH-L-151). Washington DC: Government Printing Office.

U.S. Census Bureau (2000). *Projections of residents by race, Hispanic origin and nativity: Middle series* (2,001–2,005). Washington DC: Government Printing Office.

U.S. Census Bureau (2001). The Asian and Pacific Islander population in the U.S. (PPL-146) [On-line] Available: http://www.Census.gov/population/www/socdemo/race/api.html

U.S. Surgeon Generals' Report (2001). *Mental health: Culture, race and ethnicity, Supplemental Report* [On-line]. Available: http://www.surgeongeneral.com

Yamamoto, J. (1992). Psychiatric diagnoses and neurasthenia, *Psychiatric Annals, 22*(4), 171–172.

Yi, K. (1995). Psychoanalytic psychotherapy with Asian clients: Transference and therapeutic considerations. *Psychotherapy, 32*(2), 308–316

Zheng, Y. P., Lin, K. M., Takeuchi, D., Kurasaki, K. S., Wang, Y. X., & Cheung, F. (1997). An epidemiological study of neurasthenia in Chinese Americans in Los Angeles. *Comprehensive Psychiatry, 38,* 249–259.

CHAPTER FIFTEEN

Race and the Field of Family Therapy

Robert-Jay Green

The practice of family therapy and its theoretical paradigm are undergoing momentous changes. The early pioneers' promise of a multilevel theory of family functioning is about to be realized as the field addresses intergroup race relations, the delivery of culturally attuned mental health services, and the training of multiculturally competent family therapists. In this chapter, I will sketch the contours of a "multicultural family therapy," highlighting some issues that ought to be central in its development.

Throughout, I will use examples pertaining primarily to African American families, drawing on my experiences over the last eight years as a White researcher involved in a collaborative study of ninety-five inner-city African American families of children who attend Oakland's Chapter I schools (Green, 1995). A second major source of ideas has been an ongoing multicultural curricular reform effort at the California School of Professional Psychology (CSPP), Berkeley/Alameda campus (Green, 1998). Much of what is written in this chapter applies to other disenfranchised groups such as lesbians and gays and persons with physical disabilities. There are, however, very important differences among the various ethnic, racial, and other minority groups resulting from each one's unique history and visibility vis-à-vis, the larger culture (Atkinson & Hackett, 1995; Green, 2000, 2001; Laird & Green, 1996; Sue & Sue, 1990).

A PLURALISTIC SOCIETY

According to the 1990 U.S. Census, approximately 60 million people in this country (24 percent of the population) are African American, Latino American, Asian American/Pacific Islander, or Native American. The Census Bureau conservatively estimates that by the year 2050, this number will more than double to 122 million, or 40 percent of the total U.S. population (Olmedo, 1994). The 40 percent level is close to being reached already in California and in the Southwestern states, where current racial minority populations combined are expected to exceed 50 percent of the population by the year 2050. Given that such trends are predicted to continue beyond the year 2050, it is likely that at some point in the next century, White European Americans ultimately will constitute a minority group within the total U.S. population.

The rapidly changing racial composition of the U.S. carries profound implications for the future development of our field. In the personal realm, consciousness of racial and ethnic identity (which always has been higher among racial minorities because of their visible differentness from the majority and their vulnerability to discrimination) is growing rapidly among Whites. White family therapists now find themselves increasingly living and working in multiracial environments that stimulate curiosity about their own cultural differentness from others. The changing racial composition of our everyday contexts is creating a sea of change in our consciousness, which, in turn, is affecting how we think about and do family therapy.

In contrast to the demographic trends in the U.S. population as a whole, current racial minority groups continue to be dramatically underrepresented among the ranks of family therapists. In a 1993 survey of graduate programs accredited by the American Association for Marriage and Family Therapy (AAMFT), less than 1 percent of master's degree graduates were African American during the preceding ten-year period, and only 1.8 percent of the doctoral degree graduates were African American (Wilson & Smith, 1993). In that same year, the American Family Therapy Academy (AFTA)—which is the organization of senior teachers and researchers in our field—had a membership that was only 1.4 percent African or African American; 1.1 percent Asian or Asian American; and 2.8 percent Latino or Latino-American.

The discrepancy between the proportions of people of color in the general population versus in the profession of family therapy means that racial minority families usually are treated by White family therapists, and the caseloads of White family therapists will increasingly be composed of racial minority families. For example, in 1995, the California Association of Marriage and Family Therapists (CAMFT) conducted a survey of 12,900 marriage and family therapists in California and found that *while 94 percent of marriage and family therapists in this state were Caucasian, 66 percent (two-thirds) of their clients were from other racial groups (24 percent Latino, 19 percent African American, 15 percent Asian/Pacific Islander, 6 percent Native American, 2 percent other)* (Riemersma, 1995). As a harbinger of things to come nationally, most family therapy in California already involves families of color being treated by White therapists.

Because family therapy theories tend to reflect the kinds of client populations served, I think we can expect dramatic increases in treatment concepts pertaining to therapist-client racial diversity in the near future. Race will become a major nucleus around which new developments in the theory of family therapy will emerge.

Moreover, I think that new ideas and techniques originating from this multicultural emphasis will prove valuable in all family therapy, including when White middle-class clients are being treated by White middle-class therapists. That is, the multicultural lens will bring into clearer focus the uniqueness of each race's normative family experience, including problems common to White middle-class families as a distinct cultural group. In addition, the study of therapist-client interracial differentness will help illuminate the more general process of negotiating differentness between therapist and client regardless of race. For example, it is likely to stimulate studies of how other therapist and client differences affect treatment process and outcome (for example, differences in social class background, age, gender, religion, national origin, sexual orientation, physical disability, and sociopolitical values).

In the coming years, family therapists who now feel that such questions are tangential to their everyday interests are likely to have a personal stake in the answers that unfold. They will be treating ever-growing numbers of clients who are not like themselves culturally, and they will find that the cutting-edge theories of family therapy will focus increasingly on specific interventions that are culturally attuned to specific groups' ways of being-in-the-world. In this sense, the study of race and family functioning will not be simply another peripheral vein but rather a chamber at the very heart of family therapy.

At present, we are facing a major theoretical task: to weave together multicultural theory (including factors of race, gender, ethnicity, social class, physical ability, sexual orientation, and age) and traditional family systems theory into a coherent whole (see Sue, Ivey, & Pedersen, 1996, for an analogous effort in the field of counseling psychology). This new multicultural family systems theory must link the individual, family, and cultural perspectives in a manageable way, flexible enough to encompass all manner of sociocultural diversity and practical enough to be applied in the new health care delivery and other treatment contexts.

As with earlier major innovations in our field (such as the shift from psychodynamic to structural and strategic approaches beginning in the mid-1970s, and the shift from systemic and strategic to feminist, constructionist, and narrative approaches beginning in the mid-1980s), it is a good bet that it will take about ten years for this reformation to achieve solid footing and greater acceptance. In the remainder of this chapter, I will expand on some of the themes introduced above, paying special attention to racism as a factor in the lives of racial minority group families and its implications for multicultural family theory.

CULTURE, POWER, AND THE FIELD OF FAMILY THERAPY

John Weakland, one of the founders of family therapy and a member of the group that formulated the "double bind" concept, once described the differences between family therapy and all other mental health approaches in terms of its origins in anthropology:

> I think it was very important for our work that Gregory Bateson and I were both trained anthropologically. . . . Psychiatrists, and even psychologists, to a large extent, tend to view the world in terms of pathology. If something looks strange or different, their first thought is that it is some kind of pathology. Anthropology is different. If you go out into the field in a new society, then every damned thing they do seems strange. You can't get anywhere just by saying "It's all pathological. It's all crazy!" It's *your* job to make sense out of it, no matter how crazy it looks. This produces a very different slant on the observation of behavior (Bassi, 1991, pp. 69–70).

Although the field of family therapy rapidly moved away from this cultural anthropology stance to adopt cybernetic-systems metaphors, the enduring hallmark of family therapy has been its insistence on the intelligibility and adaptiveness of psychological symptoms when viewed in a social context.

Also, early in its development, the field of family therapy incorporated an explicit analysis of power relations in the society. For example, shortly after World War II, Ackerman (another of the founders of the field of family therapy) and Jahoda (1950) coauthored a book titled *Antisemitism and Emotional Disorders: A Psychoanalytic Interpretation*. They were among the first to propose that prejudice (in this case, against Jews) was the result of unconscious defense mechanisms, particularly projection, by which individuals and social groups diverted inner frustrations, conflicts, hostility, feelings of inadequacy, and deprivations onto innocent outgroups such as racial and ethnic minorities. Later, Ackerman (1958) imported this same concept into his work with families, calling the process "prejudicial scapegoating" of the identified patient, which purportedly served the function of reducing other unresolved tensions within the family group, particularly in the parents' marriage.

Similar notions appeared in the work of other family theorists during the early to mid-1960s, including Vogel and Bell's (1968) idea of the emotionally disturbed child as the "family scapegoat"; Bowen's concept of the "family projection process" (1966) and, later, the "societal projection process" (1978); and Laing's (1965) concept of "mystification" (a term originally used by Karl Marx to describe the obfuscation of power relations that takes place in capitalist societies, which enables the continued exploitation of the proletariat by the aristocracy).

However, as historians of science have demonstrated, a field's theories and techniques tend to reflect sociopolitical developments in the society as a whole. Family therapy is no exception. Despite its auspicious anthropological beginnings and social consciousness immediately following World War II, our field's attention to social power issues waxed and waned, seemingly responsive to national trends in political attitudes and leadership.

For example, in the late 1970s and early 1980s, the whole concept of power was dismissed as nonsystemic by some of the Batesonians, rendering the field of family therapy "neutral" (and silent) when it came to confronting even the most obvious of power inequities such as racism, wife abuse, physical and sexual abuse of children, and discrimination against lesbian women and gay men. There was a kind of collective silence among White family therapists about racial inequality in the United States during the period from 1970–1990. We knew it was there; many of us had lived through and participated in the Civil Rights and antiwar movements of the 1960s.

However, like the nation's Republican presidents during the period from 1970–90 (Richard Nixon, Gerald Ford, Ronald Reagan, George Bush), White family therapists didn't talk much about race. The simple fact of the matter is members of the dominant cultural group usually have the option of ignoring or denying that racism exists unless some extreme example in the news media temporarily and painfully intrudes into awareness. This is not an option for members of minority groups whose consciousness is more or less always attuned to the possibility of becoming direct targets of discrimination (Grier & Cobbs, 1968).

What I wish to underscore here is that although our field started out with an anthropological stance and with a social analysis of power, subjugation, and prejudice in society, it soon became overly focused on intrafamilial relations. What remained of an analysis of power and scapegoating was confined mainly to within-family, parent-child relations considered separately from the larger social milieu in which families were inextricably embedded.

Documenting parallel trends in the field of psychology, Graham (1992), in an article entitled "Most of the subjects were white and middle class," reported a steady and dramatic decline in research on African Americans published in American Psychological Association (APA) journals between 1970 and 1989. For example, during the five-year period 1970–74, *203* such articles appeared, whereas in 1985–1989, only 65 such articles (one-third as many) appeared. Over the entire twenty-year period, only 3.6 percent of all published studies used an African American sample. Although I have not done a precise survey, I feel confident in saying that the percentage of articles on African Americans in the family therapy journals during this period was not much better than in the psychology journals.

By the mid- to late-1980s, however, the pendulum began to swing back in the field of family therapy. Many who initially were caught up in the pure systemic and cybernetic analogy became increasingly frustrated with the field's abstract intellectualism and inability to address the pressing social problems facing living and breathing people every day. Feminist family therapists led the way in the field's renewed interest in the analysis of power relations between the genders in both society and in the family. As Goldner (1988) pointed out, family therapists had dealt comprehensively with the issue of generational power arrangements in two and three generation families, but they did not address issues of gender-based power within the family and society, including men's violence toward women. However, in spite of their trenchant critiques, most of the White feminist authors did not extend their analysis of power relations to the domain of race relations and its implications for family life and family therapy.

Family therapists who did write about working with racial minority families tended to view the social context of racism as a set of fixed constraints (Haley, 1977; Minuchin, 1974; Minuchin, Montalvo, Guerney, Rosman, & Schumer, 1967). The therapeutic task became one of generating and selecting among behavioral options that did not involve challenging or even understanding those larger constraints. These theorists didn't, for example, advocate discussion of racial issues or racism in therapy, nor did they advocate social activism on the part of family members as a constructive self-affirming response to racism. It remained unclear, for example, how a therapist should respond if an African American client was to spontaneously make a straightforward comment about racism in the society at large or in her own personal experience. The implication, however, was that discussion of racial matters would be a distraction from the therapeutic task at hand, which was to solve a narrowly defined presenting problem by altering the intrafamilial interactions presumed to be maintaining it. Social forces beyond the family's control were to be accepted as givens; discussion of them would have been viewed as a relative waste of precious therapy time.

This model essentially required that all presenting problems be attributed to intrafamilial relations, with responsibility or blame apportioned among the family members as equitably as possible in order not to seem unfair. However, it may be extremely adaptive for racial minority families to be able to attribute some amount of causal influence to oppressive forces outside the family, to take action in regards to such oppression when feasible, and simply to assess the limits of one's responsibility for creating and maintaining family problems.

Although there have been some outstanding contributions and increasing attention being paid to matters of ethnicity and culture in our field recently, one might say these constitute only a first-order change. Much of the literature in this area has come from a small number of authors, most of whom are, themselves, members of cultural minority groups (for example, some of the contributors to McGoldrick, Giordano, & Pearce, 1996). A second-order change would seem to require that matters of race, ethnicity, social class, and prejudice become a fundamental, continual, and visible focus in the work of a majority of family therapists and researchers, including white European American family therapists and researchers.

CULTURAL "DIFFERENTNESS" VERSUS INTERCULTURAL "OPPRESSION"

Among the barriers to this shifting of the gears, some of the issues before us require a different level of analysis than the intrafamilial one. When it comes to matters of social class, race, sexual orientation, or physical disability, for example, we are talking not only about power arrangements *within* couples or families, but also about *the unequal power of some families, vis-à-vis, other families in the society.* As I discuss later in this chapter in the section on "service delivery systems," only some of the problems resulting from these inter-group inequities can be addressed with family therapy per se, whereas others may be more amenable to community-based family interventions that have a preventive or educational focus.

In this new era, we will need to distinguish clearly between matters of minority group *differentness* and matters of minority group *oppression.* I want to make very sure that we not confuse ourselves about this distinction. We will need to broaden the conversation beyond our current emphasis (which mainly involves attempts to describe *intra*cultural patterns in the different ethnic groups) to include an explicit focus on *inter*cultural relations (including prejudice, discrimination, and violence), which seem to be more difficult for us to address openly.

Although intracultural traditions, norms, and values are important to family functioning, among the most important aspects of cultural differences are the types of prejudice and discrimination experienced by various groups in a given society (racism, homophobia, sexism). These factors affect families' access to resources and abilities to cope with the tasks of raising children. A main focus should be on how cultural groups manage their differences and how some cultural groups are positioned economically and politically to control other cultural groups in the society. Our focus on different cultural patterns and historical traditions within groups often obscures our understanding of the oppressive relations between groups.

Cultural, racial, and sexual orientation differences in and of themselves are *not* problems. Prejudice, discrimination, and other forms of aggressive intercultural conflict based on these differences *are* problems. This may seem too obvious to state. However, in the past, social scientists have done great damage by viewing certain minority groups' differentness as inherently problematic or pathological. There is a long history of researchers portraying minority group families—and especially African American families, Native American families, Latino families, and gay and lesbian families—in very negative or pathological terms (Azibo, 1992; Green, Bettinger, & Zacks, 1996; Laird & Green, 1996).

For example, from the 1960s, you may remember the phrase "culturally deprived" being used to describe African American families, a term that implied that Black culture was inferior to White culture, or even that Blacks were devoid of culture, as if White culture was the only good, true, and "cultured" culture (Duckitt, 1992). Then there were the long and continuing series of research reports showing that Blacks scored lower on I.Q. tests than Whites, without acknowledging that the tests were standardized on, and culturally biased in favor of, White middle-class children.

Even now, comparative research studies (that is, studies comparing African American to White subjects) remain the most frequently utilized methods in research on African Americans, which tend to set White groups' results as the norm against which African Americans' results are evaluated (Azibo, 1992). In this regard, Graham's (1992) twenty-year survey of APA journals showed that 72 percent of research articles on African Americans were based on such race-comparative studies. It seems that researchers have been more concerned with how African Americans compare to Whites than with African Americans in their own right.

Furthermore, many of the comparative studies of the past did not adequately measure or control for socioeconomic status (Graham). Rather, they frequently compared middle-class White families to lower socioeconomic class African American families. This strategy hopelessly confounds social class and race, and yields a negatively biased picture of African Americans' functioning compared to Whites'.

In addition, previous researchers often failed to take into account certain dimensions that seem to be uniquely important to the well-being of African American families, namely: greater involvement among extended kin; the importance of the church as a source of social identity and support; more fluid boundaries in terms of household membership and child-rearing roles; and ways of socializing children to deal with racial discrimination (Boykin, 1986; McAdoo, 1988).

Finally, researchers of the past tended to attribute difficulties of African Americans to their cultural differentness from the majority group, rather than to the social oppression they face. I mean here that the amount of discrimination encountered by a minority group seems to be a larger factor in its well-functioning than is the discrepancy between the minority and majority groups' original cultures.

In this context, I would like to cite the work of Ogbu (1978, 1989), a distinguished educational anthropologist at the University of California, Berkeley. In a review of cross-national studies of immigrants, Ogbu has shown that the social position of a minority group (that is, the extent to which its opportunities are limited by the larger society) is the major determinant of that minority group's educational attainment.

In particular, Ogbu (1989) distinguishes between two types of minority groups. The first type are called voluntary, immigrant minority groups. These groups voluntarily came to the new country seeking a better life, sometimes to escape intolerable conditions in their countries of origin. Most European ethnics and Asians in the United States would be considered voluntary immigrants. Recent illustrations occurred on both the East and West coasts of the United States during 1993 when ships carrying illegal immigrants from mainland China were intercepted, and it was discovered that many families had paid as much as $30,000 for the voyage to the United States.

The second type Ogbu (1989) calls involuntary, caste-like minority groups. These groups have a history of being enslaved or colonized by the dominant cultural group. For example, African Americans, Native Hawaiians, Puerto Ricans, Native Americans, and Mexican Americans would be considered involuntary, caste-like minorities in the U.S.

In Ogbu's (1989) cross-national review, voluntary immigrant minority groups did as well or better academically than the majority group in any given country. However, the involuntary caste-like minority groups tended to be doing more poorly in school. To clarify, let me cite just a few examples from Ogbu's review.

Koreans have been studied in three locations: Korea, Japan, and the United States. In Korea and the United States, Korean children are achieving very well in school. In Japan, however, where there is a long history of discrimination against Koreans, Korean children are performing poorly in school. Clearly, this implies that there is not something intrinsic to being Korean (such as higher I.Q.) or Korean culture (such as placing a higher value on education) that leads to Koreans' higher achievement in the United States. Rather, there must be something in how Koreans are being treated in the United States versus Japan, or how Koreans view their situation in the two countries that accounts for their better school performance in the United States than in Japan (Ogbu, 1989).

Similarly, the academic achievement of Finns has been studied in two locations: Sweden and Australia. In Sweden, which colonized Finland for centuries,

Finns are performing very poorly in school. However, Finns who voluntarily immigrated to Australia are doing quite well in school. Again, the culture of origin does not in and of itself predict school achievement in these cross-national immigration comparisons (Ogbu, 1989).

Nor does dissimilarity between the culture-of-origin and culture-of-immigration predict poorer school achievement. If cultural differences (for example, between home and school) were the key, why would Koreans be doing more poorly in Japan (a more similar Buddhist culture) than in the United States (a more different Judeo-Christian culture)? Or, why would Finns do more poorly in Sweden (a more similar Scandinavian culture) than in Australia (a more different Anglo British culture)? (Ogbu, 1989).

As a final example here, West Indians have been studied in Britain, Canada, and the United States. In Britain, which colonized the West Indies, West Indians are the least academically successful minority group, whereas in Canada and the United States, West Indians are doing well academically (Ogbu, 1989).

These cross-national immigration studies imply that language differences, economic differences, and culture-of-origin differences are not the primary determinants of differential school achievement by minority groups. Rather, a minority group's relative academic success seems related to its immigration history (voluntary versus involuntary) and current status in relation to the dominant group. In particular, children from a given subcultural group will achieve more poorly if their group was colonized or enslaved historically by the dominant group (as was the case for African Americans, Native Americans, Puerto Ricans, and Mexican Americans in the United States; Koreans in Japan; Finns in Sweden; and West Indians in Britain) (Ogbu, 1989).

Based on these findings, Ogbu (1989) concludes that a minority group's historical pattern of incorporation within a given society and the current level of discrimination it faces within that society are more important to its academic success than are its pre-immigration intra-cultural patterns, language differences, or other cultural discrepancies from the majority. And from this, family therapists might conclude that issues of oppression, racial discrimination, and their psychological effects (rather than intra-group cultural traditions) should be emphasized in our attempts to understand the long-term, multigenerational functioning of minority families in America. For example, in our study of 95 African American inner-city families, we recently found that the amount of racial prejudice children experienced was significantly related to poorer academic achievement and to higher levels of problem behavior (Moore-McDowell, 1993).

We must keep in mind that members of a racial minority group have something more in common than just their traditional beliefs and family interaction patterns from their cultures or countries of origin. Despite the great diversity within a given minority group, whether they are family therapists or computer operators, judges or nurses, the members of that group share a similar potential for experiencing racial discrimination, a similar vulnerability to discrimination. Regardless of their other characteristics as individuals, skin color constitutes a fundamental organizing characteristic of their lives and tends to structure their interactions with other racial groups in the society.

The same is true for Whites. White skin color is a fundamental organizing characteristic of persons' lives, contributes to much of Whites' relative economic privilege, and structures much of their interaction with other races, including Whites' lack of interaction with other races.

I think that for members of the White majority group, it is very difficult to grasp emotionally a racial minority person's lifetime experiences in relation to prejudice and, equally important, the anticipation of and vulnerability to prejudice. For example, I think that when majority members visualize racism, they tend to picture it primarily in terms of dramatic or violent instances of hatred and aggression in cases like the Rodney King beating in Los Angeles, California, in 1991. But it is much more difficult for majority members to imagine the more common and cumulative acts of everyday discrimination, including subtle nonverbal cues and other more ambiguous signs of prejudice that constitute a basic fabric of racial minority experience.

At the same time, I think it is difficult for members of the majority group to see and to admit the extent to which they are privileged by virtue of skin color and the inequalities of race. It sometimes is painful for Whites to acknowledge that many of their opportunities for success in a competitive world are due to skin color and the many advantages that tend to go along with skin color, rather than to personal effort, talent, or other attributes of self or family.

Although I am stressing these overarching points about racial stratification and social class stratification in American society, I want to be clear that the family also has a role to play in the child's educational attainment and psychosocial functioning. Thus, even though racial discrimination is an important determinant of a minority group's relative achievement as a group, families within a given minority group still show great variability in their academic performance. Whereas the amount of societal discrimination may determine the relative academic performance of one racial group compared to other racial groups, the family also makes a significant contribution to individual children's academic performance within each racial group or within each social class.

The above findings suggest that researchers and clinicians should focus on two distinct processes: (1) how minority group families help their members cope behaviorally, emotionally, and cognitively with specific acts of discrimination and with institutionalized oppression of their group generally within American society; and (2) how patterns of family interaction are associated with the variability of behavioral, emotional, and cognitive functioning of individuals within a specific ethnic or racial group.

MODELS OF SERVICE DELIVERY

In addition to focusing our thinking on both intra-cultural and inter-cultural patterns affecting family life, the field of family therapy needs to develop more flexible, culturally attuned techniques and models of service delivery. There are large percentages of families in the United States that are in need of psychosocial help, but for whom the concept and quasi-medical trappings of "psychotherapy" are foreign and stigmatizing. Many people, especially those who are not of European descent, do not want to be associated with anything labeled "psycho" or anything labeled "therapy," both of which signal medical illness or insanity.

However, a much larger percentage of the population is open to activities such as interpersonal education, self-development, self-help, assertiveness training, parent effectiveness training, codependency groups, the various survivors' groups, immigration support groups, and other quasi-educational group activities. Quite simply, they can get help without labeling themselves, or being labeled by others, as bad or crazy. This is no small matter. Despite the repulsion highly trained family therapists often feel toward certain self-help groups and their simplistic philosophies, it is clear that these groups are attractive to many persons who would not initially seek therapy, and the groups actually provide a socializing experience rendering help more acceptable to many participants.

Such families are much more likely to take part in community-based intervention programs that have an educational, support, or preventative orientation and are delivered through ordinary community institutions such as schools, religious organizations, primary care medical facilities, and workplaces. These programs include such activities as parent education; marriage preparation; and multifamily self-help or psychoeducational groups for a wide variety of physical problems, addictions, family transitions, and serious emotional disorders. Although professional roles in these kinds of community programs (for example, family life educator, crisis counselor, community organizer, and preschool consultant) have been viewed historically as relatively low status among family therapists, we are going to have to rethink our patterns of office-based service delivery and our attachment to the "doctor" role if we are going to reach larger segments of the population that are at risk for emotional disorders.

The second arena toward which we should be drawn is prevention activities, especially: programs for pregnant teenage mothers; programs like Head Start and Healthy Start that are mandated to have family intervention components; programs like the family-school collaboration project of the Ackerman Institute (Weiss & Edwards, 1992) and Comer's (1985) family-school interventions in New Haven, Connecticut; and programs currently going under the label of "family preservation" (see Schorr, 1989, for an overview of community-oriented family and child programs). These activities involve different professional tasks than does the "therapist" role, drawing us out of our offices and out of the one-to-one mode and into tasks more associated with the roles of organizational consultant, community psychologist, and family life educator.

By way of illustration, in our research in Oakland, the median achievement test score for African American children in grades four to six was at the 36th percentile on national norms. This means that half of the children in the sample were scoring below the 36th percentile. With the decline in the manufacturing and unskilled labor sectors of the U.S. economy, and the increased growth in the service sector, a child who is scoring below the 36th percentile is probably going to have a hard time succeeding occupationally in the information age. These children are headed for difficult lives emotionally, healthwise, financially, and behaviorally in all the harsh ways that poverty and illiteracy affect self-regard, family relations, and access to health care and other services. Furthermore, many of their parents do not realize the implications of these low percentile test scores because their children still receive passing grades in their classes and graduate to the next level in school at the end of each year.

Few families in these circumstances would seek counseling to reduce the psychosocial risk factors their children face. Some of them view the trajectory of their lives and their children's lives as immutable. To almost all such families, therapy would seem ill-suited to their problems because of its social stigma (that is, a treatment for mental illness), its cost, and most important, its apparent irrelevance for solving their everyday life context problems.

We can either say so much the worse for these families, or we can say so much the worse for therapy. I vote for the latter. That is, if we want to reach the bulk of poor families, we will have to abandon traditional notions of family therapy service delivery. We will have to start thinking in terms of family intervention with a healthy coping and prevention focus, with programs beginning early in the family life cycle, with programs offering multiple social, medical, educational, and occupational services, and with programs that are available over many years in everyday settings rather than in mental health practitioners' offices. Head Start, with its family component, is a paradigmatic example of the kind of prevention programs I have in mind, although most Head Start centers are limited in terms of their availability over time and highly variable in their commitment to intensive parent involvement.

As we all know, there are many problems with family life in the United States that we would like to help change, even if families themselves do not consider those aspects of their lives problematic, or do not consider those problems suitable for therapy, or do not consider therapy suitable for their sort of family. Many of the social problems we are discussing here are caused by racism, sexism, and homophobia, which are passed down over generations in families, but the families themselves do not perceive these aspects of their lives as problematic. To affect these family linked problems, we would need to go to where the families are rather than expect them to show up in our offices. Ways of reaching such families might include educational interventions in the schools, in churches, on television, and so on.

Sexism, racism, homophobia, and other forms of prejudice are partially learned in a family context and passed down over many generations in families, but clients do not ordinarily present themselves voluntarily for treatment of their sexism, racism, or homophobia. Victims of these forms of prejudice may seek treatment, but perpetrators generally do not. This, of course, is the case for many kinds of externalizing problems. The victims of the externalizer may seek therapy, may even try to bring the externalizer for therapy, but the externalizer rarely initiates treatment and may remain resistant throughout. Therapy is essentially a context that draws and is suitable for persons with internalizing types of problems or those who are the victims of externalizers.

For example, if ever there was a family linked problem, it is White racism, inasmuch as this problem tends to be passed down through the generations in families. I know of no White family that has ever requested help to change its racism. Nor is racism considered a mental disorder (although "racist personality disorder" was actually once proposed for inclusion in DSM-IV; Hamlin, 1990). Managed care will not pay for treatment of family linked White racism, unless it is associated with a DSM diagnosis. White racism is generally not a within-family problem but might be better viewed as a problem between families, or between families nested in certain communities.

Family therapy thus cannot treat problems of White racism very effectively, if at all. Family oriented and community-based educational interventions, rather than psychotherapy, will be necessary if we wish to reduce prejudice and discrimination based on race, ethnicity, social class, gender, sexual orientation, physical disability, and other minority statuses. If White family therapists wish to be of service to racial minority families, they would do well to spend at least part of their time initiating or becoming active in community efforts to reduce racism and to insure equal opportunity for all families. There are many, many ways for mental health professionals to help families besides family therapy.

CONCLUSION

What does it mean to be a family therapist? Whom do we serve? Are we exclusively a part of the tertiary health care system or does family therapy also encompass prevention? Are we a branch of applied anthropology, human ecology, family studies, or family life education; all of which now have some of their own doctoral programs? Will we continue only to huddle in our offices waiting for individual families to request treatment, or will we move beyond family therapy to include community intervention and family social policy within our scope of practice?

As a White family therapist who has been mainly a student and sometimes a teacher of multicultural issues, I find "there has been an alarming increase in the number of things I know nothing about" (Brilliant, 1979, p. 104). Many White family therapists are like immigrants in a multicultural land. We can cling to the old clinical traditions and delay the process of acculturation, or, now that our monocultural illusions are crumbling, we can embrace a wider vision of our work.

References

Ackerman, N. W. (1958). *The psychodynamics of family life.* New York: Basic Books.

Ackerman, N. W., & Jahoda, M. (1950). *Antisemitism and emotional disorders: A psychoanalytic interpretation.* New York: Harper.

Atkinson, D. R., & Hackett, G. (1995). *Counseling diverse populations.* Dubuque, IA: Wm. C. Brown Communications.

Azibo, D.A.Y. (1992). Understanding the proper and improper usage of the comparative research framework. In A.K.H. Burlew, W. C. Banks, H. P. McAdoo, & D.A.Y. Azibo (Eds.), *African-American psychology: Theory, research, and practice* (pp. 18–27). Newbury Park, CA: Sage.

Bassi, V. (1991). *The genesis of family therapy: An oral history of the years 1945–1960.* Unpublished doctoral dissertation, California School of Professional Psychology, Alameda, CA.

Bowen, M. (1966). The use of family theory in clinical practice. *Comprehensive Psychiatry, 7,* 345–374.

Bowen, M. (1978). *Family therapy in clinical practice.* New York: Aronson.

Boykin, A. W. (1986). The triple quandary and the schooling of Afro-American children. In U. Neisser (Ed.), *The school achievement of minority children: New perspectives.* New Jersey: Lawrence Erlbaum.

Brilliant, A. (1979). *I may not be totally perfect, but parts of me are excellent, and other brilliant thoughts.* Santa Barbara, CA: Woodbridge Press.

Comer, J. P. (1985). The Yale-New Haven primary prevention project: A follow-up study. *Journal of the American Academy of Child Psychiatry, 24,* 154–160.

Duckitt, J. (1992). *The social psychology of prejudice.* New York: Praeger.

Goldner, V. (1988). Generation and gender: Normative and covert hierarchies. *Family Process, 27,* 17–31.

Graham, S. (1992). Most of the subjects were white and middle class: Trends in published research on African Americans in Selected APA journals, 1970–1989. *American Psychologist, 47,* 629–639.

Green, R.-J. (1995). High achievement, underachievement, and learning disabilities: A family systems model. In B. A. Ryan, G. R. Adams, T. P. Gullotta, R. P. Weissberg, & R. L. Hampton (Eds.), *The family-school connection: Theory, research, and practice* (pp. 207–249). Thousand Oaks, CA: Sage.

Green, R.-J. (1998). Training programs: Guidelines for multicultural transformation. In M. McGoldrick (Ed.), *Revisioning family therapy: Race, culture, and gender in clinical practice* (pp. 111–112). New York: Guilford Press.

Green, R.-J. (2000). Lesbians, gays, and family psychology: Resources for teaching and practice. In B. Greene & G. Croom (Eds.), *Education, research, and practice in lesbian, gay, bisexual, and transgender psychology: A resource manual* (pp. 207–225). Thousand Oaks, CA: Sage.

Green, R.-J. (2001). Coming out to families . . . in context. *The Family Psychologist, 17,* 11–14.

Green, R.-J., Bettinger, M., & Zacks, E. (1996). Are lesbian couples fused and gay male couples disengaged? Questioning gender straightjackets. In J. Laird & R.-J. Green (Eds.), *Lesbians and gays in couples and families: A handbook for therapists* (pp. 185–230). San Francisco: Jossey-Bass.

Grier, W., & Cobbs, P. (1968). *Black rage.* New York: Basic Books.

Haley, J. (1977). *Problem-solving therapy.* San Francisco: Jossey-Bass.

Hamlin, W. (1990). *The chains of psychological slavery: The mental illness of racism.* Unpublished manuscript, Institute for Child and Family Psychiatry, Inc., Silver Spring, MD.

Laing, R. D. (1965). Mystification, confusion, and conflict. In I. Boszormenyi-Nagy & J. L. Framo (Eds.), *Intensive family therapy* (pp. 343–363). Hagerstown, MD: Hoeber Medical Division, Harper & Row.

Laird, J., & Green, R.-J. (1996). *Lesbians and gays in couples and families: A handbook for therapists.* San Francisco: Jossey-Bass.

McAdoo, H. P. (Ed.). (1988). *Black families* (2nd ed.). Newbury Park, CA: Sage.

McGoldrick, M., Giordano, J., & Pearce, J. K. (1996). *Ethnicity and family therapy* (2nd ed.). New York: Guilford Press.

Minuchin, S. (1974). *Families and family therapy.* Cambridge, MA: Harvard University Press.

Minuchin, S., Montalvo, B., Guerney, B. G., Jr., Rosman, B. L., & Schumer, F. (1967). *Families of the slums: An exploration of their structure and treatment.* New York: Basic Books.

Moore-McDowell, J. (1993). *Inner-city African-American families' achievement practices and children's experienced prejudice: Correlates of children's academic achievement and psychosocial competence.* Unpublished doctoral dissertation, California School of Professional Psychology, Alameda, CA.

Ogbu, J. U. (1978). *Minority education and caste: The American system in cross-cultural perspective.* New York: Academic Press.

Ogbu, J. U. (1989). *Cultural models and educational strategies of non-dominant peoples (1989 Catherine Molony Memorial Lecture)*. New York: City College Workshop Center.

Olmedo, E. L. (1994). Testimony of Esteban L. Olmedo to the Subcommittee on Health and the Environment, U.S. House of Representatives' Committee on Energy and Commerce. Reprinted in *CSPP Visions, 7*(1), 15–17.

Riemersma, M. (1995, September/October). Who is the typical MFCC in California: 1995 CAMFT Survey Results. *The California Therapist,* 7–9.

Schorr, L. (1989). *Within our reach: Breaking the cycle of disadvantage.* New York: Anchor.

Sue, D. W., Ivey, A. E., & Pedersen, P. B. (1996). *A theory of multicultural counseling and therapy.* Pacific Grove, CA: Brooks/Cole.

Sue, D. W., & Sue, D. (1990). *Counseling the culturally different: Theory and practice* (2nd ed.). New York: John Wiley & Sons.

Vogel, E. F., & Bell, N. W. (1968). The emotionally disturbed child as the family scapegoat. In N. W. Bell & E. F. Vogel (Eds.), *A modern introduction to the family* (Rev. ed.) (pp. 412–427). New York: Free Press.

Weiss, H. M., & Edwards, M. E. (1992). The family-school collaboration project: Systemic interventions for school improvement. In S. L. Christenson & J. C. Conoley (Eds.), *Home-school collaboration: Enhancing children's academic and social competence.* Silver Spring, MD: National Association of School Psychologists.

Wilson, L. L., & Smith, S. M. (1993). The voices of African-American MFT students: Suggestions for improving recruitment and retention. *Journal of Marital and Family Therapy, 19,* 17–30.

CHAPTER SIXTEEN

Exploring Risky Sexual Behaviors Leading to HIV Infection

The Experience of African American Women

Eleanor Jackson-Castleberry

The African American community has been disproportionately affected by the HIV/AIDS epidemic. While they comprise only 12 percent of the general population, African Americans make up approximately 40 percent of the AIDS cases. White men constitute 85 percent of the male AIDS cases, and African American women make up approximately 60 percent of the females diagnosed with AIDS. Worldwide, the vast majority of AIDS cases in women are African and poor. From 1993–1996 HIV infection was the leading cause of death among African American women ages twenty-five to forty-four (Center for Disease Control and Prevention, 1999). HIV is primarily transmitted to African American women through IV drug use (44 percent) and heterosexual contact (37 percent) (Maldonado, 1999). In 1982 the 12 percent of United States women with AIDS fit in the exposure category of heterosexual contact, but presently over one-third are in this group, making it the fastest growing transmission method (Amaro, 1993, 1995; Berger & Vizgirda, 1993; Ehrhardt, Yingling, Zawadzki, & Martinez-Ramirez, 1992; Grinstead, Faigeles, Binson, & Eversley, 1993).

EXPLORING HIV+ AFRICAN AMERICAN WOMEN'S PAST RISKY SEXUAL BEHAVIORS

The issue of AIDS in women is also confounded by the fact that current prevention methods would control childbearing and pregnancy. In addition, women may have difficulty negotiating safe sex measures (for example, condom use) with male partners upon whom they are economically dependent (Amaro, 1995; Ehrhardt et al., 1992; Nichols, 1990; Wingood, Hunter-Gamble, & DiClemente, 1993). Although the risk of HIV infection is important, many women place it low on a list of more pressing concerns (for example, lack of food and shelter, fear of abuse, immediate health problems, drug addiction, violence, loss of child custody; Amaro, 1993, 1995; Cook, 1993; Corea, 1992; Craig, 1993; Jenkins, 1990; Johnson, 1993; Lown, Winkler, Fullilove, & Fullilove, 1993; Mays & Cochran, 1990; Quimby, 1993).

HIV education programs, which were originally designed to target the gay community, have not been as effective when applied to the African American community. Media messages and outreach programs have made it widely known that proper condom use provides protection from sexually transmitted diseases (STDs)(for example, HIV), but there are still many people who either do not or inconsistently use them (Baker, Beadnell, Gordon, Morrison, & Gillmore, 1994; Berger & Vizgirda, 1993; Bowser, Fullilove, & Fullilove, 1990; Catania et al., 1992, 1994; Cohen, 1993; Corea, 1992; Ehrhardt et al., 1992; Johnson, 1993; Patton, 1993). This is particularly alarming and confusing since HIV disease has been fatal in so many cases.

HIV disease has reached an epidemic status and continues to climb in the African American community. Apparently, the prevention and education programs have been insufficient or ineffective in reaching this group. Fullilove, Fullilove, Haynes, and Gross (1990) posit there are two major facts which increase the risk of HIV disease in this population. The first factor, reduced economic status of African American communities, results in many unemployed men. Unemployment is disruptive to families and can be an additional stressor on sexual relationships. The second factor comprises the epidemic increase of crack cocaine use in this community dramatically affecting sexual behavior (that is, casual exchanges of sex for drugs or money are more prevalent).

Other factors which impede HIV prevention include (1) inconsistent condom use; (2) perception that condom use interferes with sexual pleasure; (3) lack of sexual communication skills; (4) partner refusal to wear condoms; and (5) perception that one is not at risk for HIV infection (Baker et al., 1994; Berger & Vizgirda, 1993; Catania et al., 1994; Corea, 1992; Ehrhardt et al., 1992; Grinstead et al., 1993; Norris & Ford, 1994; Wingood et al., 1993). Further, the introduction of condom use into a sexual relationship may be viewed as distrust or admitting to sex outside of the relationship (Berger & Vizgirda; Catania et al.; Wingood et al.). If the partner refuses to use condoms, it may leave the woman feeling powerless in sexual relationships (Berger & Vizgirda; Corea; Ehrhardt et al.; Wingood et al.). Some other issues affecting this population (for example, racism, poverty, cultural pressures, oppression, gender rules, low-risk perception, social isolation) may be obstacles to effective HIV prevention (Airhihenbuwa, DiClemente, Wingood, & Lowe, 1992; Berger &

Vizgirda; Catania et al.; Cook, 1993; Corea; Ehrhardt et al.; Johnson, 1993; Quimby, 1993; Satcher, 1990; Squire, 1993; Wingood et al.).

Cook (1993) suggested that some African American women have a lower economic status and may be focusing on more pressing concerns, such as unemployment, homelessness, illiteracy, and poor health. These factors are accompanied by feelings of frustration, isolation, self-hatred, depression, powerlessness, as well as lack of access to adequate health care, which may make it easier for these individuals to be in denial of risk or perceive they are at low risk for HIV infection (Cook; Mays & Cochran, 1988; Satcher, 1990). In a study (Johnson, 1993) exploring the use of condoms by African American women with multiple sex partners, 65 percent reported they never or inconsistently used them. When condoms were used, less than 25 percent reported using them for protection against STDs. The lack of usage and negative attitude toward condoms was due to (1) male partners' low perception of risk if the women did not insist on condom use; (2) women's reduced risk perception if they are discriminating in their partner selection; and (3) personal distress due to feelings of hopelessness, low self-worth, loneliness and, possibly substance abuse. Johnson posits that these women may have multiple sex partners as a means of stress reduction and to receive more love and acceptance from others. Although health issues may be placed low on the list of priorities, a study conducted by Elder-Tabrizy, Wolitski, Rhodes, and Baker (1991) on health concerns, found that 72 percent of the African American participants cited AIDS as a primary health concern or threat.

The purpose of this study was to gain an understanding of the engagement in risky sexual behaviors by heterosexual African American women. The focus was on the intrapersonal and interpersonal processes. Heterosexual behavior was examined due to its rank as the fastest growing HIV exposure category. Information was obtained about past sexual attitudes and beliefs that led to risky behaviors.

Method

The participants were six HIV+ African American women between the ages of twenty-eight and forty-two in Central California, and paid $30 for their participation. All participants had engaged in unprotected sex with men, and believed they acquired HIV in this manner. See Table 16.1 for additional demographic information.

Individual appointments were scheduled, during which the participants completed consent forms, a demographic questionnaire, and an audio taped interview. The interview began with the following question:

> I am interested in understanding your experience of engaging in risky sexual behavior. Please begin by recalling situations in which you engaged in risky sex. As you recall these situations, relax and focus on your experience. Describe the experiences as fully as you can, taking as much time as you need.

Table 16.1. Demographic Information

Subject	Age	Marital Status	Gross Income	No. Children	Educ. Level	Risky Behavior*	DX Date	Test Reason	AIDS DX
P1	37	Single	<10K	2	11	1, 2, 3, 4	1994	PRB	No
P2	42	Single	<10K	4	11	1	1993	Symptoms	No
P3	38	Single	<10K	2	8	4, 5	1994	PRB	No
P4	28	Married	10–20K	2	11	5	1993	PRB	No
P5	42	Separated	<10K	3	11	2, 3, 4	1993	PRB/Sym.	No
P6	40	Single	<10K	3	11	1, 3	1994	PRB	No

Note. No. = number; Educ. = education; DX = diagnosis; P = participant number; *Risky Behavior codes (1 = Heterosexual contact with infected partner; PRB = past risky behavior; Sym. = symptoms; 2 = Intravenous drug use; 3 = Needle sharing [for example, tattoo]; 4 = Sex with IV drug user; 5 = Sex with Bisexual partner).

Each participant was allowed to relate her experience(s) as freely as possible, interrupted only for clarification.

Transcriptions of the participants' tapes were analyzed to ascertain meaning units, categories, and themes which were integrated to compose the fundamental structure of their experience of engaging in risky sexual behavior.

Results

The three most prevalent themes are presented with excerpts of participants' statements. It should be noted that some statements also fit into other themes.

Desire for Committed Relationship. Participants reported having unsafe sex with individuals with whom they wanted to enter into a committed relationship. When they were attracted to, in love with, or needed to feel wanted by their partner(s), risk for HIV transmission was either ignored or perceived as low. For example:

> I didn't wear protection with my kids' fathers or my boyfriend who was married to a prostitute. I should have known better, but I was in love and wanted to be with him, so I took a chance every time. Every time I had sex with him, he would give me gonorrhea. I would go to the health department and get my shot, and go right back and have sex with him again. I didn't mind going, because I liked him a lot.
>
> [and]
>
> I met a guy who was very nice to me, drove me around and listened to my problems. I needed to know someone and needed to be wanted. I thought if I could win him over, I could be with him. I wanted someone to like and want me. I had unsafe sex with him. I found out later that he wasn't looking for a commitment, so that was lost.

Trust/Fidelity. The participants assumed that they were in committed, mutually monogamous relationships. When they were not having sex outside the relationship, the participants expected their partners to do the same and believed their partners' claims of being faithful. Because the participants loved and believed in their partners, they trusted them to not engage in behaviors that would place them at risk. For example:

> When a man's in my life, I just deal with one person. He also said it was just me and him, but it was me, him and somebody else. I trusted too far in somebody that I shouldn't. Trusting him meant I wouldn't have to use a condom because he's not going to catch nothing and give it to me. I thought he was all right, he was cool, since I didn't see him with nobody, but my instincts were wrong.

Perception of Cleanliness/Health. Participants believed they would know if an individual was infected by their appearance. Prior to engaging in risky sex, participants often merely asked partners if they had any diseases, then accepted the given response. In addition, participants believed the usage of a douche after unsafe sex was sufficient protection against STDs. For example:

> The reason I never used condoms was because he was such a clean person. He bathed, and I could tell he was a clean person. He wasn't running around with a lot of women, and going to bed with every woman he sees. I could look at him and tell if he's diseased or something . . . I never thought that I would get no diseases from him.

Other themes which emerged were as follows:

1. *Kindness.* Participants reported placing themselves at risk if partners were nice; provided emotional, social and financial support; and treated them better than partners in past relationships.

2. *Accepting inappropriate behaviors in relationship.* Participants were willing to tolerate inappropriate behaviors (for example, cheating, drug abuse) from their partners in order to sustain their relationships, which included unsafe sex after contracting STDs.

3. *Substance abuse.* Some participants were abusing or addicted to illicit drugs, which impaired judgment, lowered inhibitions, and very often safer sex practices were not even taken into consideration.

4. *Prostitution.* Prostitution was a means of obtaining additional income to support the family or drug habit. Some participants felt forced to resort to prostitution since they were unemployed, undereducated, and had no other means of financial support.

5. *Condom use.* There was inconsistent condom use when participants were under the influence of drugs or partners complained about condoms interfering with sexual pleasure. Participants who engaged in prostitution often requested safer sex practices. They used condoms (1) as birth control; (2) if available; (3) if the "trick" was willing to use them; (4) if they were with someone unfamiliar; or; (5) if customer was perceived as unclean or unhealthy. With permanent partners, participants used condoms when partner was willing or until he refused, and to punish partner for being unfaithful.

6. *Inaccurate or limited AIDS knowledge.* Some participants reported having a lack of, or erroneous information about, STDs or means of HIV prevention. These participants stated they did not receive sex education in schools, from parents, or from health care professionals when consulted for STD treatment. Other participants had basic AIDS knowledge which was misapplied and distorted their risk perception.

7. *Undisclosed HIV+ status.* There were participants who reported having partners aware of their own HIV+ status, but failed to inform participants prior to engaging in risky sex. When asked their reasons for not disclosing their HIV+ status, some partners expressed fear that participants would end the relationship if the partner's HIV status was known. Others reported their partners felt no remorse over infecting the participants since the partners were also infected by other partners, who failed to disclose this information to them.

8. *Discomfort in recalling past risky behavior.* The participants expressed having negative feelings about themselves for engaging in risky behavior leading to HIV infection. They expressed anger, depression, suicidal ideation and consider themselves stupid for placing their lives at risk in the past. Many reported being able to be more assertive in present intimate relationships since their HIV+ diagnosis. However, there were participants who continued to engage in risky sex with their partners (who were aware of HIV+ status) despite the increased risk to themselves. In addition, participants expressed regret that they did not adequately protect themselves in the past.

Discussion

The themes that emerged from the participants' experiences were interrelated, forming three clusters. One cluster was composed of the following themes: desire for committed relationship, trust and fidelity, kindness, accepting inappropriate behaviors in relationship, and condom usage. The participants engaged in unprotected sex when they were in love, needed to feel connected or were trying to win over the partner to secure a relationship. The need for attachment was stronger than concerns for placing self at risk. In giving freely of themselves emotionally and physically, the women expected partners to reciprocate by being loyal, faithful, and protective of them. In relating with these partners, the participants would often overlook cheating, abuse, STD transmission, and drug addiction. They were unwilling to jeopardize the potential security offered by the desired relationship. While this method was unsuccessful in acquiring a committed relationship for any of the participants, this practice continued.

A second cluster was comprised of the following themes: substance abuse, prostitution, and condom usage. These participants had a low income, little education, and most were unemployed. Prostitution was one means to buy drugs or supplement incomes to purchase necessities. Participants used drugs as a coping mechanism for loneliness, poverty, or unemployment. The drug use led to addiction, which increased their feelings of powerlessness. Without a steady partner for economic support, some women saw no other options except prostitution to support the drug habit. They felt worse about themselves and had even less concern for their safety, especially when drugs were unobtainable and withdrawal symptoms ensued. When this occurred, the participants' entire focus was on acquiring drugs and negotiating for safe sex practices was not considered or pursued. While some women did think about requesting or insisting that condoms be used, they did not consistently practice safer sex because of their fear of jeopardizing their chances for obtaining the drugs.

The third cluster comprised of the following themes: inaccurate or limited AIDS knowledge, perception of cleanliness and health, desire for committed relationship, and substance abuse. Although a few women reported having had no education about STDs and how to protect themselves, most had basic information. They were aware that HIV was a STD, and proper condom use would provide protection. However, the women did not consistently use protection, despite their AIDS knowledge. Some hoped they would be safe with a partner who appeared to be clean and healthy. Further, some women used a douche after unprotected sex, hoping it would suffice when condoms were not used. It appears that the women distorted or misapplied accurate AIDS information in order to preserve their perception of being at low risk. The need for attachment or drugs overshadowed their concern for personal safety.

Caution should be used in interpreting the present findings given the small sample size, reliance on self-report, and demographics of the women selected for the study (for example, their low SES, education level). While the present findings provide important information to be considered in HIV prevention strategies, they are not meant to be generalizable to all African American women.

Similar to previous research findings, these African American women (1) had difficulty negotiating safe sex measures with male partners upon whom they were economically and emotionally dependent; (2) placed HIV infection lower on the list of more pressing concerns (for example, drug addiction, sustaining a relationship); (3) used condoms inconsistently with steady and casual sex partners; (4) felt powerless and inadequate in their intimate relationships; (5) had varying levels of AIDS education, ranging from none to basic, yet the informed continued to engage in risky behaviors despite their knowledge; and (6) tolerated inappropriate behaviors from their partners (for example, cheating, drugs use) in order to preserve the relationship.

The findings in this study provide further insight into risky sexual behaviors in African American women. Similar to other women in the American society, they were socialized to value connectedness. These women sought solace for life stressors through their intimate relationships. Although, they would have preferred committed monogamous partners, the women (often knowingly) placed themselves at risk in order to have a semblance of their desire. The attraction to, or love for, a partner led them to believe they could also place their safety in the partners' hands. Although some interactions with partners were temporary, abusive, or life threatening, the women continued their pursuit in the same manner. Even after contracting HIV, there were women who continued the risky behaviors.

This matter is further complicated when substance abuse is a factor. With the relationship being viewed as very important, the women in this study have resorted to substance abuse to deal with loneliness and the desire for a relationship, as well as feelings of powerlessness, inadequacy, social isolation, and poverty. While initially used as another source of comfort, the abuse led to addiction and the women resorting to self-destructive behaviors (for example, prostitution) to support the habit. The desire for relationships, intermingled with drug abuse, were the primary forces leading the women in this study to HIV infection.

In an attempt to further understand the sexual attitudes and behaviors of the participants of this study, attachment theory was reviewed. According to attachment theory, adults (like children) seek affectional bonds with significant others in order to feel safe (Ainsworth, 1989; Bowlby, 1969; Sheldon & West, 1989; West, 1994). Adult attachment was defined as "dyadic relationships in which proximity to a special and preferred other is sought or maintained to achieve a sense of security" (West, p. 19). Individuals find it comforting to be in close proximity with attachment figures during stressful times, and tend to become apprehensive and hurt if there is a loss or threat of losing the attachment. When one's efforts to connect result in failure, an individual may feel his sense of security is jeopardized, and this might lead to patterns of insecure attachment or dysfunctional attachment strategies (West).

By applying attachment theory to the women in this study, one can see how their need for affectional bonds superseded self-preservation. They utilized maladaptive attachment strategies (that is, unprotected sex) to try to secure relationships, which resulted in detrimental consequences, HIV disease.

The current methods of HIV prevention education (that is, using fear tactics and the desirability of condoms) had little or no effect on this group, due to life stressors and psychosocial issues concerning these women. Effective prevention strategies will need to address variables, such as social isolation, powerlessness, and economic dependence. Particular attention needs to be given to attachment needs and strategies, drug addiction, and the accuracy of AIDS knowledge.

References

Ainsworth, M. D. (1989). Attachments beyond infancy. *American Psychologist, 44*(4), 709–716.

Airhihenbuwa, C. O., DiClemente, R. J., Wingood, G. M., & Lowe, A. (1992). HIV/AIDS education and prevention among African Americans: A focus on culture. *AIDS Education and Prevention, 4*(3), 251–260.

Amaro, H. (1993). Reproductive choice in the age of AIDS: Policy and counseling issues. In C. Squire (Ed.), *Women and AIDS* (pp. 20–41). London: Sage.

Amaro, H. (1995). Love, sex, and power: Considering women's realities in HIV prevention. *American Psychologist, 50*(6), 437–447.

Baker, S. A., Beadnell, B., Gordon, J. R., Morrison, D. M., & Gillmore, M. R. (1994, Fall). *The women's health project: Using multiple sources of quantitative and qualitative data to inform intervention design.* Paper presented at the meeting of the American Association of Behavioral Therapy, San Diego, CA.

Berger, B., & Vizgirda, V. (1993). Prevention of HIV infection in women and children. In F. L. Cohen & J. D. Durham (Eds.), *Women, children and HIV/AIDS* (pp. 60–80). New York: Springer.

Bowlby, J. (1969). *Attachment: Volume 1 attachment and loss.* New York: Basic Books.

Bowser, B. P., Fullilove, M. T., & Fullilove, R. E. (1990). African American youth and AIDS high-risk behavior: The social context and barriers to prevention. *Youth and Society, 22*(1), 54–66.

Catania, J. A., Coates, T. J., Golden, E., Dolcini, M. M., Peterson, J., Kegeles, S., Siegel, D., & Fullilove, M. T. (1994). Correlates of condom use among Black, Hispanic, and White heterosexuals in San Francisco: The AMEN longitudinal survey. *AIDS Education and Prevention, 6*(1), 12–26.

Catania, J. A., Coates, T. J., Kegeles, S., Fullilove, M. T., Peterson, J., Marin, B., Siegel, D., & Hulley, S. (1992). Condom use in multi-ethnic neighborhoods of San Francisco: The population-based AMEN (AIDS in multi-ethnic neighborhoods) study. *American Journal of Public Health, 8*(2), 284–287.

Center for Disease Control and Prevention. (1999). *Divisions of HIV/AIDS prevention* [On-line], Available: http://www.cdc.gov/hiv/dhap.htm, Atlanta, GA: Department of Health & Human Services.

Cohen, F. L. (1993). HIV infection and AIDS: An overview. In F. L. Cohen & J. D. Durham (Eds.), *Women, children and HIV/AIDS* (pp. 3–30). New York: Springer.

Cook, S. (1993, August–October). Some barriers to HIV/AIDS prevention for African American women. *NIA: Living to Prevent AIDS, 5*(3), 5–6.

Corea, G. (1992). *The invisible epidemic.* New York: HarperCollins.

Craig, D. (1993, May–July). Crack-cocaine in the spread of HIV disease. *NIA: Living to Prevent AIDS, 5*(2), 1–2.

Ehrhardt, A. A., Yingling, S., Zawadzki, R., & Martinez-Ramirez, M. (1992). Prevention of heterosexual transmission of HIV: Barriers for women. *Journal of Psychology and Human Sexuality, 5*(1), 37–67.

Elder-Tabrizy, K., Wolitski, R. R., Rhodes, F., & Baker, J. (1991). AIDS and competing health concerns of Blacks, Hispanics and Whites. *Journal of Community Health, 16*, 11–21.

Fullilove, M. T., Fullilove, R. E., Haynes, K., & Gross, S. (1990). Black women and AIDS prevention: A view towards understanding the gender rules. *Journal of Sex Research, 27*(1), 47–64.

Grinstead, O. A., Faigeles, G., Binson, D., & Eversley, R. (1993). Sexual risk for human immunodeficiency virus infection among women in high-risk cities. *Family Planning Perspectives, 25,* 252–256, 277.

Jenkins, D. (1990, March). Effective actions for HIV education and prevention with addicts and alcoholics (active and in recovery). *HIV/AIDS Education and Prevention Project* (pp. 1–3).

Johnson, E. H. (1993). *Risky sexual behavior among African Americans.* Westport, CT: Praeger.

Lown, E. A., Winkler, K., Fullilove, R. E., & Fullilove, M. T. (1993). Tossin' and tweakin': Women's consciousness in the crack culture. In C. Squire (Ed.), *Women and AIDS* (pp. 90–105). London: Sage.

Maldonado, M. (1999). *HIV/AIDS and African American.* Washington, DC: National Minority AIDS Council.

Mays, V. M., & Cochran, S. D. (1988). Issues in the perception of AIDS risk and risk reduction activities by Black and Hispanic/Latina women. *American Psychologist, 43*(11), 949–957.

Nichols, M. (1990). Women and acquired immunodeficiency syndrome: Issues for prevention. In B. Voeller, J. M. Reinisch, & M. Gottlieb (Eds.), *AIDS and sex: An integrated biomedical and biobehavioral approach* (pp. 375–392). New York: Oxford University Press.

Norris, A. E., & Ford, K. (1994). Associations between condom experiences and beliefs, intentions, and use in a sample of urban, low-income African American and Hispanic youth. *AIDS Education and Prevention, 6*(1), 27–39.

Patton, C. (1993). "With champagne and roses": Women at risk from/in AIDS discourse. In C. Squire (Ed.), *Women and AIDS* (pp. 165–187). London: Sage.

Quimby, E. (1993). Obstacles to reducing AIDS among African Americans. *The Journal of Black Psychology, 19*(2), 215–222.

Satcher, D. (1990). Crime, sin, or disease: Drug abuse and AIDS in the African American community. *Journal of Health Care for the Poor and Underserved, 1*(2), 212–218.

Sheldon, A. E., & West, M. (1989). The functional discrimination of attachment and affiliation: Theory and empirical demonstration. *British Journal of Psychiatry, 155,* 18–23.

Squire, C. (Ed.). (1993). *Women and AIDS.* London: Sage.

West, M. L. (1994). *Patterns of relating: An adult attachment perspective.* New York: Guilford Press.

Wingood, G. M., Hunter-Gamble, D., & DiClemente, R. J. (1993). A pilot study of sexual communication and negotiation among young African American women: Implications of HIV prevention. *The Journal of Black Psychology, 19*(2), 190–203.

CHAPTER SEVENTEEN

The Impact of Skin Color and Hair Texture on Mate Selection

Implications for Interventions with African American Men and Women

Carlton W. Parks and Kamilah Marie Woodson

The origins of skin color and hair texture as mediators for the constructs of self-concept and self-esteem among African Americans date back to slavery, and the Willy Lynch Doctrine of 1712:

in my bag here, I have a fool-proof method for controlling your black slaves. I guarantee every one of you that if installed correctly, it will control the slaves at least 300 years. My method is simple, any member of your family or any overseer can use it. I have outlined a number of differences among the slaves; and I take these differences and make them bigger: I use fear, distrust, and envy for control purposes. These methods worked on my modest plantation in the West Indies, and it will work in the south. Take this simple list of differences, and think about them. On top of my list is "age," but it is there only because it starts with the letter "A," second is "color" or shade. There is intelligence, size, sex, size of plantation, status of plantation, attitude of owner, whether the slaves live in the valley, on the hill, east, west, north, south, have fine or coarse hair, or is tall or short. Don't forget, you must pitch the old black versus the young black, and the young black male against the old black male. You must use the dark skin slaves versus the light skin slaves, and the light skin slaves versus the dark skin slaves. You must use the female versus the male, and the male versus the female. You must also have your white servants and overseers

The author wishes to thank Kumea Shorter-Gooden, Ph.D. for her helpful comments during the preparation of this chapter.

distrust all blacks, but it is necessary that your slaves trust and depend on us. They must love, respect, and trust only us. The black slave, after receiving this indoctrination shall carry on and will be coming self-refueling and self-generating for hundreds of years, maybe thousands (Lynch, 1999, pp. 8–9).

Wirth and Goldhammer (1944) have discussed two reasons for the higher status enjoyed by light-skinned enslaved people in the south during slavery. First, many white slave owners were related by kinship to their light-skinned slaves. They favored them with better positions (for example, as house servants versus field slaves) and educational opportunities. Second, being a light-skinned slave increased the probability of receiving training in the skilled trades. As time progressed after slavery, this obsession with skin color and hair texture became internalized among African Americans after enslavement and served as criteria for membership in African American social organizations (for example, paper bag and comb tests) (Neal & Wilson, 1989). If your skin color was darker than the paper bag, and your hair didn't easily pass through a comb, your membership to the social organization was denied (Graham, 1999).

HISTORICAL INFLUENCES

Skin color even permeates the relationship dynamics within many African American families: "Often, it is within the family, where a variety of skin colors may be represented among individual members, that black children first learn the values attributed to differences in skin color" (Okazawa-Rey, Robinson, & Ward, 1987, p. 90). Individual family members who are perceived as being "too dark" or "too light" can become scapegoats by their family members because they look "different" (Boyd-Franklin, 1991). As African American children enter the larger social world, they carry with them this "excess baggage" that negatively impacts their interpersonal relations, and unfortunately the world often reinforces these attitudes (Okazawa-Rey et al.).

SKIN COLOR AND HAIR TEXTURE

One example of this reality is the preferential treatment light-skinned African Americans receive within the Euro-American and African American communities. The more Caucasoid their physical attributes conforms to the Euro-American standard of beauty and physical attractiveness, the more rewarding their lives are (Bond & Cash, 1992; Gatewood, 1988). Light skin color has become a criterion for the attainment of prestige within the African American and Euro-American communities (Russell, Wilson, & Hall, 1992; Wade, 1996).

Lakoff and Scherr (1984) assert "beauty is power," and many African American women rely heavily on their perceived physical attractiveness in achieving success within the social arena. Unfortunately, what is perceived as being physically attractive in the United States is based on large part on skin color and hair texture (Okazawa-Rey, Robinson, & Ward, 1987; Russell, Wilson, & Hall).

There exists data that suggest that light-skinned African Americans fare better economically, vocationally, and educationally (Hughes & Hertel, 1990; Keith & Herring, 1991). The family income of light-skinned African Americans is more than 50-percent greater than dark-skinned African Americans. Likewise, light-skinned African Americans are more likely to be employed in professional or technical positions (Keith & Herring), and their partners are more likely to have more education and higher occupational prestige than their dark-skinned counterparts (Hughes & Hertel). Interestingly, skin color predicts educational attainment, occupation, and personal and family income over and above demographic variables such as chronological age, socioeconomic status, and parental background (Keith & Herring). Chambers, Clark, Dantzler, and Baldwin (1994) have revealed that students at a historically black university with elevated levels of African self-consciousness (ASC) responded more positively to female pictures with prominent African facial features than students with medium or reduced levels of ASC.

Clearly, contextual influences play a significant role in the expression of this phenomenon. For instance, skin color is believed to have a stronger impact on sexual attractiveness than global and physical attractiveness because of the critical role it plays in the mate selection process (Cunningham, Roberts, Barbee, Druen, & Wu, 1995; Wade, 1996). Wade revealed that dark-skinned male college students' self-ratings of sexual attractiveness were higher than light-skinned male college students but female college students' ratings did not differ from one another.

When one adds sexual orientation identity status to this equation, our knowledge and awareness about issues of skin color and hair texture on mate selection is relatively scarce. Same-gender loving African American females face a "double stigma," according to Greene, White and Whitten (2000) because their physical attractiveness, self-worth, and femininity are under more critical scrutiny by the mainstream culture than among heterosexual African American females. There are few data sets (for example, Atkins, 1998; Cogan & Erickson, 1999; Rapi & Chowdhry, 1998; Rose, 1994; Rothblum, 1994) that have begun to explore the question of how body image and perceived physical attractiveness impacts the psychological functioning of lesbians, heterosexuals (Gary, 1987; Mishkind, Rodin, Silberstein, & Striegel-Moore, 1987), bisexuals, and gay men (for example, Carlat & Carmargo, 1991; Carlat, Carmargo, & Herzog, 1997; Siever, 1994). Unfortunately, these data sets have been comprised almost exclusively of Euro-Americans.

Collins (1990) and Russell, Wilson, and Hall (1992) have asserted that hair texture exerts a more prominent role in the lives of African American females than African American males. For African American females, hair texture becomes a reflection of a female's African American consciousness, socioeconomic status, and lifestyle. The literature on hair texture among African American females (Banks, 2000; Bonner, 1992; Gibson, 1995; Greene, White, & Whitten, 2000; Rooks, 1996) equates "good hair" with "manageable hair" that appears to the external world as being feminine, attractive, and easy to maintain. Typically, African American females perceive their hair as a "racial signifier," and a "badge of inferiority" (Banks). Similarly, Greene, White, and Whitten asserted that hair can be viewed as a metaphor for how African American females feel about themselves. However, Tyler (1990) questioned the further extension of this interpretation asserted by Grier and Cobbs (1968), that the hair texture(s) of African Americans and their continual attempts to dramatically alter its appearance serve as illustrations of internalized racism.

hooks (1992) discussed how the combination of the visual manipulation of the African American body image (that is, the focus on one aspect of the body or unusual body postures superimposed on long, straight hair) in the mass media projects a powerful image of sexualized imagery that communicates mixed messages to the mainstream audience concerning the "beauty" of the various prototypes of the African American female (Wyatt, 1997).

THE MATE SELECTION PROCESS AMONG AFRICAN AMERICANS

It is becoming increasingly apparent that the mate selection process among African Americans is qualitatively different than among Euro-Americans. First, due to incarceration rates, deaths, drugs, homosexuality, and other societal situations, the availability of "eligible" or "suitable" African American males is quite low. African Americans marry later and have higher rates of divorce (Tucker & Mitchell-Kernan, 1998). African Americans are spending greater portions of their lives as unmarried as is the case for the general population (James, Tucker, & Mitchell-Kernan, 1996).

When one adds to the equation the reality that many African American women will earn more their potential partners (Lichter, LeClere, & McLaughlin, 1991), Franklin and Pillow (1999) assert that African American males feel inadequate, become withdrawn while African American females feel disappointed and begin to lack respect for their male counterparts which can result in interpersonal conflict (Gary, 1987). Unfortunately, African American females are still socialized to search for a Prince Charming ideal, which results in unrealistic expectations, delusions, relationship dissatisfaction among both African American men and women which results in an out-of-wedlock birthrate at 70 percent among African American women (Bethea, 1995; Braithwaite, 1981; Cazenave, 1981; Gibbs et al., 1988; Staples, 1995; White & Cones, 1999).

Currently, 46 percent of African American men are not in the civilian labor force with 25 percent of African American men, between ages twenty and thirty, in jail, on probation, or on parole, and the mortality rate is five times higher for African American males than for African American females. Forty percent of African American men are estimated to be functionally illiterate (Chapman, 1988). The African American gender ratio, as defined by the number of males per 100 females is 88.2, and is steadily declining. "In 1975, there were 68,000 more Black female college graduates than educated Black male college graduates. Overall, the ratio of single college educated Black women to similar men is 2 to 1. As a result, some Black men are unprepared or unable to assume a positive role in the economic structure of the family. In certain categories, the ratio is as low as 38 women to every male. This gap, although wide at that time, continued to widen . . ." (Staples, 1988, p. 271).

Unfortunately, college women tend to marry highly educated males and they tend to marry less frequently than men. "The quantity and quality of available men thus influences (1) the probability that people will marry; and (2) the educational status of their mates" (Albrecht, Fossett, Cready, & Kiecolt, 1997). Suggestions that alternative strategies might need to be implemented in order to facilitate the mate selection process, are typically met with considerable resistance by African American females (Chapman, 1986). This resistance may result due to support systems of African American females as compared to African American males where males may not discuss personal problems with their male friends while African American females seek emotional support from their female friends or their families (Timmer, Veroff, & Hatchett, 1996).

Karenga (1979) described four modes through which African American males and African American females come together. They are (1) cash connection; (2) the flesh connection; (3) the force connection; and (4) the dependency connection. The cash connection is based on the notion that everything has a price and money can solve all problems. The flesh connection is based on the pursuit of sex, while the force connection is based on the notion that aggression and coercion are the best ways to resolve conflict. The dependency connection results from participation in one or all of the previously mentioned connections. Therefore, it's not too surprising that education and socioeconomic status have become major criteria given Karenga's perspective among African American males and females in determining the eligibility and suitability of potential mates, as is the case for the general population (Albrecht et al., 1997).

When one adds skin color and hair texture to the mate selection process, it becomes apparent rather quickly that the "excess baggage" unconsciously brought by African American males and females to the mate selection process sabotages the likelihood of "suitable" or "eligible" partners meeting and establishing intimate relationships. One can postulate that issues of skin color and hair texture potentially erect additional barriers for African American men and women to meet "eligible" or "suitable" mates because potential mates are prematurely screened out or deemed inappropriate due to their skin color and hair texture. Often stereotypes (for example, temperament, personality characteristics, intellectual level) are associated with skin color and hair texture. This reality is disturbing since "the problems or conflicts between Black females and males are ultimately a function of political and economic forces beyond their control, which consequently affects them emotionally" (Staples, 1988, p. 271). African American men and women "have been victimized by the whims of the dominant culture to the extent that they participate in self-defeating behaviors that are destructive to the formation of healthy relationships and unification within Black families" (Braithwaite, 1981, p. 83). These two statements relate to the availability of "suitable" and "eligible" partners as well as the impact of skin color and hair texture on the mate selection process within the African American community in the twenty-first century.

Transactional-Ecological Model for the Provision of Culturally Informed Services for African Americans Engaged in the Mate Selection Process

Jackson (1992) has proposed a treatment model for the provision of culturally informed services for African Americans. The service chain involves the African American client, family members, the African American community, and the political and economic systems that the African American client inhabits. African American professionals are expected to be involved at all levels with a focus on health promotion rather than deficits and psychopathology.

The African American clinical practice model consists of seven modules.

1. The African American helping professional
2. The African American client
3. The African American family
4. Other African American professionals
5. The African American community
6. The African American culture, political, and economic systems
7. The general environment

The ultimate goal of treatment is to facilitate the development of more adaptive functioning on the part of the African American client that will lead to more optimal functioning involving the multiple relationships within the system. To enhance therapeutic effectiveness co-joint individual, group, and family therapeutic intervention modalities may be utilized. Potential barriers to treatment effectiveness include (1) the involvement of African American professionals given potential crises in funding and support resources; (2) heterogeneity within the African American community may necessitate participant observation within the African American community by the African American helping professional to accurately assess clients; (3) distrust of the "professional competencies" of African American helping professionals; and (4) societal, political, and constitutional factors that the African American client may have little or no control over (Jackson, 1992). The philosophical underpinnings of this service-delivery model are critical and should consist of a mission, goals, and objectives that are consonant with a community-clinical psychology orientation (Crawley, 1996; Davis & Proctor, 1989; Jackson, 1992; Nelson, 1995). This may necessitate the professional training (re-education) of the staff to prepare them to effectively provide ethnically sensitive services in the community (Cheatham, 1991; Crawley; De La Cancela, 1994; Devore & London, 1993; Nelson; Washington, 1987; Woode & Lynch, 1992).

A key ingredient to service delivery would be the targeting of at-risk populations to explore issues of skin color and hair texture and their impact on the mate selection process among African Americans. It is the contention of these authors that a systemic perspective is critical to having a beneficial impact on the attitudes and behavior of African American males and females separately. The provision of culturally informed primary prevention services (Airhihenbuwa, 1992; Albee & Gullotta, 1997; Bloom, 1996; Cowen, 2000; Greene, White, & Whitten, 2000; Hill, 1999; Johnson & Birk, 1994; Ladner, 1971, 1998; Trickett, Barone, & Watts, 2000; Watts & Jagers, 1997; Wyatt, Notgrass, & Gordon, 1995) in a wide array of community- and religious-based institutions (Solomon, 1991, Wimberly, 1994) involved in coalition partnerships for health promotion (Braithwaite, 1992; Gibbs, 1991), are critical for raising the levels of consciousness and awareness of African Americans about the mate selection process. Some of the "at-risk" African American subgroups that are particularly suited to primary prevention programs include (1) couples preparing to marry; (2) adolescents who are dating; (3) parents and teachers of young children involved in the process of racial socialization (Phinney & Rotheram, 1987; Watts & Jagers; Wright, 1998); and (4) adults in middle and later adulthood involved in the mate selection process. This may necessitate the utilization of nonbiologically related providers, protectors, and role models (Lempert, 1999; White & Cones, 1999) to assist in the intergenerational transmission of values that will facilitate the mate selection process among African American men and women instead of the overreliance on same-sex African American friendship networks (Barras, 2000).

There are some themes that need to be addressed in any treatment regimen focusing on skin color and hair texture and mate selection. The meaning of skin color and hair textures for African American women should be interpreted within the context(s) of the developmental and social histories of the client from an integrated feminist-psychodynamic model (Greene, 1993). A potential barrier to treatment progress would be the inability of the therapist to engage in an intensive exploration of skin color and hair texture issues, due to their own unresolved issues (Shorter-Gooden & Jackson, 2000). The anger, guilt, and resentment frequently felt by African American women concerning these issues, and how they were dealt with within their families-of-origin and the broader African American community need to be openly expressed within a "safe environment" (Neal & Wilson, 1989). In particular, the intergenerational transmission of attitudes and beliefs concerning skin color and hair texture needs to be explored in treatment. Likewise, the impact of institutionalized racism and how historical influences dating back to slavery have shaped and molded our conceptions of beauty, physical attractiveness, and racial identity based on our notions of skin color and hair texture (particularly among their partners), needs to be systematically examined in treatment (Boyd-Franklin, 1991; Greene, White, & Whitten, 2000; White & Cones, 1999).

The impact of skin color and hair texture and the mate selection process on the expression of sexual risk taking among African American women is one of the frontiers of current psychotherapeutic intervention modalities. Wyatt et al. (1997) has revealed the need for a more comprehensive assessment of past victimization histories and cultural factors on African American women's sexual risk taking. It is becoming increasingly apparent that partner influences related to sexual risk taking (Campbell, 1995; Mays & Cochran, 1993; Wade, 1994; Wingood & DiClemente, 1998) are predictors of the expression of sexual risk taking behaviors among African American men and women. Likewise, relationship partner status is a potent predictor of sexual risk taking behavior among African American women (St. Lawrence et al., 1998). Once again, the systematic assessment of the impact of skin color and hair texture as mediators of sexual risk taking among African American women needs to be a part of any ethnically sensitive treatment plan. Finally, attachment histories (Barras, 2000; Lyons-Ruth & Jacobvitz, 1999), and child sexual abuse histories (Wyatt, Guthrie, & Notgrass, 1992) are related to subsequent sexual re-victimization. At-risk groups of African American women and their perceptions of the impact of skin color and hair texture on their sexual risk taking behavior needs to be assessed in treatment. It is becoming apparent that women who struggle with their low self-esteem and poor self-concepts—possibly as a result of their skin color and hair texture—are more likely to take sexual risks as a result of the skin color and the hair texture of their sexual partner, which can potentially threaten their physical health. These provocative hypotheses need to be empirically validated so they can inform primary preventive and psychotherapeutic intervention modalities for African American men and women engaged in mate selection.

References

Airhihenbuwa, C. O. (1992). Health promotion and disease prevention strategies for African-Americans: A conceptual model. In R. L. Braithwaite & S. E. Taylor (Eds.), *Health issues in the Black community* (pp. 267–280). San Francisco: Jossey-Bass.

Albee, G. W., & Gullotta, T. P. (Eds.). (1997). *Primary prevention works: Issues in Children's and families' lives* (Vol. 6). Thousand Oaks, CA: Sage.

Albrecht, C. M., Fossett, M. A., Cready, C. M., & Kiecolt, K. J. (1997). Mate availability, women's marriage prevalence, and husbands' education. *Journal of Family Issues, 18*(4), 429–452.

Atkins, D. (Ed.). (1998). *Looking queer: Body image and identity in lesbian, bisexual, gay, and transgender communities.* Binghamton, NY: Harrington Park Press.

Banks, I. (2000). *Hair matters: Beauty, power, and black women's consciousness.* New York: New York University Press.

Barras, J. R. (2000). *Whatever happened to daddy's little girl: The impact of fatherlessness on Black women.* New York: Ballantine.

Bethea, P. D. (1995). African-American women and the male-female relationship dilemma: A counseling perspective. *Journal of Multicultural Counseling and Development, 23*, 87–95.

Bloom, M. (1996). *Primary prevention practices: Issues in children's and families' lives* (Vol. 5). Thousand Oaks, CA: Sage.

Bond, S., & Cash, T. F. (1992). Black beauty: Skin color and body images among African-American college women. *Journal of Applied Social Psychology, 22*(11), 874–888.

Bonner, B. (1992). *For colored girls who've considered weaves when the chemicals became too ruff.* New York: Three Rivers Press.

Boyd-Franklin, N. (1991). Recurrent themes in the treatment of African-American women in group psychotherapy. *Women and Therapy, 11*(2), 25–40.

Braithwaite, R. L. (1981). Interpersonal relations between Black males and Black females. In L. E. Gary (Ed.), *Black men* (pp. 83–97). Beverly Hills, CA: Sage.

Braithwaite, R. L. (1992). Coalition partnerships for health promotion and empowerment. In R. L. Braithwaite & S. E. Taylor (Eds.), *Health issues in the Black community* (pp. 321–337). San Francisco: Jossey-Bass.

Campbell, C. A. (1995). Male gender roles and sexuality: Implications for women's AIDS risk and prevention. *Social Science Medicine, 41*(2), 197–210.

Carlat, D. J., & Camargo Jr., C. A. (1991). Review of bulimia nervosa in males. *American Journal of Psychiatry, 148*(7), 831–843.

Carlat, D. J., Camargo Jr., C. A., & Herzog, D. B. (1997). Eating disorders in males: A report on 135 patients. *American Journal of Psychiatry, 154*(8), 1127–1132.

Cazenave, N. A. (1981). Black men in America: The quest for "manhood." In H. P. McAdoo (Ed.), *Black families* (pp. 176–185). Beverly Hills, CA: Sage.

Chambers Jr., J. W., Clark, T., Dantzler, L., & Baldwin, J. A. (1994). Perceived attractiveness, facial features, and African self-consciousness. *Journal of Black Psychology, 20*(3), 305–324.

Chapman, A. B. (1986). *Mansharing: Choice or dilemma?* New York: William Morrow.

Chapman, A. B. (1988). Male-female relations: How the past affects the present. In H. P. McAdoo (Ed.), *Black families* (2nd ed., pp. 190–200). Newbury Park, CA: Sage.

Cheatham, H. E. (1991). Empowering Black families. In H. E. Cheatham & J. B. Stewart (Eds.), *Black families: Interdisciplinary perspectives* (pp. 373–393). New Brunswick, NJ: Transaction Publishers.

Cogan, J., & Erickson, J. (Eds.). (1999). *Lesbians, levis, and lipstick: The meaning of beauty in our lives.* Binghamton, NY: Harrington Park Press.

Collins, P. H. (1990). *Black feminist thought: Knowledge, consciousness, and the politics of empowerment.* New York: Routledge.

Cowen, E. L. (2000). Community psychology and routes to psychological wellness. In J. Rappaport & E. Seidman (Eds.), *Handbook of community psychology* (pp. 79–99). New York: Kluwer Academic/Plenum.

Crawley, B. H. (1996). Effective programs and services for African-American families and children: An African-centered perspective. In S. L. Logan (Ed.), *The Black family: Strengths, self-help, and positive change* (pp. 112–130). Boulder, CO: Westview Press.

Cunningham, M. R., Roberts, A. R., Barbee, A. P., Druen, P. B., & Wu, C. H. (1995). "Their ideas of beauty are, on the whole, the same as ours": Consistency and variability in the cross-cultural perception of female physical attractiveness. *Journal of Personality and Social Psychology, 68*, 261–279.

Davis, L. E., & Proctor, E. K. (1989). *Race, gender, and class: Guidelines for practice with individuals, families, and groups.* Englewood Cliffs, NJ: Prentice Hall.

DeLa Cancela, V. (1994). "Coolin": The psychosocial communication of African and Latino men. In D. J. Jones (Ed.), *African-American males: A critical link in the African-American family* (pp. 33–44). New Brunswick, NJ: Transaction Publishers.

Devore, W., & London, H. (1993). Ethnic sensitivity for practitioners: A practice model. In H. P. McAdoo (Ed.), *Family ethnicity: Strength in diversity* (pp. 317–331). Newbury Park, CA: Sage.

Franklin II, C. W., & Pillow, W. (1999). Single and married: The Black male's acceptance of the Prince Charming ideal. In R. Staples (Ed.), *The Black family: Essays and studies* (6th ed., pp. 87–102). Belmont, CA: Wadsworth.

Gary, L. E. (1987). Predicting interpersonal conflict between men and women: The case of Black men. In M. S. Kimmel (Ed.), *Changing men: New directions in research on men and masculinity* (pp. 232–243). Newbury Park, CA: Sage.

Gatewood, W. B. (1988). Aristocrat of color: South and North and the Black elite, 1880–1920. *Journal of Southern History, 54*, 3–19.

Gibbs, J. T., Brunswick, A. F., Connor, M. E., Dembo, R., Larson, T. E., Reed, R. J., & Solomon, B. (Eds.). (1988). *Young, black, and male in America: An endangered species.* New York: Auburn House.

Gibbs, J. T. (1991). Developing intervention models for Black families: Linking theory and research. In H. E. Cheatham & J. B. Stewart (Eds.), *Black families: Interdisciplinary perspectives* (pp. 325–351). New Brunswick, NJ: Transaction Publishers.

Gibson, A. L. (1995). *Growing up Black and female in America.* New York: Harlem Press.

Graham, L. O. (1999). *Our kind of people: Inside America's Black upper class.* New York: HarperCollins.

Greene, B. (1993). Psychotherapy with African-American women: Integrating feminist and psychodynamic models. *The Journal of Training and Practice in Professional Psychology, 7*(1), 49–66.

Greene, B., White, J. C., & Whitten, L. (2000). Hair texture, length, and style as a metaphor in the African-American mother-daughter relationship: Considerations in psychodynamic psychotherapy. In L. C. Jackson & B. Greene (Eds.), *Psychotherapy with African-American women: Innovations in psychodynamic perspectives and practice* (pp. 166–193). New York: Guilford Press.

Grier, W. H., & Cobbs, P. M. (1968). *Black rage.* New York: Bantam Books.

Hill, R. B. (1999). *The strengths of African-American families: Twenty-five years later.* Lanham, MD: University Press of America.

hooks, b. (1992). *Black looks: Race and representation.* Boston: South End Press.

Hughes, M., & Hertel, B. R. (1990). The significance of color remains: A study of life chances, mate selection, and ethnic consciousness among Black Americans. *Social Forces, 68*(4), 1105–1120.

Jackson, A. M. (1992). A theoretical model for the practice of psychotherapy with Black populations. In A. K. Hoard-Burlew, W. C. Banks, & D. A. Azibo (Eds.), *African-American psychology, theory, research, and practice* (pp. 321–330). Newbury Park, CA: Sage.

James, A. D., Tucker, M. B., & Mitchell-Kernan, C. (1996). Marital attitudes, perceived mate availability, and subjective well-being among partnered African-American men and women. *Journal of Black Psychology, 22*(1), 20–36.

Johnson, P., & Birk, T. A. (1994). The role of African-American owned radio in health promotion: Community service projects targeting young African-American males. In D. J. Jones (Ed.), *African-American males: A critical link in the African-American family* (pp. 85–94). New Brunswick, NJ: Transaction Publishers.

Karenga, M. (1979). On Wallace's myths: Wading thru troubled waters. *The Black Scholar, 10*(8/9), 36–39.

Keith, V. M., & Herring, C. (1991). Skin tone and stratification in the Black community. *American Journal of Sociology, 97*, 760–778.

Ladner, J. A. (1971). *Tomorrow's tomorrow: The Black woman.* New York: Doubleday/Anchor Books.

Ladner, J. A. (1998). *Timeless values for African-American families: The ties that Bind.* New York: John Wiley & Sons.

Lakoff, R. T., & Scherr, R. L. (1984). *Face value: Politics of beauty.* Boston: Routledge, Kegan, & Paul.

Lempert, L. B. (1999). Other fathers: An alternative perspective on African-American community caring. In R. Staples (Ed.), *The Black Family: Essays and studies* (pp. 189–201). Belmont, CA: Wadsworth.

Lichter, D. T., LeClere, F. B., & McLaughlin, D. K. (1991). Local marriage markets and the marital behavior of Black and White women. *American Journal of Sociology, 96,* 843–867.

Lynch. W. (1999). The untold "story" 1712. In W. Lynch, *The Willie Lynch letter and the making of a slave* (pp. 5–9). Chicago: Lushena Books.

Lyons-Ruth, K., & Jacobvitz, D. (1999). Attachment disorganization: Unresolved loss, relational violence, and lapses in behavioral and attentional strategies. In J. Cassidy & P. R. Shaver (Eds.), *Handbook of attachment: Theory, research, and clinical applications* (pp. 520–554). New York: Guilford Press.

Mays, V. M., & Cochran, S. D. (1993). Ethnic and gender differences in beliefs about sex partner questioning to reduce HIV risk. *Journal of Adolescent Research, 8*(1), 77–88.

Mishkind, M. E., Rodin, J., Silberstein, L. R., & Striegel-Moore, R. H. (1987). The embodiment of masculinity: Cultural, psychological, and behavioral dimensions. In M. S. Kimmel (Ed.), *Changing men: New directions in research on men and masculinity* (pp. 37–52). Newbury Park, CA: Sage.

Neal, A. M., & Wilson, M. L. (1989). The role of skin color and features in the Black community: Implications for Black women and therapy. *Clinical Psychology Review, 9,* 323–333.

Nelson, J. (1995). Working with inner-city tribes: Collaborating with the enemy or finding opportunities for building community? In L. Combrinck-Graham (Ed.), *Children in families at risk: Maintaining the connections* (pp. 3–31). New York: Guilford Press.

Okazawa-Rey, M., Robinson, T., & Ward, J. V. (1987). Black women and the politics of skin color and hair. *Women and Therapy, 6*(1/2), 89–102.

Phinney, J. S., & Rotheram, M. J. (Eds.). (1987). *Children's ethnic socialization: Pluralism and development.* Newbury Park, CA: Sage.

Rapi, N., & Chowdhry, M. (Eds.). (1998). *Acts of passion: Sexuality, gender, and performance.* Binghamton, NY: Harrington Park Press.

Rappaport, J. (1994). Empowerment as a guide to doing research: Diversity as a positive value. In E. J. Trickett, R. J. Watts, & D. Birman (Eds.), *Human diversity: Perspectives on people in context* (pp. 359–382). San Francisco: Jossey-Bass.

Rooks, N. M. (1996). *Hair raising: Beauty, culture, and African-American women.* New Brunswick, NJ: Rutgers University Press.

Rose, S. (1994). Sexual pride and shame in lesbians. In B. Greene & G. M. Herek (Eds.), *Lesbian and gay psychology: Theory, research, and clinical applications* (pp. 71–83). Thousand Oaks, CA: Sage.

Rothblum, E. D. (1994). Lesbians and physical appearance: Which model applies? In B. Greene & G. M. Herek (Eds.), *Lesbian and gay psychology: Theory, research, and clinical applications* (pp. 84–97). Thousand Oaks, CA: Sage.

Russell, K., Wilson, M., & Hall, R. (1992). *The color complex: The politics of skin color among African-Americans.* New York: Anchor Books/Doubleday.

Shorter-Gooden, K., & Jackson, L. C. (2000). The interweaving of cultural and intrapsychic issues in the therapeutic relationship. In L. C. Jackson & B. Greene (Eds.), *Psychotherapy with African-American women: Innovations in psychodynamic perspectives and practice* (pp. 15–32). New York: Guilford Press.

Siever, M. D. (1994). Sexual orientation and gender as factors in socioculturally acquired vulnerability to body dissatisfaction and eating disorders. *Journal of Consulting and Clinical Psychology, 62*(2), 252–260.

Solomon, B. B. (1991). Counseling Black families at inner-city church sites. In H. E. Cheatham & J. B. Stewart (Eds.), *Black families: Interdisciplinary perspectives* (pp. 353–372). New Brunswick, NJ: Transaction Publishers.

Staples, R. (1988). An overview of race and marital status. In H. P. McAdoo (Ed.), *Black families* (2nd ed., pp.187–189). Newbury Park, CA: Sage.

Staples, R. (1995). Socio-cultural factors in Black family transformation: Toward a redefinition of family functions. In C. K. Jacobson (Ed.), *American families: Issues in race and ethnicity* (pp. 19–27). New York: Garland Publishing.

St. Lawrence, J. S., Eldridge, G. D., Reitman, D., Little, C. E., Shelby, M. C., & Brasfield, T. L. (1998). Factors influencing condom use among African-American women: Implications for risk reduction interventions. *American Journal of Community Psychology, 26*(1), 7–28.

Timmer, S. G., Veroff, J., & Hatchett, S. (1996). Family ties and marital happiness: The different marital experiences of Black and White newly wed couples. *Journal of Social and Personal Relationships, 13*(3), 335–359.

Trickett, E. J., Barone, C., & Watts, R. J. (2000). Contextual influences in mental health consultation. In J. Rappaport & E. Seidman (Eds.), *Handbook of community psychology* (pp. 303–330). New York: Kluwer Academic/Plenum.

Tucker, M. B., & Mitchell-Kernan, C. (1998). Psychological well-being and perceived marital opportunity among single African-American, Latina, and White women. *Journal of Comparative Family Studies, 29*(1), 57–72.

Tyler, B. M. (1990). Black hairstyles: Cultural and socio-political implications. *Western Journal of Black Studies, 14*(4), 235–250.

Wade, B. H. (1994). The gender role and contraceptive attitudes of young men: Implications for future African-American families. In D. J. Jones (Ed.),

African-American males: A critical link in the African-American family (pp. 57–65). New Brunswick, NJ: Transaction Publishers.

Wade, T. J. (1996). The relationships between skin color and self-perceived global, physical, and sexual attractiveness, and self-esteem for African-Americans. *Journal of Black Psychology, 22*(3), 358–373.

Washington, C. S. (1987). Counseling Black men. In M. Scher, M. Stevens, G. Good, & G. Eichenfield (Eds.), *Handbook of counseling and psychotherapy with men* (pp. 192–202). Newbury Park, CA: Sage.

Watts, R. J., & Jagers, R. J. (Eds.). (1997). *Manhood development in urban African-American communities.* Binghamton, NY: Haworth Press.

White, J. L., & Cones III, J. H. (1999). *Black man emerging: Facing the past and seizing a future in America.* New York: W.H. Freeman.

Wimberly, E. P. (1994). Pastoral counseling with African-American men. In D. J. Jones (Ed.), *African-American males: A critical link in the African-American family* (pp. 77–84). New Brunswick, NJ: Transaction Publishers.

Wingood, G. M., & DiClemente, R. J. (1998). Partner influences and gender-related factors associated with noncondom use among young adult African-American women. *American Journal of Community Psychology, 26*(1), 29–51.

Wirth, L., & Goldhammer, H. (1944). The hybrid and the problem of miscegenation. In O. Klineberg (Ed.), *Characteristics of the American Negro* (pp. 253–369). New York: Harper & Row.

Woode, M. K., & Lynch, K. B. (1992). Effective intervention strategies for producing Black health care providers. In R. L. Braithwaite & S. E. Taylor (Eds.), *Health issues in the Black community* (pp. 281–297). San Francisco: Jossey-Bass.

Wright, M. A. (1998). *I'm chocolate, you're vanilla; Raising healthy Black and biracial children in a race-conscious world: A guide for parents and teachers.* San Francisco: Jossey-Bass.

Wyatt, G. E. (1997). *Stolen women: Reclaiming our sexuality, taking back our lives.* New York: John Wiley & Sons.

Wyatt, G. E., Guthrie, D., & Notgrass, C. M. (1992). Differential effects of women's child sexual abuse and subsequent sexual revictimization. *Journal of Consulting and Clinical Psychology, 60*(2), 167–173.

Wyatt, G. E., Notgrass, C. M., & Gordon, G. (1995). The effects of African-American women's sexual revictimization: Strategies for prevention. In C. Swift (Ed.), *Sexual assault and prevention: Sociocultural context of prevention* (pp. 111–134). Binghamton, NY: Haworth Press.

Wyatt, G. E., Tucker, M. B., Romero, G. J., Carmona, J. V., Newcomb, M. D., Waymant, H. A., Loeb, T. B., Solis, B. M., & Mitchell-Kernan, C. (1997). Adapting a comprehensive approach to African-American women's sexual risk taking. *Journal of Health Education, 28*(6), 52–60.

CHAPTER EIGHTEEN

Religiosity and Racial Identity Attitudes

Clinically Relevant Factors in Psychotherapy with African Americans

Elizabeth Davis-Russell

As more multicultural clients have come into the mental health system, particularly in psychotherapy, questions have been raised about how psychotherapy should be conducted with these clients. In trying to come to grips with such a difficult question, there has been a plethora of materials that offer advice and direction. In 1984 Jones, looking at the literature, then concluded that what existed was not very useful because of the generalities of what was presented. Therapists were told that they needed knowledge and experience with ethnic minority clients; they needed to modify their techniques; that their communications with the clients needed to be respectful and be consistent with the client's frame of reference; and that they should be prepared to intervene more directly in the client's life.

As we have entered the twenty-first century, our discussions now seem to include two important concepts that had not held the kind of prominence they now do. These are cultural competence and context. How culturally competent is the psychotherapist who enters into a psychotherapy relationship with, in this case, an African American client? What is the context of the client? What is his/her social background or environmental context? What is his/her racial and ethnic identity? What is her/his educational level? What are his/her conceptualizations of psychological conflict and psychotherapy? And one, often neglected factor in psychotherapy as it has been historically done, is what are his/her religious or spiritual beliefs and practices?

I contend that a culturally competent psychotherapist must be knowledgeable about the client's context. This chapter will focus on two of those contextual factors which I believe have particular relevance to success in psychotherapy with African Americans. These are religious or spiritual beliefs and practices, and racial identity attitudes. Some empirical data will be presented to support this position. Allport (1950) points out the quandary of modern empirical psychology. While psychology had some ties with religion, there was a sharp separation made from religion. Allport points out that this separation is absurd because both psychology and religion deal with the human mind. To see them at odds with each other presents us with an untenable position, making it difficult to fully explain the depth of human thinking and feeling.

As observers and scholars note, within African American communities, religion, and especially the black church, has a prominence enjoyed by very few other institutions. Racism has had far-reaching control within this society. Manifestations of such control can be observed in the lack of control that African Americans have over many institutions and agencies. But, the black church represents one of few institutions over which they do have control, and religiosity provides an emotional and psychological haven. Sanchez-Hucles (2000) points out that this allegiance to the black church is also accompanied by a valuing of a sense of spirituality, whether that is evident in regular church attendance or not. "Most African Americans have been exposed to the idea that there is a creator, a master plan, and meaning to the challenges of living" (Sanchez-Hucles, p. 21). Some have chosen to see this prominent role of religion as "escapist" and "otherworldly" providing African Americans with palliative promises of better days to come in "a land flowing with milk and honey." But Taylor and Chatters (1991) remind us that

> Historical and current evidence attests to the fact that black religious thought and organized religion has consistently functioned as a foundation for social action and reform. . . . Deeply held religious beliefs were incorporated into the ideological core and principles of the struggle for civil and human rights and, further, provided the strategy and human resolution to participate in organized protest (that is, civil disobedience, protest marches). . . . The weight of evidence attests to the fact that, while black religious traditions are dedicated to the spiritual lives and concerns of individuals, black religious thought and experience remain deeply committed to the political and social betterment and advancement of black Americans, individually and collectively (p. 122).

While historically the predominant focus has been on the Black church as the medium through which religious, social, and political activity occurs, there have been some more recent voices speaking and writing about spirituality. Paris defines spirituality as the animating and integrative power that constitutes the principal frame of meaning for individual and collective experiences. . . . the integrating center of their power and meaning. The distinguishing feature of African spirituality, as opposed to other groups, is that it is always integrally connected with the dynamic movement of life . . . in the struggle for survival . . . [as well as] the union of those forces of life that have the power within to threaten and destroy life . . . or to preserve and enhance it" (as cited in Jones, 1999, p. 295).

This conception of spirituality seems to be specifically African American. It is said to be more "scripturally based, concerned with the prayer and God-conscious experiences of Black people in the United States, and focused on social concerns, social justice, practical charity, and political involvement" (Downey, 1993) necessitated by an African American cultural history of oppression (Jones, 1999, p. 298).

Brookins (1999) and others put forth a conception of a spiritual community, which has its origins in traditional African religions and philosophy. This spiritual community is said to have a unifying force, bringing together people of African descent according to a communal framework. It is one "defined by the values and ideals related to human aspirations, and that provide meaning to life" (Jones, 1999, p. 33). They argue that even though one's spirituality is demonstrated in one's practices, seemingly diverse practices share commonalities, which can be attributed to traditional African religions and practices (Brookins).

But are there religious or spiritual implications for mental health for African Americans? Many have examined what they see as benefits of a religion for mental health in African Americans (Akbar, 1979; Edwards, 1987; Gary, 1987; Griffifth, English, & Mayfield, 1980, as cited in Jones, 1999; Smith, 1981, as cited in Jones, 1999). They provide empirical data that one of the primary components (that is, first-ranked characteristics of African American psychological health) is a spiritual or religious ideology. For their participants, the centrality of spirituality seems to support the idea that African Americans are a spiritual people.

In a later study designed to define Black/African American psychological health from an African American perspective, Edwards (1999) points out that the spiritual component of psychological health is a distinguishing feature from European American definitions. The participants in her study indicated that self-knowledge and other references to self, such as respect and acceptance, were aspects of a spiritual orientation. They did not see these as separate. They also saw self, in relationship to and embedded within spirituality as an overriding framework. Edwards argues that this would potentially negate "self-centered" and "narcissistic" strivings and interpretations of psychological health. She also points out that it is also distinctive from other European American interpretations in that it links psychological health with spirituality, ethics, and morality.

In the beginning of this chapter, I raised the possibility of another contextual factor being relevant to success in psychotherapy with African Americans. That is racial identity attitudes. I shall briefly examine some of the relevant nigrescence literature in general, followed by a specific look at the Cross model, and then focus on empirical data obtained by this author in a study of religiosity and racial identity attitudes.

Cross, Parham, and Helms (1999) state that "psychologically speaking, the social history of African Americans has been dominated by two compelling processes; deracination, or the attempt to erase Black consciousness, and nigrescence, or the struggle for Black self-awareness" (p. 4). Cross, one of the early authors of a nigrescence model, points out that nigrescence is derived from French and means "to become Black." This conversion from Negro to Black is evident in the lives and works of Black Americans throughout their history in the United States.

There have been many nigrescence models in the literature, with the years 1968–76 seeing a bourgeoning in this literature. Working independently, and sometimes competitively, the outcomes in terms of the phenomena being studied, showed great similarity. Nigrescence models tend to have four or five stages . . . and the common point of departure is not the change process per se, but an analysis of the identity to be changed. The person is first described as functioning in an ongoing steady-state (Stage 1), with a deracinated or "Negro identity"; following this, some event or series of events compel the person to seek and be a part of change (Stage 2); this is followed by psychological metamorphosis (Stage 3); and finally, the person is described as having internalized the new Black identity and enters another steady-state (Stage 4). The period of metamorphosis or transition is depicted as an intense struggle between the "old" and emerging "new" self; consequently, the process writers depict the change process as being informed by, rather than divorced from, the character of the identity to be transformed (Cross, Parham, & Helms, 1999, p. 7). An examination of the models conveys the implication that the Stage 1 identity is indicative of some level of impaired mental health. (Cross, Parham, & Helms). It is the stage that is indicative of a deracinated personality, which in turn, influences cognitions, affects, and behaviors. Specifically, there is "an aggressive assimilation-integration agenda linked not only to the search for a secure place in the socio-economic mainstream, but motivated as well by a desperate attempt to escape from the implications of being a "Negro" (p. 8). The person at this stage views being Black as "an obstacle, problem or stigma, and seldom a symbol of culture, tradition or struggle." She or he is thus preoccupied with thoughts of how to overcome her stigma, or how she or he can assist Whites in discovering that she or he is "just another human being." The Stage 1 person is described as one whose reference group is Whites, "and will do almost anything to overcome the stigma of race, in order to obtain White approval" (p. 8).

Because there is little identification with the group, a Stage 1 person is described as "an uncompromising individualist," who places emphasis on the progress of individuals rather than the group.

All nigrescence models see in Stage 2 an encounter that has the effect of "pulling the rug" from under the feet of the person operating with the Stage 1 or Negro identity (Cross, Parham, & Helms, 1999). This is seen as a two-step process that involves "first, experiencing and personalizing the event and, secondly, beginning to reinterpret the world as a consequence of the encounter" When the individual comes to the end of this stage she is "not depicted as having obtained the new identity, but as having made the decision to start the journey toward the new identity" (p. 9). Cross, Parham, and Helms (1999) see Stage 3 as encompassing "the most sensational aspects of Black identity development, as it is the vortex of psychological metamorphosis" (p. 9). This is seen as "the period of transition in which the struggle to destroy all vestiges of the 'old' perspective occurs simultaneously with an equally intense concern to clarify the personal implications of the 'new' frame of reference" (p. 9).

Having lost patience with the past, the boundaries and essence of the old self are truncated, collapsed, and codified in very pejorative terms, images, and emotions. On the other hand he/she is unfamiliar with the new self, for that is exactly what he/she hopes to become; thus, the person is forced to erect simplistic, glorified, highly romantic and speculative images of what he or she assumes the new self will be like. "Under the spell of this dynamic, the person can be vicious in attacks on aspects of the old self that appear in others or her/himself, and he or she may even appear bizarre in his or her affirmation of the new self" (Cross, Parham, & Helms, 1999, p. 10).

All of the nigrescence models present a fourth or fifth stage. This stage usually describes the "habituation and internalization" of the individual's new identity (Cross, Parham, & Helms). Whereas the previous stage was rife with tension, emotionality, and defensiveness, calmness and a secure demeanor are more characteristic of this stage. The conflicts experienced between the old identity and the new one get resolved at this stage. (Cross et al.). Thus, feelings about one's Blackness now represent a strong and positive springboard from which one can interact with the White world. One's racial identity now takes its balanced place with other aspects of one's total identity, including one's national identity. There is the recognition that one is "neither solely Black nor American, he or she is very much an African American" (p. 13).

Given the implications for affective behavior at the various stages, the question as to the impact of racial identity attitudes and religiosity was pursued. The current study uses the Racial Identity Attitude Scale (RIAS) which is based on Cross's model. In his model, he (1991) states that the Pre-encounter stage covers a broad range of attitudes. These range from low salience to social stigma, where "race is a hassle, a problem, an imposition," to anti-Black, where one's sense of Blackness is seen as a "mark of oppression." These attitudes may be fused with some other Pre-encounter characteristics. These include, among others, mis-education, which can distort the nature of discourse on Black cultural historical issues and other Black challenges and problems. Cross contends that the "most damning aspect of mis-education is not necessarily poor mental health but the development of a world view and cultural-historical perspective that can inhibit knowledge about, and thus the capacity to be an advocate for, the cultural, political, economic, and historical interests of Black people" (p. 193). In its most extreme form, this mis-education causes a "great deal of skepticism about the abilities and capacities of Black leaders, Black businesses, and Black professionals, and an equal degree of romanticism and near mysticism concerning the capacities and talents of Whites" (p. 193).

Another characteristic of Pre-encounter persons is their eurocentric perspective, which values European art, music, and beauty as measures of cultural "correctness." Spotlight or rage anxiety is also characteristic of Pre-encounter persons. This is a concern that things are "too Black" (Cross, 1991). This anxiety is especially acute in the company of Whites, or when events or efforts of Blacks are organized and public.

Pre-encounter Blacks have an assimilation-integration perspective. This perspective causes them to superficially analyze racism, placing the blame on Blacks' unwillingness to fit in and become part of the system. Such a perspective frames their opposition to pluralistic and multicultural education as being "unnecessary, wasteful, or somehow inferior" (Cross, 1991, p. 196).

Pre-encounter Blacks may have the same value structure as Blacks at other stages, but differ in their value orientation (Cross, 1991). They "place priority on organizations and causes that have low race salience and/or little nationalistic import, while Blacks who are deeper into nigrescence stress high race salience, activities and organizations" (p. 197).

One's identity provides stability and predictability, and provides a buffer against the effects of rapid and dramatic changes to it. Some experience shakes this stability and predictability leading to a resocialization or transformation. This event can be a startling racial incident, imprisonment, or contact with someone at an advanced stage, or it may be a series of small encounters that "chip away" at one's world view culminating in the push toward nigrescence (Cross, 1991). There are two steps in this encounter, experiencing an encounter and personalizing it (Cross). An encounter must have a personal impact in a powerful way to move the individual toward nigrescence. During this period, the individual compares his/her insight with the Pre-encounter life she or he has been living. The discrepancy jolts the individual into a new consciousness. Accompanying this new consciousness is a great range of emotions. These include guilt at him/herself, anger toward Whites, and general anxiety.

These can be energizing factors (Cross). The encounter stage signifies the death of the Pre-encounter person and the birth of the Afrocentric person (Cross).

As indicated, this is a transitional stage, therefore there can be consequences. The internal struggles of the old and new identities may result in rejection of the new identity with a return to the Pre-encounter stage. Continuing struggle with White racism may cause the individual who is in the throes of the immersion-emersion stage to become fixated at this stage and adopt some "variant of the whitey as devil philosophy" (Cross, 1991, p. 208).

Another negative consequence of the immersion-emersion stage is "dropping-out." Persons who enter this stage with vulnerable and unstable general personalities may experience some depression or anomie (Cross, 1991). Yet, others who are psychologically healthy may drop out because this stage represented a phase that is no longer relevant in their lives.

At Stage 4, Internalization, the new identity becomes internalized. Cross (1991) points out that

> from a psychodynamic point of view, the internalized identity seems to perform three dynamic functions in a person's everyday life: (1) to defend and protect the person from psychological insults that stem from having to live in a racist society; (2) to provide a sense of belonging and social anchorage; (3) to provide a foundation or point of departure for carrying out transactions with people, cultures, and situations beyond the world of Blackness (p. 210).

This stage represents a foundation upon which one can then build a more expansive sense of self that is inclusive of religion and other identity concerns. "The person feels calmer, more relaxed, more at ease with self. An inner peace is achieved, as Weusi anxiety is transformed into Weusi pride (Black pride) and Weusi self-acceptance (Black self-acceptance)" (Cross, 1991, p. 210).

While nigrescence isn't a "process that lends itself to the needs of personal identity therapy," given that great emotionality is associated with conversion, it's necessary for clinicians to be familiar with their clients' racial identity and attendant characteristics to avoid making misdiagnoses. The present study was intended to provide some empirical data to inform those decisions.

METHODOLOGY

The participants were 179 African Americans from five different states in the Midwestern, Western, and Northeastern regions of the United States. Three-fourths of the participants were female. All of the participants identified themselves as African Americans, even though a small number of them were born outside of the United States. The average age range was forty to forty-nine, and the average income range was above $40,000. Average level of education was a bachelor's degree, and the most often reported religion was Christianity.

Instruments

Two instruments were used in this study: the Religious Orientation Scale and the RIAS. The Religious Orientation Scale is a twenty-item scale that deals with various types of religious ideas and social opinions. The items have multiple choices and the respondent is asked which choice corresponds most closely with his/her feelings. The RIAS is a fifty-item Likert Scale, with five points on the scale, and requires the respondent to rate the item from Strongly Disagree to Strongly Agree.

Procedures

Letters were sent to Black churches, sororities, and professional groups in metropolitan areas of four states in the Western, Northeastern, and Midwestern regions of the United States. The letter stated the purpose of the research (to study social attitudes) and requested an "audience" at a meeting of the church, sorority, or professional group to answer questions about the research and to request volunteers. The investigator and her research assistants (all African Americans) then attended the meetings designated by the institution or organization, and made identical presentations and responded to questions. The groups were told that they could fill out the questionnaires at the meetings or mail them in to the researcher. When volunteers filled out the instruments at the meetings, the participation was much higher than when they mailed in their responses. Having them fill out the instruments and demographic material without names and depositing them in a box near the door preserved their anonymity.

Results

Two hundred and fifty responses were received out of 500 given out, a response rate of 50 percent. Because the focus was on the middle class, and that was defined in terms of income, those individuals whose income fell below $25,000 were eliminated. This eliminated some respondents. Others responses could not be used because they were filled out improperly. Seventy-six responses were eliminated. Data were analyzed for the remaining 174 respondents.

Demographic analyses indicate that the sample contained more females (64 percent). The participants' average age range was forty to forty-nine with at least a B.A. degree; they earned an average salary of $40,000; they were predominantly Christian; and they generally were born in the United States.

Income Differences

There was a difference in place of birth. Those participants born in the United States tended to have higher incomes than those born outside of the United States ($r = 0.42$; $p < 0.01$). Those with higher income levels also tended to have higher educational levels ($r = 0.42$; $p < 0.01$). The older the participants, the higher their income levels.

Age Differences

Age, education, and income showed some relationship to one another. The higher the age, the higher the education level ($p < 0.05$; $r = 0.17$). Also, the higher the age, the higher the income level ($p < 0.01$; $r = 0.30$), and the higher the income, the higher the education level ($p < 0.01$; $r = 0.42$).

Data from the Religious Orientation Scale showed 60 percent of the participants tended to be intrinsic, while 40 percent tended to be extrinsic. Those who were intrinsic tended to view churchgoing, the role of religion in their lives, and the role of the church and prayers differently from those who tended to be extrinsic. The following is more characteristic of the intrinsic. These participants said they were keenly aware of the presence of God, attended church once a week, and also tended to agree that their religious beliefs lie behind their approach to life ($r = 0.34$; $p < 0.01$). Those participants who agreed that religion provides meaning of life tended to disagree that it does not matter so much what one believes so long as one leads a moral life ($r = 0.18$; $p < 0.05$). They agreed that they carry their religion over into all their other dealings in life ($r = 0.31$; $p < 0.01$), and agreed that their religious beliefs lie behind their approach to life ($r = 0.36$; $p < 0.01$). They also agreed that prayers have the same meaning and personal emotion when said alone and during services, and also viewed religion as a comfort ($r = 0.26$; $p < 0.01$). Those who agreed that religion offers comfort also tended to agree that prayer is to secure happiness and peacefulness in life ($r = 0.34$; $p < 0.01$).

The extrinsic participants said that they attended church once a week, but said their interest in religion is because of its congenial social activities. Those whose interest in religion because of its congenial social activities tended to view church membership as helping to establish oneself in the community ($r = 0.49$; $p < 0.01$). They stated that they tended not to carry their religion over into other dealings in life ($r = 0.22$; $p < 0.01$). Those who felt that there were many more important things in their life despite their religious beliefs, also tended to agree that membership at church helps to establish a person in the community ($r = 0.35$; $p < 0.01$). Those who refused to let religious considerations influence everyday affairs felt that there were many more important things in their life, despite their religious beliefs, and they also tended to agree that membership at church helps to establish a person in the community ($r = 0.35$; $p < 0.01$). They viewed the purpose of prayer as being to secure a happy and peaceful life ($r = 0.24$; $p < 0.01$), but they also tended not to view prayers said alone as having the same meaning as prayers said during services ($r = 0.26$; $p < 0.01$). They agreed that it does not matter what they believe so long as they lead a moral life ($r = 0.21$; $p < 0.01$), and they were less likely to agree that their religious beliefs are what lie behind their approach to life ($r = 0.22$; $p < 0.01$). They agreed that they are less likely to read literature about their faith, and are less likely to carry their religion to their dealings in life ($r = 0.29$; $p < 0.01$). They agreed that they found it necessary to compromise their religious beliefs in order to protect social and economic well-being ($r = 0.29$; $p < 0.01$). Those who disagreed that it is important for them to spend time in religious thought and meditation are less likely to carry their religion into their dealings in life ($r = 0.22$; $p < 0.01$).

Gender

The results of the study did indicate gender differences both in religiosity and in racial identity attitudes. Males tended to be more extrinsic that females on religion. Females tended to agree that they are keenly aware of the presence of God, and that it is important to spend time in religious thought and meditation ($r = 0.22$; $p < 0.01$). Females also agreed that their religious beliefs inform their approach to life, and that they carry their religion over to all their other dealings in life, and that religion offers them comfort when sorrows and misfortune strike. They also agreed that the purpose of prayer is to secure happiness and peacefulness in life ($r = 0.34$; $p < 0.01$). Males tended to see church membership as a means of establishing one's presence in the community, and tended not to agree with the position that religion offers them comfort when sorrows and misfortune strike ($r = 0.31$; $p < 0.01$). They are less likely to carry their religious beliefs over into all areas of their lives ($r = 0.30$; $p < 0.01$). Younger participants tended to endorse that they rarely or never read literature about faith or church ($r = 0.25$; $p < 0.01$).

There are some similarities that cut across those who tended to respond as intrinsic and those who tended to respond as extrinsic in this study. There is a general set of religious beliefs. This shows some consistency with Edwards's findings (1999) from her study, which sought to define the characteristics of Black or African American psychological health from an African American perspective. Edwards found in her population that the highest ranked characteristic of psychological health was "Ideological and Belief Reference." For her participants, characteristics of psychological health included spiritual awareness, racial identity awareness (awareness of whom one is as an African

American), interpersonal relationships, and strategies for daily living. Important themes raised were "Spiritual guidance, needing a belief in God, being in touch with a Supreme Being, and strong cultural identity" (Edwards). Sanchez-Hucles (2000) also stresses the importance of a belief in a Supreme Being for African Americans.

Another similarity among the participants of the present study is the role of the church and attendance at church. Church attendance is seen as important, and the role of the church as a social institution is prominent. It is the place where one goes not only for spiritual guidance but also, as the place where one establishes one's self in the community. This is also an important theme stressed by Sanchez-Hucles (2000).

The role of prayer is also a similar theme across participants. The desire for a happy, peaceful life through prayers, whether said alone or in the company of others, is stated as important.

Across groups in this study, the importance of leading a moral life was stressed. This finding is consistent with the findings of Edwards (1999) who found that her participants ranked moral worth as their second-highest characteristic of psychological health. Here moral worth was closely related to Godliness and compassion, and "provided aspects of a general philosophical orientation which called for needing a belief in God, seeking spiritual guidance, and a need for treating one's fellow man correctly" (p. 295). These results highlight two important facts: that spirituality is seen as a foundation to psychological health, and that spirituality or religiosity is connected to ethics and morality. This reconnection of spirit to ethics and morality presents a more balanced and comprehensive view of psychological health (Edwards, 1987) and is distinctly different from eurocentric conceptualizations of psychological health.

The gender differences in this study show some similarities to Edwards's findings. In this study, women were more intrinsic, and in Edwards's study, women made more references to religious themes of psychological health, such as the importance of religion, a belief in God, being in prayer and Godliness. When Neighbors et al., (1983) findings are combined with these and Edwards's findings, we can no longer ignore the fact that African Americans, and especially African American women, see their religiosity, their churches, and their ministers as important factors in their lives. Therefore, their reliance on faith and prayer can't be excluded as important variables in psychotherapy.

Since the present study also looked at racial identity attitudes, the results are summarized. Data from the RIAS showed that 34 percent of the sample received scores that placed them at the Internalization stage. According to the RIAS, these individuals see themselves as having crystallized their racial identity attitudes. Thirty percent of the participants had scores that placed them at the Immersion stage, indicating that these individuals are immersed in a Black world as they attempt to define a Black identity. Twenty-two percent of the participants had scores that placed them at the Encounter stage indicating that these individuals have decided to adopt a Black perspective. Fourteen percent of the participation had scores that placed them at the Pre-encounter stage indicating that the individuals identify with a Euro-American world view (see Table 18.1).

Gender Differences

Males tended to score higher on the Pre-encounter scales. Examination of the data revealed some interactions between the scores on the RIAS and the Religious Orientation Scale. Those who agreed that being a church member is to establish a person in the community also tended to have higher scores on RIAS-ENC ($r = 0.17$; $p < 0.05$) and RIAS-IMM ($r = 0.20$; $p < 0.01$), and they tended not to agree that religion offers them comfort when sorrows and misfortune strike. Those who refuse to let religious considerations influence their everyday affairs tended to score high on RIAS-ENC ($r = 0.16$; $p < 0.05$). They are also less likely to carry their religious beliefs to all areas of their lives ($r = 0.30$; $p < 0.01$).

Those who view the church as a congenial social activity tended to score high on RIAS-IMM ($r = 0.16$; $p < 0.05$). Those who view the church as a place to formulate social relationships also tended to score high on RIAS-PRE ($r = 0.28$; $p < 0.01$) and RIAS-IMM ($r = 0.15$; $p < 0.05$). They also tended to view religion as offering comfort and peace ($r = 0.22$; $p < 0.01$). They were less likely to carry their religion over into their dealings in life ($r = 0.23$; $p < 0.01$). The higher the score on RIAS-ENC, the more likely participants were to agree that the purpose of prayer is to secure a happy and peaceful life ($r = 0.20$; $p < 0.01$). Also, those who believe religion offers meaning to life tended to score high on RIAS-ENC ($r = 0.16$; $p < 0.05$) and they tended to carry their religion over into other dealings in life ($r = 0.22$; $p < 0.01$).

The data on the RIAS indicate that on this sample of African Americans, there is a distribution across the stages of racial identity. If as has been stated, Cross (1991) is describing a complex interaction between feelings, cognitions, attitudes, and behaviors; then we can conclude that at various epochs in the lives of African Americans, any set of these complex interactions of feelings, cognitions, attitudes, and behaviors may have salience. Since a clinician relies on the client's feelings, cognitions, attitudes, and behaviors to make diagnoses and develop treatment plans, I contend that these processes can be enhanced,

Table 18.1. Participants Breakdown by Stage

Stage	Number	Percent
Pre-encounter	24	14
Encounter	38	22
Immersion	52	30
Internalization	60	34

and better and more accurate diagnoses and more effective treatment plans can be effectuated if the clinician understands her client's world views. What these and other data show, is that generally for African Americans, spirituality or religiosity and world views are important factors that clinicians need to include in their understanding of their clients.

References

Akbar, N. (1979). Awareness: The key to Black mental health. In W. D. Smith, K. H. Burlew, M. H. Mosley, & W. M. Whitney (Eds.), *Reflections on Black psychology* (pp. 13–21). Washington, DC: University Press of America.

Allport, G. W. (1950). *The individual and his religion: A psychological interpretation.* New York: Macmillan.

Brookins, C. C. (1999). *African/Community Psychology: Exploring the foundations of a progressive paradigm.* In R. L. Jones (Ed.), Advances in African American Psychology. Hampton, VA: Cobb & Henry.

Cross Jr., W. E. (1991). *Shades of Black: Diversity in African-American identity.* Philadelphia: Temple University Press.

Cross Jr., W. E., Parham, T. A., & Helms, J. E. (1991). The stages of Black identity development: Nigrescence models. In R. L. Jones (Ed.), *Black psychology* (3rd ed., pp. 319–338). Berkeley, CA: Cobb & Henry.

Cross Jr., W. E., Parham, T. A., & Helms, J. E. (1999). Nigrescence Revisted: Theory and Research. In R. L. Jones (Ed.), *African American identity development* (pp. 3–71). Hampton, VA: Cobb & Henry.

Dana, R. H. (1998). *Understanding cultural identity in intervention and assessment.* Thousand Oaks, CA: Sage.

Downey, M. (Ed.). (1993). *The new dictionary of Catholic spirituality.* Collegeville, MN: The Liturgical Press.

Edwards, K. L. (1987). Exploratory study of Black psychological health. *Journal of Religion and Health, 26*(1), 73–80.

Edwards, K. L. (1999). African American definitions of self and psychological health. In R. L. Jones (Ed.), *Advances in African American psychology* (pp. 287–312). Hampton, VA: Cobb & Henry.

Gary, L. (1987). Religion and mental health in an urban Black community. *Urban Research Review, 11*(2), 5–7; 14.

Jackson, J. S. (Ed.). (1991). *Life in Black America.* Newbury Park, CA: Sage.

Jenkins, A. H. (1995). *Psychology and African Americans: A humanistic approach* (2nd ed.). Needham Heights, MA: Allyn & Bacon.

Jones, R. L. (Ed.). (1999). *Advances in African American psychology.* Hampton, VA: Cobb & Henry.

Neighbors, H. W. (Ed.). (1991). Mental health. In H. W. Neighbors (Ed.), *Life in Black America.* Thousand Oaks, CA: Sage.

Neighbors, H. W., & Jackson, J. S. (Eds.). (1996). *Mental Health in Black America*. Thousand Oaks, CA: Sage.

Neighbors, H. W., Jackson, J. S., Bowman, P. J., & Gurin, G. (1983). Stress, coping and Black mental health: Preliminary findings from a national study. *Prevention in Human Services, 2*, 5–29.

Ramseur, H. P. (1991). Psychologically healthy blacks adults. In R. L. Jones (Ed.), *Black psychology* (3rd ed., pp. 353–378). Berkeley, CA: Cobb & Henry.

Ridley, C. R. (1995). *Overcoming unintentional racism in counseling and therapy: A practitioner's guide to intentional intervention*. Thousand Oaks, CA: Sage.

Sanchez-Hucles, J. (2000). *The first session with African Americans: A step-by-step guide*. San Francisco: Jossey-Bass.

Taylor, R. J., & Chatters, L. M. (1991). Religious life. In J. S. Jackson (Ed.), *Life in Black America* (pp. 105–123). Newbury Park, CA: Sage.

White, J. L., & Parham, T. A. (1990). *The psychology of Blacks: An African-American perspective* (2nd ed.). Englewood Cliffs, NJ: Prentice Hall.

CHAPTER NINETEEN

Coming Out to Family . . . In Context

Robert-Jay Green

To expand on what Nancy Boyd-Franklin and others have written about how African American parents can prepare their children for the discrimination they'll face in society, let's think about the analogous situation for lesbian, gay, bisexual, transgender (LGBT) children and youths. A fundamental difference is that LGBT children grow up in families in which the parents ordinarily do not share the same minority group status as their LGBT child. This difference has profound implications for family life.

Typically, in other cultural groups that face discrimination, parents and children share the same vulnerability to prejudice in the outside world, and parents are able to socialize and prepare their children to deal with that oppression. Ordinarily, minority group parents and their children are on the same side against the oppressive forces in society, and parents take a protective role. By contrast, for LGBT children and youths, their parents can't prepare them for the discrimination they will face, and the parents don't face the same oppression themselves. Parents and children can end up on different sides of the discrimination equation, with the parents becoming oppressors and siding with other oppressive forces against their own child. Thus, at best, most LGBT children and youths have to "go it alone" in their families when it comes to understanding their sexual orientation and the discriminatory situation in society for people with that sexual orientation. At worst, some LGBT children and youths are truly "living with the enemy."

One consequence of this difference between heterosexual parents and LGBT children is that almost every LGBT person has to face *the possibility* that they will be disowned by their own family (Weston, 1991). This is an existential crisis for almost every person who comes out to their parents because he or she doesn't know in advance how well the parents, siblings, and grandparents will react or whether he or she will be disowned. As a result, LGBT people become aware in a very personal and tangible way that family relationships in adulthood are much more volitional than most heterosexual people assume. Most heterosexuals grow up sort of easily counting on the fact that their family relations are going to last for the persons' lifetimes. It is very unusual for a heterosexual person to think or worry: "my parents might disown me at some point; they may entirely cut off all contact with me; they may diminish contact with me simply because of who I am—not for something I did—but for who I am." By contrast, LGBT people ordinarily have to face that possible consequence around the time they are claiming their sexual orientation and deciding whether to come out to their parents. A corollary of this unique existential position in their families is that it opens the mind of LGBT people to the possibility that they will need to find in their lives other primary sources of social support than their family. In fact, research on social support for LGBT people shows that their families are not the main source. One caveat to this research—like most psychological research—is that it has been done predominantly using white middle-class populations in urban areas of the United States. What the research on these samples has shown is that, when asked to rank order, what are their sources of social support other than their partners in couple relationships, white middle-class LGBT people list (1) lesbian and gay friends; (2) lesbian and gay organizations; (3) heterosexual friends; (4) co-workers; (5) siblings; (6) boss; (7) mother; (8) other relatives; (9) father; and (10) mainstream church (Bryant & Demian, 1994). Most striking in this list, perhaps, is that LGBT people report that they get more support from coworkers than from any family members and that they get more support from their bosses than from their mothers or fathers! If you ask heterosexuals this same question, they typically will list family members first.

As a result of this difference, LGBT adults typically form very close networks of friends, and sometimes these networks of friends have what is called high density: meaning that not only are you friends with these six people, but these six people are also friends of each other, so that the interconnection among friends takes on a family like quality to it. These interconnected social networks of LGBT people are sometimes called "families of choice" (Weston, 1991).

The optimal situation is where a LGBT person would have a family of choice that provides a strong source of social support and also have the social support of their family members as well. But what we might think of as full family support and acceptance is not ordinarily the case. My own impression of this is that while probably 10–15 percent, of families ever reach some deep level of comfort around the issue of their child being LGBT and whereas probably 10–15 percent totally or almost totally reject their LGBT child, the remaining 70–90 percent show varying degrees of acceptance (Savin-Williams, 2001). In other words, the typical outcome is not really what we would think of as "full acceptance" but is really more like "tolerance." Parents may accept the LGBT person bringing a partner home for the holidays. They may be cordial and friendly to the partner up to a point. But often, there are crucial ways in which the LGBT person's sexual orientation sets that person's relationships apart from the rest of the family. For example, parents may treat the LGBT offspring's partner as a sort of "friend of the family" rather than as a bona fide family member akin to a son-in-law or daughter-in-law (Weinstein, 1996).

One thing I have been concerned about lately is that there seems to be a normative ideology among family therapists that it is always "good" (that is, mentally healthy) for LGBT clients to come out to their families, without regard for the sociocultural context (LaSala, 2000; Green, 2000). In many family therapy circles (particularly Bowenian circles) the decision to keep a major secret like this from your family is almost inconceivable because family therapists typically value open communication, differentiation of self, and authenticity so highly in family life.

However, if you look at LGBT people around the world—in all of Asia, all of the Islamic world, and all of Latin America (and even in all of the United States prior to the 1960s)—the vast majority of LGBT people are not out to their families. Most LGBT in these countries get married heterosexually and carry on their lives in secret from heterosexuals, including from their own family members. Although there are nascent gay rights movements in almost all parts of the world now, it still is true that most LGBT people in the world lead double lives at work and in their families of origin. Thus, what is unthinkable to most family therapists—the keeping of this major secret from one's family—is and has been de rigueur for most LGBT people throughout history and in most parts of the world now.

At the extreme, in some countries that are dominated by totalitarian regimes (sometimes with religious fundamentalist ideologies), homosexuality is still punishable by death. Obviously, coming out to certain fundamentalist religious parents might be so physically dangerous that it would not be "mentally healthy" to do so. Most LGBT people choose *not* to come out to their families or anyone else in totalitarian nations for fear that the information will be revealed in the community and will lead to their imprisonment or execution. This maintenance of the secret obviously has nothing to do with being a "differentiated" or "mentally healthy" person, it has to do with survival.

It is easy to point to other parts of the world where there is life-threatening homophobia, but even in many, many communities in the United States, there is still virulent homophobia or subgroups of the community that are violently

homophobic, such that LGBT people are scared for their lives and afraid to disclose to their family members because the information may filter out into the
community, putting the LGBT person at risk for violence, persecution at work,
or even murder. Sometimes the violence is perpetrated by members of the LGBT
person's own family.

These situations of life-threatening violence are, of course, extreme situations
in the United States nowadays, but they are used to illustrate that the decision
to come out to parents can't be reduced to matters of self-differentiation, mental health, or self-esteem alone. It's not that simple. One really needs to take a
much more complex view of what are the determinants and the consequences of
coming out. These determinants certainly include factors in the individual, such
as differentiation of self, self-esteem, general assertiveness, conventionality, self-
awareness of sexual orientation, life history of sexual behavior, and clarity of
sexual identity. These detriments also include factors in the nuclear and
extended family, such as general cohesiveness, frequency of contact with family
members in the present, ability to deal with conflict, attitudes toward sexuality
in general and homosexuality in particular; as well as factors in the family's
unique sociocultural niche, including variables such as race, ethnicity, social
class, religious affiliation, and legal or political factors (Green, 2000).

LGBT offspring do not usually come out to both parents at the same time.
Typically, they come out to siblings first, then mother, and fathers last. About
25 percent of LGBT people report not being out to their mothers, and about half
report not being out to their fathers (Savin-Williams, 2001). Other factors
involved in the decision to come out or the consequences of coming out to a specific family member include: (1) the *salience* of the parents as a source of social
support, social identity, economic support (not all parents are equally important
to an adult offspring); (2) the availability of nonfamily sources of social and economic support; and (3) the individual's appraisal of the anticipated cost-benefits
to themselves, to the family member, and to their relationship (Green, 2000b).
LGBT people tend to be quite aware, long before the disclosure, of their parents'
attitudes around issues such as gender roles, sexual behavior, homosexuality,
nonconformity, politics, and religion; and they use this knowledge to decide
whether and how to come out and to anticipate the parents' responses.

It is very hard to predict the consequences of coming out in terms of its
effects on family relationships and on the individual's mental health. Most families react very negatively at first, but many become more tolerant or accepting
over time (Crosbie-Burnett, Foster, Murray, & Bowen, 1996; Savin-Williams,
1996, 2001). Another common pattern seems to be "no change"—that is, the
parent-child relationships don't change much one way or the other, for better
or worse, over the long run. The family that was mostly distant and conflict-
avoidant before the disclosure is likely to remain so afterwards. The parents who

were intrusive and critical before the disclosure are not likely to become suddenly (or even eventually) more respectful of boundaries and more accepting of individuality, just in response to this new information. One can expect the disclosure of homosexuality to be filtered through the family's usual coping mechanisms to a large extent, as well as the family's specific attitudes about gender and sexuality (Laird & Green, 1996).

In terms of the stance family therapists should adopt, I think we should take a "pro-choice" position on coming out (Green, 2000b). It is my opinion that coming out to family members is a very individualized decision and that mental health professionals should not take a stance for or against coming out in a generic sense. We should be able to consider the set of issues in each particular dyadic relationship in the family and be open to exploring that unique mix of factors: the pros and cons and the likely advantages and risks of coming out, and not take a moralistic, judgmental position that implies it is good or bad, or necessary for that person to come out. We can't assume, based on some of the risks of disclosure I've described above, that keeping such a secret from one's parents is inevitably going to be deleterious to one's mental health or future relationships. We have to look at each parent-child dyadic relationship in the context of the entire family and its sociocultural niche.

In particular, we should consider the potentially very dangerous consequences for adolescents in the process of coming out. About 50 percent of LGBT adolescents of color in a mostly working class sample in New York City reported that they were physically threatened or physically hurt by their family members because they were LGBT (Savin-Williams, 1994). Therefore, with our adolescent clients, we have to carefully assess for potential physical harm, ejection from the household, loss of economic support, and potential emotional abuse from parents or siblings if the young person chooses to come out to them or is suddenly forced out of the closet by third parties or circumstances.

The disclosure of homosexual orientation is not necessarily like other secrets adolescents might reveal to their parents because it so profoundly shakes the parents' whole sense of the world order and the gender order. Also, the disclosure of homosexual orientation often falls into a net of inconsistent and usually erroneous assumptions the parents' hold about homosexuality, and there is almost no way to predict what these assumptions might be (Savin-Williams, 1996). For example, upon learning that her Chinese American son was gay, one mother assumed that he must be going regularly to "rave" parties and doing drugs, which she had read about in a local newspaper. The parents of another man from Panama, upon being told that he was gay, accused him of being a transvestite who worked the streets as a prostitute, apparently because these were the only kind of openly gay men the parents were aware of in Panama City at the time.

These examples illustrate that information the offspring is trying to transmit about her or his LGBT orientation is sometimes drastically transformed and distorted in the parents' minds. Much of what parents know about homosexuality is limited to the same old "bill of goods" we all were sold about it during our childhoods, along with some new information from the media in the areas of civil rights, gay pride parades, and gay lifestyle pieces on television and in newspapers. It seems that about half of the contemporary mainstream media coverage tends to focus on the most incendiary and scandalous episodes, the most shocking dress and behavior, so that parents are left with almost equal amounts of biased and unbiased information.

Thus, the journey from initial disclosure to tolerance to genuine parental acceptance is usually very long and usually incomplete. It is important that family therapists, along with LGBT clients in therapy, take a realistic view of what can be accomplished and also take a long-term perspective of ten, twenty, thirty years (Iasenza, Colucci, & Rothberg, 1996). Some families never budge an inch from their initial negative reactions, and others travel a very long way indeed. It is important to mention here a new trend likely to gain momentum. The contemporary LGBT social movement in the United States is now moving firmly in the direction of more emphasis on couples and on having children (Ariel & McPherson, 2000; Green, 2000a; Laird & Green, 1996). Younger LGBT adults (especially young lesbians) usually assume that someday they will be in a long-term couple relationship and will raise children in the context of that couple relationship. An ancillary consequence of this shift is that the children of these LGBT parents will likely provide a re-unifying bridge to the grandparental generation (that is, there already is some evidence that parents of LGBT adults provide greater support and are more involved with their LGBT adult children when grandchildren arrive) (Laird & Green, 1996).

Therefore, in the future, we will probably see stronger linkages across three generations in the families of LGBT adults who have children, and these linkages will undoubtedly produce greater connectedness as well as some of the usual problems that occur between parents and grandparents (Laird & Green, 1996). In addition, family therapists will be called upon to treat many more LGBT couples and their children in the future. Along these lines, we recently started a specialized LGBT family therapy program, the Alternative Family Institute, which is part of the California School of Professional Psychology (CSPP) (see website http://www.altfamily.org for more information about the kinds of services LGBT couples and families need as well as links to related resources on the web).

In summation, this author believes that coming out to parents is a personal decision that we should help clients explore, just as we would with any other major life decision, without taking an a priori stand "for" or "against." Our clients' sociocultural niches vary so greatly and the research on coming out to parents is so limited to middle-class and White samples at this point, that it is virtually impossible to make generalizations about diverse parents' likely responses to the disclosure in the United States, let alone in other parts of the world. The only thing we can say with some certainty, based on a fair amount of research on predominantly White middle-class samples, is that parents whose initial reactions are not extremely rejecting do seem to become somewhat more tolerant over long stretches of time (Savin-Williams, 2001). For clients who already have come out to their parents and not been totally rejected, we can probably help them by taking a longer-term perspective on family relationships than we or they are used to taking (Iasenza, Colucci, & Rothberg, 1996). We should view their therapy as only one leg of a much longer family journey.

References

Ariel, J., & McPherson, D. W. (2000). Therapy with lesbian and gay parents and their children. *Journal of Marital and Family Therapy, 26,* 421–432.

Bryant, A. S., & Demian. (1994). Relationship characteristics of American gay and lesbian couples: Findings from a national survey. *Journal of Gay and Lesbian Social Services, 1,* 101–117.

Crosbie-Burnett, M., Foster, T. L., Murray, C. I., & Bowen, G. L. (1996). Gays' and lesbians' families of origin: A social-cognitive-behavioral model of adjustment. *Family Relations, 45,* 397–403.

Green, R.-J. (2000a). Guest editor's introduction to the special section on "Gay, lesbian, and bisexual issues in family therapy" (pp. 407–468). *Journal of Marital and Family Therapy, 26,* 407–408.

Green, R.-J. (2000b). Lesbians, gay men, and their parents: A critique of LaSala and the prevailing clinical "wisdom." *Family Process, 39,* 257–266.

Iasenza, S., Colucci, P. L., & Rothberg, B. (1996). Coming out and the mother-daughter bond: Two case examples. In J. Laird & R.-J. Green (Eds.), *Lesbians and gays in couples and families: A handbook for therapists* (pp. 123–136). San Francisco: Jossey-Bass.

Laird, J., & Green, R.-J. (Eds.). (1996). *Lesbians and gays in couples and families: A handbook for therapists.* San Francisco: Jossey-Bass.

LaSala, M. (2000). Lesbians, gay men, and their parents: Family therapy for the coming out crisis. *Family Process, 39,* 67–81.

Savin-Williams, R. C. (1994). Verbal and physical abuse as stressors in the lives of lesbian, gay male, and bisexual youths: Associations with school problems, running away, substance abuse, prostitution, and suicide. *Journal of Consulting and Clinical Psychology, 62,* 261–269.

Savin-Williams, R. C. (1996). Self-labeling and disclosure among gay, lesbian, and bisexual youths. In J. Laird & R.-J. Green (Eds.), *Lesbians and gays in couples and families: A handbook for therapists* (153–182). San Francisco: Jossey-Bass.

Savin-Williams, R. C. (2001). *Mom, dad. I'm gay: How families negotiate coming out.* Washington, DC: American Psychological Association.

Weston, K. (1991). *Families we choose: Lesbians, gays, kinship.* New York: Columbia University Press.

Weinstein, D. L. (1996). No place in the family album. *Journal of Feminist Family Therapy, 8,* 63–67.

PART FOUR

TRAINING

CHAPTER TWENTY

Preparation for Training

Assessing Attitudes Toward Difference Using the ISI

Elizabeth Davis-Russell

As the United States began to increase its level of activity in global affairs, and as demographic shifts began to become more pronounced within the nation, a plethora of "cultural sensitivity" training programs began to emerge and flourish. As this training flourished it became apparent that the trainers neglected "the phenomenology of training" (Bennett, 1986, p. 179); the subjective experience of the trainees. One of the observations that Bennett makes is that intercultural sensitivity is not natural to any single culture. Therefore, one's ability to develop intercultural sensitivity requires new awareness and new attitudes. Trainers therefore need to know how the attitude of intercultural sensitivity develops so that they can facilitate movement in that direction through their training.

Bennett (1986) proposed a developmental model of intercultural sensitivity that is a stage model with each stage representing a way of experiencing difference. The model is based on the assumption that movement occurs from the left side of the continuum, more ethnocentric, to the right side, toward more relative treatments of difference, ethnorelativism. A brief description of these stages is in order.

STAGE 1: DENIAL OF DIFFERENCE

In this stage Bennett (1986) proposes that one sees no difference at all or employs wide categories in perceptual differences among people. It is Bennett's contention that the ability not to see difference occurs when physical or social isolation precludes significant contact. This enables one's view of the world to remain unchallenged and becomes central to her reality. Parochialism is prominent at this stage. When there is the ability to perceive difference, this is done at a minimal level without discrimination. The example that Bennett gives is the recognition that Asians are different from Westerners without the recognition that Asian cultures are different in any way from one another. Bennett points out that in extreme cases of denial, difference may be attributed to subhuman status.

STAGE 2: DEFENSE AGAINST DIFFERENCE

At this stage one perceives some threat to the centrality of one's world view. The individual utilizes some strategies in an attempt to counter this perceived threat. The most common defense strategy, according to Bennett (1986), is the denigration of difference. This involves negative stereotyping. It is important to note that although misinformation may accompany the denigration, the central factor is not ignorance but ethnocentrism.

Another strategy that the individual assumes, according to Bennett (1986), is to adopt a stance of cultural superiority. Rather than denigrating other cultures, one simply assumes that his culture is the "acme of some evolutionary scheme" (p. 180). This maneuver automatically assigns a lower status to cultural difference while allowing the defender to be "tolerant" of those cultures' attempts to develop. Bennett sees this stage as the easiest to diagnose because the individual makes overt statements of hostility toward other cultures. Sometimes these statements of hostility may be masked by requests for confirmation that one particular group is really troublesome.

Critical factors in the manifestation of these defensive strategies are the relationship of the group to which one belongs and the institution with which one is affiliated. Group pressure may exacerbate the denigration and discourage more sensitive individuals from standing out against such group pressure. Because some institutions teach that some cultures are evil or subhuman, the individual who is affiliated with such institutions may be more vociferous to demonstrate her allegiance to the institution.

But there is another phase to this stage that is less obvious. The individual may exhibit strong pride in his culture and sees that as a standard or goal for the entire world.

STAGE 3: MINIMIZATION

At this stage, as Bennett (1986) sees it, the individual's last-ditch effort to preserve the centrality of her own world view causes him to "bury differences under the weight of cultural similarities" (p. 181). Even though cultural difference is acknowledged, it is trivialized. This occurs in two forms. In the first form—physical universalism—human behavior is viewed as mainly innate, and the awareness of basic human patterns of behavior is seen as sufficient to ensure successful understanding and communication.

In the second form—transcendent universalism—all human beings, whether they know it or not, are products of some single transcendent principle, law, or imperative. Bennett (1986) points out that minimization may serve the function of preserving a kind of "enlightened ethnocentrism" that sounds interculturally sensitive while allowing persons to avoid the sense of incompetence that might arise from confronting cultural unknowns.

STAGE 4: ACCEPTANCE

At this stage differences are acknowledge and respected. They are perceived as fundamental, necessary, and preferable in human affairs. Differences are not evaluated; they simply exist. Bennett (1986) postulates that there are two levels. At the first level there is an acceptance of behavioral differences, including language, communication style, and nonverbal patterns. At the second level there is an acceptance of the underlying cultural value differences that may represent profoundly different organizations of reality. There is a shift from differences being seen as a thing to a process. One example he gives is that people do not have values, they value. At this level, people are seen as dynamic cocreators of their realities. People bring enjoyment to the recognition and experience of differences. These are people who seem to tolerate ambiguity.

STAGE 5: ADAPTATION

At this stage people show adaptation of their behavior and to differences. Evident is empathy, where one sees a temporary shift in the frame of reference so that one behaves as if one were the other person. Also evident is cultural pluralism, where there is the ability to shift into two or more rather complete cultural world views.

STAGE 6: INTEGRATION

At this stage, according to Bennett, people begin to apply ethnorelativism to their own identity. The epitome of a person at this stage is the multicultural person who is always in the process of becoming a part of and apart from other cultures.

This model forms the theoretical basis upon which the Intercultural Sensitivity Inventory (ISI) was developed. The present study was designed to test the validity and reliability of the ISI.

ITEM CONSTRUCTION

Using Bennett's definitions and descriptions of the stages of his developmental model, 150 questions were developed to form six scales. The first three scales (1) Denial of Difference; (2) Defense Against Difference; and (3) Minimization of Difference are designed to measure different kinds of ethnocentric attitudes, while the other three scales, (1) Acceptance of Difference; (2) Adaptation to Difference; and (3) Integration of Difference are designed to measure different kinds of ethnorelativistic attitudes. The questions were then subjected to Q-sort. Twenty professional psychologists were provided with the questions and asked to sort the items into the categories, including a "Doesn't Fit Any Category" category. The items (sixty-nine) with the highest consistent sorting were retained. Inter-rater reliability was 0.95. The sixty-nine items were then used to develop a four-point Likert scale ranging from "Strongly Disagree" to "Strongly Agree."

Methodology

A total of 518 participants were administered the ISI. The participants were graduate students, law enforcement officers, mental health workers, business executives, teachers, and other educators. They ranged in age from twenty-five to fifty-six. In order to assess test-retest reliability, 163 participants were administered the intercultural sensitivity instrument two times separated by two weeks. The first test administration was coded with a one and the second test was encoded with a two. These were matched by the last four digits of social security numbers. One hundred sixty-three matches were found ($n = 90$ males with a mean age of 30.19, $n = 71$ females with a mean age of 30.64, and $n = 2$ with no gender reported). One hundred twenty participants were undergraduate and graduate students, fourteen were police officers, twelve were mental health workers, six were business executives, and two were educators. Sixteen subjects did not report their occupation.

Internal consistency of items comprising the six pretest scores and the six posttest scores was evaluated with Cronbach's Alpha. A Pearson Product Moment Correlation comparing pretest scores with posttest scores for each of the six scales evaluated test-retest reliability. The internal consistency of the pretest scores ranged from 0.66 to 0.82. The internal consistency of the posttest scores ranged from 0.63 to 0.84 as reflected in Table 20.1. Test-retest reliability for the six scales ranged from 0.65 to 0.84 as reflected in Table 20.2.

Establishing Norms for Various Populations. The general population norms are reflected in Table 20.1 below.

Norms for the different ethnic groups involved were determined. Following is an examination of the differences in the means and standard deviations between ethnic groups that were obtained when norming the data, implementing a listwise regression analysis (see Tables 20.2–20.6).

The means of each variable of each ethnicity was compared with the overall means of all the ethnic groups combined. There were no significant differences found with regards to their means and standard deviations. When comparing any two ethnicities, there were also no significant differences found between any two ethnic groups. This means that the general population norms are applicable to the samples of any of the ethnic groups involved in the study.

Table 20.1. Population Means and Standard Deviations

Variable	Mean	Standard Deviation
Denial	27.94	4.78
Defense	27.53	5.99
Minimization	25.51	3.99
Acceptance	34.58	3.59
Adaptation	23.13	2.68
Integration	30.49	3.81

Total population $N = 327$.

Table 20.2. African American Means and Standard Deviations

Variable	Mean	Standard Deviation
Denial	26.23	5.04
Defense	24.46	5.75
Minimization	24.52	3.86
Acceptance	34.77	2.65
Adaptation	24.08	2.18
Integration	32.23	3.35

African American $N = 13$.

Table 20.3. Asian American Means and Standard Deviations

Variable	Mean	Standard Deviation
Denial	27.46	4.85
Defense	25.33	5.36
Minimization	26.13	4.14
Acceptance	34.33	3.51
Adaptation	23.92	2.55
Integration	31.00	3.09

Asian American $N = 24$.

Table 20.4. Euro-American Means and Standard Deviations

Variable	Mean	Standard Deviation
Denial	28.40	4.73
Defense	27.93	6.24
Minimization	25.24	4.14
Acceptance	34.89	3.64
Adaptation	23.17	2.71
Integration	30.56	3.96

Euro-American $N = 212$.

Table 20.5. Native American Means and Standard Deviations

Variable	Mean	Standard Deviation
Denial	27.00	4.73
Defense	27.80	5.71
Minimization	25.53	3.46
Acceptance	34.80	3.49
Adaptation	22.53	3.20
Integration	30.40	3.74

Native American $N = 15$.

Table 20.6. Hispanic Means and Standard Deviations

Variable	Mean	Standard Deviation
Denial	27.76	5.63
Defense	28.19	6.28
Minimization	27.10	3.79
Acceptance	33.52	3.68
Adaptation	22.48	2.38
Integration	29.90	3.05

Hispanic $N = 21$.

Factor Analysis

Prior to analysis, posttest scores were filtered from the database. The sixty-nine ISI responses were checked for missing values. Seven participants failed to answer eight or more questions on the ISI questionnaire and were filtered from the database. The mean substitution method was used for the fifty-seven participants who failed to answer six or fewer items. Three hundred twenty seven cases were available for factor analysis.

The sixty-nine items of the ISI questionnaire were submitted to a Principal Components (factor analysis specifying a varimax rotation). The determinant of the correlation matrix was 0.0000000. The determinant is a coefficient ranging in value from zero to one and represents the amount of variance in a correlation matrix that is left over after covariances are removed. High values mean that there is not a lot of relationship among the variables in the data set. Lower values reflect more correlation with which to work. A zero determinant, however, may be problematic. Zero determinant usually reflect sets of variables that are too highly correlated ($r > 0.90$) and can result in problems in the matrix algebra solution analogous to dividing by zero in scalar algebra. A review of the correlation matrix failed to identify variables that were too highly correlated. The 0.0000000 value may be attributed to the effects of rounding.

The Kaiser-Meyer-Olkin (KMO) Measure of Sampling Adequacy was 0.88135. The KMO measure is an index form comparing the magnitudes of the observed correlation coefficients. A partial correlation is the linear association between two variables, apart from that which arises from a shared association with all other variables. Large KMO coefficients (above 0.50) mean that a sufficiently large amount of the variance between pairs of variables can be explained by the other variables.

The Bartlett Test of Sphericity was significant, X2 ($68, N = 327$) = 7973.58 ($p > 0.001$). The hypothesis that the population correlation matrix is an identity matrix can be rejected. An identity matrix is a correlation matrix with all diagonal elements = 1.00 and all of diagonal elements = 0 (meaning there is no relationship among the variables in the population). If Bartlett's test is significant, factor analysis can proceed on the assumption that there is a relationship among the variables in the population from which the sample was taken.

The initial statistics were examined to determine the number of factors based solely on the relationship among the sixty-nine ISI items. The system default specifies that the number of factors that exist may be determined by the number of eigenvalues that are greater than one. A factor with an eigenvalue of one represents the proportion of variance of the average single variable in the data set. The default factor solution specifies twenty factors and accounts for 64 percent of the variance of the sixty-nine-item correlation matrix. An examination of the initial statistics; however, revealed that eleven of the twenty factors had eigenvalues between 1.0 and 1.43 suggesting that they be ignored. A reasonable estimate of nine factors is made based on eigenvalues greater than 1.5. Nine factors account for 45 percent of the variance of the sixty-nine-item correlation matrix.

Examination of the scree plot often provides a visual method of estimating the number of variables. This data provided a scree plot that suggests that five factors best describe the correlation matrix. Five factors account for 36 percent of the variance of the sixty-nine-item correlation matrix. A six-factor solution using the full sixty-nine-item data set was specified by theory and accounted for 39 percent of the variance of the sixty-nine-item correlation matrix. The factor structure, however, was not comparable to the original factor structure of the pilot study.

The communalities of six-factor structure were examined to identify ISI items that are weakly related to the six factors. Eight ISI items (7, 8, 9, 23, 25, 32, 39 and 45) had less than 25 percent of their variance explained by the six factors. They were removed from the second analysis. The second analysis also specified that minimum rotated factor loadings be set to 0.35. This procedure was repeated until a six-factor solution having ISI loading at 0.35 or higher on each of their respective factors. Additionally, the communalities were maintained at 0.25 or higher.

The next phase of the factor analysis involved correlation of the ISI items with the five factors. A satisfactory solution presents when the ISI items are correlated higher with their respective factor than with any other factor. The first correlation revealed that ISI items fifty-eight, forty-four, and fifty-four failed this test. These items were removed from the analysis and the principal components process was repeated. A satisfactory six-factor solution was obtained with a high sampling adequacy, KMO = 0.89.

The internal consistency of the items loading on each factor was satisfactory. Alpha ranged from 0.47 to 0.88 in the initial model and ranged from 0.52 to 0.88 in the final model.

DISCRIMINANT FUNCTION ANALYSIS

The efficacy of a six-factor structure to differentiate among the five occupation groups was evaluated using a discriminant function analysis. Two sets of discriminant scores were generated. The first set was based on the factor scores of the starting six-factor model and one set from the final six-factor model.

The hypothesis that in the population, the means of all discriminant functions in all groups are really equal and zero is rejected for both six-factor models. The first discriminant function for each model accounts for the majority of the variance. Functions two, three, and four do not contribute significantly to group discriminant score differences. In the initial model the occupation groups account for 80 percent of the variance in discriminant scores. In the final model, however, the occupation groups account for 76 percent of the variance of discriminant scores.

In the starting six-factor model factors one, two, and three have the highest correlation with function one and are the factors that best discriminate between occupation groups. In the final model factors one, two, three, and four have the highest correlation with function 1, and are the factors that best discriminate between occupations. This mean that Denial, Defense, Minimization, and

Acceptance are the ones that best discriminate between occupations, and that generally, people in these occupational groups seem to hold similar attitudes towards difference.

Classification of subjects based on scores on the various factors requires that a probability estimate of the proportion of each occupation category be made. This is accomplished by

- inserting an estimate of the proportion of each occupation category in the population based on census data or other external data source
- estimating the proportion of each occupation category based on the sample proportion
- assigning equal proportions to each occupation category.

Two sets of classification results were generated. The first was based on an estimate of the proportion of each occupation category based on the sample proportion and the second set based on equal proportions of each occupation category. The classification results were about equal for both factor models. However, classifications based on prior probability estimates were substantially different from those based on equal sample proportions.

We can conclude a number of things. The reliability and the validity of the ISI have been established. This means that we can measure aspects of intercultural sensitivity through an instrument such as the ISI (after dropping those items that did not meet the statistical criteria). This, in turn, enables us to change our practices. We can identify appropriate training for different levels of ethnorelativism; and we can then customize training for the specific populations, making training consistent with the identified levels. This is a definite improvement from past practices where training has been universal.

References

Bennett, M. J. (1986). A developmental approach to training for intercultural sensitivity. *International journal of intercultural relations, 7,* 179–196.

CHAPTER TWENTY-ONE

A Heuristic Model of Managing Emotions
In Race Relations Training

Billy E. Vaughn

Psychologists in the inner cities are currently challenged by diversity in communities, the workplace, schools, and clinical settings. Professionals, such as community psychologists, are in the best position to confront threats to the social fabric of society, but can do so only to the extent that they are trained to plan and disseminate effective interventions (Lorion, 1992). Diversification of psychology in the wake of these realities inevitably affects research, practice, and training (Vaughn, 1988; Stricker et al., 1990). The increased inclusion of human diversity courses in the core psychology curriculum holds promise for training the competence psychologists need in contemporary professional life (Vaughn, Eulert, & Trybus, 1997).

Americans are ill prepared to confront their racial attitudes and those in the field of psychology are no exception. The author's experiences suggest that laudable efforts to introduce multicultural competency within psychology programs are inconsistent with the majority of the students' training expectations and professional goals. This conclusion is based on more than ten years of teaching diversity within predominantly White ethnic American psychology departments, scholarly exchanges with other professionals who are dedicated to teaching diversity, and knowledge of relevant literature.[1]

A classroom exercise the author uses supports the point that multicultural competency is not related to the professional goals of most White ethnic psychology students. Students are instructed to visualize themselves ten years after completion of their degree. The majority confess that they are surprised to discover that their future professional identity does not include serving people who are racially different from themselves. They also indicate that they consider themselves nonprejudiced, and do not view diversity training is needed for their professional development. The students support elective courses emphasizing race and culture, but are not in support of required multicultural courses. White ethnic Americans do not have a monopoly on aversive reactions to learning about multiculturalism, but they constitute the majority of the psychology student population.

A lack of appreciation for race relations training leads to negative reactions toward mandatory instruction, especially when combined with normal ambivalence toward racial matters (Gaertner & Dovidio, 1986). Many of my trainees rationalize their negative reactions by claiming that race relations courses are subjective and opinionated, even though I clearly ground the subject matter in theory and empirical research. Such perceptions are partly derived from the controversy in higher education about multiculturalism in the core curriculum (D'Souza, 1991) and a poor understanding of teaching emotionally charged participants among trainers. The controversy and poor instruction promote resistance.

Teaching strategies for managing emotional responses to the race relations course often reflect instructor multicultural competency, rather than principled instruction based on empirically driven methodology (Vaughn, 1994a, 1994b). The study of emotion has received little focus in psychology until recently, while countless anecdotes indicate that emotions run high in the work of psychologists who deal with such behaviors on a regular basis, which include community psychologists, clinicians, and health psychologists.

Goleman (1995) provides convincing evidence that emotional intelligence can be more important than I.Q. Presumably, the abilities to govern one's own emotions and negotiate others' feelings are hallmarks of higher mental functioning in practical life. Insight into the nature of emotion and its implications for race relations instruction is needed to train professional competency, develop interventions, and conduct research.

An empirically based framework that describes the relationships among emotional reactions, racial attitude, and learning can stimulate scholarly debate while offering insights into improved race relations instruction. The recent increased interest in the study of emotion has been limited to laboratory studies, most of which are not easily generalized to race relations instruction. The insights presented in this chapter are the result of combining the author's expertise in cognitive psychology, recent research findings, and teaching experiences.

A HISTORICAL LINK BETWEEN EMOTION
AND RACE RELATIONS TRAINING

The emergence of broad-based race relations training can be traced to the period of criticism and accompanying shifts in assumptions about people of color. The Black power movement challenged Americans to seek solutions to historical racial tensions. In response, the military and higher education institutions introduced race relations training during the 1970s. Psychologists directly involved in cross-cultural training used their expertise to arrange structured environments for interracial contact (Helms, 1990). Community psychologists were at the forefront of confronting inequality at systemic levels, such as in community mental health (Newbrough, 1992a).

The military provides the best data for understanding early race relations training methods and outcomes. A broad and vigorous training program was required of all recruits in the military's attempt to integrate a large, diverse, and racially segregated organization (Day, 1983). Basic training included at least two weeks of race relations instruction using an experiential learning format. Confrontational techniques were common (Day, 1983). It was assumed that all White ethnics needed confrontation to get them emotionally involved in healing their racism. Many White recruits became more open to close contact with racial Minorities as a result of the training. Others either did not change noticeably or became more prejudiced. A few changed to the extent that they became crusaders against all forms of racism and discrimination. This led to adjustment problems with peers and family members. Others were more apprehensive about interracial contact as a result of the training. Little research existed at the time to provide insight into how emotional reactions to diversity training influenced learning, but recent research indicates that confronting racial beliefs is discomforting (Devine et al., 1991). Military officials grew concerned about many of the recruits' emotional reactions to the training among those who became crusaders and those who became more prejudiced. This led to a shift toward less focus on race relations and discouraging confrontational techniques (Day). Educational institutions witnessed a decline in race relations courses offered at the same time partly due to a decrease in Black militancy.

The recent resurgence of required race relations training is in response to the realities of changing demographics and emergence of an international marketplace. Higher education and the business community are presently leading the way.[2] Training intercultural competency to build a diverse workforce and to compete in a global economic community is considered good business for companies and the higher education institutions competing to prepare future workers (Ferdman & Brody, in press). The contemporary instructional focus is on human diversity in general rather than race in particular, which is a reflection of awareness of a range of identity groups contributing to society. The reduced emphasis on racial awareness is not due to improved race relations. It is more likely that the focus on diversity is an effort to reduce emotional reactions to the course. Race remains a controversial topic bounded by emotions, such as guilt, shame, threat, and resentment, associated with unresolved historical issues, including segregation and equal opportunity. De-emphasizing the importance of race is little more than a fruitless attempt to avoid confronting interracial discomfort (Katz, Wachenhut, & Glen Hass, 1986).

Avoiding racial issues is further played out in racial differences in training preference. The author notices that psychology students of color tend to value the race relations training, whereas most of the White ethnic American trainees tend to favor diversity courses. One reason is that the students feel included under the general topic of diversity. Diversity can include people who are obese, learning disabled, and religious. Students do not resist when the course content has personal meaning. The general diversity course may be easier to teach when race is de-emphasized, but often at the cost of students learning how to meet the challenge of their social and professional lives. These challenges include managing emotions and intercultural affairs.

Goleman (1995) argues in his book, *Emotional Intelligence*, that ignoring emotional competence will prove harmful to society. Emotions, according to Goleman, are distinct from rational thinking, but the two must be "exquisitely coordinated" if a person is to act with integrity. "But, when passions surge the balance tips: it is the emotional mind that captures the upper hand, swamping the rational mind" (p. 9). The Los Angeles disturbances and the Rodney King beating in 1991, are examples of emotional highjackings that people regret in rational hindsight. Americans will not make progress in managing the diversity unless they collectively deal with their emotional reactions to race. Richard Brislin, the cultural diversity trainer, supports this claim in that ignoring emotion excludes an important component of intercultural competency development (Brislin & Yoshida, 1994). It is difficult to learn such competencies by trial and error or by having good intentions.

The Nature of Race Relations Training Resistance

D'Souza (1991) argues that legitimate challenges to the intellectual and moral infrastructure of academia are at the heart of multicultural education resistance and renewed racial tension on American campuses. The *Frontline* documentary, "Racism 101," depicts racial tension on American college campuses as a product of White ethnic Americans' resistance to Minority student demands for inclusive education (*Frontline*, 1988).[3] Doing away with mandatory diversity courses is considered one key to overcoming interracial problems on college campuses. A major problem with introducing multicultural curriculum is the sociopolitical arena in which the subject matter is embedded.

Most psychology instructors teach from a positivist perspective, which assumes that the information presented represents objective and universal knowledge of human behavior (Fried, 1993). The objective-universalism assumption is shared by both students and faculty. In contrast, the race relations course is an emotionally latent, constructivist instructional context in which knowledge is assumed to be bounded by political correctness and ethnocentrism (Fried). This justifies resistance to such courses. The resistance challenges instructors of mandatory race relations courses in their efforts to coordinate with students. Successful teaching requires them to learn how to employ emotion management skills. However, the positivist instructional arrangement is not much different in reality. The appearance of objectivity and generalization, along with the perception of legitimacy, disguise the constructive nature of the well-established course (for example, statistics). It is also a socially constructed activity created by people attempting to coordinate with one other in more or less meaningful situations (Kollock & O'Brien, 1994). Differences in emotional reactions to courses are a function of both instructor and student attitudes.

Diversity experts interpret White ethnic American students' emotional reaction to mandatory diversity courses in terms of one of the following: (1) a form of resistance that students need to overcome in order to achieve multicultural competency (Brislin & Yoshida, 1994; Gay, 1984); (2) an aversive reaction to intrapsychic conflict about race (Kovel, 1970); or (3) a lack of White identity awareness (Helms, 1990). Some race relations instructors assume that emotion is a healthy and necessary part of competency development. Others believe emotion retards learning and, therefore, should be avoided or controlled as much as possible. Between the extremes is the assumption that emotional discharge is inevitable in the course because Americans lack intercultural competence (Brislin & Yoshida).

A Taxonomy of Racial Attitudes

A racial attitude is composed of beliefs about racial groups, issues, or objects, affective association with those beliefs, and corresponding behaviors. Few White ethnic Americans harbor the stereotypes and aversion toward other races that were prevalent in the 1950s. Modern racial attitudes are better explained by poor social skills (Devine et al., 1991), social dominance orientation (Pratto, Sidanius, Stallworth, & Malle, 1994), and ambivalence (Katz et al., 1986, 1975, 1973). Instructors must take into account differences in White ethnic racial attitudes and subtle distinctions that influence corresponding emotional reactions to racial issues. A racial attitude classification system is needed to better understand the variations in response to mandatory race relations instructions to overcome historical challenges to the courses and integrate the subject into psychology training. Table 21.1 represents a taxonomy of attitudes

Table 21.1 Taxonomy of Racial Attitudes Among White Ethnic Americans.

	Conventional	Defensive	Ambivalent	Egalitarian	Integrative
Beliefs	Political and economic conservatism	Political and economic conservatism	Political and economic moderatism	Political and economic liberalism	Political and economic liberalism
	High in social dominance orientation	High in social dominance orientation	Medium social dominance orientation	Low social dominance orientation	Low social dominance orientation
	Zero-sum interracial contact view	Zero-sum interracial contact view	Assume a colorblind view in interracial contact	Assume a color-conscious view of interracial contact	Treats each person as an individual, yet color consciousness
Affect	Opposition to equality ideologies and policies	Opposition to equality ideologies and policies	Egalitarian and oppositional views about equality ideologies and policies	Egalitarian views about equality ideologies and policies	Egalitarian views about equality ideologies and policies
	Belief-behavior discrepancy leads to antipathy, anger and irritation toward others	Belief-behavior discrepancy leads to threat and fear of others	Belief-behavior discrepancy leads to guilt, shame, and self-criticism	Belief-behavior discrepancy leads to depression, sadness, and self-criticism	Belief-behavior discrepancy leads to humor and self-criticism
	Aversion to interracial interactions	Discomfort in interracial interactions	Discomfort in interracial interactions	Comfort in interracial interactions	Solace in interracial interactions
Behavior	Automatic prejudice response	Automatic prejudice response	Automatic prejudice response	Controlled nonprejudice response	Automatic nonprejudice response
	In-group favoritism based on personal standards	In-group favoritism with concerns about social norms	Concerned about social norms	Nonprejudice standards	Nonprejudice standards
	Lacks interracial interaction skills	Lacks interracial interaction skills	Few interracial interaction skills	Intermediate interracial interaction skills	Expert interracial interaction skills

among trainees in a racial and ethnic diversity course:

- Conventionals
- Defensives
- Ambivalents
- Egalitarians
- Integratives

The categories depict White ethnic Americans as varying in racial attitudes and intercultural interaction skills. Emotional response to race relations instruction is assumed to be directly related to prejudice level and interracial skills such that the competent low-prejudiced people are the least resistant. It should be noted that individuals may have characteristics that appear to defy the boundaries of any one category which is consistent with other racial and ethnic identity classification systems (Helms, 1990).

Recent prejudice research findings provide insight into the nature of White ethnic emotional responses to race relations training. Patricia Devine and colleagues investigated emotional reactions to awareness of personal prejudice information among hundreds of White ethnic American undergraduate students (Devine & Monteith, 1993; Devine, Monteith, Zuwerink, & Elliot, 1991; Monteith, Devine, & Zuwerink, 1993). Devine et al. (1991), provided participants with scenarios of interracial encounters which they used to first rate what they *should* do in the imagined racial encounter (for example, an African American sits next to you on a bus). They were then instructed to rate the extent to which they *would* actually do as they believe they should. The majority of their participants' ratings, regardless of prejudice level, showed a discrepancy between their personal standards (that is, "shoulds") and behaviors (that is, "woulds"). Results indicated that the high-prejudiced participants tolerated more prejudice as evidenced by significantly higher should ratings (that is, they believe prejudice toward a Black person in contact situations is justified) compared to their low-prejudice counterparts. Low-prejudiced participants were more egalitarian in their "should" ratings, but their higher "would" responses revealed more prejudice behaviors than those dictated by their personal standards.

Devine et al. (1991), employed an affective measure to investigate how awareness of discrepancies from personal standards affected participants' sense of self. Participants received response feedback informing them of the extent to which their ratings were consistent. Awareness of inconsistencies had emotional consequences that differed as a function of prejudice level and amount of discrepancy. A factor analysis of the affect characteristic data isolated six factors that account for the differences:

- Negative self
- Discomfort

- Positive feelings
- Negative other
- Threatened
- Depressed

The overall results support the claims that most White ethnic Americans harbor inconsistent racial attitudes; they are not conscious of it, and discomfort occurs with awareness. Their results influenced the ways in which differences in White ethnic American attitudes are categorized for the present purposes.

A combination of research, teaching experience, and scholarly insights is the basis for the category distinctions. Conventionals, Defensives, Ambivalents, Egalitarians, and Integratives account for roughly 2 percent, 25 percent, 60 percent, 10 percent, and 3 percent of the White ethnic American student population, respectively. The category percentages are based on teaching experience and recent research findings. Hundreds of student journals from the author's cultural diversity courses covering topics, such as race relations, ethnicity, prejudice, and discrimination, served as data in determining the categories and percentages in each. The small percentage of Egalitarians and Integratives support the claim that multicultural competency training is needed in psychology education and training. Devine et al. (1991), provided empirical support for the categories in their racial prejudice study. They found that 71 percent of their 101 participants had inconsistent "should-would" discrepancy scores. The remaining 29 percent were consistent in attitude and evenly represented across prejudice levels. Table 21.1 categories are based on the assumption consistency between prejudice attitude and behaviors as the primary factor in identifying prejudice. People with consistent nonprejudice standards and behaviors are on one end of the continuum while those with consistent prejudice standards and behaviors are on the other end. Those in the middle are considered representative of the majority of Americans who want to show solidarity with social equality norms, but struggle with lingering prejudice.

Conventional and Defensive people may be difficult to identify. They know that outward expression of prejudice violates social equality norms. One result is that it is difficult to measure prejudice. Devine and colleagues employed the Modern Racism Scale (McConahay, Hardee, & Batts, 1981) which is one of the most reliable. However, it does not overcome the social desirability response problem common to racial attitudes measures (McConahay, 1986). Pratto and colleagues demonstrated that their social dominance scale is a reliable mirror into the otherwise elusive White ethnic racial attitude (Pratto, Sidanius, & Stallworth, 1993; Pratto et al., 1994; Sidanius, Pratto, & Bobo, 1994). Social dominance orientation (SDO) refers to the degree to which an individual favors his own social group over another (Pratto et al., 1994). Pratto et al. (1994), state that they "came to postulate the existence of SDO not by thinking about 'personality' in the traditional, individualistic sense, but by thinking about how group-based human social life is" (p. 755). Low scores correlate with egalitarian beliefs (for example, I believe in racial integration). High-SDO scores correlate with cultural elitism, anti-Black racism, and Nationalism. The researchers found support for their claim that high-SDO people rely on superior-inferior legitimizing myths such as social Darwinism and meritocracy to justify their beliefs. High SDOs endorse social policies that legitimize inequality, such as welfare reform, anti-affirmation action referendums, and discontinuing school busing. Their data indicate that racial prejudice is more prevalent than most attitude measures are sensitive enough to capture. SDO also gives us insight into differences in prejudice among White ethnics.

Conventionals are high in racial prejudice and social dominance. Their prejudice standards are consistent with their behaviors (Devine et al., 1991). Conventionals believe that society should be stratified in favor of certain groups even if it is costly those who are not able to compete (Pratto, Sidanius, Stallworth, & Malle, 1994). High SDOs tend to be conservative and ethnocentric (Bodenhausen, 1993; Esses, Haddock, & Zanna, 1993; Pratto & John, 1991, Pratto et al., 1994). Sidanius, Pratto, and Bobo (1994) demonstrated that high social dominance is related to the belief that inter-group interactions are inherently based on winner-loser competitive relations. White ethnic high status is viewed as a byproduct of the group's superior contributions to society.

Ironically, Conventionals are often unaware of their ethnocentrism (Brislin & Yoshida, 1994; Gaertner & Dovidio, 1986). This is especially true of groups for which they find aversive (Esses et al., 1993; Katz et al., 1986, McConahay, 1986). However, awareness of a discrepancy between their racial beliefs and behavior leads to anger, irritation, or disgust toward the target group, rather than self-criticism (Jones, 1986). Focusing on the target of prejudice, or blaming the victim, is characteristic of the Negative Other affect Devine et al. (1991), found in their study. Conventionals may use racial stereotypes about criminal behavior or cleanliness to justify not wanting to sit next to a Black person on a bus. In this way, their well-established stereotypes are held as facts in managing discomfort.

Conventionals automatically use stereotypes in racial matters (Devine et al., 1991). They are sensitive equality norms, but will deliberately discriminate in order to preserve White ethnic privileges. Apologies or reparations for historical American injustices, such as slavery, are considered unnecessary. Central to their racial attitude is an antimiscegeny stance. They abhor interracial marriage and biracial offspring, and avoid interracial contact as much as possible. Avoidance protects their stereotypes and maintains a false sense of equity and fairness toward others (Fiske & Ruscher, 1993). The race relations course is viewed as irrelevant to psychology and an imposition on personal values.

Defensives are high in social dominance orientation, but believe being a good American requires supporting the equality principle (Gaertner & Dovidio, 1986). However, their prejudice attitude is inconsistent with their desire to fit into social norms (Devine et al., 1991). The result is that prejudiced thoughts are a source of discomfort. A major obstacle to resolving their dissonance is difficulty in accepting the legitimacy of world view different from their own (Bennett, 1986). Defensives feel concerned, frustrated, tense, distressed, and anxious with awareness of a discrepancy between their personal standards and actual behaviors. They rely more on stereotypes as a self-esteem management feedback defense, which corresponds to the Threatened factor identified by Devine et al. (1991).

A major problem is that the Defensive person's prejudiced thoughts automatically come to mind in interracial encounters or racial matters. The Defensive will avoid interracial encounters as much as possible as a result. The use of presumably nonracial stereotypes, such as criminality and poverty are used in justifying not sitting next to a Black person on a bus. Unlike Conventionals, Defensives believe that some African Americans are good people, as long as they accept and follow White ethnic standards of conduct. The race relations course is avoided, if possible, in order to protect against others discovering their true beliefs.

Research by Katz and colleagues established the existence of ambivalence (Katz, Cohen, & Glass, 1975; Katz, Glass, & Cohen, 1973; Katz, Glass, Lucido, Cohen, & Farber, 1979). *Ambivalents* are moderate in social dominance because they both equality and social dominance beliefs (Katz, Wachenhut, & Glen Hass, 1986). They differ from Defensives in that they truly believe that all people are similar apart from superficial differences. Their colorblind perspective is the basis for treating other racial groups equally and assuming that equality is inherently good for everyone.

Awareness of race-related belief-behavior discrepancies cause Ambivalents to experience affect that corresponds to the Discomfort, Threat, and Negative Self factors identified by Devine et al. (1991). Feeling distress, frustration, anxiety, and uneasiness are associated with Discomfort. Ambivalents fear exposing their poor intercultural skills to others. Guilt, shame, and disappointment occur when they expose themselves. Defensives will not prefer to sit next to the Black person on the bus, but will do so if necessary to save face.

The Ambivalent is both curious about other world views and uncomfortable with not knowing how to judge differences fairly (Esses et al., 1993). A colorblind perspective is used to minimize the discomfort associated with the awkwardness and anxiety experienced in interracial contact. Schofield's (1986) study of the colorblind perspective in an interracial educational setting led her to the conclusion that it facilitates discrimination under the disguise of fairness. She found that it enables teachers and administrators greater freedom of action while avoiding the strain of making insensitive decisions. A colorblind perspective is ideal for Ambivalents because they avoid feeling unfair for using White ethnic standards in judging and treating racially different people.

Automatic prejudice responses are difficult for Ambivalents to control during contact with people of color, especially with those who have not assimilated White ethnic culture. Ambivalents are open to contact with racial Minorities, but limit it to White ethnic social contexts or racial Minorities who "act White" (Fiske & Ruscher, 1993). Their restricted contact maintains a colorblind perspective and allows them to behave according to their personal standards without guilt and shame. The Ambivalent prefers to avoid race relations courses, but enters mandatory courses with trepidation due to uncertainty about how much their poor intercultural skills will be exposed.

Egalitarians renounce prejudice because they believe human diversity enriches society and personal life (Bennett, 1986). Race is considered a factor that can't be ignored in American race-conscious society. Their characteristics are typical of low social dominance orientation persons. A considerable amount of self-esteem is associated with their open-minded personal standards. Egalitarians experience self-critical guilt and shame when they notice disparities between personal nonprejudice standards and actual behaviors. The inconsistencies make them realize that they have not mastered their internalized ideals. The affect they experience with discrepancy awareness corresponds to the Negative Self factor identified by Devine et al. (1991). Unlike Negative Other (Conventionals), Threatened (Defensives), and Discomfort (Ambivalents), Negative Self affect motivates one to resolve the discrepancies by learning the behaviors that are consistent with personal standards (Devine, 1993). However, they are not always prepared to deal with the guilt, shame, and distress self-criticism activates (Brislin & Yoshida, 1994; Monteith, 1991). A healthier sense of self in discrepancy situations comes with continued commitment to learning, experience, and personal growth.

Egalitarians often feel that other White ethnics don't understand them. They suffer from a sense of marginality or the feeling that their unique open-minded attitude prevents them from fully identifying with White ethnic Americans. This is not surprising since most White ethnics and Minority group members consider White ethnics who denounce racism and engage in extensive interracial contact as existing out of the mainstream (Helms, 1990) and difficult to relate to (Bennett, 1986). Some Egalitarians cope with marginality by resenting White ethnic ideology, and choosing to actively fight against racism, discrimination, and oppression (cf. Helms, 1990; Bennett, 1986). Others try to abandon their racial identity by embracing and indulging in a different ethnic group's cultural practices.

Egalitarians seek equal status relationships and cooperative goals with people of color (Fiske & Ruscher, 1993). Many Egalitarians are activists who participate in anti-racism demonstrations and are members of anti-racism organizations. They have learned to control stereotyped responses to members of other racial groups. Race relations courses are welcomed, especially classes that teach them interracial competency. They aren't always prepared for challenges to their views and the accompanying compunction.

Little research exists that provides the insight needed to support the *Integrative* individual's characteristics. It is easy to consider the Integrative as someone who is merely on the upper end of the Egalitarian racial attitude continuum. The author's teaching and professional experience suggests that their achievement level sets them apart from the others. Integratives are few in number because a considerable amount of personal growth is necessary to develop their characteristics which may reach well into adult life (Devine & Monteith, 1993; Helms, 1990; Tatum, 1994).

Integratives have taken a nonprejudiced stance and acquired the knowledge and skills needed to form a consistent racial attitude. They cherish achieving equal status interracial interactions and intimate contact with people of different races, and are not threatened by nonWhite ethnic social norms. Their color-conscious perspective reflects a need to interact with people who are different, rather than a need to stereotype or compete. Integratives have also worked through their own issues concerning feeling marginalized, resulting in a reflective view of diversity and being an American (Bennett, 1986).

They seldom experience inconsistencies in their personal nonprejudiced standards and corresponding behaviors. Their occasional interracial social foibles lead to optimism, which corresponds to the Positive appraisal factor in discrepancy awareness identified by Devine et al. (1991). The Integrative finds humor instead of discomfort in their personal standards-behavioral discrepancies. They reflect on their foibles in a continual effort to refine their interracial skills. The difference between the Integrative and other identities is that it includes multicultural competence beyond managing emotional responses to diversity and concern for social norms. Equal status and cooperative goal contact with people of color are essential in relationships for Integratives (Fiske & Ruscher, 1993). This reflects the cumulative outcomes of self-exploration, self-confrontation in earlier personal bouts with personal ambivalence, defensiveness, and risk taking. Factors identified as important for achieving interdependent workplace relationships are relevant to understanding the Integrative. Scholarly insights into characteristics of inclusive organizations support these claims about the Integrative (Kelly, Azelton, Burzette, & Mock, 1994). Kelly et al. (1994), identify four factors that characterize an inclusive organization: (1) extensive interaction; (2) learning and practicing social skills; (3) individual accountability; and (4) valuing joint goals. They indicate that workplace social norms are needed that promote interdependent or equitable relations. The focus is "not on the qualities of individuals per se but rather on how the qualities of a supportive context enable individuals to become resources for one another" (p. 426). It is argued here that the four factors are easily translated into interracial competence at the individual level.

Interracial relationships give the Integrative a sense of meaning and self-satisfaction. It is their empathy-without-prejudice stance that makes them outstanding. The Integrative is known for constantly trying to empathize in making attributions about others, even other White ethnics. This often includes being objective as possible and tolerating the ambiguity common in interracial encounters (Brislin & Yoshida, 1994; Gudykunst, 1991). Integratives welcome racial diversity training as an opportunity to refine their skills and engage in interracial interactions.

The present paper assumes that poor intercultural skills and poor emotion management maintain racial distance and is the basis for even low-prejudiced White ethnic American students' avoidance response to mandatory diversity training. Most White ethnic Americans are distant from other racial groups because it serves to protect their nonprejudiced self-image against the threat of having to show competence. Devine (1996) states that:

> although low prejudiced people are highly motivated to respond without
> prejudice, there are few guidelines for "how to do the intergroup thing well."
> As a result, many experience doubt and uncertainty about how to express their
> nonprejudiced attitudes in intergroup situations. . . . Under these circumstances,
> they become socially anxious; this anxiety disrupts the typically smooth
> coordinated aspects of social interactions (p. 11).

White ethnics with poor interracial communication skills tend to engage in nonverbal behaviors, such as decreased eye contact and awkward speech patterns, in intercultural interactions. These are "exactly the types of subtle responses that have typically been interpreted as signs of prejudice or antipathy" (Devine, 1996, p. 11). Mandatory race relations courses upstage intercultural skills which threaten both high- and low-prejudiced White ethnic Americans, but for different reasons. The overall result is that the opportunities the course offers for achieving the competency is viewed instead as a source of anxiety.

The taxonomy of White ethnic American attitudes toward racial diversity reflect varying responses to required race relations training. Research indicates that the White ethnic Americans are better at managing their emotional responses and resistance to ethnic diversity when they are secure with and aware of their racial identity and its consequences for diversity-related experiences (Helms, 1990; Rotheram & Phinney, 1987). Racial awareness influences perceptions of uncertainty, unpredictability, and personal control over experiences in mandatory training (Brislin & Yoshida, 1994). In general, Conventionals, Defensives, and Ambivalents are the most resistant to racial diversity, while Egalitarians and Integratives seek out opportunities to build their interracial knowledge and skills.

THE HEURISTIC MODEL OF EMOTION IN RACE RELATIONS TRAINING

The heuristic model described here is limited to a description of White ethnic American emotional reaction to diversity training. This group is targeted more than other racial groups because their majority status and norms are threatened by efforts to achieve equality (Farley, 1988; Merger, 1991).[4] In addition, this group represents the largest population among psychology graduate trainees. The model is also limited to emotional reactions to race relations training, although implications for reactions to other types of diversity instruction are apparent. Poor race relations continue to threaten the social fabric of American society as evidenced by inner-city riots and protest marches. An understanding of affective associations to race relations provides insight into managing emotions in other diversity courses.

Table 21.1 depicts the sequence of events that influence White ethnic American students' emotional reactions to the mandatory race relations course. A student's (1) racial attitude; (2) interracial interaction ability; (3) professional goals; and (4) self-esteem management opportunities determines the emotional response. Students are assumed to evaluate their emotional reactions at onset for relevant attributions in decision making (Mandler, 1984). Corollary assumptions are that negative emotional reactions automatically activate stereotypes about the source (Bodenhausen & Kramer, 1990a, 1990b; Kim & Baron, 1988; Smith, 1993) and that high affect reduces learning (Hamilton, Stroessner, & Mackie, 1993; Pratto & John, 1991; Wilder, 1993).

White ethnic graduate students either become resistant, ambivalent, or open once they discover a race relations course is required. Integrative and Egalitarian students are comfortable with race relations training and support it as a requirement. They remain supportive and optimistic even if the course does not fully meet their expectations because they are committed to the subject matter. Defensive and Conventional students will automatically experience resistance because such courses are viewed as lacking professional relevance and oppositional to expressions of conservative values (Esses et al., 1993; Devine & Monteith, 1993). The Ambivalents resist if this is considered the best way to protect themselves against feeling bad for not being interracially competent.

Resistance is a coping strategy for dealing with anxiety caused by feeling attacked (Fein & Spencer, 1997). Kogod (1991) characterizes several types of resistant behaviors associated with diversity training, including (1) expressing the opinion that the training is not necessary; (2) open expression of the view that other critical priorities should take precedence over racial and ethnic issues; (3) avoiding discussion of personal diversity-related beliefs and experiences; and (4) an aversion to labels and stereotyping used to characterize social group differences. The fate of resistant students' initial reactions depends on the instructor's ability to manage emotion (Fried, 1993). Successful intervention is a complicated process influenced by instructional factors, such as the trainer's interracial competency, teaching ability, type of intervention, classroom atmosphere, classroom racial composition, and the institution's racial climate (Banks, 1994).

The use of confrontation will increase resistance. The author's experience indicates that most instructors who espouse confrontation techniques assume that disgruntled students are signs that their instruction is successful.

These instructors take comfort in assuming that somewhere during the students' professional careers they will look back and realize that the mandatory training paid off. What they fail to understand is that emotions can diminish students' intellectual involvement and learning (Bodenhausen, 1993; Hamilton, Stroessner, & Mackie, 1993; Luria, 1932, 1976; Wilder, 1993). For example, the cognition and emotion research literature suggests that high negative affect associated with racial attitudes leads to faulty attributions (Hamilton, Stroessner, & Mackie, 1993), reliance on stereotypes in affect appraisal (Wilder, 1993), and a tendency to be more aware of undesirable than desirable instructor traits (Pratto & John, 1991).

Numerous studies have shown that self-esteem influences racial attitude (Crocker & Schwartz, 1985). For example, Crocker and Schwartz employed the minimal inter-group method to show differences in emotion management between high and low self-esteem participants. Low self-esteem White ethnic Americans tended to discriminate against out-groups in order to enhance their self-image. Those with high self-esteem discriminated less, but derogated out-group members in an effort to maintain a positive sense of self under esteem threat conditions (Tabachnik, Crocker, & Alloy, 1983). Crocker and Luhtanen (1990) also demonstrated that White ethnic Americans with high racial group membership self-esteem will engage in in-group and out-group esteem-enhancing acts, such as downward comparison, when their group identity is threatened. One implication is that the African American instructor who focuses solely on racism among European Americans will cause White ethnic students to experience collective resistance in order to maintain esteem maintenance.

Self-esteem is managed by creating a safe environment in which students feel that what they say and do will not be held against them. This is one reason that most diversity trainers and instructors use a considerable amount of time establishing ground rules at the beginning of working with a new group. Judith H. Katz and Frederick A. Miller of The Kaleel Jamison Consulting Group are professional diversity trainers who believe that effective group work is directly a function of the rules members agree on to guide their efforts (Miller & Katz, 1995). It is critical that group members feel others will support and validate them even when they make mistakes. The instructor will succeed in making the mandatory course a good experience to the extent that students feel this way. Students will then volunteer to learn from the course.

In summary, the heuristic model characterizes how racial attitude is associated with differences in White ethnic emotional responses to mandatory race relations training. The more negative the racial attitude, the more initial resistance. Instructors with poor intervention strategies for managing emotions tend to experience increased resistance and decreased learning. Successful intervention requires effective strategies for increasing a sense of self-esteem.

INTERVENTION STRATEGIES

A detailed discussion of the range of intervention strategies available is beyond the scope of this chapter. This brief overview of a teaching strategy the author developed for managing emotion in race relations training is provided. The successful teaching model is described as the Listen, Lean, Empathize, and Learn (LLEL) model. Course objectives are characterized as providing students with opportunities to acquire the social competencies. The competencies are discussed in the context of human service delivery skills in order to specify their importance in professional development. The Kaleel Jamison Consulting Group trust-building activity, Learning Community Behaviors, which emphasizes the importance of flexible thinking, risk-taking, and being supportive of others is used to set up ground rules for student interactions. It is also used to establish a community of learning and inquiry.

An ability to listen to and empathize with people of different points of view is presented as intercultural competencies. Listening is defined as the ability to allow a person to talk while the listener pays enough attention to paraphrase accurately what was heard. Exercises are used with students to improve their ability to listen in order to increase their awareness of personal reactions to differences. Students learn how to refrain from "butting in" in order to "straighten the person out." The instructor models the listening skill by first creating an atmosphere within which students are allowed to say whatever they think and protecting their rights to do so. Once students take the risk to speak their mind, the instructor listens to each comment without interruption. Each comment is paraphrased by the instructor to make certain that he understood and the student knows what the student was saying, he was heard. Students who take risks are told that their comments are considered a gift to the class as a way to encourage others to disclose. The instructor never criticizes what a person says. A classroom rule is that fellow students can ask questions in response to comments in order to get qualification or relate similar beliefs and experiences, but critical comments are discouraged unless they include self-reflection (for example, Your beliefs make me realize that I am different from you.). By demonstrating that the instructor can put personal values and beliefs aside while listening to controversial statements, students learn how to listen and lean into personal discomfort. Modeling also helps the other students feel that they can trust that the instructor is not interested in punishing those who may have "politically incorrect" views.

Self-confrontation, listening skill, and emotion management are presented as characteristics of critical thinking skills that are associated with intercultural competence. Students are trained to listen to people with points of views different their own, with emphasis on leaning into the discomfort differences create: empathetic listening and critical self-reflection. Empathic critical self-reflection involves exploring personal reactions to differences from multiple points of view. Students are taught that the first rule in learning to empathize with someone you disagree with is to trust that most people have good intentions, but lack the competency to show it (Devine & Monteith, 1993). They want to be liked and leave a good impression. For this reason, most people who know their views are different try not to say things others will find offensive. Students who can't control their need to take issue with fellow students' disclosures are asked to consider why it is so difficult to listen to views they do not agree with, and how their impulse will affect their critical thinking in professional life.

The LLEL approach maintains students' self-esteem because they are less concerned about having conflicting values or experiencing personal attacks for being different. Conventionals and Defensives prefer this teaching strategy because they are able to say whatever is on their minds instead of being silenced by political correctness assumptions. They need evidence that their personal standards are not evaluated by the instructor in a negative manner. The course is often the first opportunity they have had to explore their views openly and without constraints. Implementation of the LLEL approach led to increase risk-taking as evidenced by conservative views being expressed in class discussions and journals and greater appreciation for the course based on teaching evaluation data. This provides a foundation for students to think critically about their views and the extent to which they reflect their ideal personal and professional standards.

Instructional content that presents topics from a balanced perspective provides Conventionals and Defensives with opportunities to have their own views validated, thus encouraging critical thinking, risk-taking, and increased involvement (see Vaughn, 1994a, for a detailed discussion). The more Conventionals and Defensives believe that the more their views are heard and objectively judged, the more likely they will trust the process. Not surprisingly, they feel less threatened once they are volunteers instead of compulsory recruits. The more conservative students become allies with their liberal counterparts in arranging for a learning experience everyone values as each person achieves professional competence.

The LLEL method both directly and indirectly assists Ambivalents in dealing with their discomfort. They have opportunities to learn that others are still trying to work on their interracial competence. Others can teach them how to close the gap between their personal standards and behaviors.

The overall goal is to provide the entire class and its individual students with as much opportunity to get involved in the training as possible. Individual students are allowed to make progress suitable to their own potential, while using the range of racial attitudes in the classroom as a yardstick by which they can assess personal growth.

Race relations instructors and trainers are challenged by student emotional responses. Avoiding emotions and the issues that activate them ignore their presence and diminish instructional effectiveness. At the same time, managing emotion requires understanding differences in racial attitudes. Some instructors have a natural ability to manage student emotions and get them to volunteer to learn in mandatory race relations courses (Mayton et al., 1994; Ponterotto & Pedersen, 1994; Rokeach, 1973). Most, however, are ill equipped for the challenges of race relations training. Without training and experience, intervention strategies are likely to do more harm than good to the students and the course. It is imperative that the instructor has an arsenal of intervention skills to harness emotionally charged situations for instructional purposes.

The expert provides a supportive context within which students of different attitudes can express and confront their beliefs in a climate of respect and trust (Vaughn, 1994b). This requires allowing students to be heard in a community of inquiry that respects a diversity of viewpoints (Ponterotto & Pedersen, 1994). The trainer's ability to diagnose emotions and readily employ management skills are the keys to a successful course. Community psychology offers a number of role models and training strategies for learning these knowledge and skills.

The heuristic model presented in this chapter offers a tool for understanding and managing White ethnic American negative emotional responses to mandatory race relations training. The model is based on the research literature, professional expertise, and classroom teaching experience. Individual differences in emotional reactions to the mandatory course are characterized along with the interaction between intervention strategy and resistance. The model is limited in that it does not include racial minority student emotional reactions or American attitudes toward people who prefer same-sex partners. Future efforts to understand emotional responses to instruction need to address these areas, as well as discern the empirical utility of the model.

Endnotes

1. The term White ethnic American refers to all Caucasian people who are American and of European descent.

2. Ethnicity is assumed to be an important part of each and every person's behavior. The term minority refers to a group of people who are (1) distinct in physical characteristics; (2) identify themselves as distinct from other social groups; (3) has less power than one or more majority groups; (4) tend to intermarry; and (5) they have less control over their own destiny (Feagin, 1984). Thus, these group characteristics define minority status more than population size.

3. Ethnic diversity refers to a society of identifiable social groups characterized by shared unique socio-psychological norms and practices. Race is often used interchangeable with ethnicity. For example, many Jewish Americans identify

themselves as members of a racial, rather than ethnic, group. This demonstrates the constructive nature of definitions in reflecting identity and the difficulty of using group labels.

4. It is recognized that students are more aversive toward gay and lesbian issues, as demonstrated in the research by Devine and others (1991). Sexual preference probably arouses more emotional reactions because moral indignation toward people of alternative sexual orientations continues to be widely supported, whereas racial aversion can no longer be morally defended (Devine et al., 1991). However, studying emotional reactions to race can assist in improving sexual preference instruction.

References

Banks, J. A. (1994). *Multicultural education: Theory and practice.* (3rd ed.). Boston: Allyn & Bacon.

Bennett, J. (1986). Modes of cross-cultural training: Conceptualizing cross-cultural training as education. *International Journal of Intercultural Relations, 10,* 117–134.

Bodenhausen, G. V. (1993). Emotions, arousal, and stereotypic judgments: A heuristic model of affect and stereotyping. In D. Mackie & D. Hamilton (Eds.), *Affect, cognition, and stereotyping: Interactive processes in group perception* (pp. 13–37). San Diego, CA: Harcourt, Brace, & Jonanovich.

Bodenhausen, G. V., & Kramer, G. P. (1990a, June). *Affective states trigger stereotypic judgments.* Paper presented at the annual convention of the American Psychological Society, Dallas.

Bodenhausen, G. V., & Kramer, G. P. (1990b). *Affective states and the heuristic use of stereotypes in social judgment.* Unpublished manuscript, Michigan State University, East Lansing.

Boettiger, J., Perry, W., Steiny, N., Vaughn, B. E., & Williams, R. (1988). *Quality of student life in the California School of Professional Psychology system.* San Francisco: Board of Trustee of the California School of Professional Psychology.

Brislin, R., Cushner, K., Cherrie, C., & Yong, M. (1986). *Intercultural interactions.* Newbury Park, CA: Sage.

Brislin, R., & Yoshida, T. (1994). *Intercultural communication training: An introduction.* Thousand Oaks, CA: Sage.

Cooley, C. H. (1994). Learning who we are by imagining how we appear to others. In P. Kollock & J. O'Brien (Eds.), *The production of reality* (pp. 266–268). Thousand Oaks, CA: Pine Forge Press.

Crocker, J., & Luhtanen, R. (1990). Collective self esteem and ingroup bias. *Journal of Personality and Social Psychology, 58*(1), 60–67.

Crocker, J., & Schwartz, I. (1985). Prejudice and ingroup favoritism in a minimal intergroup situation: Effects of self esteem. *Journal of Personality and Social Psychology, 11*(4), 379–386.

Day, H. R. (1983). Race relations training in the military. In D. Landis & R. Brislin (Eds.), *Handbook of Intercultural training, Vol. II: Issues in training methodology* (pp. 241–289). New York: Pergamon Press.

Devine, P. G. (1996). Breaking the prejudice habit. In *Psychological science agenda science briefs.* Washington, DC: APA Science Directorate.

Devine, P. G. (1993). The role of discrepancy-associated affect in prejudice reduction. In D. M. Mackie & D. L. Hamilton (Eds.), *Affect, cognition, and stereotyping: Interactive processes in group perception* (pp. 317–370). San Diego, CA: Academic Press.

Devine, P. G., & Monteith, M. J. (1993). The role of discrepancy-associated affect in prejudice reduction. In D. Mackie & D. Hamilton (Eds.), *Affect, cognition, and stereotyping: Interactive processes in group perception* (pp. 137–166). San Diego, CA: Harcourt, Brace, & Jonanovich.

Devine, P. G., Monteith, M. J., Zuwerink, J. R., & Elliot, A. J. (1991). Prejudice with and without compunction. *Journal of Personality and Social Psychology, 60,* 817–830.

D'Souza, D. (1991). *Illiberal Education: The politics of race and sex on the campus.* New York: The Free Press.

Esses, V. M., Haddock, G., & Zanna, M. P. (1993). Values, stereotypes, and emotions as determinants of intergroup attitudes. In D. Mackie & D. Hamilton (Eds.), *Affect, cognition, and stereotyping: Interactive processes in group perception* (pp. 137–166). San Diego, CA: Harcourt, Brace, & Jonanovich.

Farley, J. E. (1988; 1982). *Majority-minority relations.* (2nd ed.). Englewood Cliffs, NJ: Prentice Hall.

Feagin, (1984). *Race and ethnic relations.* (3rd ed.). Englewood Cliffs, NJ: Prentice Hall.

Fein, S., & Spencer, S. (1997). Prejudice as self-image maintenance: Affirming the self through derogating others. *Journal of Personality and Social Psychology, 73*(1), 31–44.

Ferdman, B. M. & Brody, S. E. (1996). Models of diversity training. In D. Landis & R. Bahgat (Eds.), *Handbook of intercultural training* (2nd Ed.). Thousand Oaks, CA: Sage.

Fiske, S. T., & Ruscher, J. B. (1993). Negative interdependence and prejudice: Whence the affect? In D. Mackie & D. Hamilton (Eds.), *Affect, cognition, and stereotyping: Interactive processes in group perception* (pp. 239–268). San Diego, CA: Harcourt, Brace, & Jonanovich.

Fried, J. (1993). Bridging emotion and intellect: Classroom diversity in process. *College Teaching, 41*(4) 123–128.

Frontline (1988). *Racism 101: Racial prejudice on American university campuses.* Nova.

Gay, G. (1984). Implications of selected models of ethnic identity development for educators. *The Journal of Negro Education, 54*(1), 43–52.

Gaertner, S. L., & Dovidio, J. F. (1986). The aversive form of racism. In J. Dovidio & S. Gaertner (Eds.), *Prejudice, discrimination, & racism* (pp. 61–90). San Diego, CA: Academic Press.

Goleman, D. (1995). *Emotional intelligence: Why it can matter more than IQ.* New York: Bantam.

Gudykunst, W. (1991). *Bridging differences.* Newbury Park, CA: Sage.

Hamilton, D. L., Stroessner, S. J., & Mackie, D. M. (1993). The influence of affect in stereotyping: The case of illusory correlations. In D. Mackie & D. Hamilton (Eds.), *Affect, cognition, and stereotyping: Interactive processes in group perception* (pp. 39–62). San Diego, CA: Harcourt, Brace, & Jonanovich.

Helms, J. E. (1990). *Black and white identity: Theory, research, and practice.* Westport, CT: Praeger.

Jones, J. M. (1986). Racism: A cultural analysis of the problem. In J. Dovidio & S. Gaertner (Eds.), *Prejudice, discrimination, and racism* (pp. 270–314). San Diego, CA: Academic Press.

Katz, I., Cohen, S., & Glass, D. (1975). Some determinants of cross-racial helping behavior. *Journal of Personality and Social Psychology, 32,* 964–970.

Katz, I., Glass, D., & Cohen, S. (1973). Ambivalence, guilt, and the scapegoating of minority group victims. *Journal of Personality and Social Psychology, 9,* 423–436.

Katz, I., Glass, D. C., Lucido, D. J., Cohen, S., & Farber, J. (1979). Harm doing and victim's racial or orthopedic stigmas as determinants of helping behavior. *Journal of Personality, 47,* 340–364.

Katz, I., Wachenhut, J., & Glen Hass, R. (1986). Racial ambivalence, value duality, and behavior. In J. Dovidio & S. Gaertner (Eds.), *Prejudice, discrimination, and racism* (pp. 35–60). San Diego, CA: Academic Press.

Katz, J., & Miller, F. (1995). Cultural diversity as a developmental process: The path from monocultural club to inclusive organization. *Consulting, 2,* 40–47.

Kelly, J. G., Azelton, L. S., Burzette, R. G., & Mock, L. O. (1994). Creating social settings for diversity: An ecological thesis. In E. Trickett, R. Watts, & D. Birman (Eds.), *Human diversity* (pp. 359–382). San Francisco: Jossey-Bass.

Kim, H. S., & Baron, R. S. (1988). Exercise and illusory correlation: Does arousal heighten stereotypic processing? *Journal of Experimental Social Psychology, 24,* 366–380.

Kogod, S. K. (1991). *A workshop for managing diversity in the workplace.* San Diego, Calif.: Pfeiffer.

Kollock, P., & O'Brien, J. (1994). *The production of reality.* Thousand Oaks, CA: Pine Forge Press.

Kovel, J. (1970). *White racism: A psychohistory.* NY: Pantheon.

Landis, D., Brislin, R. (Eds.). (1983). *Handbook of intercultural training* (Vols. 1–3). Elmsford, NY: Pergamon.

Lennon, T., & Bagwell, O. (Producers). (1988). Racism 101. *Frontline.* Alexandria, VA: PBS.

Lorion, R. P. (1992). Community Psychology in the 1990s: Reflections from the Editor. *Journal of Community Psychology, 20*, 3–6.

Luria, A. (1932; 1976). *The nature of human conflict.* NY: Liveright.

Mandler, G. (1984). *Mind and body: The Psychology of emotion and stress.* New York: Norton.

Mayton II, D. M., Loges, W. E., Ball-Rokeach, S. J., & Grube, J. W. (1994, Winter). Human values and social issues: Current understanding and implications for the future. *Journal of Social Issues, 50*(4), 1–9.

McConahay, J. B. (1986). Modern racism, ambivalence, and the modern racism scale. In J. Dovidio & S. Gaertner (Eds.), *Prejudice, discrimination, and racism* (pp. 91–126). San Diego, CA: Academic Press.

McConahay, J. B., Hardee, B. B., & Batts, V. (1981). Has racism declined? It depends on who's asking and what is asked. *Journal of Conflict Resolution, 25,* 563–579.

Merger, M. (1991). *Race and ethnic relations.* Belmont, CA: Wadsworth.

Miller, F. A. & Katz, J. H. (1995). Cultural diversity as a developmental process: The path from monocultural club to inclusive organization, *The 1995 Annual: Volume 2, Consulting* (267–281). San Diego: Pfeiffer & Company.

Monteith, M. J. (1991). *Self-regulation of stereotypical responses: Implications for progress in prejudice reduction efforts.* Unpublished doctoral dissertation, University of Wisconsin-Madison.

Monteith, M. J., Devine, P. G., & Zuwerink, J. R. (1993). Self-directed versus other-directed affect as a consequence of prejudice-related discrepancies. *Journal of Personality and Social Psychology, 64*(2), 198–210.

Newbrough, J. R. (1992). Community psychology for the 1990s. *Journal of Community Psychology, 20*, 7–9.

Ponterotto, J. G., & Pedersen, P. B. (1994, February). *Fighting prejudice and racism: A racial/ethnic identity-based intervention program.* Paper presented at the annual Teachers College winter Round Table in Cross-cultural Counseling and Psychotherapy, New York.

Pratto, F., & John, O. P. (1991). Automatic vigilance: The attention-grabbing power of negative social information. *Journal of Personality and Social Psychology, 61*(3), 380–391.

Pratto, F., Sidanius, J., Stallworth, L. M. (1993). Sexual selection and the sexual and ethnic basis of social hierarchy. In L. Ellis (Ed.), *Social stratification and socioeconomic inequality: A comparative biosocial analysis* (pp. 111–137). NY: Praeger.

Pratto, F., Sidanius, J., Stallworth, L., & Malle, B. (1994). Social dominance orientation: A personality variable predicting social and political attitudes. *Journal of Personality and Social Psychology, 67*(4), 741–763.

Rokeach, M. (1973). *The nature of human values.* New York: Free Press.

Rotheram, M. J., and Phinney, J. S. (1987). Ethnic behavior patterns as an aspect of identity. In J. S. Phinney and M. J. Rotheram (Eds.), *Children's ethnic socialization: Pluralism and development* (pp. 180–200). Newbury Park, CA: Sage.

Schofield, J. (1986). Causes and consequences of the color-blind perspective. In J. Dovidio & S. Gaertner (Eds.), *Prejudice, Discrimination, and Racism.* San Diego, CA: Academic Press.

Sidanius, J., Pratto, F., Bobo, L. (1994). Social dominance orientation and the political psychology of gender: A case of invariance? *Journal of Personality and Social Psychology, 67*(6), 998–1011.

Smith, E. R. (1993). Social identity and social emotions: Towards new conceptualizations of prejudice. In D. Mackie & D. Hamilton (Eds.), *Affect, cognition, and stereotyping: Interactive processes in group perception* (pp. 297–313). San Diego, CA: Harcourt, Brace, & Jonanovich.

Stricker, G., Davis-Russell, E., Bourg, E., Durante, E., Hamilton, R., McHolland, J., Polite, K., & Vaughn, B. (1990). *Toward ethnic diversification in psychology education and training.* Washington, DC: American Psychological Association.

Tabachnik, N., Crocker, J., & Alloy, L. B. (1983). Depression, social comparison, the false consensus effect. *Journal of Personality and Social Psychology, 58*(1), 60–67.

Tatum, B. D. (1994). Teaching white students about racism: The search for white allies and the restoration of hope. *Teachers College Record, 95*(4), 463–476.

Vaughn, B. E. (1988). Incorporating multicultural issues in professional training. *National Council of Schools of Professional Psychology Newsletter,* 3–8. Washington, DC: NCSPP.

Vaughn, B. E. (1994a, Fall). *Harnessing the multicultural debate in the classroom, in Thought and Action, 10*(2), 37–46.

Vaughn, B. E. (1994b). Teaching cultural diversity courses from a balanced perspective. *Exchanges: Newsletter of the California State University System Institute for Teaching and Learning, 5*(2), 17–18.

Vaughn, B. E., Eulert, D., & Trybus, R. (1997). Earning the right to serve. In J. Grip et al. (Eds.), *Evaluation and research in professional psychology training.* Washington, DC: National Council of Professional Schools of Psychology.

Wilder, D. A. (1993). The role of anxiety in facilitating stereotypic judgment of outgroup behavior. In D. Mackie & D. Hamilton (Eds.), *Affect, cognition, and stereotyping: Interactive processes in group perception* (pp. 87–110). San Diego, CA: Harcourt, Brace, & Jonanovich.

THE EDITOR

Elizabeth Davis-Russell is provost and vice president for Academic Affairs at the State University of New York College at Cortland. Prior to that she was with the California School of Professional Psychology (CSPP) for thirteen years as a professor, director of the Cross Cultural Psychology Proficiency, dean for Academic and Professional Affairs, and presidential associate. She was one of the original founders of the Multicultural, Education, Research, Intervention, and Training (MERIT) Institute of CSPP and served as its director for two years. During her tenure with CSPP, she developed curricula and programs in ethnic minority mental health and cross-cultural psychology.

Prior to her tenure at CSPP, Davis-Russell was an associate professor at the Chicago School of Professional Psychology, where she developed the Center for Intercultural Clinical Psychology, a center devoted to research, education and training, and service in cross-cultural psychology.

Davis-Russell is a Fellow of the American Psychological Association, Society for the Study of Ethnic Minority Issues. Prior publications include edited books, articles, and chapters on multicultural issues in education and training and treatment.

THE CONTRIBUTORS

Diane Adams, Ph.D. is a professor at the California School of Professional Psychology at Alliant International University, Alameda, California. Dr. Adams served as the first director of the MERIT Institute at the California School of Professional Psychology.

Mary A. Bachran, Psy.D. is director of Southwest Colorado Mental Health Center. Dr. Bachran is an alumna of the California School of Professional Psychology, Fresno, California.

Leena Banerjee, Ph.D. is affiliated with the Psy.D. program and the Multicultural Community Clinical Psychology Emphasis area at the Los Angeles campus of Alliant International University. Dr. Banerjee was contacted by the World Education Encyclopedia's publishers, and wrote about the Maldives Islands, an archipelago of 1,190 small islands in the Indian Ocean, one of the world's most economically disadvantaged nations.

Hanya Bluestone, Ph.D. is an alumna of the California School of Professional Psychology, Fresno, California.

Elaine A. Burke, Ph.D. is a member of Alliant International University, California School of Professional Psychology, Los Angeles campus, Los Angeles, California.

William W. Chien, Psy.D. graduated from the California School of Professional Psychology, in Los Angeles, California. He has lectured extensively on Psychotherapy and Mental Health Treatment with Asian Americans at the University of California, Irvine. Between 1994 and 1996, Dr. Chien initiated and completed all phases of a doctoral level empirical study that examined the relationship between ethnic identity development and the perception of prejudice in Chinese American college students. He has co-chaired the Asian Faculty and Staff Association at the University of California, Irvine, in facilitating monthly group meetings to discuss and address concerns of UCI Asian faculty and staff. Dr. Chien is a member of the American Psychological Association, the Asian American Psychological Association and a member of the University of California, Irvine Asian Faculty and Staff Association.

Renae K. Chung, M.A. is a fourth-year Clinical Psy.D. graduate student at the California School of Professional Psychology at Alliant International University, Fresno, in the cross-cultural emphasis area. Ms. Chung received her M.A. in clinical psychology from CSPP in the fall of 2000. She received her B.A. from Ohio State University in 1998.

Harriet Curtis-Boles has a Ph.D. in clinical psychology and is a licensed marriage, family and child counselor. She has worked in mental health administration as the clinical director of an outpatient mental health agency, has provided consultation and training in addressing racism, managing diversity, and treating multicultural populations to community organizations, and is an associate professor at Alliant International University, California School of Professional Psychology. In her capacity as associate professor, she has specialized in courses addressing intercultural awareness, communication, and intervention and legal and ethical issues in clinical settings. She supervises research of students working with multicultural populations covering a wide range of topics including acculturation and mental health attitudes, the impact of violence exposure on African American youth and the development of culturallly sensitive mentoring programs for at-risk Asian American youth. She has conducted research and published articles addressing critical concerns of the African American community.

Elizabeth Davis-Russell, Ed. D., Ph.D. is provost and vice president for Academic Affairs at the State University of New York College at Cortland. Prior to that she was with the California School of Professional Psychology for thirteen years as a professor, director of the Cross Cultural Psychology Proficiency, dean for Academic and Professional Affairs, and presidential associate. She was one of the original founders of the MERIT Institute of CSPP and served as its director for two years. During her tenure with CSPP she developed curricula and programs in ethnic minority mental health and cross-cultural psychology.

Robert-Jay Green, Ph.D. is a member of the clinical psychology faculty at the San Francisco Bay campus of Alliant International University, California School of Professional Psychology. He, along with another professor, Paul Werner, Ph.D., developed a model of family relations and an assessment device for it, called the California Inventory for Family Assessment (CIFA). He has received the 2001 Award for Distinguished Contributions to Family Systems Research from the American Family Therapy Academy.

Judith Holloway, Ph.D. is a professor in the Multicultural Community Clinical Psychology Program at the California School of Professional Psychology, Alliant International University, Los Angeles campus, Los Angeles, California.

Eleanor Jackson-Castleberry, Ph.D. is an alumna of the California School of Professional Psychology, Fresno, California. She is now director of Training, Counseling and Psychological Services, Humboldt State University.

Paula B. Johnson, Ph.D. is a member of Alliant International University, California School of Professional Psychology, Los Angeles campus, Los Angeles, California.

Debra M. Kawahara, Ph.D. is a professor at Alliant International University, School of Social and Policy Studies, Cultural and Human Behavior Program, in San Diego, California.

Sue A. Kuba, Ph.D. is a full professor at Alliant International University, California School of Professional Psychology, Fresno, California. Dr. Kuba has served as interim dean and program director for the Clinical Psy.D. program in her role on the Fresno campus.

Glenn I. Masuda, Ph.D. is a member of Alliant International University, California School of Professional Psychology, Los Angeles campus, Los Angeles, California.

Richard H. Mendoza, Ph.D. is a member of Alliant International University, California School of Professional Psychology, Los Angeles campus, Los Angeles, California.

Carlton W. Parks, Ph.D. is a professor in the Multicultural Community-Clinical Psychology Program at the California School of Professional Psychology and the School of Education of Alliant International University, Los Angeles campus, Los Angeles, California.

Kenneth Polite, Ph.D. is a member of Alliant International University, California School of Professional Psychology, Los Angeles campus, Los Angeles, California.

Kumea Shorter-Gooden, Ph.D. is a professor in the Multicultural Community Clinical Psychology Program at the California School of Professional Psychology, Alliant International University, Los Angeles campus, Los Angeles, California.

Shelley J. Stokes, Ph.D. is a professor of psychology at the California School of Professional Psychology at Alliant International University, Fresno, and former director of the Psychological Service Center. His experience as a clinician and administrator in county mental health programs and private practice is extensive. Dr. Stokes is a graduate of the three-year advanced training program of the Masterson institute in psychoanalytic psychotherapy of the disorders of the self, and has made numerous presentations on the subject. He has previously been an active member in the National Association of Black Psychologists and has had a long-standing interest in cultural issues tracing back to his dissertation work in 1980 on "Racism and Cognitive Structure: Reconceptualization of Constructs, Measurement, and the Development of Paradigmatic Fit."

Kimlin Tam Ashing, Ph.D. is a member of Alliant International University, California School of Professional Psychology, Los Angeles campus, Los Angeles, California.

Sylvie Taylor, Ph.D. is a member of Alliant International University, California School of Professional Psychology, Los Angeles campus, Los Angeles, California.

Billy E. Vaughn, Ph.D. is an associate professor at Alliant International University, San Diego, California. He is in the Community Health and Behavior program.

Kamilah Marie Woodson, M.A. is a doctoral candidate in Clinical Psychology at the California School of Professional Psychology at Alliant International University, Los Angeles, California. In 1994, she received her B.A. in psychology from the University of Michigan in Ann Arbor. Her clinical and research interests include mate-selection strategies among African Americans, multicultural urban community health psychology, and interpersonal violence.

Gale Young, Ph.D. is associate dean of the School of Arts and Sciences at California State University, Haywood. Dr. Young is also a faculty member in Communications, and has written extensively in multicultural communications.

INDEX

DATE DUE